W9-CEH-089

The
NYSTROM
DESK ATLAS

HERFF JONES
NYSTROM

CONTENTS

2014 Update of Names and Boundaries
© 2008, 2004, 2003, 1994 Herff Jones, Inc.
4719 W. 62nd St., Indianapolis, IN 46268

All rights reserved. No part of this book may be reproduced or transmitted in any form or by any means, electronic or mechanical, including photocopying, recording, or by any information storage and retrieval system, without permission in writing from the publisher.

Printed in U.S.A.

10 9 8 7 6   17 16 15 14

Print: ISBN: 978-0-7825-1188-8   Product Code: 9AD
E-book: ISBN: 978-0-7825-1637-1   Product Code: SL5-AD-NA

To order: www.herffjonesnystrom.com or 800-621-8086

Statistics and estimates are from government and United Nations sources: populations for the most recent available date, other data averaged over the three most recent available years.

Photo Credits

front cover © Jean-Paul Pelissier/Reuters/Corbis; **back cover** top: © Radu Sigheti/Reuters/Corbis, bottom © AFP/Getty Images; **7** © German Aerospace Center (DLR), Physical World left: © Photo Researchers/First Light, right: © Keren Su/Corbis, Human World left: Reuters/Corbis, right: © epa/Corbis; **14** left: © Dietrich Rose/zefa/Corbis; right: © Craig Lovell/Corbis, **15** left: © Herbert Spichtinger/zefa/Corbis; right: © Panorama Stock/First Light, **16** © Crack Palinggi/Reuters/Corbis; **17** © Photo Researchers/First Light; **18** © Cousteau Society/Getty Images; **20** © Walter Geiersperger/Corbis; **21** © Adam Woolfitt/Corbis; **24** © Lester Lefkowitz/Corbis; **25** © Paul A. Souders/Corbis; **26** © Tom Stoddart/Getty Images; **28** left: © Royalty-Free/Corbis, right: © Andre Gallant/Getty Images; **29** left: © Keren Su/Corbis, top right: " Corbis, bottom right: Owen Franken/Corbis; **30** top: © Andy Hibbert/Ecoscene/Corbis, bottom: © David Hiser/Getty Images; **31** left: © NASA, right: © NASA; **33** epa/Corbis;

34 © China Newsphoto/Reuters/Corbis; **36** © Reuters/Corbis; **38** © Enrique Marcarian/Reuters/Corbis; **40** all Balance of Trade graphs throughout atlas: Golden Dollar Reverse image courtesy United States Mint; **42** © Sucheta Das/Reuters/Corbis; **44** © Jean-Paul Pelissier/Reuters/Corbis; **45** © Gavin Hellier/Robert Harding World Imagery/Corbis; **50** left: © Theo Allofs/zefa/Corbis, right: © Dave Gleiter; **51** © Mark Segal/Getty Images; **52** © William W. Bacon/Alaska Stock; **53** © Paula Bronstein/Getty Images; **57** © Philip & Karen Smith/Getty Images; **59** © John Sylvester/First Light; **60** © Ron Watts/Corbis; **67** © Christian Lamontagne/First Light; **74** © Cameron Davidson/Getty Images; **75** © Frans Lanting/Corbis; **76** © Photowood Inc/Corbis; **77** © Larry Ulrich; **78** left: © Lester Lefkowitz/Corbis, right: © Mitchell Funk/Getty Images; **102** left: © Dave G. Houser/Post-Houserstock/Corbis, right: © Bob Krist/Corbis; **105** © Doug Armand/Getty Images; **106** © Danny Lehman/Corbis; **108** © Trujillo-Paumier/Getty Images; **110** © Marcos Delgado/epa/Corbis; **111** © James Marshall/Corbis; **116** © Georg Gerster/Photo Researchers/First Light; **117** © Wolfgang Kaehler/Corbis; **120** Jacques Jangoux; **121** © Colin Samuels/Getty Images; **125** © Daniel Berehulak/Getty Images; **128** © James Marshall/Corbis; **129** © Radu Sigheti/Reuters/Corbis; **131** © Werner Bollmann/A.G.E. Foto Stock/First Light; **132** © Gideon Mendel/Corbis; **133** © John and Lisa Merrill/Corbis; **139** © Tibor Bognar/Corbis; **142** © Robert Francis/Getty Images; **144** © Paul McErlane/Getty Images; **149** © Belousov Vitaly/ITAR-TASS/Corbis; **150** © Oliver Strewe/Getty Images; **151** © Steve Kaufman/Corbis; **157** © Adrian Masters; **159** © Martin Puddy/Getty Images; **162** © Claro Cortes IV/Reuters/Corbis; **165** left: © WorldSat International, right: © WorldSat International; **166** © Earl & Nazima Kowall/Crobis; **169** © Tibor Bognar/Corbis; **170** © Robert Nickelsberg/Getty Images; **171** © AFP/Getty Images; **174** © Theo Allofs/zefa/Corbis; **176** © D. Holdsworth/Getty Images; **177** © Peter Adams/Getty Images; **178** © Stephanie Lamy/Corbis; **179** © Will Burgess/Reuters/Corbis; **181** top: © Frans Lemmens/zefa/Corbis, bottom: © Chris Rainier/Corbis; **182** © Paul A. Souders/Corbis; **183** © B. & C. Alexander/First Light

How to Use This Atlas

The Nystrom Desk Atlas is a collection of maps—and much more. Its reference and thematic maps, graphs, photos, and explanatory text explore key concepts and processes. These tools will help you understand important environmental, humanitarian, economic, and cultural issues affecting the world today. To get the most out of *The Nystrom Desk Atlas*, follow these steps.

A

Get acquainted with the three styles of **REFERENCE MAPS** in this atlas. See the **Political Relief**, **Land Cover**, and **Elevation** maps of the world on pages 8–13. Their **detailed legends** are on page 6.

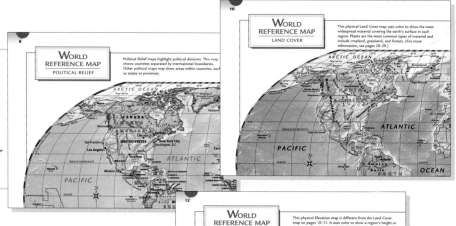

B

Check out **WORLD MATTERS** on pages 14–44. They provide a foundation for understanding themes that are repeated throughout the atlas.

1. Look at the **title**, which tells you what the two-page spread is about.

2. Then read the **introduction**. It provides an overview of the theme addressed on the spread.

3. Look at the maps. Their **legends** explain what the main colors and symbols on the map mean. Always read the legend before examining a map.

4. Also look at the **graphs**, **photos**, and **diagrams**. Read their captions too. They help you understand the significance of each image.

5. Watch for **Geodes**, which are nuggets of geographic facts. Some define important terms; others provide helpful examples.

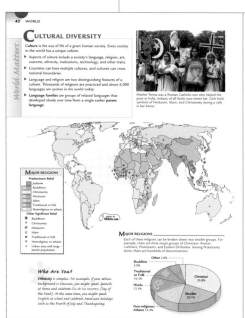

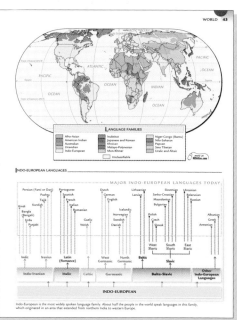

For each continent, start with the first page, the **CONTINENT OVERVIEW**. It provides key facts and shows the areas covered by regional maps.

Locator maps show the location of the continent in relation to the world or a region in relation to the continent or a larger region.

Area comparisons compare the size of a continent, country, or state with the familiar size and shape of the contiguous United States.

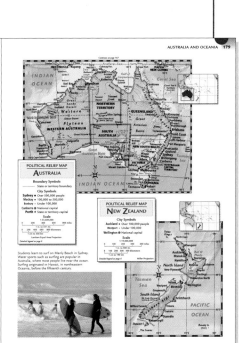

D

Then page through the section. First you'll find reference maps, followed by thematic maps for the full continent, and then maps for regions on the continent.

Diagrams illustrate concepts that are difficult to show in a map, graph, or photo.

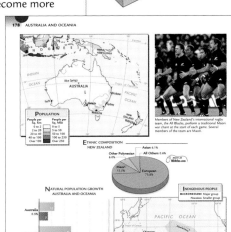

Thematic maps focus on single topics or themes. Often the patterns on one thematic map become more meaningful when compared to the patterns on another. The five types of recurring thematic maps are shown on page 6.

Graphs summarize facts in a visual way, making it easier to see trends and make comparisons. Four recurring graphs appear throughout the atlas: Climographs, Balance of Trade, Natural Population Growth, and Ethnic Composition.

Regional maps are provided for nearly every populous part of the world. Because they appear at larger scales than maps of continents, they can name more cities and show more features.

Photos show people and places in a geographic context. Some provide examples of map categories. Others bring abstract ideas to life.

Cross sections show slices of the earth, to make landscapes easier to comprehend. Their exaggerated height and depth make features easy to see.

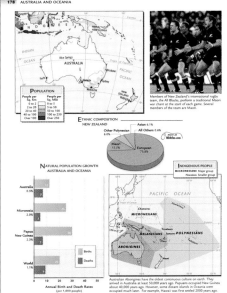

Other Reference Tools

Map projections used in *The Nystrom Desk Atlas* are described and explained on pages 184–185.

Country Tables, organized by continent, list key facts about every country in the world.

Unfamiliar terms in **bold** type are defined in context. Other terms are defined in the **Glossary**.

The complete **Index** gives the page, latitude and longitude, and description of every place named on the maps.

The **Thematic Index** lists thematic maps and graphs by theme.

This symbol lets you know that the website **NystromDeskAtlas.com** has more maps, graphs, and/or photos on the topic.

E

Finally, read **ISSUES TODAY**. Each article looks at a global issue that has particular relevance for the continent or region—from two perspectives.

POLITICAL RELIEF MAPS
(For more information about Political Relief maps, see pages 8–9.)

Boundary Symbols
- Continental boundary
- International boundary
- Disputed or undefined boundary
- Small country
- State, province, or territory boundary

Lettering Styles
- EUROPE — Continent
- *INDIAN OCEAN* — Ocean
- *Himalayas* — Land feature
- *Lake Victoria* — Water feature
- **CANADA** — Country
- **TEXAS** — State, province, or territory
- (U.S.) — National affiliation

City Symbols
- Shanghai ● — A city's population is shown by numbers in the legend and by the relative size of its symbol and lettering.
- Vancouver ●
- Cairns ●
- Dakar ⊗ — National capital
- Atlanta ★ — State, province, or territory capital

Other Symbols
- Land beyond the subject area
- Polar sea ice
- Water and sea floor
- Lake and river
- Dry or seasonal lake and river
- Waterfall
- Canal
- Dam
- △ Mountain peak
- 🛣(80) U.S. Interstate highway
- Trans-Canada Highway
- (101) Other highway

LAND COVER MAPS
(For more information about Land Cover maps see pages 10–11 and 28–29.)

Boundary Symbols
- Continental boundary
- International boundary
- Disputed or undefined boundary
- Small country
- State, province, or territory boundary

Lettering Styles
- EUROPE — Continent
- *INDIAN OCEAN* — Ocean
- *Himalayas* — Land feature
- *Lake Victoria* — Water feature
- CANADA — Country
- TEXAS — State, province, or territory
- (U.S.) — National affiliation

City Symbols
- Shanghai ● — A city's population is shown by the relative size of its symbol and lettering.
- Vancouver ●
- Cairns ●
- Dakar ⊗ — National capital
- Atlanta ★ — State, province, or territory capital

Other Symbols
- Land beyond the subject area
- Polar sea ice
- Water and sea floor
- Lake and river
- Dry or seasonal lake and river
- Waterfall
- Canal
- Dam
- ▲ Mountain peak
- Wetland
- Sand dunes

ELEVATION MAPS
(For more information about Elevation maps, see pages 12–13 and 14–15.)

Boundary Symbols
- Continental boundary
- International boundary
- Disputed or undefined boundary
- Small country
- State, province, or territory boundary

Lettering Styles
- EUROPE — Continent
- *INDIAN OCEAN* — Ocean
- *Himalayas* — Land feature
- *Lake Victoria* — Water feature
- CANADA — Country
- TEXAS — State, province, or territory
- (U.S.) — National affiliation

City Symbols
- Shanghai ● — A city's population is shown by the relative size of its symbol and lettering.
- Vancouver ●
- Cairns ●
- Dakar ⊗ — National capital
- Atlanta ★ — State, province, or territory capital

Other Symbols
- Land beyond the subject area
- Ice covered land
- Water
- Lake and river
- Dry or seasonal lake
- Waterfall
- Canal
- Dam
- ▲ Mountain peak

Thematic Maps

Thematic maps focus on single topics or themes, and the subject can be anything that is mappable. The following thematic maps appear throughout the atlas.

PRECIPITATION
(See pages 20–21.)

CLIMATE
(See pages 22–23.)

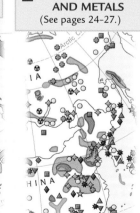

ENERGY RESOURCES AND METALS
(See pages 24–27.)

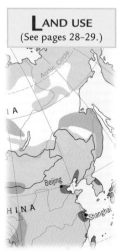

LAND USE
(See pages 28–29.)

POPULATION
(See pages 32–33.)

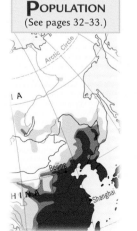

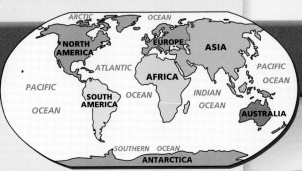

WORLD

Mauna Kea

Earth is known as the "blue planet" because 71 percent of its surface is covered with water. The planet has five oceans and seven continents.

PHYSICAL FEATURES

Landforms
Longest mountain range: Andes Mountains
4,500 mi. (7 200 km)

Largest plain: West Siberian Plain
1,200,000 sq. mi. (3 000 000 sq. km)

Earthquakes
Deadliest: 830,000 people
Shansi, China, January 23, 1556

Strongest: 9.5 on Richter scale
Valdivia, Chile, May 22, 1960

Average Ocean Depth
12,200 ft. (3 730 m)

Average Temperature
59°F (15°C)

Most Abundant Metal
Aluminumn (8.1% of Earth's crust)

World Extreme If measured from base to peak, Mauna Kea in Hawaii—33,476 feet (10 203 meters) tall—would be the tallest mountain in the world. This computer-generated image shows the mountain above and below sea level.

Physical World
- Landforms, Plates, and Oceans
  pages 14–19
- Weather and Climate
  pages 20–23
- Resources, Land Cover, and Environment
  pages 24–31

CULTURAL FEATURES

Population
7,100,000,000

Population Density
Most densely populated: Monaco
43,390.7 per sq. mi. (16 688.7 per sq. km)

Least densely populated: Greenland
0.1 per sq. mi. (0.03 per sq. km)

Life Expectancy
Longest: Andorra 83.5 years

Shortest: Swaziland 33.2 years

GDP (Gross Domestic Product) per Capita
Highest: Luxembourg US$58,900

Lowest: East Timor US$400

Human World
- Population, Health, and Food
  pages 32–37
- Economics
  pages 38–41
- Cultures and Migration
  pages 42–44

more at
NDAtlas.com
For more maps and graphs of the World, go to NystromDeskAtlas.com

7

WORLD REFERENCE MAP
POLITICAL RELIEF

Political Relief maps highlight political divisions. This map shows countries separated by international boundaries. Other political maps may show areas within countries, such as states or provinces.

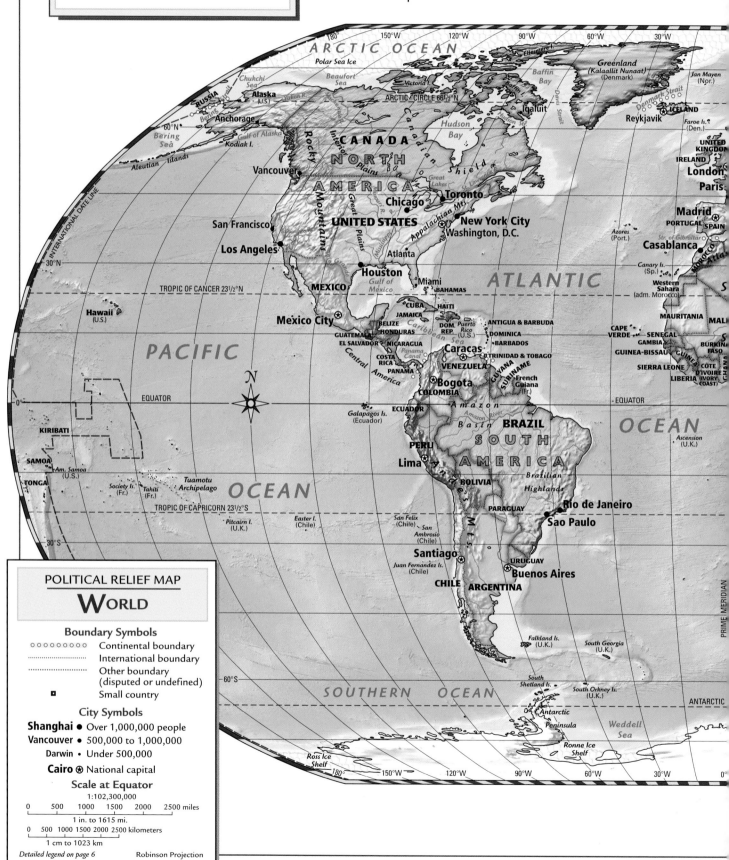

POLITICAL RELIEF MAP
WORLD

Boundary Symbols
∘∘∘∘∘∘∘∘∘ Continental boundary
·············· International boundary
·············· Other boundary (disputed or undefined)
▣ Small country

City Symbols
Shanghai ● Over 1,000,000 people
Vancouver ● 500,000 to 1,000,000
Darwin · Under 500,000
Cairo ⊛ National capital

Scale at Equator
1:102,300,000
0 500 1000 1500 2000 2500 miles
1 in. to 1615 mi.
0 500 1000 1500 2000 2500 kilometers
1 cm to 1023 km

Detailed legend on page 6   Robinson Projection

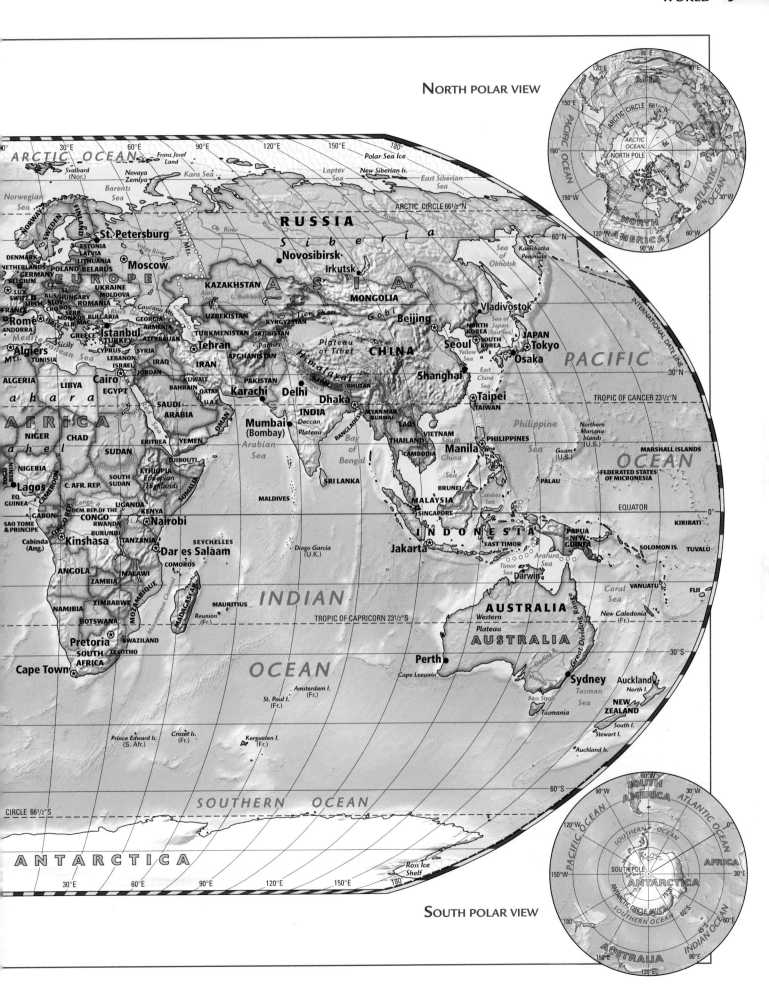

NORTH POLAR VIEW

ARCTIC OCEAN

30°E 60°E 90°E 120°E 150°E 180°

Svalbard
(Nor.) Franz Josef
Land Kara Sea Laptev
Sea New Siberian Is. Polar Sea Ice East Siberian
Sea

Norwegian
Sea Novaya
Zemlya Barents
Sea Yenisey River ARCTIC CIRCLE 66½°N

NORWAY FINLAND **RUSSIA** *Siberia*

St. Petersburg ESTONIA Ob River Sea of
Okhotsk Kamchatka
Peninsula 60°N

DENMARK LATVIA Volga River **Moscow** Novosibirsk Irkutsk
NETHERLANDS LITHUANIA Ural Mts. Amur River
GERMANY POLAND BELARUS KAZAKHSTAN A S I A
BELGIUM **EUROPE** UKRAINE L. Balkhash MONGOLIA Vladivostok Sea of
LUX AUS HUNGARY MOLDOVA KYRGYZSTAN Tien Shan Gobi Beijing NORTH Japan
SWITZ SLOV ROMANIA UZBEKISTAN Seoul KOREA (East Sea) **JAPAN**
LIECH CRO SERB. GEORGIA TAJIKISTAN Pamirs Plateau SOUTH Tokyo
FRANCE MON BOS BULGARIA ARMENIA of Tibet **CHINA** KOREA Osaka **PACIFIC**
Rome ITALY ALB. MAC. TURKMENISTAN Shanghai Yellow East
ANDORRA GREECE Istanbul AZERBAIJAN AFGHANISTAN Sea China 30°N
Sicily TURKEY **Tehran** Himalayas Sea Taipei
Mediterr CYPRUS LEBANON SYRIA NEPAL TAIWAN TROPIC OF CANCER 23½°N
Algiers Atlas Sea ISRAEL IRAQ IRAN PAKISTAN BHUTAN
Mts. TUNISIA JORDAN Karachi **Delhi** Dhaka MYANMAR Philippine
ALGERIA LIBYA **Cairo** KUWAIT Dhaka (BURMA) Sea Northern
ahara EGYPT BAHRAIN U.A.E. **INDIA** BANGLADESH LAOS Mariana **OCEAN**
QATAR SAUDI Deccan VIETNAM Islands
A F R I C A SAUDI OMAN **Mumbai** Plateau Bay THAILAND (U.S.)
NIGER CHAD ARABIA (Bombay) of South Guam MARSHALL ISLANDS
ahel ERITREA YEMEN *Arabian* Bengal CAMBODIA **Manila** China (U.S.) FEDERATED STATES
NIGERIA SUDAN DJIBOUTI *Sea* SRI LANKA PHILIPPINES Sea OF MICRONESIA
TOGO SOUTH ETHIOPIA BRUNEI PALAU
BENIN C. AFR. REP. SUDAN Ethiopian MALDIVES MALAYSIA Celebes EQUATOR 0°
Lagos CAMEROON Highlands SOMALIA SINGAPORE Sea KIRIBATI
EQ. GABON DEM. REP. OF THE UGANDA **I N D O N E S I A** PAPUA
GUINEA CONGO KENYA **Nairobi** EAST TIMOR NEW SOLOMON IS. TUVALU
SAO TOME RWANDA L. Victoria Jakarta GUINEA
& PRINCIPE BURUNDI Timor Arafura
Cabinda **Kinshasa** TANZANIA SEYCHELLES Diego Garcia Sea Sea
(Ang.) Dar es Salaam (U.K.) Darwin VANUATU
ANGOLA COMOROS Coral FIJI
ZAMBIA MALAWI **I N D I A N** **AUSTRALIA** Sea
NAMIBIA ZIMBABWE MOZAMBIQUE MAURITIUS Western New Caledonia
BOTSWANA MADAGASCAR Reunion TROPIC OF CAPRICORN 23½°S Plateau (Fr.)
Pretoria SWAZILAND (Fr.) **AUSTRALIA** 30°S
SOUTH LESOTHO **OCEAN** **Perth** Great Dividing Range
Cape Town AFRICA Cape Leeuwin Darling R. **Sydney** Auckland
Amsterdam I. Murray R. North I.
St. Paul I. (Fr.) Bass Strait **NEW** Tasman
(Fr.) Tasmania **ZEALAND** Sea
Prince Edward Is. Crozet Is. Kerguelen I. South I.
(S. Afr.) (Fr.) (Fr.) Stewart I.
Auckland Is.

SOUTHERN OCEAN 60°S

CIRCLE 66½°S

A N T A R C T I C A

30°E 60°E 90°E 120°E 150°E 180° Ross Ice
Shelf

SOUTH POLAR VIEW

WORLD REFERENCE MAP
LAND COVER

This physical Land Cover map uses color to show the most widespread material covering the earth's surface in each region. Plants are the most common types of material and include cropland, grassland, and forests. (For more information, see pages 28–29.)

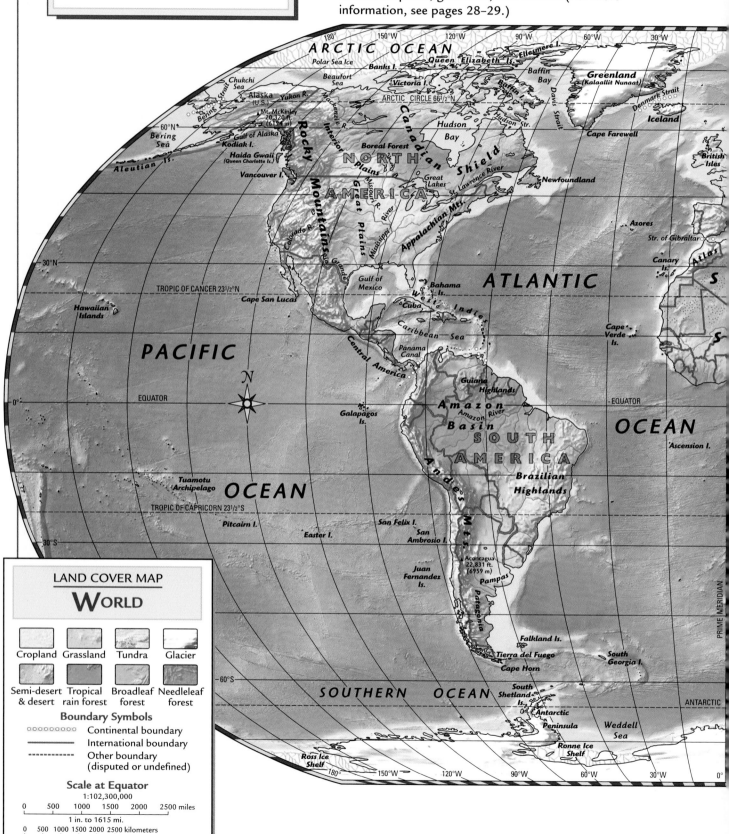

LAND COVER MAP
WORLD

Cropland   Grassland   Tundra   Glacier

Semi-desert   Tropical   Broadleaf   Needleleaf
& desert   rain forest   forest   forest

Boundary Symbols

○○○○○○○○○   Continental boundary
──────────   International boundary
- - - - - - -   Other boundary
(disputed or undefined)

Scale at Equator

1:102,300,000

0   500   1000   1500   2000   2500 miles

1 in. to 1615 mi.

0   500 1000 1500 2000 2500 kilometers

1 cm to 1023 km

Detailed legend on page 6   Robinson Projection

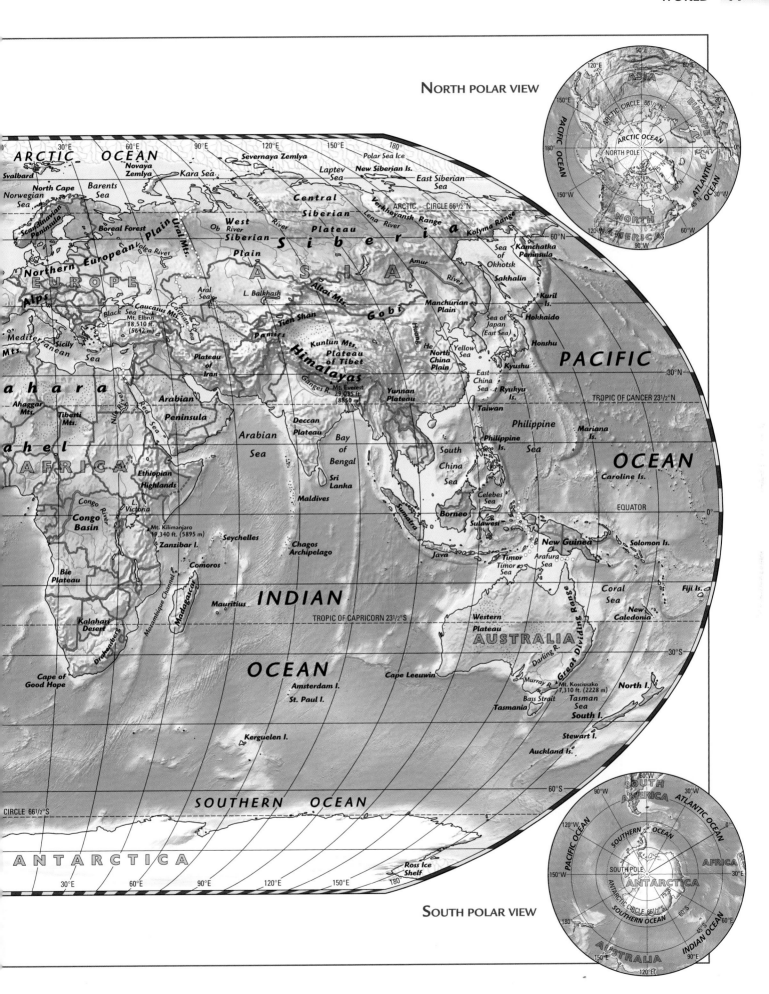

NORTH POLAR VIEW

ASIA
EUROPE
PACIFIC OCEAN
ARCTIC CIRCLE 66½°N
ARCTIC OCEAN
NORTH POLE
ATLANTIC OCEAN
NORTH AMERICA

ARCTIC OCEAN
Svalbard
Novaya Zemlya
Kara Sea
Severnaya Zemlya
Polar Sea Ice
Laptev Sea
New Siberian Is.
East Siberian Sea
North Cape
Norwegian Sea
Barents Sea
Scandinavian Peninsula
Central
Siberian
Plateau
Verkhoyansk Range
ARCTIC CIRCLE 66½°N
Kolyma Range
Boreal Forest
Northern European Plain
Ural Mts.
Ob River
Yenisey River
West Siberian Plain
S i b e r i a
A S I A
Amur River
Sea of Okhotsk
Kamchatka Peninsula
EUROPE
Volga River
Aral Sea
Caspian Sea
L. Balkhash
Altai Mts.
Gobi
Manchurian Plain
Sakhalin
Kuril Is.
Hokkaido
Alps
Caucasus Mts.
Mt. Elbrus
18,510 ft.
(5642 m)
Black Sea
Tien Shan
Pamirs
Kunlun Mts.
Plateau of Tibet
Huang He
Sea of Japan (East Sea)
Honshu
PACIFIC
Mediterranean Sea
Sicily
Plateau of Iran
Himalayas
Ganges R.
Mt. Everest
29,035 ft.
(8850 m)
North China Plain
Yellow Sea
Kyushu
East China Sea
Ryukyu Is.
30°N
S a h a r a
Ahaggar Mts.
Tibesti Mts.
Red Sea
Nile River
Arabian Peninsula
Deccan Plateau
Yunnan Plateau
Taiwan
TROPIC OF CANCER 23½°N
a h e l
AFRICA
Arabian Sea
Bay of Bengal
South China Sea
Philippine Is.
Philippine Sea
Mariana Is.
OCEAN
Ethiopian Highlands
Sri Lanka
Caroline Is.
Congo River
Congo Basin
L. Victoria
Mt. Kilimanjaro
19,340 ft. (5895 m)
Zanzibar I.
Maldives
Seychelles
Chagos Archipelago
Celebes Sea
Borneo
Sulawesi
EQUATOR
0°
Bie Plateau
Comoros
Sumatra
Java
New Guinea
Solomon Is.
Mauritius
Madagascar
Mozambique Channel
INDIAN
Timor
Timor Sea
Arafura Sea
Coral Sea
Fiji Is.
Kalahari Desert
Drakensberg
TROPIC OF CAPRICORN 23½°S
Western Plateau
AUSTRALIA
Great Dividing Range
New Caledonia
30°S
Cape of Good Hope
OCEAN
Amsterdam I.
St. Paul I.
Cape Leeuwin
Murray R.
Darling R.
Mt. Kosciuszko
7,310 ft. (2228 m)
North I.
Bass Strait
Tasman Sea
Tasmania
South I.
Kerguelen I.
Stewart I.
Auckland Is.
60°S
CIRCLE 66½°S
SOUTHERN OCEAN
ANTARCTICA
Ross Ice Shelf

30°E   60°E   90°E   120°E   150°E   180°

SOUTH POLAR VIEW

SOUTH AMERICA
ATLANTIC OCEAN
PACIFIC OCEAN
SOUTHERN OCEAN
SOUTH POLE
AFRICA
ANTARCTICA
ANTARCTIC CIRCLE 66½°S
SOUTHERN OCEAN
AUSTRALIA
INDIAN OCEAN

WORLD REFERENCE MAP
ELEVATION

This physical Elevation map is different from the Land Cover map on pages 10–11. It uses color to show a region's height or depth above or below sea level. (For more information, see pages 14–15.)

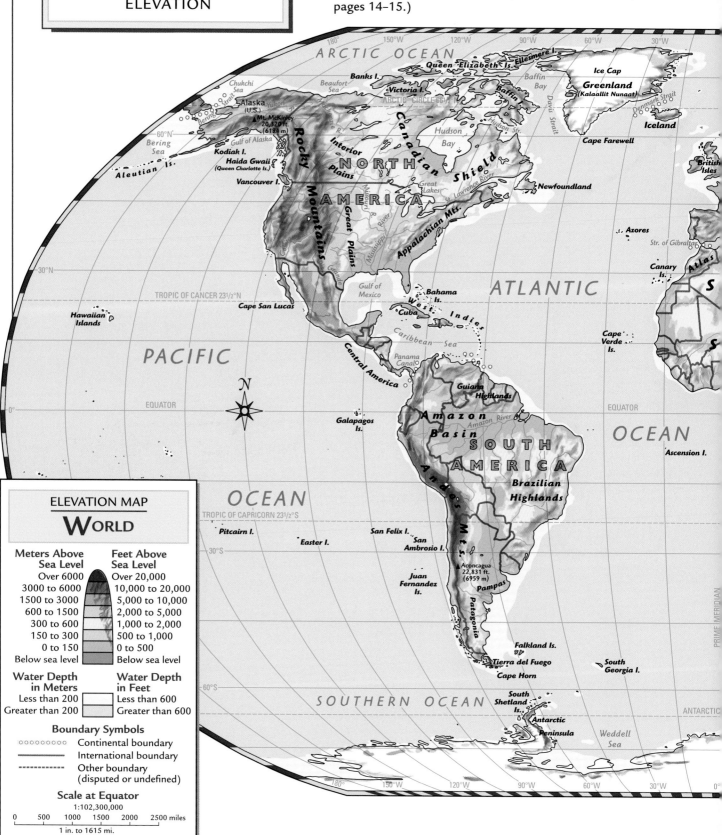

ELEVATION MAP
WORLD

Meters Above Sea Level	Feet Above Sea Level
Over 6000	Over 20,000
3000 to 6000	10,000 to 20,000
1500 to 3000	5,000 to 10,000
600 to 1500	2,000 to 5,000
300 to 600	1,000 to 2,000
150 to 300	500 to 1,000
0 to 150	0 to 500
Below sea level	Below sea level

Water Depth in Meters	Water Depth in Feet
Less than 200	Less than 600
Greater than 200	Greater than 600

Boundary Symbols

∘∘∘∘∘∘∘∘∘ Continental boundary

⎯⎯⎯⎯⎯ International boundary

‑ ‑ ‑ ‑ ‑ ‑ Other boundary (disputed or undefined)

Scale at Equator
1:102,300,000

0   500   1000   1500   2000   2500 miles

1 in. to 1615 mi.

0   500 1000 1500 2000 2500 kilometers

1 cm to 1023 km

Detailed legend on page 6   Robinson Projection

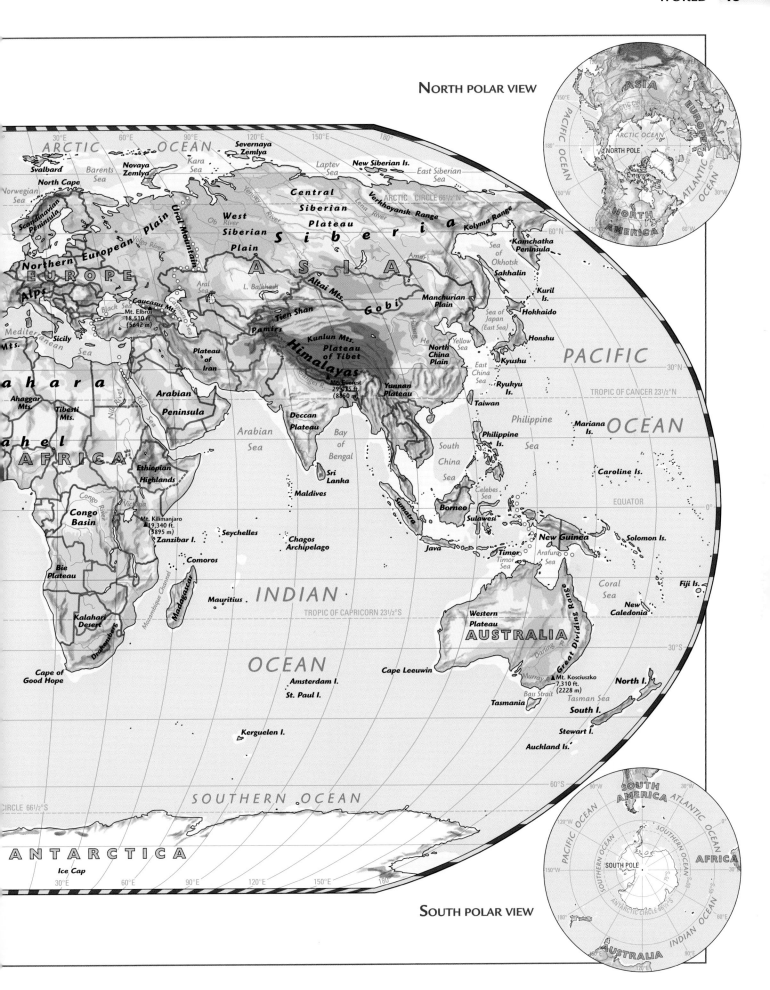

ASIA
EUROPE
PACIFIC OCEAN
ARCTIC CIRCLE
ARCTIC OCEAN
NORTH POLE
ATLANTIC OCEAN
NORTH AMERICA

ARCTIC OCEAN
30°E 60°E 90°E 120°E 150°E 180°
Svalbard
Severnaya Zemlya
Novaya Zemlya
Kara Sea
Laptev Sea
New Siberian Is.
East Siberian Sea
Norwegian Sea
North Cape
Barents Sea
ARCTIC CIRCLE 66½°N
Scandinavian Peninsula
Central Siberian Plateau
Verkhoyansk Range
Kolyma Range
60°N
Northern European Plain
West Siberian Plain
Ural Mountains
S i b e r i a
Sea of Okhotsk
Kamchatka Peninsula
Volga River
Ob River
Yenisey River
Lena River
Amur River
Sakhalin
EUROPE
A S I A
Kuril Is.
Alps
Aral Sea
L. Balkhash
Altai Mts.
Gobi
Manchurian Plain
Sea of Japan (East Sea)
Hokkaido
Caucasus Mts.
Mt. Elbrus 18,510 ft. (5642 m)
Black Sea
Caspian Sea
Tien Shan
Pamirs
Kunlun Mts.
Plateau of Tibet
Huang He
North China Plain
Yellow Sea
Honshu
Mediterranean Sea
Sicily
Himalayas
Mt. Everest 29,035 ft. (8850 m)
Yunnan Plateau
East China Sea
Kyushu
Ryukyu Is.
PACIFIC
Mts.
Plateau of Iran
Ganges R.
Taiwan
30°N
ahara
Ahaggar Mts.
Tibesti Mts.
Arabian Peninsula
Deccan Plateau
Bay of Bengal
South China Sea
Philippine Sea
Philippine Is.
Mariana Is.
OCEAN
TROPIC OF CANCER 23½°N
Nile River
Red Sea
Arabian Sea
ahel
AFRICA
Ethiopian Highlands
Sri Lanka
Caroline Is.
Congo River
L. Victoria
Maldives
Celebes Sea
EQUATOR
Congo Basin
Mt. Kilimanjaro 19,340 ft. (5895 m)
Zanzibar I.
Seychelles
Chagos Archipelago
Sumatra
Borneo
Sulawesi
Java
New Guinea
Solomon Is.
Bie Plateau
Comoros
Timor
Arafura Sea
Madagascar
Mauritius
INDIAN
Timor Sea
Coral Sea
Fiji Is.
Kalahari Desert
Mozambique Channel
TROPIC OF CAPRICORN 23½°S
Western Plateau
New Caledonia
Drakensberg
OCEAN
Amsterdam I.
St. Paul I.
Cape Leeuwin
AUSTRALIA
Great Dividing Range
Darling R.
30°S
Cape of Good Hope
Murray R.
Mt. Kosciuszko 7,310 ft. (2228 m)
North I.
Tasmania
Bass Strait
Tasman Sea
South I.
Kerguelen I.
Stewart I.
Auckland Is.
60°S
SOUTHERN OCEAN
CIRCLE 66½°S
A N T A R C T I C A
Ice Cap
30°E 60°E 90°E 120°E 150°E 180°

SOUTH AMERICA
ATLANTIC OCEAN
PACIFIC OCEAN
SOUTHERN OCEAN
AFRICA
SOUTH POLE
ANTARCTIC CIRCLE 66½°S
INDIAN OCEAN
AUSTRALIA

World Matters

ELEVATION AND LANDFORMS

Elevation is the measure of land's height or depth above or below sea level. **Landforms** are the physical features of the landscape. Most extensive landforms have patterns of high, low, or changing elevation.

▶ Most vast, level landforms are sections of the relatively flat tectonic plates that make up the continents.

▶ High landforms are produced when plates collide and push up the earth's crust or the magma below.

▶ Other landforms are carved or deposited by wind, water, and living beings.

▶ **Relief** is the difference between the highest and lowest elevation of a feature or region. Shading on a map shows landforms with rugged relief, such as mountains and hills.

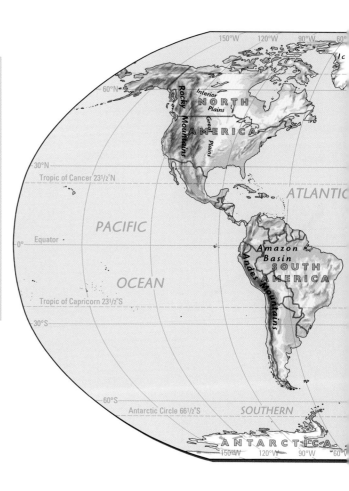

Every Breath You Take

The higher you travel above sea level, the thinner the air is and the less oxygen you get with each breath. That is why climbers aiming for the world's highest peaks must first acclimatize or get accustomed to the oxygen level at one elevation range before attempting the next.

A **Mountains** can be single peaks or part of a range. The summit of Lhotse Mountain in Nepal lies at 27,940 feet (8516 meters). Lhotse is part of the Himalayas, the highest mountain range in the world. (For more information, see page 157.)

B **Plateaus** are vast areas of relatively flat land at high elevation. The Plateau of Tibet, located in China, is the world's highest plateau. It has an average elevation of more than 14,800 feet (4500 meters).

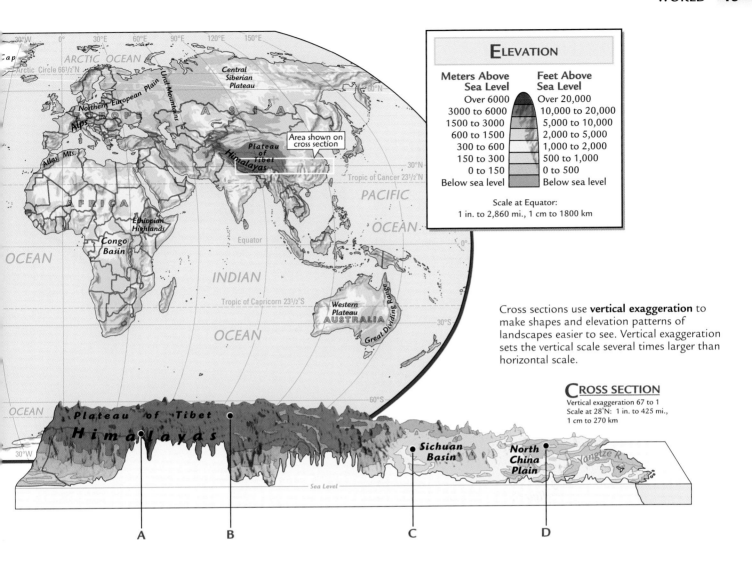

ELEVATION

Meters Above Sea Level	Feet Above Sea Level
Over 6000	Over 20,000
3000 to 6000	10,000 to 20,000
1500 to 3000	5,000 to 10,000
600 to 1500	2,000 to 5,000
300 to 600	1,000 to 2,000
150 to 300	500 to 1,000
0 to 150	0 to 500
Below sea level	Below sea level

Scale at Equator:
1 in. to 2,860 mi., 1 cm to 1800 km

Cross sections use **vertical exaggeration** to make shapes and elevation patterns of landscapes easier to see. Vertical exaggeration sets the vertical scale several times larger than horizontal scale.

CROSS SECTION
Vertical exaggeration 67 to 1
Scale at 28°N: 1 in. to 425 mi.,
1 cm to 270 km

C **Basins** are low areas surrounded by higher ground. The Sichuan Basin, along the Yangtze River in southern China, is surrounded by rugged mountains. It has an elevation range between 700 and 2,500 feet (200 and 750 meters).

D **Plains** are broad stretches of nearly level land, usually found at low elevations. The fertile lowlands of the North China Plain have the best farmland in China. The elevation of the North China Plain ranges from 0 to 500 feet (0 to 150 meters) above sea level.

World Matters

THE MOVING EARTH

The land and water features of the earth appear stable, but actually they move between 1 to 5 inches (2.5 to 15 centimeters) each year.

▶ The earth's crust is made up of about 30 **plates** that float above the molten interior of the planet. Lighter, thicker areas of the plates form the continents. Denser, thinner areas form the ocean floors.

▶ Plates slide along, bump into, and move away from each other.

▶ **Earthquakes** and **volcanoes** are common near the boundaries between plates. When an earthquake takes place beneath the ocean, a massive, destructive wave called a **tsunami** may result.

In 2005 an earthquake shook the town of Gunung Sitoli in Indonesia. With a magnitude of 8.7, it destroyed homes and offices and wrecked power lines and sewage systems. Over 900 people died in this quake.

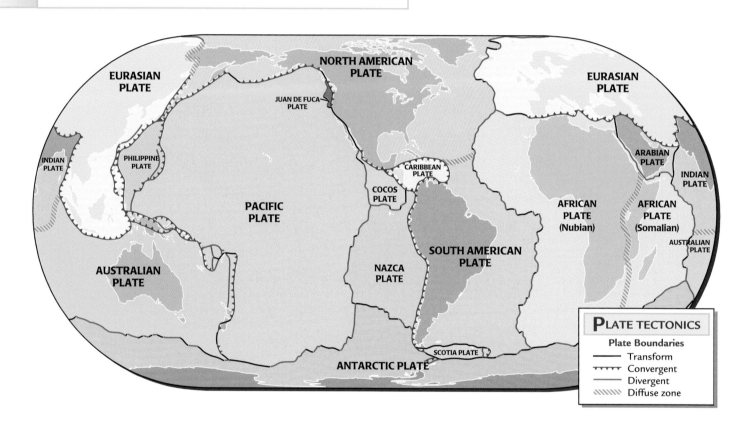

EURASIAN PLATE

NORTH AMERICAN PLATE

JUAN DE FUCA PLATE

EURASIAN PLATE

INDIAN PLATE

PHILIPPINE PLATE

ARABIAN PLATE

INDIAN PLATE

CARIBBEAN PLATE

COCOS PLATE

PACIFIC PLATE

AFRICAN PLATE (Nubian)

AFRICAN PLATE (Somalian)

AUSTRALIAN PLATE

AUSTRALIAN PLATE

SOUTH AMERICAN PLATE

NAZCA PLATE

SCOTIA PLATE

ANTARCTIC PLATE

PLATE TECTONICS

Plate Boundaries
— Transform
⊤⊤⊤⊤ Convergent
— Divergent
░░░░ Diffuse zone

TRANSFORM PLATE BOUNDARIES

These plates move side-by-side—sometimes in opposite directions, sometimes in the same direction. This type of plate movement can cause earthquakes.

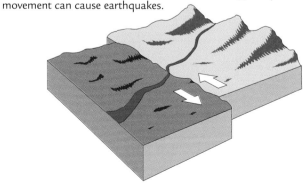

CONVERGENT PLATE BOUNDARIES

When one plate moves under another plate—**subduction**—earthquakes and volcanoes can occur. In the long run, the subducted plate will disappear. Convergent plates can be found near South America and the coasts of Asia, and in the western Pacific.

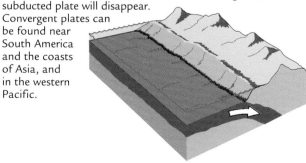

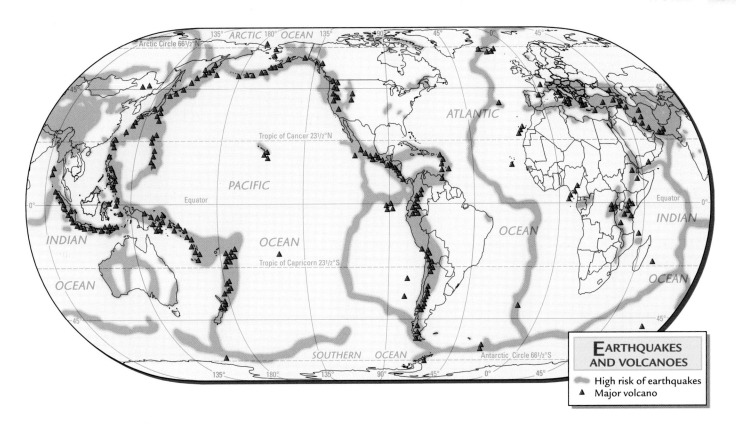

EARTHQUAKES AND VOLCANOES

- High risk of earthquakes
- ▲ Major volcano

Location, Location

Why does one earthquake with a magnitude of 9.0 cause over 283,000 deaths, while another quake of the same magnitude results in none? It's all in the location. When a quake strikes near a populous area without earthquake-resistant buildings, death rates are high. Depth of the quake and stability of the overlying rock also can affect the death rate.

DIVERGENT PLATE BOUNDARIES

These plates move away from each other in opposite directions. The Mid-Atlantic Ridge is on a divergent plate boundary. This movement causes the Atlantic Ocean to widen by about 1.5 miles (2.5 kilometers) every 100,000 years.

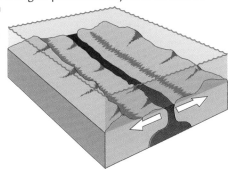

The volcano at Soufriere Hills on the West Indian island of Montserrat buried villages and destroyed the capital city of Plymouth.

World Matters

OCEANS

Ocean waters cover about 71 percent of the earth's surface. There is only one world ocean, but the continents divide the ocean into five distinct parts—the five oceans named on the map.

▶ A **continental shelf** is submerged land found just beyond the coastlines of the continents. A shelf may extend 19 to 190 miles (30 to 300 kilometers) from shore.

▶ **Abyssal plains** are the vast, flat stretches of ocean floor.

▶ The deepest parts of the ocean are **trenches**, which often lie 2 to 2.5 miles (3.2 to 4.0 kilometers) below the plains.

▶ The vast majority of sea exploitation—including fishing and gas and oil drilling—occurs on the continental shelf. Coastal areas are in the greatest danger of pollution.

Divers off the coast of Indonesia explore the ocean depths. The deep ocean remains the most mysterious and least-explored habitat on Earth. The deepest known spot is in the Mariana Trench east of the island of Guam. It plummets more than 6.8 miles (11 kilometers) below sea level.

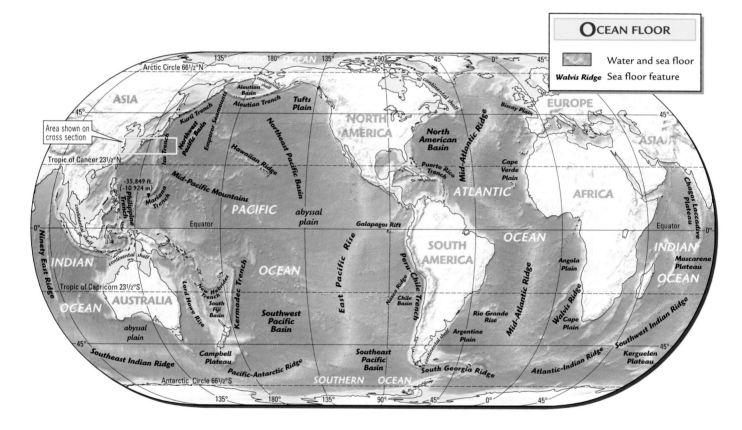

OCEAN FLOOR

Water and sea floor
Walvis Ridge Sea floor feature

CROSS SECTION

Vertical exaggeration 14 to 1
Scale at 28°N: 1 in. to 250 mi., 1 cm to 158 km

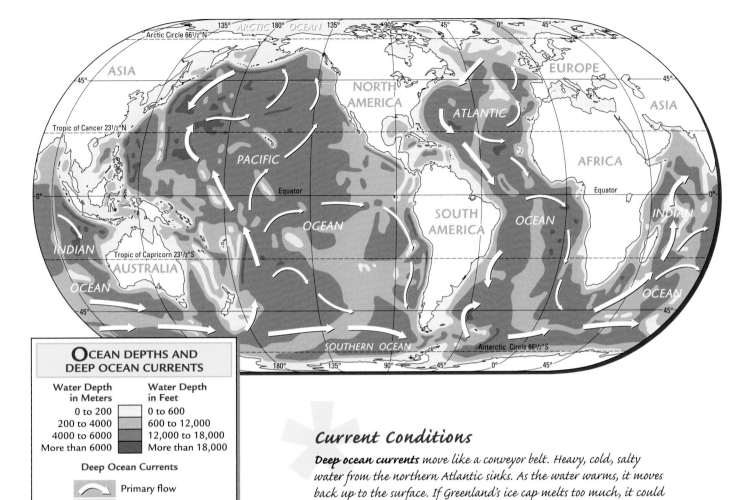

OCEAN DEPTHS AND DEEP OCEAN CURRENTS

Water Depth in Meters		Water Depth in Feet
0 to 200		0 to 600
200 to 4000		600 to 12,000
4000 to 6000		12,000 to 18,000
More than 6000		More than 18,000

Deep Ocean Currents

Primary flow

Secondary flow

Current Conditions

Deep ocean currents move like a conveyor belt. Heavy, cold, salty water from the northern Atlantic sinks. As the water warms, it moves back up to the surface. If Greenland's ice cap melts too much, it could cause the conveyor belt to shut down.

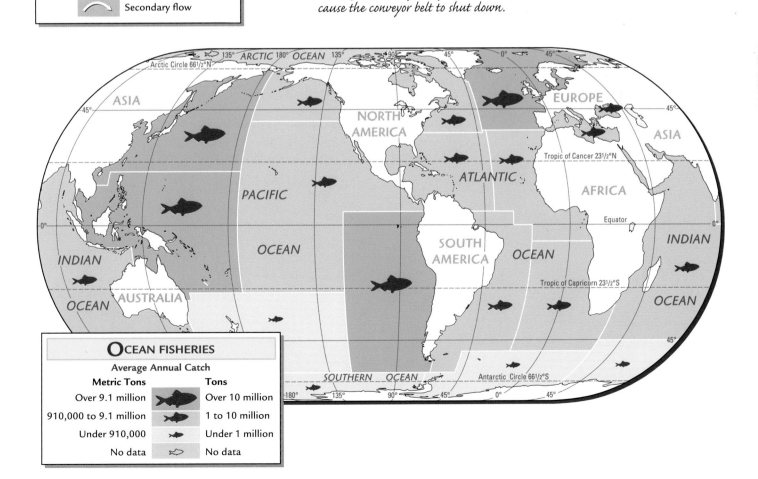

OCEAN FISHERIES

Average Annual Catch

Metric Tons		Tons
Over 9.1 million		Over 10 million
910,000 to 9.1 million		1 to 10 million
Under 910,000		Under 1 million
No data		No data

WEATHER PATTERNS

Weather is the condition of the atmosphere at a given time and place. Weather involves temperature, precipitation, humidity, wind, and other factors.

▶ **Temperature** is a measure of how hot or cold the air is near Earth's surface.

▶ **Precipitation** includes rain, snow, sleet, and hail. Although, on average, 10 inches (25.4 centimeters) of snow equals about 1 inch (2.5 centimeters) of rain, the actual ratio varies. Dry, powdery snow equals less rain than wet, heavy snow.

▶ **Humidity** is the amount of water vapor in the air, affecting the level of comfort and chance that clouds will form.

▶ **Seasonal winds** affect weather patterns by moving warm, cold, moist, or dry air to a region. (See the monsoon maps on page 158.)

Salzburg, Austria, is located in the Alps. Its winters are cold with an average temperature in January of 29°F (-2°C). Winters there are snowy and drier than its summers.

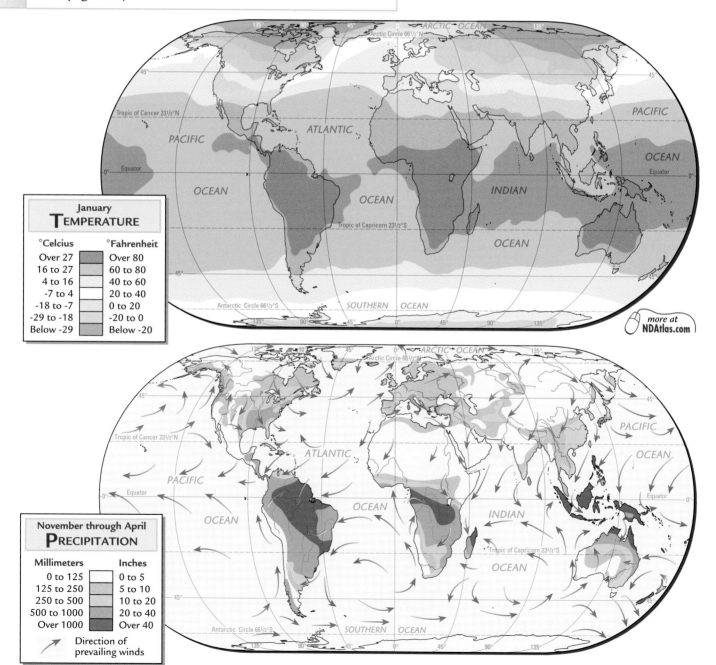

January TEMPERATURE

°Celcius	°Fahrenheit
Over 27	Over 80
16 to 27	60 to 80
4 to 16	40 to 60
-7 to 4	20 to 40
-18 to -7	0 to 20
-29 to -18	-20 to 0
Below -29	Below -20

more at NDAtlas.com

November through April PRECIPITATION

Millimeters	Inches
0 to 125	0 to 5
125 to 250	5 to 10
250 to 500	10 to 20
500 to 1000	20 to 40
Over 1000	Over 40

➚ Direction of prevailing winds

SUN AND SEASONS

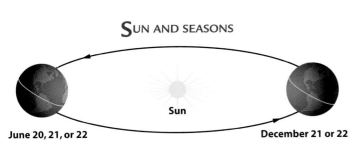

June 20, 21, or 22   **December 21 or 22**

The axis of the earth is tilted 23½°. From March through September, the Northern Hemisphere is tilted toward the sun and temperatures rise. The Southern Hemisphere gets warmer from September through March, when it is tilted toward the sun.

Summers in Salzburg are warm, with an average temperature in July of 64°F (18°C). In summer the city experiences *Schnürlregen*, a heavy downpour that suddenly appears and then disappears.

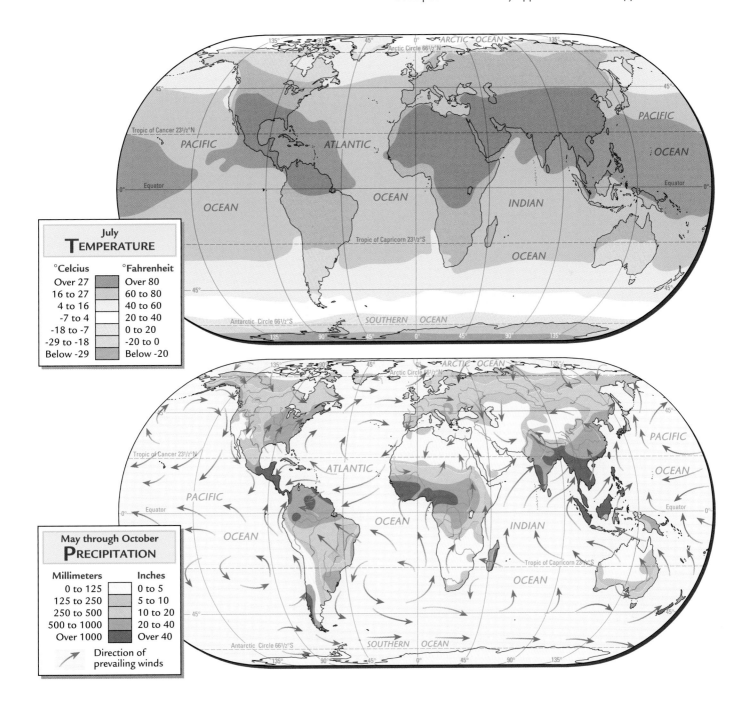

July TEMPERATURE

°Celcius	°Fahrenheit
Over 27	Over 80
16 to 27	60 to 80
4 to 16	40 to 60
-7 to 4	20 to 40
-18 to -7	0 to 20
-29 to -18	-20 to 0
Below -29	Below -20

May through October PRECIPITATION

Millimeters	Inches
0 to 125	0 to 5
125 to 250	5 to 10
250 to 500	10 to 20
500 to 1000	20 to 40
Over 1000	Over 40

↗ Direction of prevailing winds

World Matters

CLIMATE

While **weather** describes an area's atmosphere at a *specific* time, **climate** describes the usual weather pattern of a region over a *period* of time. Elevation, latitude, distance from oceans, and surface currents help determine a region's climate.

▶ Temperature and moisture decrease with **elevation**.

▶ **Latitude** affects temperature. Regions within the **Tropics of Cancer** and **Capricorn** receive direct sunlight and are warmer than polar areas within the **Arctic** and **Antarctic Circles**.

▶ Earth's rotation and the coasts of the continents drive most **surface currents** in a circular pattern, transferring warm ocean water near the Equator to higher northern and southern latitudes.

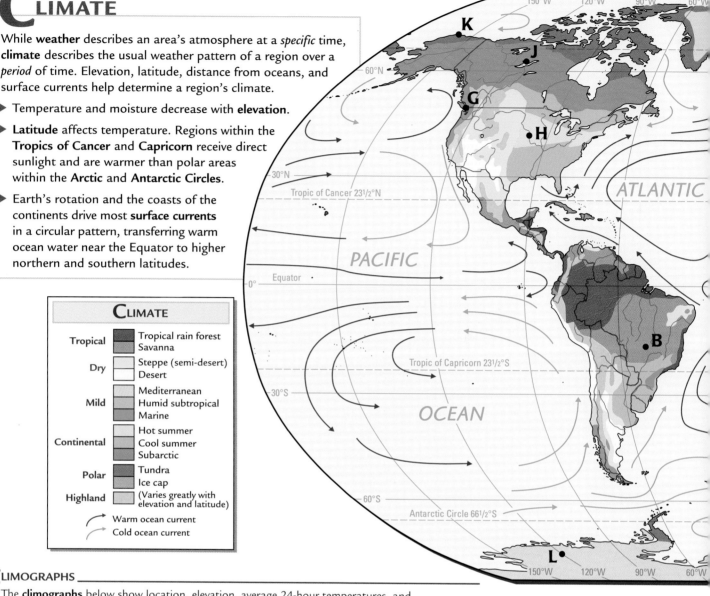

CLIMATE

Tropical	Tropical rain forest
	Savanna
Dry	Steppe (semi-desert)
	Desert
Mild	Mediterranean
	Humid subtropical
	Marine
Continental	Hot summer
	Cool summer
	Subarctic
Polar	Tundra
	Ice cap
Highland	(Varies greatly with elevation and latitude)

→ Warm ocean current
→ Cold ocean current

CLIMOGRAPHS

The **climographs** below show location, elevation, average 24-hour temperatures, and average monthly rainfall for several places. Letters refer to locations on the map. Colors indicate climate type. Curved lines show temperatures, while bars represent rainfall.

more at NDAtlas.com

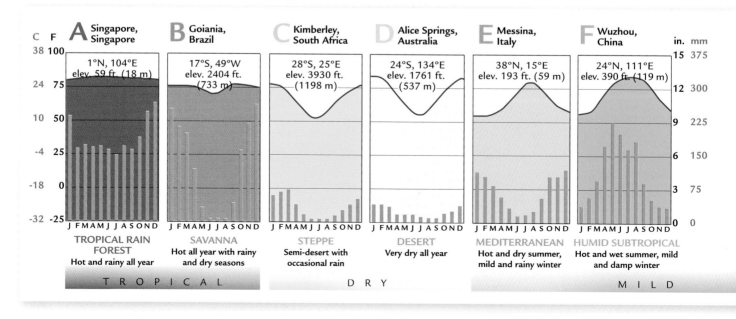

A Singapore, Singapore
1°N, 104°E
elev. 59 ft. (18 m)
TROPICAL RAIN FOREST
Hot and rainy all year

B Goiania, Brazil
17°S, 49°W
elev. 2404 ft. (733 m)
SAVANNA
Hot all year with rainy and dry seasons

C Kimberley, South Africa
28°S, 25°E
elev. 3930 ft. (1198 m)
STEPPE
Semi-desert with occasional rain

D Alice Springs, Australia
24°S, 134°E
elev. 1761 ft. (537 m)
DESERT
Very dry all year

E Messina, Italy
38°N, 15°E
elev. 193 ft. (59 m)
MEDITERRANEAN
Hot and dry summer, mild and rainy winter

F Wuzhou, China
24°N, 111°E
elev. 390 ft. (119 m)
HUMID SUBTROPICAL
Hot and wet summer, mild and damp winter

TROPICAL   DRY   MILD

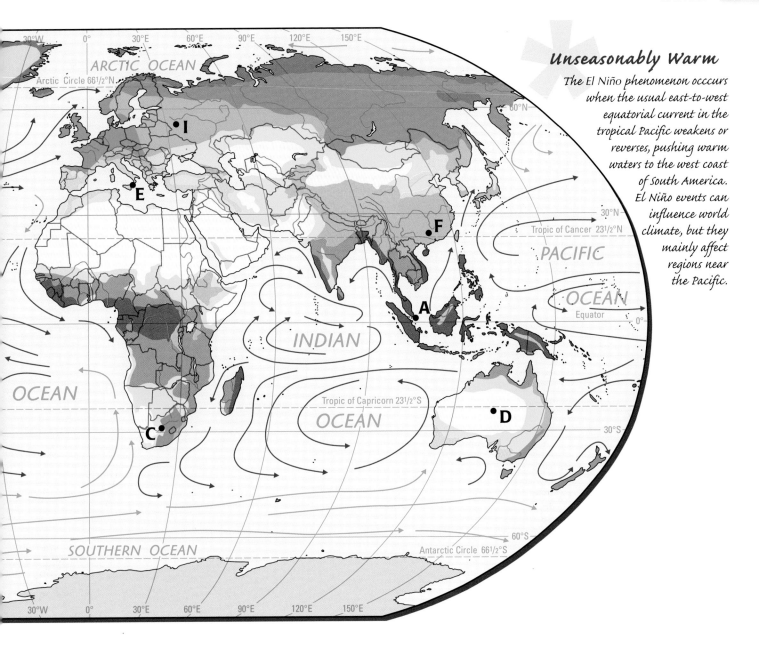

Unseasonably Warm

The El Niño phenomenon occcurs when the usual east-to-west equatorial current in the tropical Pacific weakens or reverses, pushing warm waters to the west coast of South America. El Niño events can influence world climate, but they mainly affect regions near the Pacific.

ARCTIC OCEAN
Arctic Circle 66½°N
PACIFIC
Tropic of Cancer 23½°N
INDIAN
OCEAN
Equator
OCEAN
Tropic of Capricorn 23½°S
OCEAN
SOUTHERN OCEAN
Antarctic Circle 66½°S

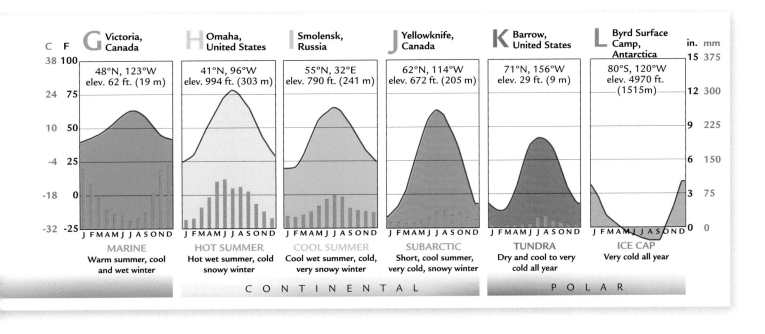

	G Victoria, Canada	H Omaha, United States	I Smolensk, Russia	J Yellowknife, Canada	K Barrow, United States	L Byrd Surface Camp, Antarctica
	48°N, 123°W elev. 62 ft. (19 m)	41°N, 96°W elev. 994 ft. (303 m)	55°N, 32°E elev. 790 ft. (241 m)	62°N, 114°W elev. 672 ft. (205 m)	71°N, 156°W elev. 29 ft. (9 m)	80°S, 120°W elev. 4970 ft. (1515m)
	MARINE	HOT SUMMER	COOL SUMMER	SUBARCTIC	TUNDRA	ICE CAP
	Warm summer, cool and wet winter	Hot wet summer, cold snowy winter	Cool wet summer, cold, very snowy winter	Short, cool summer, very cold, snowy winter	Dry and cool to very cold all year	Very cold all year

C F 38 100 / 24 75 / 10 50 / -4 25 / -18 0 / -32 -25

in. mm 15 375 / 12 300 / 9 225 / 6 150 / 3 75 / 0 0

C O N T I N E N T A L   P O L A R

World Matters

ENERGY RESOURCES

Oil (petroleum), natural gas, coal, and uranium fill most of the world's energy requirements. All but uranium are **fossil fuels** because they come from prehistoric plants and animals. All four are **consumable**—once used, they cannot be renewed.

▶ **Coal** is abundant and cheap. Countries use more than 5 billion tons (4.5 billion metric tons) of coal each year. Coal combustion, however, accounts for 35 percent of worldwide carbon dioxide emissions.

▶ **Uranium** is a radioactive metal. Nuclear power plants use this energy source to generate electricity.

▶ **Renewable energy resources** are an important alternative to fossil fuels. They include hydroelectricity, biomass, and geothermal, ocean thermal, solar, and wind energy.

This solar power plant is in California. It provides electricity 24 hours a day by capturing energy from the sun during the day and converting it into electrical power.

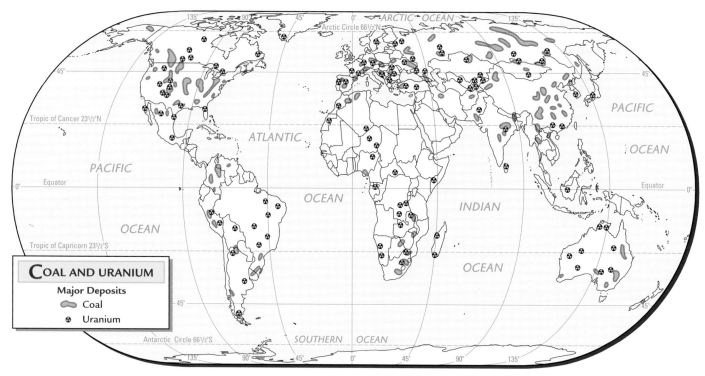

COAL AND URANIUM

Major Deposits
- Coal
- Uranium

COAL

Leaders in World **PRODUCTION**
- 29.0% **China**
- 20.7% **United States**
- 7.5% **India**
- 7.0% **Australia**
- 5.2% **Russia**

Leaders in World **CONSUMPTION**
- **China** 27.1%
- **United States** 20.3%
- **India** 8.0%
- **Germany** 5.2%
- **Russia** 4.6%

URANIUM

Leaders in World **PRODUCTION**
- 30.1% **Canada**
- 20.9% **Australia**
- 8.8% **Kazakhstan**
- 8.5% **Niger**
- 8.3% **Russia**

Leaders in World **CONSUMPTION**
- **United States** 30.1%
- **France** 15.5%
- **Japan** 12.5%
- **Germany** 5.3%
- **Russia** 5.3%

SOURCES OF WORLD ENERGY

Oil is the most-used energy source in the world today. Hydroelectricity is the only major energy source that is renewable. (For more information, see pages 78, 142, and 160–161.)

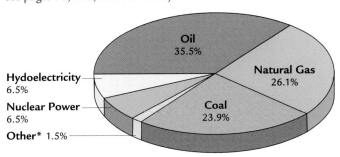

Oil
35.5%

Natural Gas
26.1%

Hydoelectricity
6.5%

Nuclear Power
6.5%

Coal
23.9%

Other* 1.5%

*Other includes: geothermal, ocean thermal, solar, wind, and biomass (wood, ethanol from corn or sugar, biodiesel from vegetable oils, methane made from waste)

Almost 79 percent of the electricity in Macedonia comes from fossil fuels. This particular power plant uses coal.

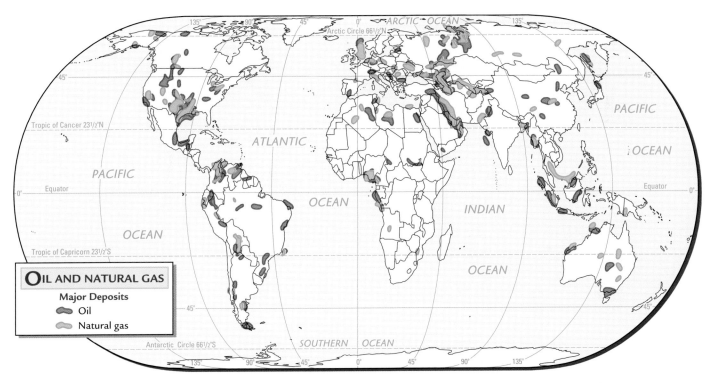

OIL AND NATURAL GAS

Major Deposits
- Oil
- Natural gas

OIL

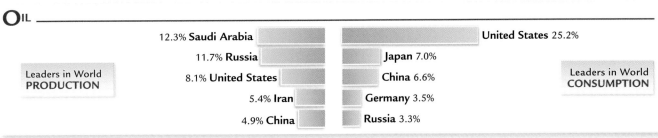

Leaders in World PRODUCTION

12.3% **Saudi Arabia**
11.7% **Russia**
8.1% **United States**
5.4% **Iran**
4.9% **China**

United States 25.2%
Japan 7.0%
China 6.6%
Germany 3.5%
Russia 3.3%

Leaders in World CONSUMPTION

NATURAL GAS

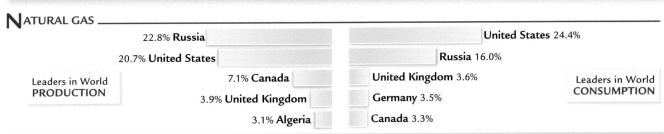

Leaders in World PRODUCTION

22.8% **Russia**
20.7% **United States**
7.1% **Canada**
3.9% **United Kingdom**
3.1% **Algeria**

United States 24.4%
Russia 16.0%
United Kingdom 3.6%
Germany 3.5%
Canada 3.3%

Leaders in World CONSUMPTION

World Matters

METALS

Metals are natural resources whose properties include strength, hardness, and conductivity. Metals such as iron and copper are in products that people use daily. The metal industry employs about 70 million people worldwide.

▶ **Copper** is responsible for conducting electrical currents in most homes, buildings, and telephone systems.

▶ **Gold** and **silver** are valuable metals. They are used in dentistry and electronics, as well as in jewelry and coins.

▶ **Iron** is one of the most abundant and commonly used metals in the world. It is used to produce **steel** and products made from steel, such as cars, bridges, and ships.

▶ **Nickel**, **tin,** and **zinc** are often used as coatings to protect steel from rust and corrosion.

Gold mining is an intricate, but rewarding, process. Here, a refinery worker pours gold at a mine in South Africa.

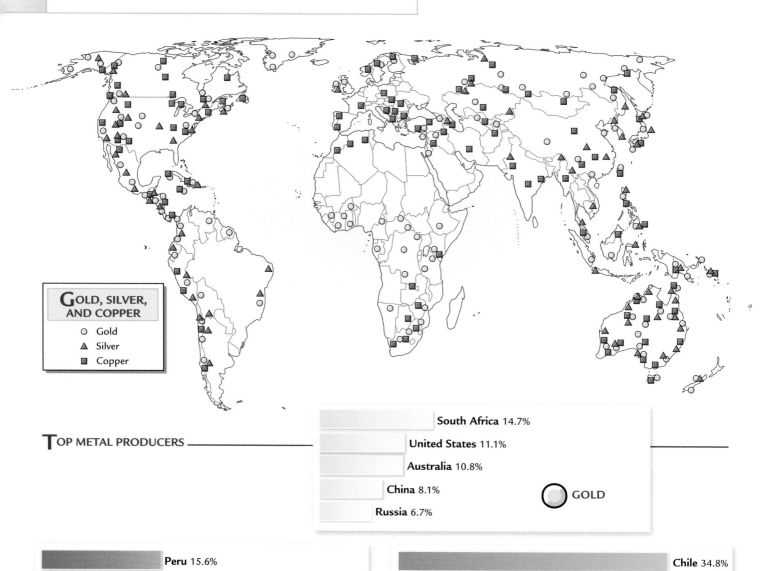

GOLD, SILVER, AND COPPER
- ○ Gold
- ▲ Silver
- ■ Copper

TOP METAL PRODUCERS

South Africa 14.7%
United States 11.1%
Australia 10.8%
China 8.1%
Russia 6.7%

○ GOLD

Peru 15.6%
Mexico 14.2%
China 12.5%
Australia 10.9%
Canada 7.2%

▲ SILVER

Chile 34.8%
United States 8.8%
Indonesia 7.9%
Australia 6.3%
Peru 5.9%

■ COPPER

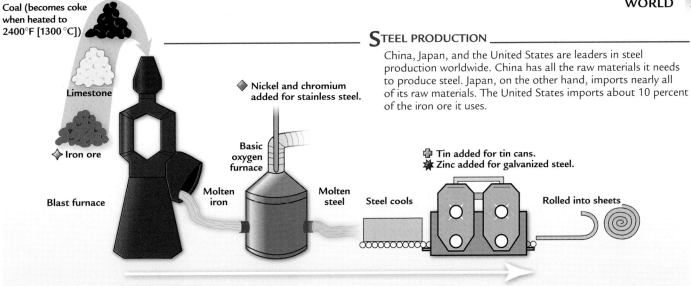

Coal (becomes coke when heated to 2400°F [1300°C])

Limestone

Iron ore

Blast furnace

Molten iron

◆ Nickel and chromium added for stainless steel.

Basic oxygen furnace

Molten steel

✚ Tin added for tin cans.
✷ Zinc added for galvanized steel.

Steel cools

Rolled into sheets

STEEL PRODUCTION

China, Japan, and the United States are leaders in steel production worldwide. China has all the raw materials it needs to produce steel. Japan, on the other hand, imports nearly all of its raw materials. The United States imports about 10 percent of the iron ore it uses.

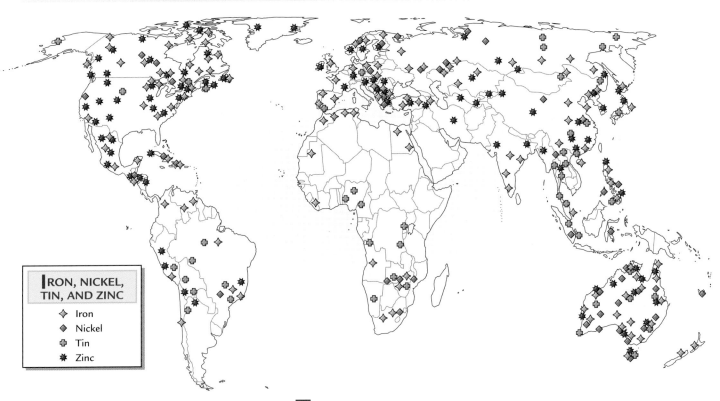

IRON, NICKEL, TIN, AND ZINC

- ◆ Iron
- ◆ Nickel
- ✚ Tin
- ✷ Zinc

TOP METAL PRODUCERS

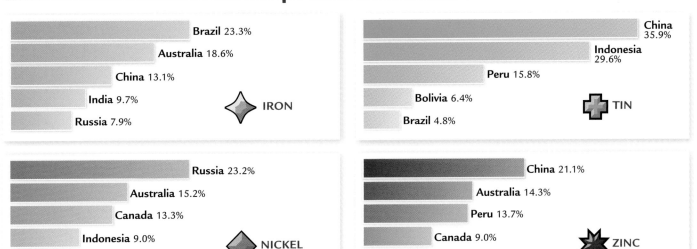

IRON
- Brazil 23.3%
- Australia 18.6%
- China 13.1%
- India 9.7%
- Russia 7.9%

TIN
- China 35.9%
- Indonesia 29.6%
- Peru 15.8%
- Bolivia 6.4%
- Brazil 4.8%

NICKEL
- Russia 23.2%
- Australia 15.2%
- Canada 13.3%
- Indonesia 9.0%
- New Caledonia (Fr.) 8.0%

ZINC
- China 21.1%
- Australia 14.3%
- Peru 13.7%
- Canada 9.0%
- United States 8.3%

World Matters

USING THE LAND

Land cover, such as desert or cropland, is the most common ground cover found in a given area, though most areas also may contain other types of land cover. **Land use**, such as farming or herding, is the most economically valuable human use of land in a given area, though the area often has other uses as well.

▶ Land cover often affects the way an area's land can be used.

▶ At nearly a third of the world's total land cover, **forests** are the most prevalent land cover on Earth.

▶ **Urban areas** are cities and their surrounding suburbs. Although urban areas are home to about half the world's population, they are the least widespread use of land on Earth.

Tundra

No widespread use

B **Tundra** is used for **nomadic herding** or has **no widespread use** at all. In spring and summer, the frozen soil thaws 1 to 10 feet (0.3 to 3 meters) below the surface, allowing only small plants and low shrubs to grow. This tundra is in far northern Canada.

Needleleaf forest

Forestry

A **Needleleaf forests**, as well as **tropical rain forests** and **broadleaf forests**, are used for **forestry**. Only half of the world's original forests remain standing. Canada is home to one-tenth of them.

Cartography 101

How do you map land cover? With a combination of high-tech sources and cartographic techniques. Satellite imagery and scientific analysis provide a detailed picture of the land. Then map makers adjust colors and add shading.

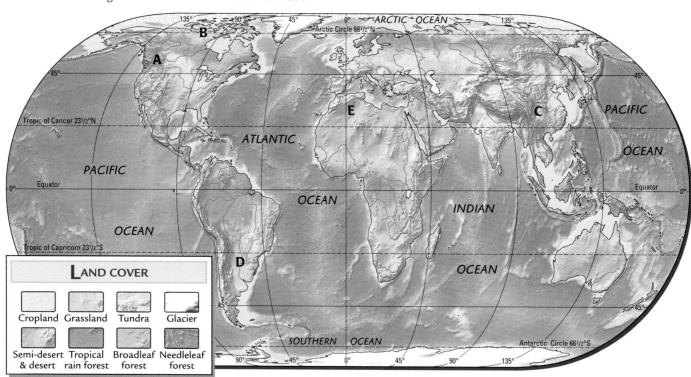

ARCTIC OCEAN
Arctic Circle 66½°N
B
A
45°
PACIFIC
Tropic of Cancer 23½°N
ATLANTIC
E
C
OCEAN
PACIFIC
Equator
OCEAN
INDIAN
OCEAN
D
OCEAN
Tropic of Capricorn 23½°S
45°
SOUTHERN OCEAN
Antarctic Circle 66½°S

LAND COVER

Cropland Grassland Tundra Glacier

Semi-desert & desert Tropical rain forest Broadleaf forest Needleleaf forest

Grassland

Ranching or herding

D **Grasslands** are primarily used for **ranching or herding**. Ranching often takes place on land too dry to farm. This gaucho is herding cattle on the plains of northern Argentina.

Cropland

Commercial farming

C **Cropland** is used for **subsistence farming** or **commercial farming**. Subsistence farmers only are able to raise enough food for their families. Commercial farms raise enough food to sell. These terraced commercial rice fields in China maximize the use of hilly land.

Semi-desert & desert

Nomadic herding

E **Desert** and **semi-desert** are typically used for **nomadic herding** or have **no widespread use**. Nomadic herders seasonally move their animals to fresh grazing areas and water. This herder leads camels across the Sahara in Algeria.

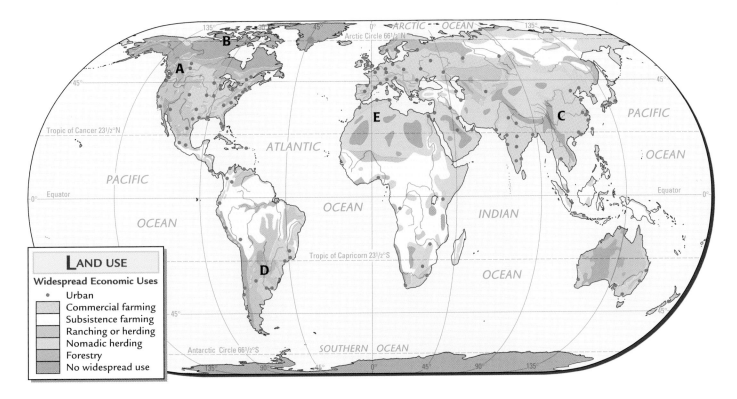

LAND USE

Widespread Economic Uses
- Urban
- Commercial farming
- Subsistence farming
- Ranching or herding
- Nomadic herding
- Forestry
- No widespread use

World Matters

ENVIRONMENTAL ISSUES

The **environment**, the natural world that we inhabit with all other living things, is affected and often harmed by human activities.

▶ **Acid rain** is precipitation that contains sulfuric, nitric, or other acids. This precipitation, caused by the burning of fossil fuels, can kill plants and make lakes too acidic for fish.

▶ **Tropical rain forests** are shrinking at an alarming rate due to logging, mining, and clearing land for agriculture.

▶ **Global warming** is the increase in the temperature of the earth's atmosphere. Rates of global warming in recent decades are significantly greater than rates of naturally occurring climate change. Scientists have concluded that human activities, such as burning fossil fuels and clearing forests, are the cause.

Acid rain is not only harmful to the environment, but also to statues and buildings made of marble or limestone. Acid rain has severely eroded this stone carving in England.

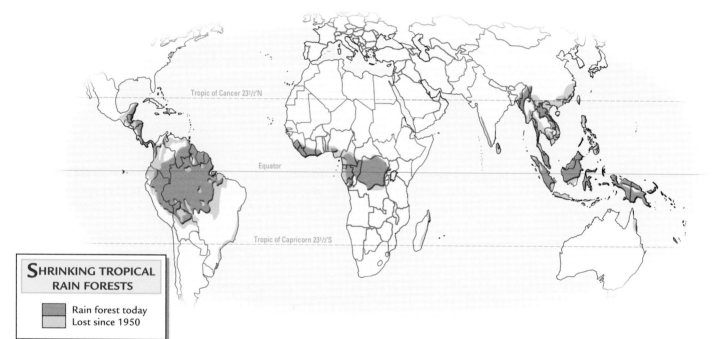

Tropic of Cancer 23¹/₂°N

Equator

Tropic of Capricorn 23¹/₂°S

SHRINKING TROPICAL RAIN FORESTS

- Rain forest today
- Lost since 1950

Deforestation has reduced tropical rain forests on nearly every continent since 1950. Every year about 32 million acres of the earth's forests are lost as forest lands are cleared for other uses. (For more information, see page 120.)

These Guatemalan farmers cut rain forests to grow crops. In just a few years the soil will lose its fertility and farmers move on to clear more land. Such slash-and-burn farming is the most prevalent and destructive form of deforestation.

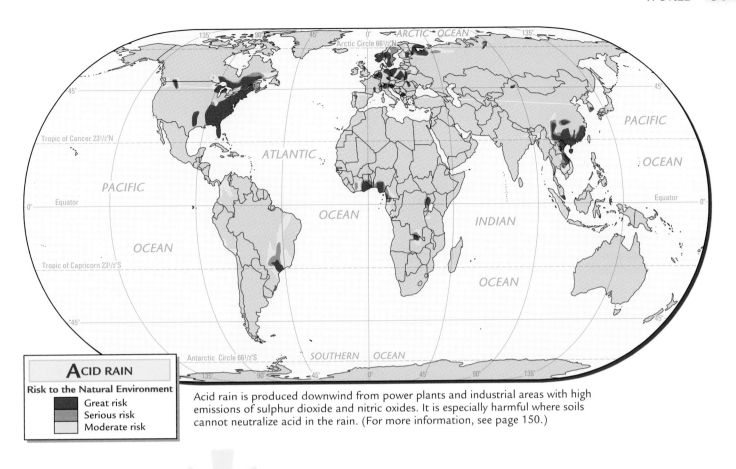

ACID RAIN

Risk to the Natural Environment
- ■ Great risk
- ■ Serious risk
- ☐ Moderate risk

Acid rain is produced downwind from power plants and industrial areas with high emissions of sulphur dioxide and nitric oxides. It is especially harmful where soils cannot neutralize acid in the rain. (For more information, see page 150.)

Rising Costs

Tuvalu is a small island country in the western Pacific Ocean near the Equator. As the oceans rise due to global warming, Tuvalu may soon be underwater, forcing its inhabitants to evacuate. By the year 2050, several island countries will spend more than 10 percent of their gross domestic product each year to combat the earth's rising water levels.

GLOBAL WARMING AND SEA ICE

The polar ice cap expands and contracts every year, melting to its smallest size in September, before freezing weather returns. Compare the ice cap in 1979 and 2005. More ice melts now because polar summers are warmer and longer. Melting sea ice does not raise the water level, but melting glaciers do.

more at NDAtlas.com

September 1979

September 2005

World Matters

GROWING POPULATION

Earth is home to more than 6.5 billion people. Its population continues to grow by about 80 million people per year.

▶ **Population density** is the average number of people living in a square mile or square kilometer of a region. The world's population density is about 114 people per square mile (44 per square kilometer).

▶ **Overpopulation** occurs when a population has outgrown an area's resources, such as land and water. Large parts of India, China, and Nigeria are overpopulated.

▶ **Natural population growth** is calculated by subtracting the total deaths from the total births in an area. It does not include migration to or from the area. The world has a growth rate of 1.1 percent.

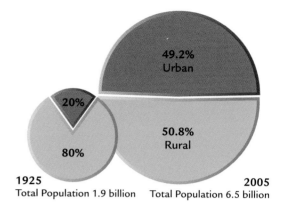

1925
Total Population 1.9 billion

2005
Total Population 6.5 billion

URBANIZATION

The world's urban population has more than quadrupled in the past 50 years. As farming becomes more efficient, people move to cities in search of jobs. Nearly half of the world's population now lives in urban areas.

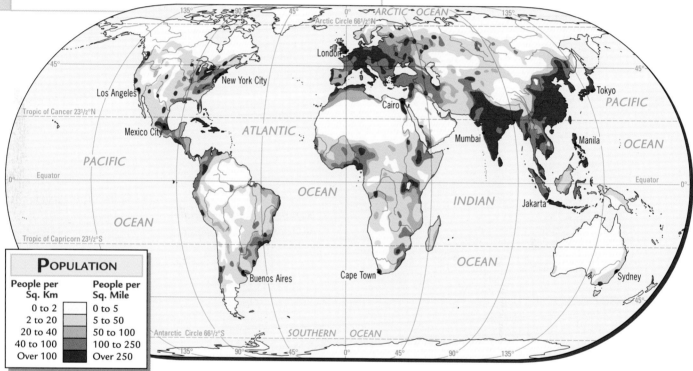

POPULATION

People per Sq. Km	People per Sq. Mile
0 to 2	0 to 5
2 to 20	5 to 50
20 to 40	50 to 100
40 to 100	100 to 250
Over 100	Over 250

Ups and Downs

There is an inverse relationship between prosperity and population. When people have access to quality health care and proper nutrition, they live longer. When women are educated, employed, and can expect that their children will survive childhood, they tend to have fewer children.

more at **NDAtlas.com**

POPULATION PYRAMIDS

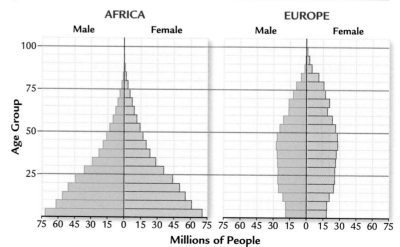

Most of Africa's population is young. This is in stark contrast to the population of Europe, which has nearly four times as many people over the age of 64 as Africa.

more at **NDAtlas.com**

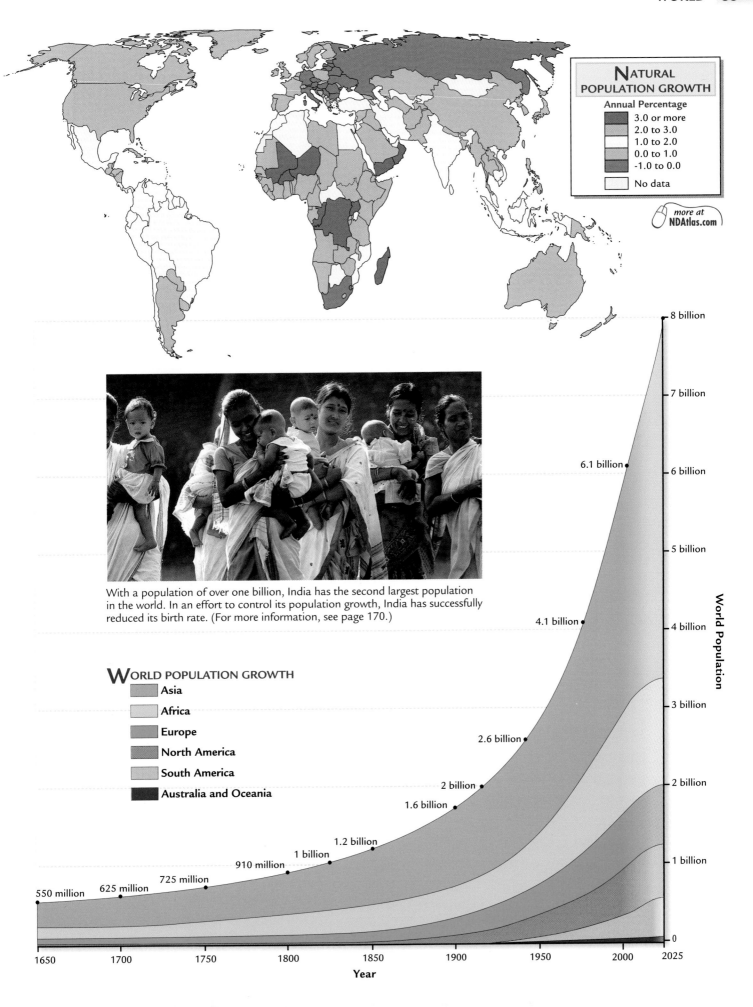

NATURAL
POPULATION GROWTH
Annual Percentage

- 3.0 or more
- 2.0 to 3.0
- 1.0 to 2.0
- 0.0 to 1.0
- -1.0 to 0.0
- No data

more at NDAtlas.com

With a population of over one billion, India has the second largest population in the world. In an effort to control its population growth, India has successfully reduced its birth rate. (For more information, see page 170.)

WORLD POPULATION GROWTH

- Asia
- Africa
- Europe
- North America
- South America
- Australia and Oceania

World Population

- 8 billion
- 7 billion
- 6 billion
- 5 billion
- 4 billion
- 3 billion
- 2 billion
- 1 billion
- 0

6.1 billion

4.1 billion

2.6 billion

2 billion

1.6 billion

1.2 billion

1 billion

910 million

725 million

625 million

550 million

Year
1650 1700 1750 1800 1850 1900 1950 2000 2025

World Matters

HEALTH CONCERNS

Better access to clean water and health care increases life expectancy. However, more than one billion people lack safe drinking water, and one-third of the world's population has no access to needed medicine.

▶ **Life expectancy** is the average number of years a person is expected to live. It is based on the death rates of specific age groups in a given population.

▶ In the developing world, rural water sources are more polluted than urban water sources. Eighty percent of all sickness in the developing world is attributed to water–related illnesses.

▶ Prevention controls disease. For example, smallpox killed an approximate 300 million people in the twentieth century, but the disease was eradicated by 1979 through a global vaccination program.

Immunization programs have drastically reduced the spread of infectious diseases, such as diphtheria and polio, worldwide. In China, a meningitis outbreak led this child to a local vaccination center.

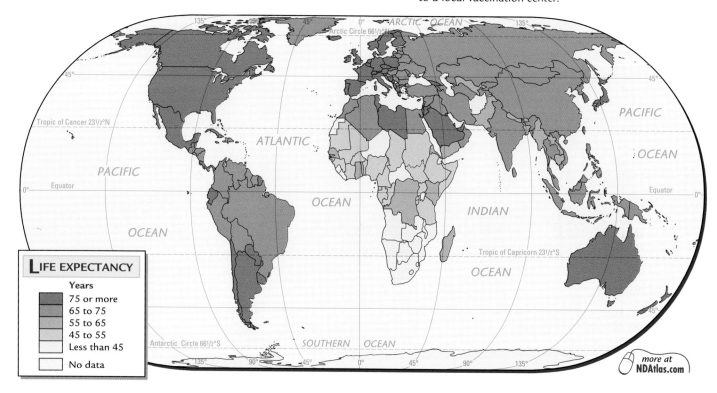

LIFE EXPECTANCY

Years
- 75 or more
- 65 to 75
- 55 to 65
- 45 to 55
- Less than 45
- No data

more at NDAtlas.com

LEADING CAUSES OF DEATH

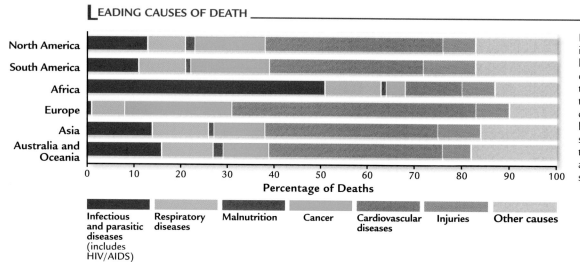

North America
South America
Africa
Europe
Asia
Australia and Oceania

Percentage of Deaths

Infectious and parasitic diseases (includes HIV/AIDS) · Respiratory diseases · Malnutrition · Cancer · Cardiovascular diseases · Injuries · Other causes

Disease caused by infection and parasites kill more people in developing countries than in other parts of the world. Wealthier countries have better health care systems, so more people die there from diseases associated with aging, such as heart disease.

 more at NDAtlas.com

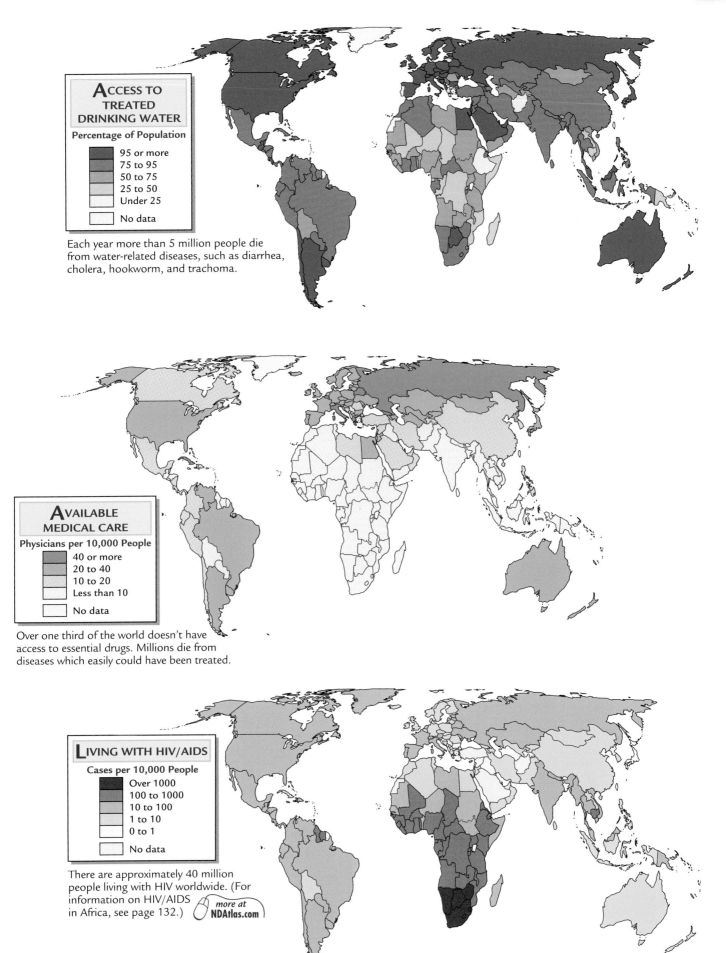

ACCESS TO TREATED DRINKING WATER

Percentage of Population

- 95 or more
- 75 to 95
- 50 to 75
- 25 to 50
- Under 25
- No data

Each year more than 5 million people die from water-related diseases, such as diarrhea, cholera, hookworm, and trachoma.

AVAILABLE MEDICAL CARE

Physicians per 10,000 People

- 40 or more
- 20 to 40
- 10 to 20
- Less than 10
- No data

Over one third of the world doesn't have access to essential drugs. Millions die from diseases which easily could have been treated.

LIVING WITH HIV/AIDS

Cases per 10,000 People

- Over 1000
- 100 to 1000
- 10 to 100
- 1 to 10
- 0 to 1
- No data

There are approximately 40 million people living with HIV worldwide. (For information on HIV/AIDS in Africa, see page 132.)

more at **NDAtlas.com**

FEEDING THE WORLD

World agriculture is capable of providing everyone on Earth with 2720 Calories a day (more calories than the average 2100 recommended by the American Red Cross). Even so, 800 million people go to bed hungry every night.

▶ Labeled as the number one health risk worldwide by the United Nations, world hunger affects one in seven people.

▶ War, drought and other natural disasters, and disease escalate world hunger by destroying crops and killing heads of households.

▶ New varieties of crops, such as high-yield rice and wheat and disease-resistant cassava, are helping increase productivity in developing countries.

In 1992 drought and civil war caused widespread suffering in Somalia. An estimated 270,000 people starved to death. About 70 percent of all Somalians still suffer from hunger.

CALORIES AND DIET

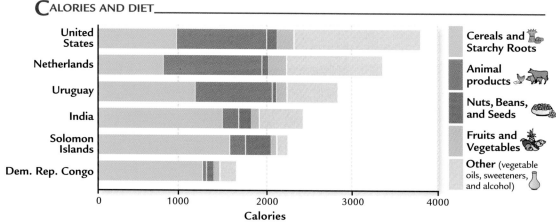

United States
Netherlands
Uruguay
India
Solomon Islands
Dem. Rep. Congo

0   1000   2000   3000   4000
Calories

Cereals and Starchy Roots

Animal products

Nuts, Beans, and Seeds

Fruits and Vegetables

Other (vegetable oils, sweeteners, and alcohol)

When a society gets wealthier, it shifts from a diet of grains to one with more meat, oils, sugars, and alcohol. Calorie consumption also increases.

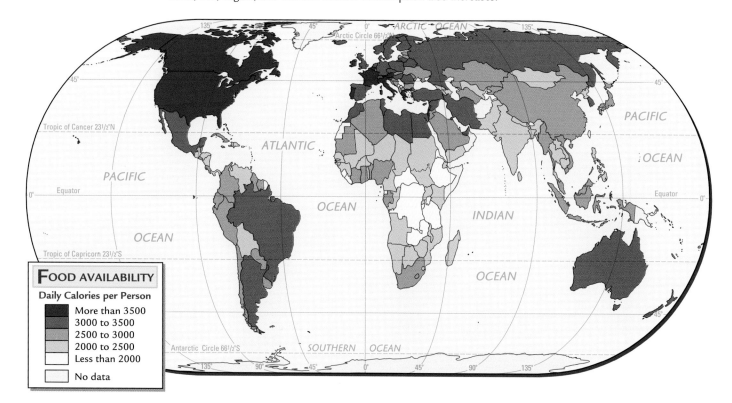

FOOD AVAILABILITY

Daily Calories per Person

- More than 3500
- 3000 to 3500
- 2500 to 3000
- 2000 to 2500
- Less than 2000
- No data

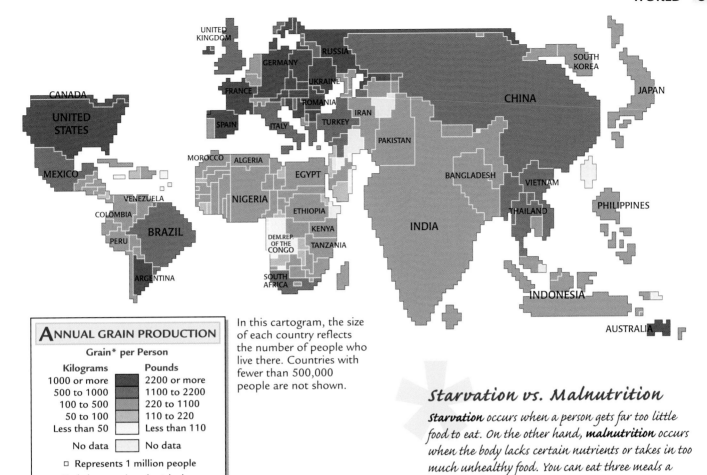

ANNUAL GRAIN PRODUCTION

Grain* per Person

Kilograms		Pounds
1000 or more		2200 or more
500 to 1000		1100 to 2200
100 to 500		220 to 1100
50 to 100		110 to 220
Less than 50		Less than 110
No data		No data

□ Represents 1 million people

*Includes corn, rice, wheat, barley, millet, oats, rye, and sorghum

In this cartogram, the size of each country reflects the number of people who live there. Countries with fewer than 500,000 people are not shown.

Starvation vs. Malnutrition

Starvation occurs when a person gets far too little food to eat. On the other hand, **malnutrition** occurs when the body lacks certain nutrients or takes in too much unhealthy food. You can eat three meals a day and still be malnourished.

STAPLE FOOD PRODUCTION

Staple foods are the major food sources of particular regions. They are typically energy-rich, inexpensive, and easy to maintain over a long period of time. Most of the world's people rely on grains such as rice, wheat, oats, or millet as their main food sources. In humid tropical and sub-tropical regions, root vegetables such as cassava are staple foods.

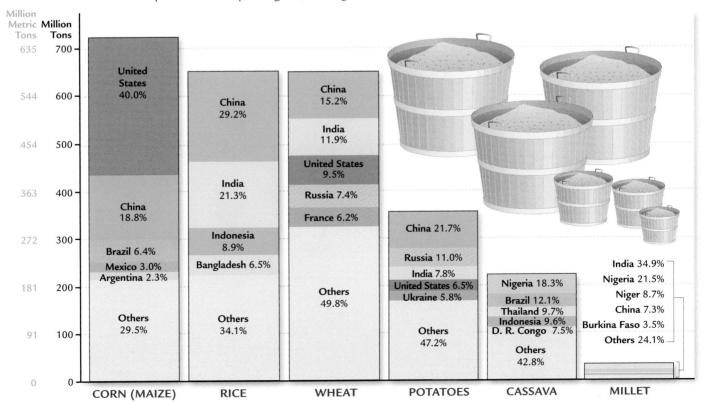

CORN (MAIZE)
- United States 40.0%
- China 18.8%
- Brazil 6.4%
- Mexico 3.0%
- Argentina 2.3%
- Others 29.5%

RICE
- China 29.2%
- India 21.3%
- Indonesia 8.9%
- Bangladesh 6.5%
- Others 34.1%

WHEAT
- China 15.2%
- India 11.9%
- United States 9.5%
- Russia 7.4%
- France 6.2%
- Others 49.8%

POTATOES
- China 21.7%
- Russia 11.0%
- India 7.8%
- United States 6.5%
- Ukraine 5.8%
- Others 47.2%

CASSAVA
- Nigeria 18.3%
- Brazil 12.1%
- Thailand 9.7%
- Indonesia 9.6%
- D. R. Congo 7.5%
- Others 42.8%

MILLET
- India 34.9%
- Nigeria 21.5%
- Niger 8.7%
- China 7.3%
- Burkina Faso 3.5%
- Others 24.1%

World Matters

RICH AND POOR

When people cannot afford basic human needs, such as food and housing, they are living in **poverty**. Poverty has different meanings in different parts of the world.

▶ **Absolute poverty** is poverty that threatens a person's life. In global terms, this is a household earning less than the equivalent of US$1 a day. Disease, hunger, and child labor plague people living in absolute poverty.

▶ **Relative poverty** is having fewer resources than others in a community or country. Countries define their national poverty lines differently.

▶ In the United States, a person living in poverty earns less than $9,645 a year, or $26 a day. According to the U.S. Census Bureau, more than 35 million Americans live below the U.S. poverty line.

In Buenos Aires, Argentina, this shanty-town is home to 20,000 poverty-stricken residents. It is separated by railroad tracks from the city's wealthiest neighborhood, visible in the background.

CONCENTRATION OF WEALTH

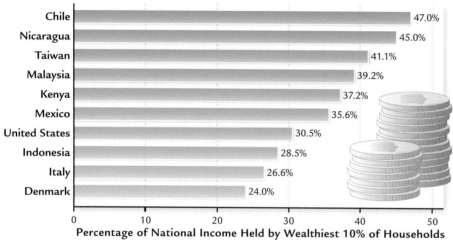

Country	Percentage
Chile	47.0%
Nicaragua	45.0%
Taiwan	41.1%
Malaysia	39.2%
Kenya	37.2%
Mexico	35.6%
United States	30.5%
Indonesia	28.5%
Italy	26.6%
Denmark	24.0%

0   10   20   30   40   50
Percentage of National Income Held by Wealthiest 10% of Households

In many countries the largest portion of wealth is controlled by a small portion of the population. This **disparity of income** can lead to social unrest.

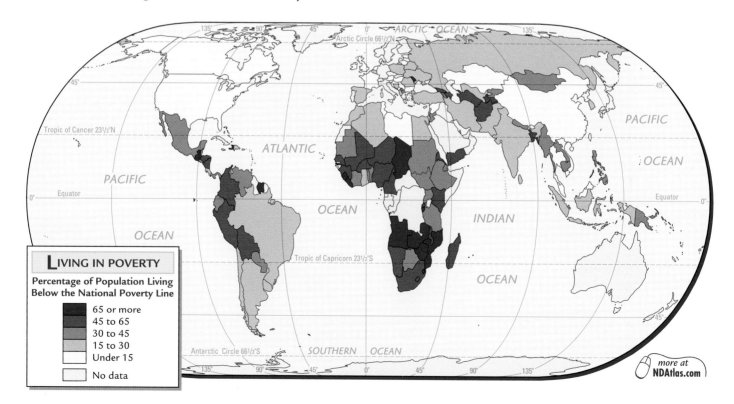

LIVING IN POVERTY

Percentage of Population Living Below the National Poverty Line

- 65 or more
- 45 to 65
- 30 to 45
- 15 to 30
- Under 15
- No data

more at NDAtlas.com

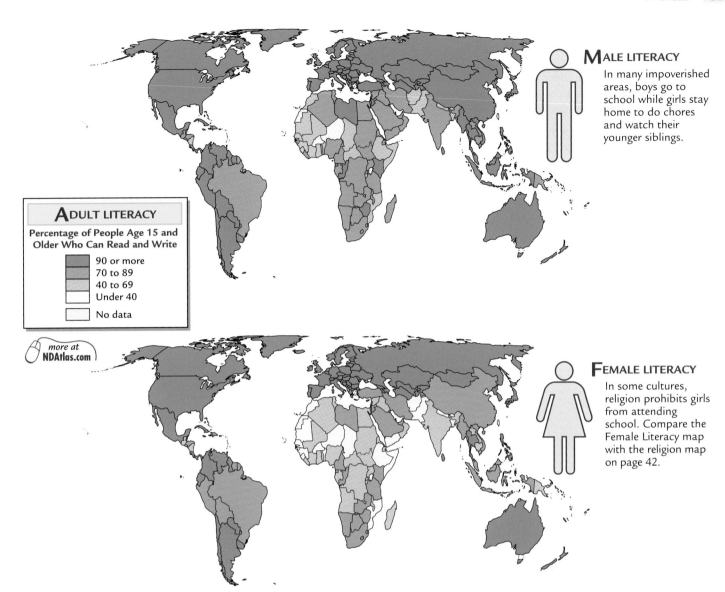

MALE LITERACY

In many impoverished areas, boys go to school while girls stay home to do chores and watch their younger siblings.

ADULT LITERACY

Percentage of People Age 15 and Older Who Can Read and Write

- 90 or more
- 70 to 89
- 40 to 69
- Under 40
- No data

more at NDAtlas.com

FEMALE LITERACY

In some cultures, religion prohibits girls from attending school. Compare the Female Literacy map with the religion map on page 42.

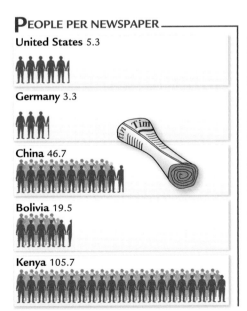

PEOPLE PER NEWSPAPER

United States 5.3

Germany 3.3

China 46.7

Bolivia 19.5

Kenya 105.7

The proportion of newspapers to people is more an indicator of literacy than of wealth. However, a population's level of education can affect its wealth.

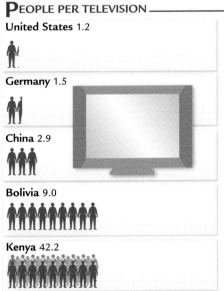

PEOPLE PER TELEVISION

United States 1.2

Germany 1.5

China 2.9

Bolivia 9.0

Kenya 42.2

The proportion of televisions to people is a strong indicator of wealth. While many homes in the United States have a television in nearly every room, some countries do not have a television in most communities.

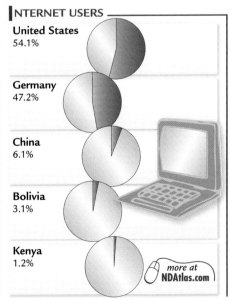

INTERNET USERS

United States 54.1%

Germany 47.2%

China 6.1%

Bolivia 3.1%

Kenya 1.2%

more at NDAtlas.com

As our world continues to become more technologically sophisticated, access to information is increasingly vital to economic prosperity.

World Matters

GLOBAL ECONOMY

As products, services, and money circulate around the world at a rapid rate, most countries have become economically interdependent, forming a **global economy**.

▶ **Gross Domestic Product**, or GDP, is the value of all goods and services produced within a country in a year. The United States accounts for one-fifth of the world's GDP.

▶ A **trade deficit** occurs when a country's imports exceed its exports. A **trade surplus** occurs when a country's exports exceed its imports.

▶ **Free trade** allows people to buy and sell goods across international borders without restrictions. It provides consumers with the cheapest possible goods, but cheaper imports may threaten domestic jobs.

more at NDAtlas.com

BALANCE OF TRADE
UNITED STATES

Total Exports
US$ 819 billion

Canada 23.1%
All Others 42.3%
European Union 21.1%
Mexico 13.5%

Total Imports
US$ 1,526 billion

European Union 19.1%
All Others 39.8%
Canada 17.0%
China 13.8%
Mexico 10.3%

Balance of trade is the value of a country's exports minus the value of its imports. The United States has ten times the trade deficit of any other country in the world.

more at NDAtlas.com

NATIONAL PRODUCTIVITY

GDP in US$ Billion

- Over 1,000
- 100 to 1,000
- 10 to 100
- 1 to 10
- Under 1
- No data

□ Represents 1 million people

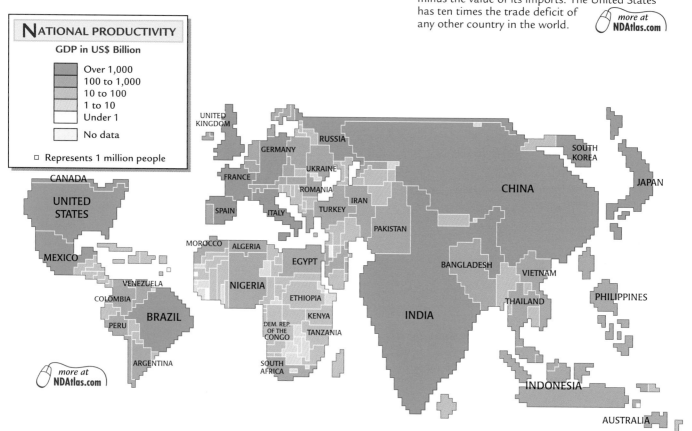

more at NDAtlas.com

SINGLE-COMMODITY ECONOMIES

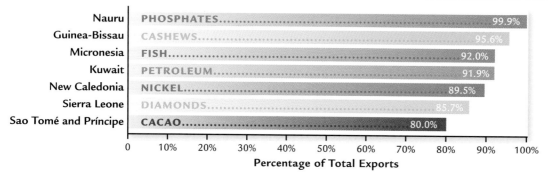

Country	Commodity	Percentage of Total Exports
Nauru	PHOSPHATES	99.9%
Guinea-Bissau	CASHEWS	95.6%
Micronesia	FISH	92.0%
Kuwait	PETROLEUM	91.9%
New Caledonia	NICKEL	89.5%
Sierra Leone	DIAMONDS	85.7%
Sao Tomé and Príncipe	CACAO	80.0%

Percentage of Total Exports

Many countries rely on a single natural resource or crop for 80 percent or more of their exports. These countries run the risk of becoming dependent on other countries for goods and services. Their economies also are vulnerable to sudden changes in international prices and demands for their key commodity.

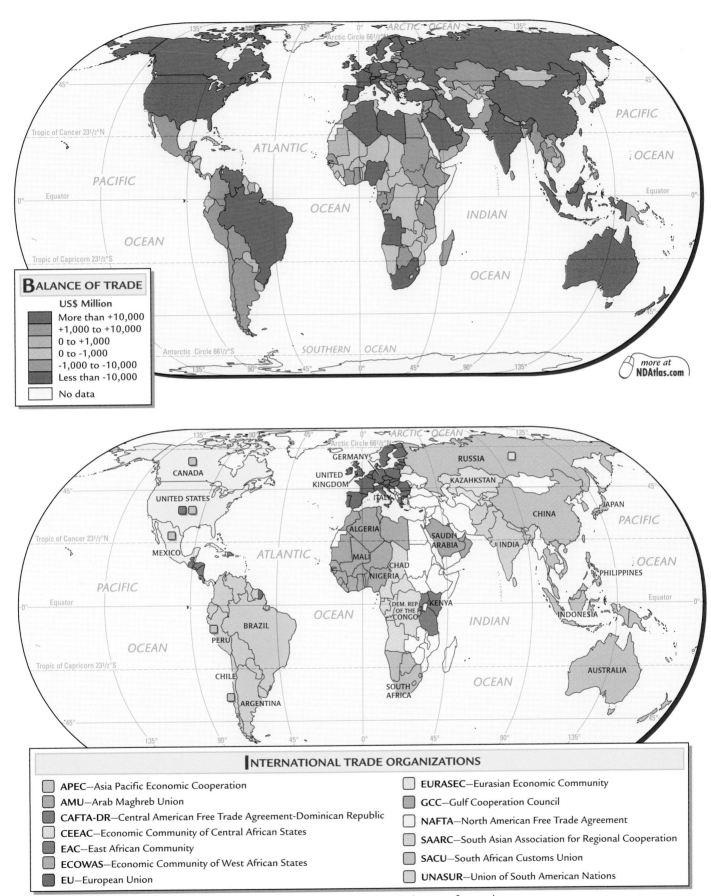

BALANCE OF TRADE

US$ Million

- More than +10,000
- +1,000 to +10,000
- 0 to +1,000
- 0 to -1,000
- -1,000 to -10,000
- Less than -10,000
- No data

more at NDAtlas.com

INTERNATIONAL TRADE ORGANIZATIONS

- **APEC**—Asia Pacific Economic Cooperation
- **AMU**—Arab Maghreb Union
- **CAFTA-DR**—Central American Free Trade Agreement-Dominican Republic
- **CEEAC**—Economic Community of Central African States
- **EAC**—East African Community
- **ECOWAS**—Economic Community of West African States
- **EU**—European Union
- **EURASEC**—Eurasian Economic Community
- **GCC**—Gulf Cooperation Council
- **NAFTA**—North American Free Trade Agreement
- **SAARC**—South Asian Association for Regional Cooperation
- **SACU**—South African Customs Union
- **UNASUR**—Union of South American Nations

Trade organizations are established by agreements between governments to increase free trade.
NAFTA and EU are among the wealthiest and most influential trade organizations in the world.
(For more information, see pages 51 and 141.)

CULTURAL DIVERSITY

Culture is the way of life of a given human society. Every society in the world has a unique culture.

▶ Aspects of culture include a society's language, religion, art, customs, ethnicity, institutions, technology, and other traits.

▶ Countries can have multiple cultures, and cultures can cross national boundaries.

▶ Language and religion are two distinguishing features of a culture. Thousands of religions are practiced and about 6,000 languages are spoken in the world today.

▶ **Language families** are groups of related languages that developed slowly over time from a single earlier **parent language**.

Mother Teresa was a Roman Catholic nun who helped the poor in India. Indians of all faiths now revere her. Girls hold symbols of Hinduism, Islam, and Christianity during a rally in her honor.

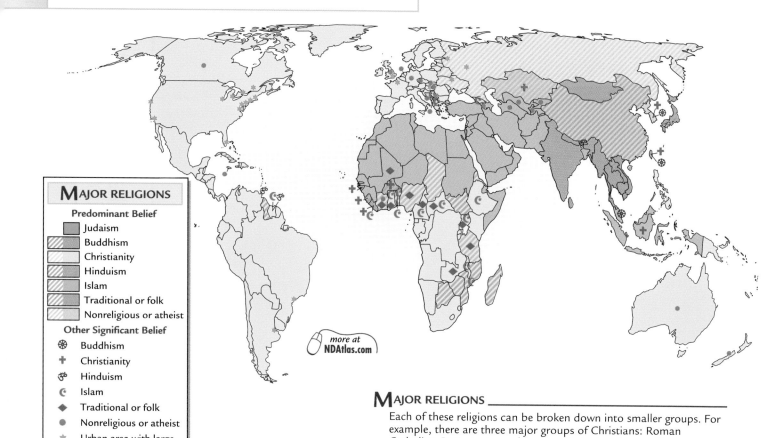

MAJOR RELIGIONS

Predominant Belief
- Judaism
- Buddhism
- Christianity
- Hinduism
- Islam
- Traditional or folk
- Nonreligious or atheist

Other Significant Belief
- ❀ Buddhism
- ✝ Christianity
- ॐ Hinduism
- ☾ Islam
- ◆ Traditional or folk
- ● Nonreligious or atheist
- ✳ Urban area with large Jewish population

more at NDAtlas.com

Who Are You?

Ethnicity is complex. For example, if your ethnic background is Mexican, you might speak Spanish at home and celebrate Día de los Muertos (Day of the Dead). At the same time, you might speak English at school and celebrate American holidays such as the Fourth of July and Thanksgiving.

MAJOR RELIGIONS _____

Each of these religions can be broken down into smaller groups. For example, there are three major groups of Christians: Roman Catholics, Protestants, and Eastern Orthodox. Among Protestants alone, there are hundreds of denominations.

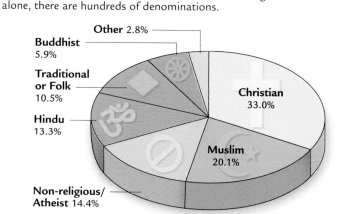

- **Other** 2.8%
- **Buddhist** 5.9%
- **Traditional or Folk** 10.5%
- **Hindu** 13.3%
- **Non-religious/ Atheist** 14.4%
- **Christian** 33.0%
- **Muslim** 20.1%

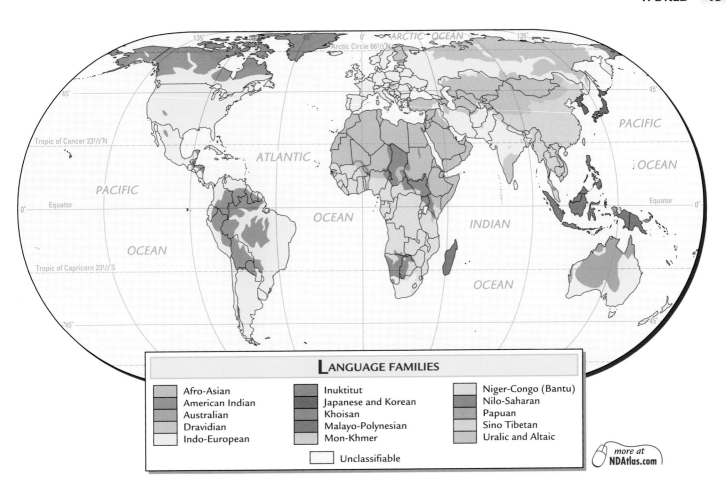

LANGUAGE FAMILIES

- Afro-Asian
- American Indian
- Australian
- Dravidian
- Indo-European
- Inuktitut
- Japanese and Korean
- Khoisan
- Malayo-Polynesian
- Mon-Khmer
- Niger-Congo (Bantu)
- Nilo-Saharan
- Papuan
- Sino Tibetan
- Uralic and Altaic

Unclassifiable

more at NDAtlas.com

INDO-EUROPEAN LANGUAGES

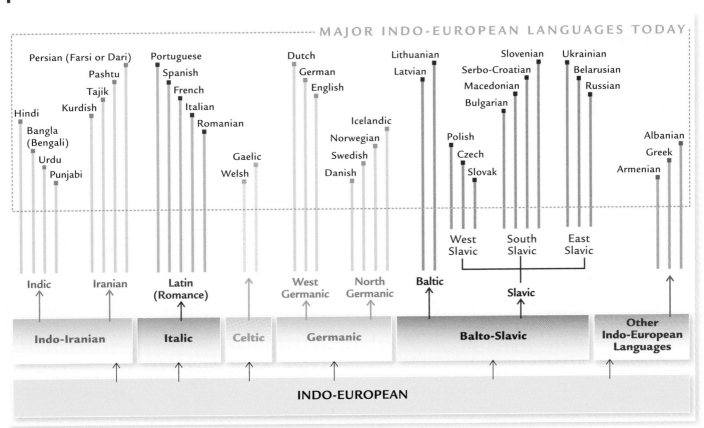

— MAJOR INDO-EUROPEAN LANGUAGES TODAY —

Indo-Iranian
- Indic: Hindi, Bangla (Bengali), Urdu, Punjabi
- Iranian: Persian (Farsi or Dari), Pashtu, Tajik, Kurdish

Italic
- Latin (Romance): Portuguese, Spanish, French, Italian, Romanian

Celtic
- Gaelic, Welsh

Germanic
- West Germanic: Dutch, German, English
- North Germanic: Icelandic, Norwegian, Swedish, Danish

Balto-Slavic
- Baltic: Lithuanian, Latvian
- Slavic:
  - West Slavic: Polish, Czech, Slovak
  - South Slavic: Slovenian, Serbo-Croatian, Macedonian, Bulgarian
  - East Slavic: Ukrainian, Belarusian, Russian

Other Indo-European Languages
- Albanian, Greek, Armenian

INDO-EUROPEAN

Indo-European is the most widely spoken language family. About half the people in the world speak languages in this family, which originated in an area that extended from northern India to western Europe.

World Matters

HUMAN MIGRATION

People have moved to new places throughout history. Today, with improvements in transportation, people can move farther and faster than ever before.

▶ People often leave their old homes in search of better economic, political, or religious opportunities. These attractions to new homes are called **pull factors**.

▶ Some people leave their old homes to escape natural disasters, persecution, or war. These are called **push factors**.

▶ People can move to new locations within their country (**migration**) or move to another country (**immigration**).

Cultural differences between immigrants and their new countries often lead to conflicts. Here immigrants from North Africa protest proposed restrictions on religious dress, including Muslim head scarves, in French schools.

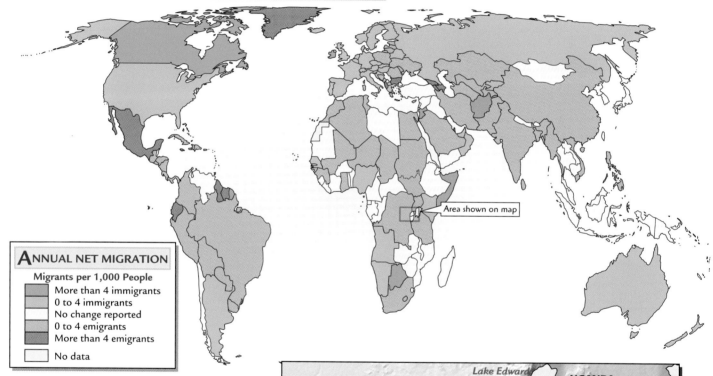

Area shown on map

ANNUAL NET MIGRATION

Migrants per 1,000 People

- More than 4 immigrants
- 0 to 4 immigrants
- No change reported
- 0 to 4 emigrants
- More than 4 emigrants
- No data

Safe Away from Home

People leave their home countries for many reasons. **Refugees** are fleeing for their lives. **Emigrants** leave by their own choice. The difference is very important. Refugees are protected by international agreements and may be supported by the world community. Emigrants do not have these protections.

ZAIRE-RWANDA MIGRATION

⇠	from Rwanda
⇢	from Zaire/Dem. Rep. of the Congo

April 1994	Civil war and genocide break out in Rwanda.
July 1994	Civil war ends, some return home.
1996	Civil war breaks out in Zaire.
1997	Government overthrown, Democratic Republic of the Congo established.

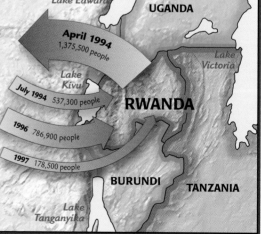

ZAIRE
(Dem. Rep. of the Congo since 1997)

Lake Edward — UGANDA

April 1994 — 1,375,500 people

Lake Kivu

July 1994 — 537,300 people

RWANDA

1996 — 786,900 people

1997 — 178,500 people

Lake Victoria

BURUNDI — TANZANIA

Lake Tanganyika

Genocide and revolution in Rwanda led to a huge refugee crisis, which helped undermine the government of neighboring Zaire. Zaire's collapse, in turn, provoked another refugee crisis in the opposite direction.

NORTH AMERICA

North America includes two of the world's largest countries: Canada and the United States. People with ancestors from Europe, Africa, Asia, and the Americas share the plains and mountainous regions of North America.

PHYSICAL FEATURES

Mountains
Highest peak: Mt. McKinley 20,320 ft. (6 194 m)
Longest range: Rocky Mountains 3,000 mi. (4 800 km)

Largest Island
Greenland 836,330 sq. mi. (2 166 066 sq. km)

Largest Lakes
Lake Superior 31,700 sq. mi. (82 100 sq. km)★
Lake Huron 23,000 sq. mi. (59 600 sq. km)★
Lake Michigan 22,300 sq. mi. (57 800 sq. km)★

Longest Rivers
Mississippi-Missouri System 3,741 mi. (6 020 km)★
Mackenzie 2,635 mi. (4 241 km)★

Other Key Physical Features
Great Basin
Great Plains
Coastal Plains
Colorado Plateau
Plateau of Mexico
Canadian Shield
Labrador Peninsula
Yucatan Peninsula
Florida Peninsula

CULTURAL FEATURES

Population 518,300,000

Largest Countries
By area: Canada 3,855,103 sq. mi. (9 984 670 sq. km)★
United States 3,676,487 sq. mi. (9 522 058 sq. km)★
By population: United States 304,059,728

Population Density
Most densely populated: Barbados 1,686 people per sq. mi. (651 per sq. km)
Least densely populated: Greenland 0.1 people per sq. mi. (0.03 per sq. km)

Largest Urban Areas
Mexico City, Mexico 19,460,000★
New York City, United States 19,425,000★
Los Angeles, United States 12,762,000★

★ Among the world's largest. See the inside front cover.

 more at NDAtlas.com
For more maps, graphs, and photos of North America, go to NystromDeskAtlas.com.

AREA COMPARISON

■ North America
9,348,000 sq. mi.
(24 211 000 sq. km)

Contiguous United States
3,021,295 sq. mi.
(7 825 112 sq. km)

World Extreme Nuuk (Godthab), the smallest capital in the world, is located on the world's largest island, Greenland. A self-governing dependency of Denmark, Greenland (Kalaallit Nunaaat) is also the largest possession in the world.

REGIONAL MAPS OF NORTH AMERICA

Greenland

CANADA

1

2

UNITED STATES

2

3

MEXICO

CUBA

NICARAGUA

PANAMA

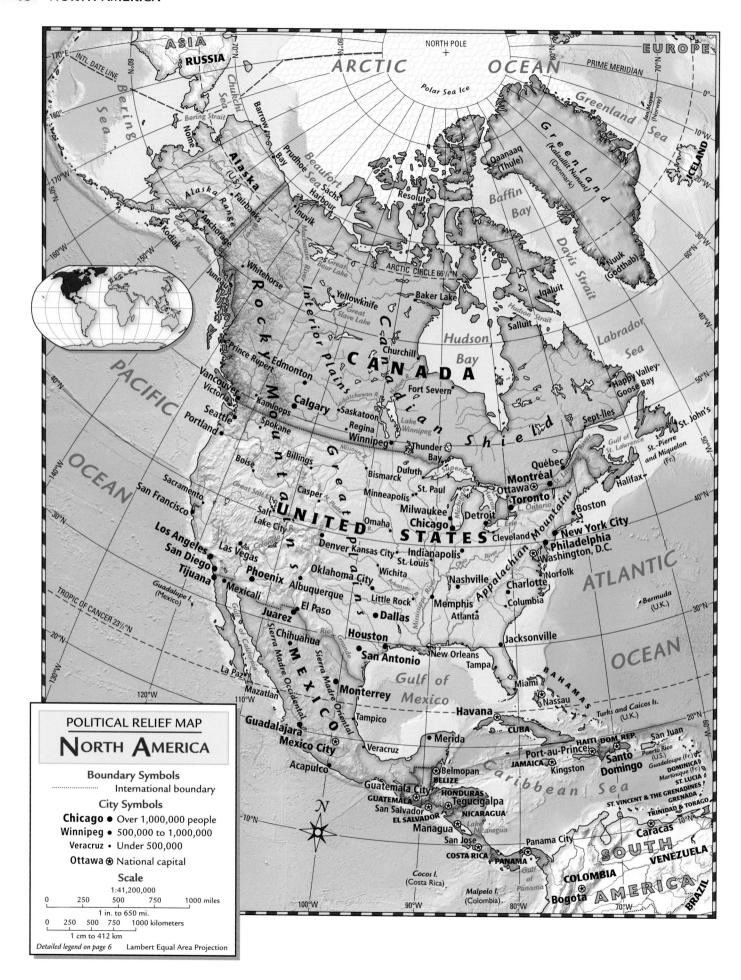

POLITICAL RELIEF MAP
NORTH AMERICA

Boundary Symbols
.... International boundary

City Symbols
Chicago ● Over 1,000,000 people
Winnipeg ● 500,000 to 1,000,000
Veracruz · Under 500,000
Ottawa ⊗ National capital

Scale
1:41,200,000

0   250   500   750   1000 miles

1 in. to 650 mi.

0   250   500   750   1000 kilometers

1 cm to 412 km

Detailed legend on page 6   Lambert Equal Area Projection

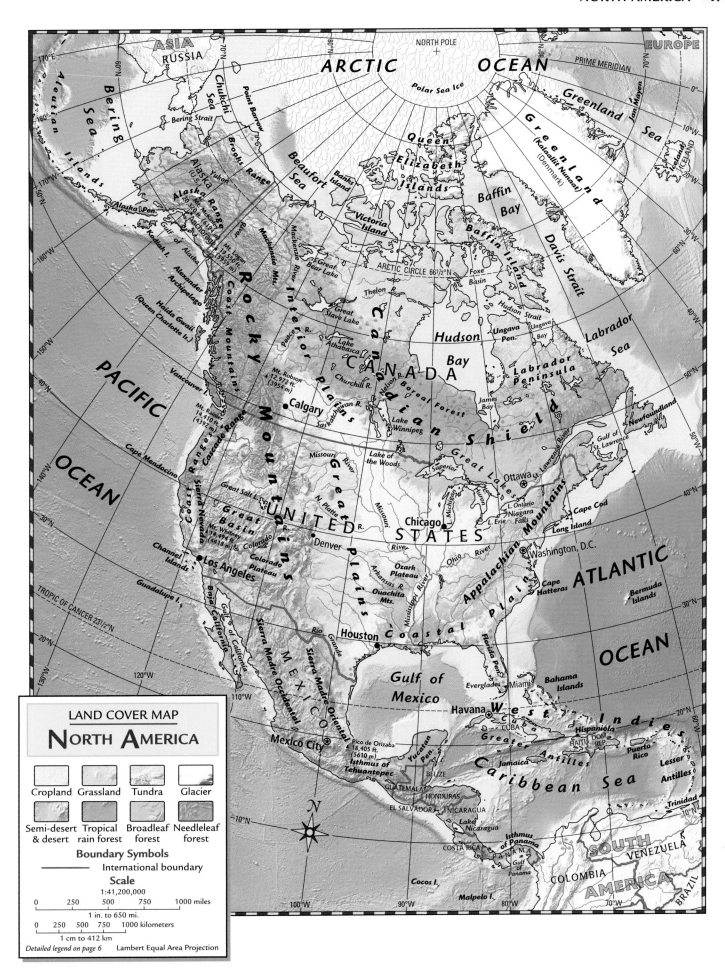

ASIA
RUSSIA

ARCTIC OCEAN
NORTH POLE
Polar Sea Ice

EUROPE
PRIME MERIDIAN

Aleutian Islands
Bering Sea
Chukchi Sea
Point Barrow
Bering Strait
Beaufort Sea
Banks Island
Queen Elizabeth Islands
Greenland (Kalaallit Nunaat) (Denmark)
Greenland Sea
Jan Mayen
ICELAND

Alaska Range
Brooks Range
Yukon River
Mt. McKinley 20,320 ft. (6194 m)
Anchorage
Gulf of Alaska
Kodiak I.
Alexander Archipelago
Haida Gwaii (Queen Charlotte Is.)
Vancouver I.
Mackenzie Mts.
Mackenzie River
Great Bear Lake
ARCTIC CIRCLE 66½°N
Victoria Island
Baffin Bay
Baffin Island
Foxe Basin
Hudson Strait
Davis Strait

Thelon
Great Slave Lake
Lake Athabasca
Peace R.
Churchill R.
CANADA
Canadian Shield
Hudson Bay
Ungava Pen.
Ungava Bay
Labrador
Labrador Sea

PACIFIC OCEAN

Cape Mendocino
Coast Ranges
Cascade Range
Mt. Robson 12,972 ft. (3954 m)
Mt. Rainier 14,410 ft. (4392 m)
Calgary
Rocky Mountains
Interior Plains
Boreal Forest
Nelson R.
Saskatchewan R.
Great Slave Lake
James Bay
Great Lakes
Labrador Peninsula
Newfoundland
Gulf of St. Lawrence

Guadalupe I.
TROPIC OF CANCER 23½°N
Channel Islands
Los Angeles
Sierra Nevada
Mt. Whitney 14,494 ft. (4418 m)
Great Basin
Colorado Plateau
Colorado R.
UNITED STATES
Great Salt L.
Denver
N. Platte R.
Great Plains
Missouri River
Missouri R.
Lake of the Woods
Lake Winnipeg
L. Superior
L. Michigan
L. Huron
L. Ontario
L. Erie
Niagara Falls
Chicago
Ottawa
St. Lawrence River
Cape Cod
Long Island
Washington, D.C.
Appalachian Mountains
Ozark Plateau
Arkansas R.
Ouachita Mts.
Ohio River
Mississippi River
Coastal Plain
Cape Hatteras
ATLANTIC OCEAN
Bermuda Islands

Baja California
Gulf of California
Sierra Madre Occidental
Sierra Madre Oriental
MEXICO
Rio Grande
Houston
Gulf of Mexico
Florida Pen.
Everglades
Miami
Bahama Islands
Havana
CUBA
West Indies
Greater Antilles
HAITI
DOM. REP.
Hispaniola
Puerto Rico
Lesser Antilles

Mexico City
Pico de Orizaba 18,405 ft. (5610 m)
Isthmus of Tehuantepec
Yucatan Pen.
BELIZE
GUATEMALA
HONDURAS
EL SALVADOR
NICARAGUA
Lake Nicaragua
COSTA RICA
Isthmus of Panama
PANAMA
Gulf of Panama
Cocos I.
Malpelo I.
Caribbean Sea
Jamaica
Trinidad
SOUTH AMERICA
VENEZUELA
COLOMBIA
BRAZIL

N

LAND COVER MAP
NORTH AMERICA

Cropland   Grassland   Tundra   Glacier

Semi-desert & desert   Tropical rain forest   Broadleaf forest   Needleleaf forest

Boundary Symbols
——— International boundary

Scale
1:41,200,000

| 0 | 250 | 500 | 750 | 1000 miles |

1 in. to 650 mi.

| 0 | 250 | 500 | 750 | 1000 kilometers |

1 cm to 412 km

Detailed legend on page 6   Lambert Equal Area Projection

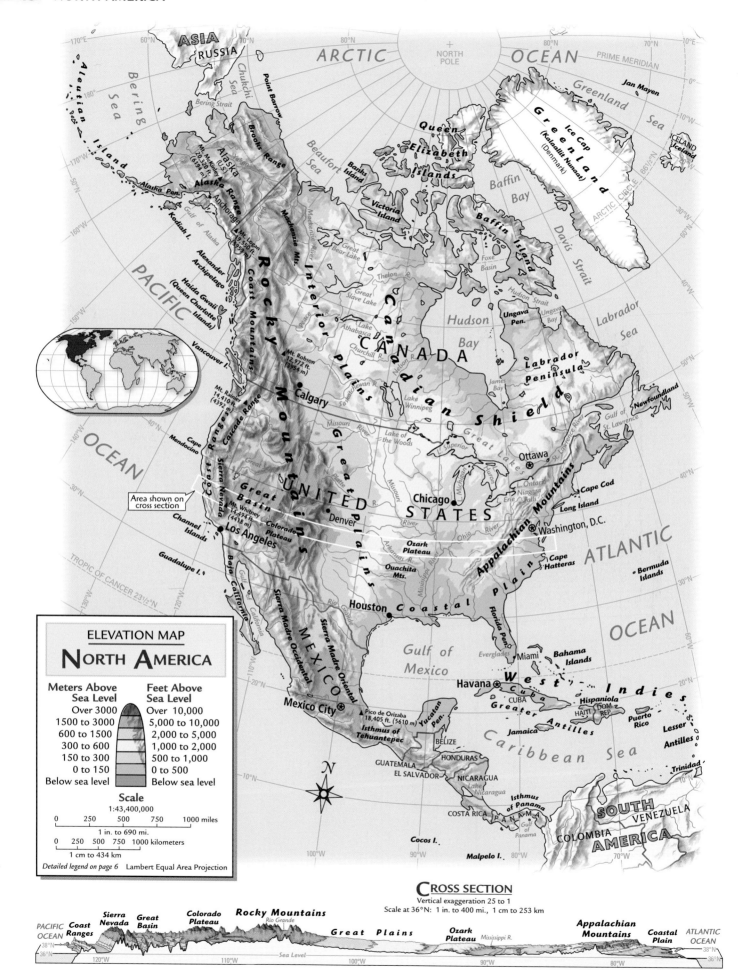

ASIA
RUSSIA

ARCTIC OCEAN
PRIME MERIDIAN
NORTH POLE

Bering Strait
Point Barrow
Chukchi Sea
Beaufort Sea
Banks Island
Queen Elizabeth Islands
Victoria Island

Greenland Sea
Jan Mayen
Greenland
Ice Cap
Greenland
(Kalaallit Nunaat)
(Denmark)
ARCTIC CIRCLE 66½°N
ICELAND
Iceland

Aleutian Islands
Bering Sea
Brooks Range
Alaska (U.S.)
Mt. McKinley 20,320 ft. (6194 m)
Alaska Range
Anchorage
Alaska Pen.
Kodiak I.
Gulf of Alaska
Mt. Logan 19,550 ft. (5959 m)
Alexander Archipelago
Haida Gwaii (Queen Charlotte Islands)

Mackenzie Mts.
Mackenzie River
Great Bear Lake
Great Slave Lake
Thelon
Lake Athabasca
Churchill R.

Baffin Bay
Baffin Island
Foxe Basin
Hudson Strait
Ungava Pen.
Ungava Bay

Davis Strait
Labrador Sea

PACIFIC OCEAN

Vancouver I.

Mt. Robson 12,972 ft. (3954 m)

Calgary

Coast Mountains
Rocky Mountains
Interior Plains

Saskatchewan R.
Lake Winnipeg
Lake of the Woods

CANADA
Canadian Shield
James Bay

Hudson Bay

Labrador Peninsula

Gulf of St. Lawrence
Newfoundland

Cape Mendocino
Cascade Range
Mt. Rainier 14,410 ft. (4392)
Sierra Nevada
Great Basin
Mt. Whitney 14,494 ft. (4418 m)
Channel Islands
Los Angeles
Colorado Plateau
Denver
Great Plains

Superior
L. Michigan
Huron
L. Ontario
Niagara Falls
Erie
Ottawa
St. Lawrence River

UNITED STATES
Chicago

Washington, D.C.
Appalachian Mountains
Cape Cod
Long Island

Guadalupe I.
TROPIC OF CANCER 23½°N

Area shown on cross section

Missouri River
Platte River
Ohio River
Arkansas R.
Ozark Plateau
Ouachita Mts.
Mississippi River

ATLANTIC OCEAN
Cape Hatteras
Bermuda Islands

Baja California
Gulf of California
Sierra Madre Occidental
Sierra Madre Oriental
Rio Grande
Houston
Coastal Plain
Florida Pen.
Everglades
Miami
Bahama Islands

MEXICO
Mexico City
Pico de Orizaba 18,405 ft. (5610 m)
Isthmus of Tehuantepec
Yucatan Pen.

Gulf of Mexico
Havana
Cuba
Greater Antilles
Jamaica
Hispaniola
HAITI
DOM. REP.
Puerto Rico
West Indies
Lesser Antilles
Caribbean Sea

GUATEMALA
EL SALVADOR
BELIZE
HONDURAS
NICARAGUA
Lake Nicaragua
COSTA RICA
PANAMA
Isthmus of Panama
Gulf of Panama

Cocos I.
Malpelo I.

Trinidad
SOUTH AMERICA
VENEZUELA
COLOMBIA

ELEVATION MAP
NORTH AMERICA

Meters Above Sea Level	Feet Above Sea Level
Over 3000	Over 10,000
1500 to 3000	5,000 to 10,000
600 to 1500	2,000 to 5,000
300 to 600	1,000 to 2,000
150 to 300	500 to 1,000
0 to 150	0 to 500
Below sea level	Below sea level

Scale
1:43,400,000

0   250   500   750   1000 miles

1 in. to 690 mi.

0   250   500   750   1000 kilometers

1 cm to 434 km

Detailed legend on page 6   Lambert Equal Area Projection

N

CROSS SECTION
Vertical exaggeration 25 to 1
Scale at 36°N: 1 in. to 400 mi., 1 cm to 253 km

PACIFIC OCEAN
Coast Ranges
Sierra Nevada
Great Basin
Colorado Plateau
Rocky Mountains
Rio Grande
Great Plains
Ozark Plateau
Mississippi R.
Appalachian Mountains
Coastal Plain
ATLANTIC OCEAN
Sea Level
38°N
36°N
120°W
110°W
100°W
90°W
80°W
38°N
36°N

RAIN SHADOW EFFECT

When moist warm air meets a mountain range, it rises, cools, and creates clouds that rain on the **windward** side of the mountain. The air then becomes drier as it descends the opposite **leeward** side of the mountain. Few clouds reach the leeward side, so it is relatively dry. Astoria lies near the Pacific Coast on the windward side of the Cascade Range, while Sunnyside lies on the leeward side.

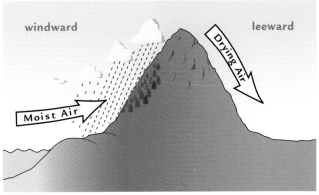

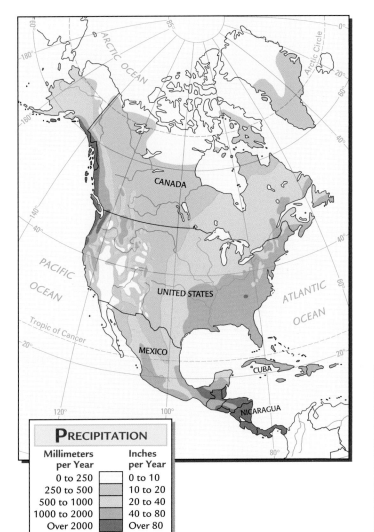

PRECIPITATION

Millimeters per Year	Inches per Year
0 to 250	0 to 10
250 to 500	10 to 20
500 to 1000	20 to 40
1000 to 2000	40 to 80
Over 2000	Over 80

CLIMOGRAPHS

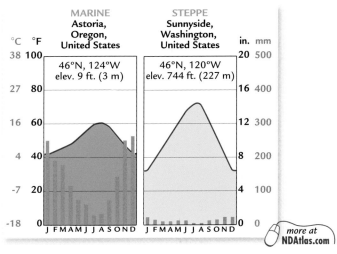

MARINE
Astoria, Oregon, United States
46°N, 124°W elev. 9 ft. (3 m)

STEPPE
Sunnyside, Washington, United States
46°N, 120°W elev. 744 ft. (227 m)

more at
NDAtlas.com

CLIMATE

Tropical	Tropical rain forest
	Savanna
Dry	Steppe (semi-desert)
	Desert
Mild	Mediterranean
	Humid subtropical
	Marine
Continental	Hot summer
	Cool summer
	Subarctic
Polar	Tundra
	Ice cap
Highland	(Varies greatly with elevation and latitude)

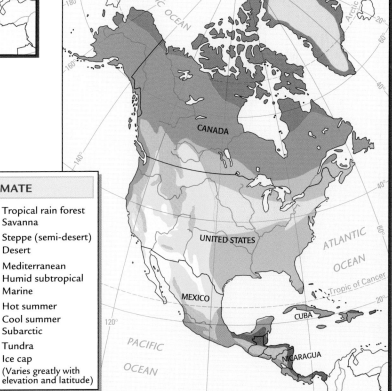

A Smoggy Day

Combine calm winds and a sunny day with nitrogen oxides from car and factory exhaust fumes and volatile organic compounds and you get **smog**. Any city can have smog, but it's especially a problem when smog is trapped by nearby mountains, as in Los Angeles, Denver, and Mexico City. In fact, Mexico City has the worst levels of smog in the world.

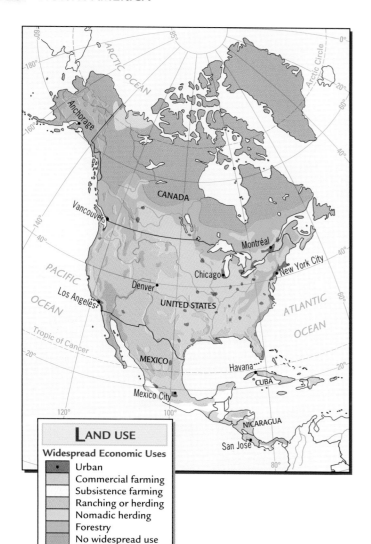

LAND USE

Widespread Economic Uses

- Urban
- Commercial farming
- Subsistence farming
- Ranching or herding
- Nomadic herding
- Forestry
- No widespread use

Wheat grows throughout the Great Plains of the United States and Canada, making North America one of the world's leading wheat producers.

Waves of Grain

North America is one of the world's leading agricultural exporters, shipping corn, soybeans, wheat, and other crops to Europe, Japan, and China. The United States and Canada rank first and third in wheat exports, while the United States ranks first in soybean exports.

The Trans-Alaska Pipeline System transports oil from northern Alaska to an ice-free port in southern Alaska, where it can be shipped to the contiguous states and eastern Asia. North America is home to three of the world's top ten oil producers—the United States, Mexico, and Canada.

ENERGY RESOURCES AND METALS

- Coal
- Oil (petroleum)
- Natural gas
- Uranium
- Aluminum (bauxite)
- Copper
- Gold
- Iron
- Lead
- Manganese
- Nickel
- Silver
- Tin
- Zinc

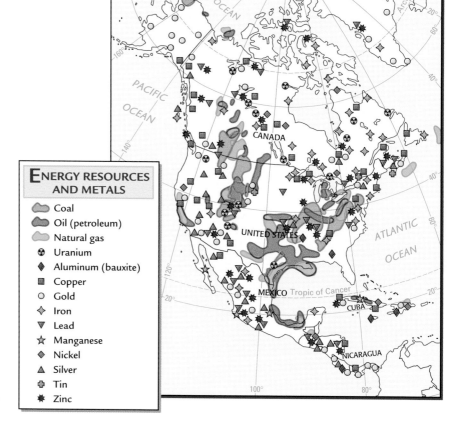

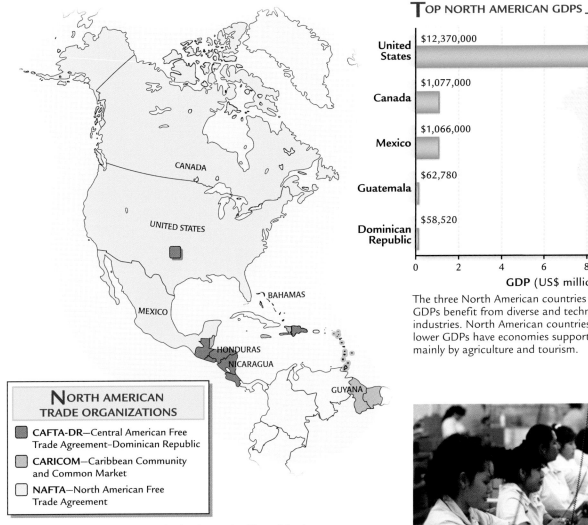

TOP NORTH AMERICAN GDPS

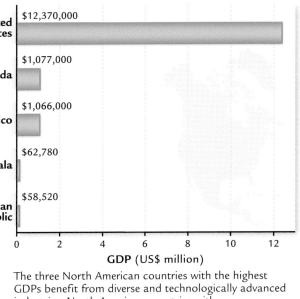

Country	GDP
United States	$12,370,000
Canada	$1,077,000
Mexico	$1,066,000
Guatemala	$62,780
Dominican Republic	$58,520

GDP (US$ million)

The three North American countries with the highest GDPs benefit from diverse and technologically advanced industries. North American countries with lower GDPs have economies supported mainly by agriculture and tourism.

more at NDAtlas.com

NORTH AMERICAN TRADE ORGANIZATIONS

- **CAFTA-DR**—Central American Free Trade Agreement–Dominican Republic
- **CARICOM**—Caribbean Community and Common Market
- **NAFTA**—North American Free Trade Agreement

Trade organizations encourage the buying and selling of foreign goods from member countries by reducing or eliminating tariffs and other restrictions on imports. Trade agreements can increase employment opportunities and economic growth.

Mexico's *maquiladoras* are industrial plants owned by foreign corporations. These factories often assemble American-made parts. The finished products are then usually exported back to the United States.

BALANCE OF TRADE

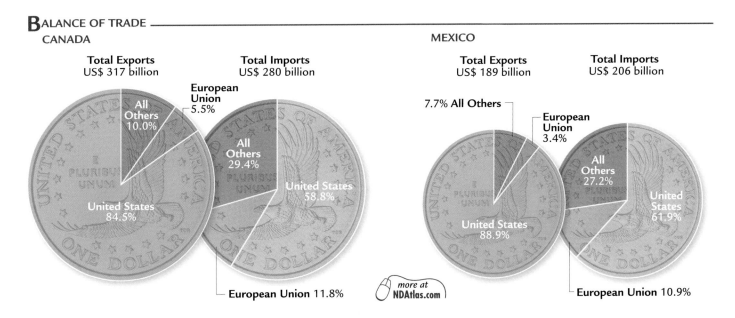

CANADA

Total Exports
US$ 317 billion

- All Others 10.0%
- European Union 5.5%
- United States 84.5%

Total Imports
US$ 280 billion

- All Others 29.4%
- United States 58.8%
- European Union 11.8%

more at NDAtlas.com

MEXICO

Total Exports
US$ 189 billion

- 7.7% All Others
- European Union 3.4%
- United States 88.9%

Total Imports
US$ 206 billion

- All Others 27.2%
- United States 61.9%
- European Union 10.9%

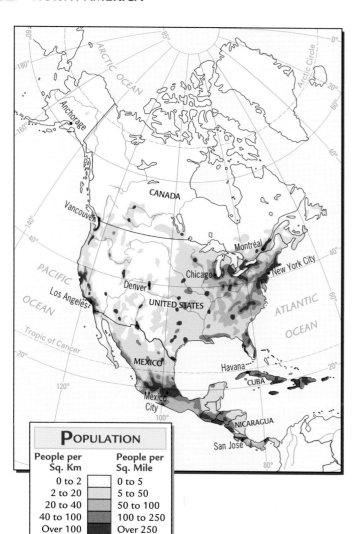

NATURAL POPULATION GROWTH NORTH AMERICA

Haiti
2.5%
- Births: 37
- Deaths: 12

Mexico
1.6%
- Births: 21
- Deaths: 5

United States
0.6%
- Births: 14
- Deaths: 8

World
1.1%
- Births: 20
- Deaths: 9

Births

Deaths

0 10 20 30 40 50

Annual Birth and Death Rates
(per 1,000 people)

POPULATION

People per Sq. Km	**People per Sq. Mile**
0 to 2	0 to 5
2 to 20	5 to 50
20 to 40	50 to 100
40 to 100	100 to 250
Over 100	Over 250

Inuit live in some of the coldest places on Earth: Alaska, northern Canada, Greenland, and eastern Siberia. Many of these indigenous people still engage in traditional activities, such as hunting and fishing.

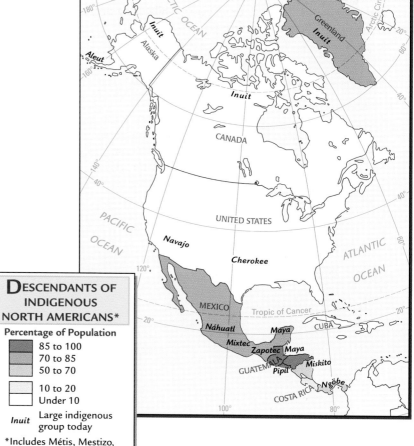

DESCENDANTS OF INDIGENOUS NORTH AMERICANS*

Percentage of Population
- 85 to 100
- 70 to 85
- 50 to 70
- 10 to 20
- Under 10

Inuit Large indigenous group today

*Includes Métis, Mestizo, and Garifuna

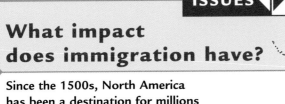

ISSUES ◀▶ TODAY

What impact does immigration have?

Since the 1500s, North America has been a destination for millions of voluntary and involuntary immigrants. The overwhelming majority of North Americans are descendants of immigrants from Europe, Africa, or Asia. Do immigrants have a positive or negative impact on their host countries? There are many perspectives on this issue. Here are two of them.

ANNUAL NET MIGRATION
Migrants per 1,000 People

- More than 4 immigrants
- Up to 4 immigrants
- No change reported
- Up to 4 emigrants
- More than 4 emigrants
- Immigrants to the United States

304,000 Asians
147,000 Europeans
54,000 Africans
66,000 South Americans
327,000 Middle Americans

GREENLAND (Den.)
Alaska (U.S.)
CANADA
UNITED STATES
MEXICO
CUBA
HAITI
DOMINICAN REPUBLIC
JAMAICA
EL SALVADOR
NICARAGUA

Immigrants improve a country.

- Immigration expands the economy. About 70 percent of immigrants who arrive in the United States are at their peak employment age, ready to pay taxes and make purchases.

- Immigrants earn about US$240 billion annually and pay about US$90 billion in taxes, while using only about US$5 billion in public benefits each year.

- Often immigrants fill gaps in the workforce, taking jobs that are deemed undesirable.

- Many immigrants have training that benefits the country. More than a third of all immigrants to Canada have college degrees.

- Historically, every group of immigrants has integrated with and contributed to the culture at large. Some famous immigrants include physicist Albert Einstein, industrialist and philanthropist Andrew Carnegie, and author Isabel Allende.

IMMIGRANTS IN THE UNITED STATES

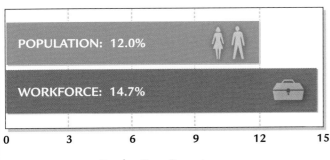

POPULATION: 12.0%

WORKFORCE: 14.7%

0   3   6   9   12   15

Foreign Born Percentage

Immigrants often arrive looking for jobs. They make up a larger percentage of the labor force than of the population.

Immigration disrupts society.

- Some immigrants do not integrate their customs and values with those of their host country.

- Immigrants strain the education system with special needs. Ontario, Canada's most populous province, spends about US$200 million a year on immigrant ESL (English as a Second Language) students.

- Governments try to prevent illegal immigrants from entering their countries. The United States spends about US$4.5 billion annually securing its borders.

- Immigrants drain resources intended for a country's citizens. About 3.2 million immigrants in the United States are enrolled in Medicaid, a program that provides health care to low-income individuals.

- Illegal immigrants take jobs from citizens and from immigrants who entered their host countries legally. In the United States, about 7.2 million workers are illegal immigrants.

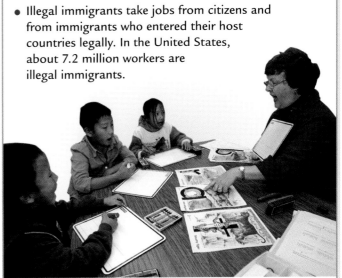

Laotian immigrants receive daily small-group speech lessons in their California school. About 25 percent of all people in California are immigrants.

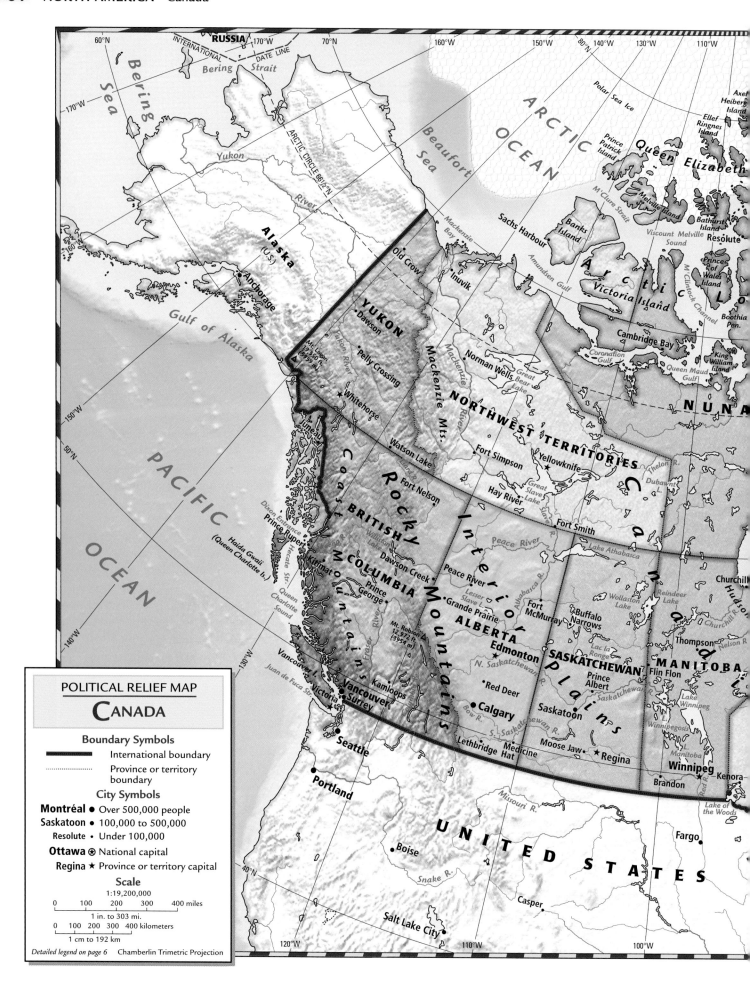

RUSSIA

Bering Strait

INTERNATIONAL DATE LINE

ARCTIC OCEAN

Bering Sea

Polar Sea Ice

Axel Heiberg Island

Prince Patrick Island

Ellef Ringnes Island

Queen Elizabeth

Yukon

ARCTIC CIRCLE 66½°N

Alaska (U.S)

Anchorage

Beaufort Sea

Mackenzie Bay

Sachs Harbour

Banks Island

Melville Island

M'Clure Strait

Bathurst Island

Resolute

Viscount Melville Sound

Prince of Wales Island

Arctic

Inuvik

Old Crow

Victoria Island

Amundsen Gulf

M'Clintock Channel

Boothia Pen.

Gulf of Alaska

YUKON

Dawson

Mt. Logan 19,550 ft. (5,959 m)

Pelly Crossing

Yukon River

Whitehorse

Juneau

Mackenzie River

Norman Wells

Great Bear Lake

Coronation Gulf

Cambridge Bay

King William Island

Queen Maud Gulf

NUNA

PACIFIC OCEAN

Dixon Entrance

Prince Rupert

Haida Gwaii (Queen Charlotte Is.)

Coast Mountains

Hecate Str.

Watson Lake

Mackenzie Mts.

NORTHWEST TERRITORIES

Fort Simpson

Yellowknife

Great Slave Lake

Thelon R.

Dubawnt L.

Fort Nelson

Hay River

Fort Smith

Great Slave Lake

Queen Charlotte Sound

BRITISH COLUMBIA

Kitimat

Williston Lake

Rocky Mountains

Dawson Creek

Peace River

Peace River

Lesser Slave L.

Athabasca R.

Lake Athabasca

Canada

Reindeer Lake

Churchill

Hudson

Prince George

Fraser River

Mt. Robson 12,972 ft. (3,954 m)

Grande Prairie

Fort McMurray

Wollaston Lake

Buffalo Narrows

Thompson

Nelson R.

Churchill R.

Interior Plains

ALBERTA

Edmonton

Lac la Ronge

SASKATCHEWAN

Flin Flon

MANITOBA

Vancouver I.

Kamloops

Red Deer

N. Saskatchewan R.

Saskatoon

Prince Albert

Saskatchewan R.

Lake Winnipeg

Juan de Fuca Str.

Victoria

Vancouver

Surrey

Calgary

Bow R.

S. Saskatchewan R.

Moose Jaw

Winnipegosis

L. Manitoba

Seattle

Lethbridge

Medicine Hat

Regina

Winnipeg

Brandon

Kenora

Portland

Red R.

Lake of the Woods

Missouri R.

UNITED STATES

Fargo

Boise

Snake R.

Casper

Salt Lake City

POLITICAL RELIEF MAP

CANADA

Boundary Symbols

—————— International boundary

·············· Province or territory boundary

City Symbols

Montréal ● Over 500,000 people

Saskatoon ● 100,000 to 500,000

Resolute · Under 100,000

Ottawa ⊛ National capital

Regina ★ Province or territory capital

Scale

1:19,200,000

| 0 | 100 | 200 | 300 | 400 miles |

1 in. to 303 mi.

| 0 | 100 | 200 | 300 | 400 kilometers |

1 cm to 192 km

Detailed legend on page 6 Chamberlin Trimetric Projection

0°W 70°W 60°W 50°W 40°W 30°W 20°W

ICELAND

ARCTIC CIRCLE 66½°N

60°N

80°N

70°N

20°W

30°W

50°N

40°W

G r e e n l a n d
(Kalaallit Nunaat)
(Denmark)

Islands

Ellesmere Island

Kane
Basin

Qaanaaq (Thule)

Baffin
Bay

Devon Island

Somerset
Island

Lancaster Sound

Clyde River

Davis Strait

Denmark Strait

Cape Farewell

Nuuk (Godthab)

wland

Baffin Island

Gulf of Boothia

Kugaaruk

Prince
Charles I.

Foxe

Cumberland Sound

VUT

Melville
Peninsula

Basin

Foxe
Peninsula

Iqaluit

Frobisher Bay

Southampton
Island

Foxe Channel

N

Chesterfield
Inlet

Coats
Island

Hudson Strait

Cape
Chidley

Labrador
Sea

ATLANTIC

OCEAN

Rankin Inlet

Mansel
Island

Salluit

Hudson

Ungava
Peninsula

Ungava
Bay

50°N

40°W

Bay

Belcher
Islands

R. aux Feuilles

R. George

NEWFOUNDLAND

AND

LABRADOR

Bay

Fort Severn

Kuujjuaq

Smallwood
Res.

Lowlands

Severn R.

Kuujjuarapik

L a b r a d o r   P e n i n s u l a

Happy Valley-
Goose Bay

Churchill R.

St. John's

Winisk R.

James
Bay

Akimiski
I.

QUÉBEC

S

h

i

Labrador City

Res.
Manicouagan

Corner Brook

Newfoundland

Cape Race

Albany R.

Moosonee

e

l

d

Mistassini

Sept-Îles

Anticosti
Island

St.-Pierre and
Miquelon
(France)

50°W

ONTARIO

Saguenay

Gulf of
St. Lawrence

PRINCE
EDWARD
ISLAND

Charlottetown

Cape
Breton
Island

40°N

L.
Nipigon

Val-d'Or

Québec

St. Lawrence River

NEW
BRUNSWICK

Fredericton

NOVA SCOTIA

Sable Island
(Nova Scotia)

Thunder Bay

Lake Superior

Sault
Ste. Marie

Sudbury

Ottawa R.

Gatineau

Montréal

Saint John

Halifax

L.
Nipissing

Georgian
Bay

Ottawa

Bay of Fundy

Yarmouth

Cape Sable

Minneapolis

Lake Michigan

Lake Huron

L. Simcoe

Kingston

Boston

Mississippi R.

Toronto

L. Ontario

Mississauga

Hamilton

Buffalo

New York City

Detroit

Windsor

Niagara
Falls

Chicago

Lake Erie

90°W 80°W 70°W 60°W

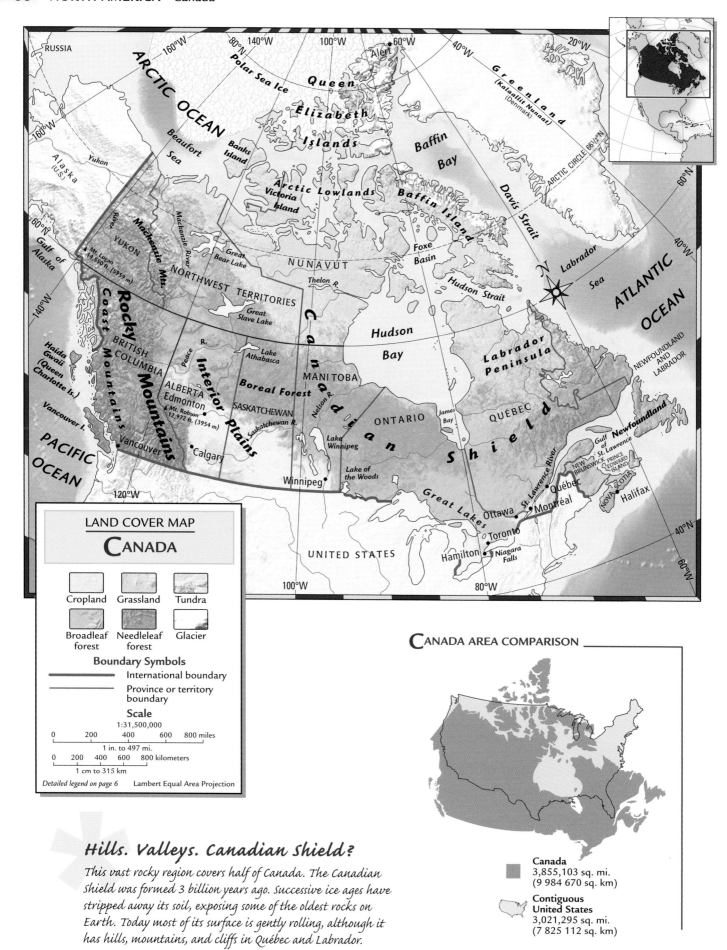

RUSSIA

ARCTIC OCEAN

Polar Sea Ice

Queen

Alert

Elizabeth

Islands

Beaufort Sea

Banks Island

Greenland
(Kalaallit Nunaat)
(Denmark)

Baffin Bay

Alaska (U.S.)

Yukon

Arctic Lowlands

Victoria Island

Baffin Island

Davis Strait

ARCTIC CIRCLE 66½°N

Mackenzie River

Mt. Logan
19,550 ft. (5959 m)

YUKON

Mackenzie Mts.

Great Bear Lake

NUNAVUT

NORTHWEST TERRITORIES

Foxe Basin

Labrador Sea

Gulf of Alaska

Rocky Mountains

Coast Mountains

BRITISH COLUMBIA

Great Slave Lake

Thelon R.

Hudson Strait

ATLANTIC OCEAN

Haida Gwaii (Queen Charlotte Is.)

Peace R.

Interior Plains

Lake Athabasca

Hudson Bay

Labrador Peninsula

NEWFOUNDLAND AND LABRADOR

Vancouver I.

ALBERTA

Edmonton

Mt. Robson
12,972 ft. (3954 m)

SASKATCHEWAN

Boreal Forest

Saskatchewan R.

Nelson R.

MANITOBA

ONTARIO

James Bay

QUÉBEC

Canadian Shield

PACIFIC OCEAN

Vancouver

Calgary

Lake Winnipeg

Gulf of St. Lawrence

Newfoundland

NEW BRUNSWICK

PRINCE EDWARD ISLAND

Winnipeg

Lake of the Woods

Great Lakes

St. Lawrence River

Québec

Montréal

NOVA SCOTIA

Halifax

Ottawa

Toronto

Hamilton

Niagara Falls

UNITED STATES

LAND COVER MAP
CANADA

Cropland   Grassland   Tundra

Broadleaf forest   Needleleaf forest   Glacier

Boundary Symbols

International boundary

Province or territory boundary

Scale

1:31,500,000

0   200   400   600   800 miles

1 in. to 497 mi.

0   200   400   600   800 kilometers

1 cm to 315 km

Detailed legend on page 6   Lambert Equal Area Projection

CANADA AREA COMPARISON

Canada
3,855,103 sq. mi.
(9 984 670 sq. km)

Contiguous United States
3,021,295 sq. mi.
(7 825 112 sq. km)

Hills. Valleys. Canadian Shield?

This vast rocky region covers half of Canada. The Canadian Shield was formed 3 billion years ago. Successive ice ages have stripped away its soil, exposing some of the oldest rocks on Earth. Today most of its surface is gently rolling, although it has hills, mountains, and cliffs in Québec and Labrador.

The Coast Mountains tower over Vancouver, Canada's third largest metropolitan area. Located near the Pacific Ocean, Vancouver has a relatively mild climate that allows its seaport, Canada's busiest, to remain free of ice year-round.

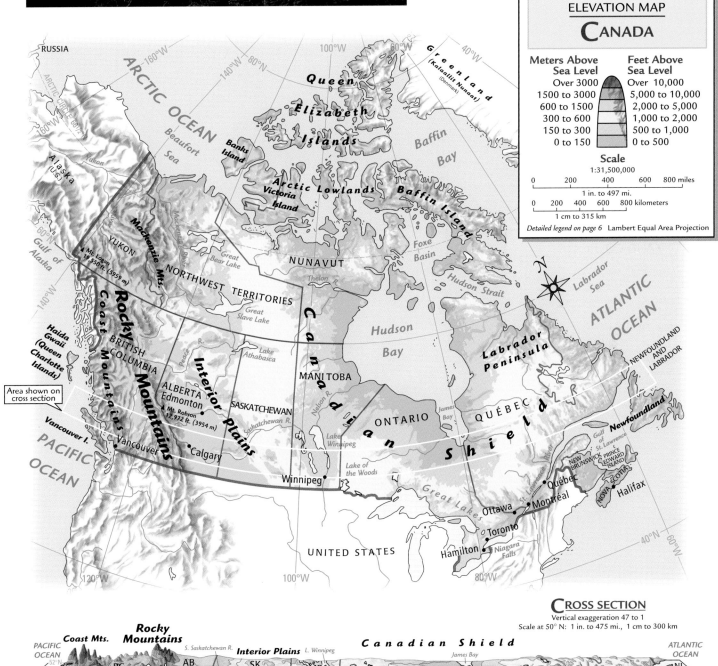

ELEVATION MAP

CANADA

Meters Above Sea Level	Feet Above Sea Level
Over 3000	Over 10,000
1500 to 3000	5,000 to 10,000
600 to 1500	2,000 to 5,000
300 to 600	1,000 to 2,000
150 to 300	500 to 1,000
0 to 150	0 to 500

Scale
1:31,500,000

0   200   400   600   800 miles

1 in. to 497 mi.

0   200   400   600   800 kilometers

1 cm to 315 km

Detailed legend on page 6   Lambert Equal Area Projection

RUSSIA

ARCTIC OCEAN

ARCTIC CIRCLE 66½°

Greenland (Kalaallit Nunaat) (Denmark)

Queen Elizabeth Islands

Beaufort Sea

Banks Island

Baffin Bay

Alaska (U.S.)

Yukon

Arctic Lowlands

Victoria Island

Baffin Island

Gulf of Alaska

YUKON

Mackenzie Mts.

NORTHWEST TERRITORIES

Great Bear Lake

Mackenzie River

NUNAVUT

Foxe Basin

Rocky

Coast

Mountains

Mountains

Thelon

Hudson Strait

Labrador Sea

ATLANTIC OCEAN

Haida Gwaii (Queen Charlotte Islands)

BRITISH COLUMBIA

Great Slave Lake

Hudson Bay

Labrador Peninsula

NEWFOUNDLAND AND LABRADOR

Area shown on cross section

Interior Plains

Peace R.

ALBERTA Edmonton

Lake Athabasca

Mt. Robson 12,972 ft. (3954 m)

Mt. Logan 19,550 ft. (5959 m)

SASKATCHEWAN

Saskatchewan R.

MANITOBA

Nelson R.

ONTARIO

James Bay

QUÉBEC

Newfoundland

Vancouver I.

Vancouver

Calgary

Lake Winnipeg

PACIFIC OCEAN

Winnipeg

Lake of the Woods

Great Lakes

St. Lawrence River

Gulf of St. Lawrence

NEW BRUNSWICK PRINCE EDWARD ISLAND

Québec

Montréal

NOVA SCOTIA

Halifax

UNITED STATES

Ottawa

Toronto

Hamilton

Niagara Falls

CROSS SECTION
Vertical exaggeration 47 to 1
Scale at 50° N: 1 in. to 475 mi., 1 cm to 300 km

PACIFIC OCEAN

Coast Mts.

Rocky Mountains

S. Saskatchewan R.

Interior Plains

L. Winnipeg

Canadian Shield

James Bay

ATLANTIC OCEAN

BC

AB

SK

MB

ON

QC

NL

Sea Level

120°W   110°W   100°W   90°W   80°W   70°W   60°W

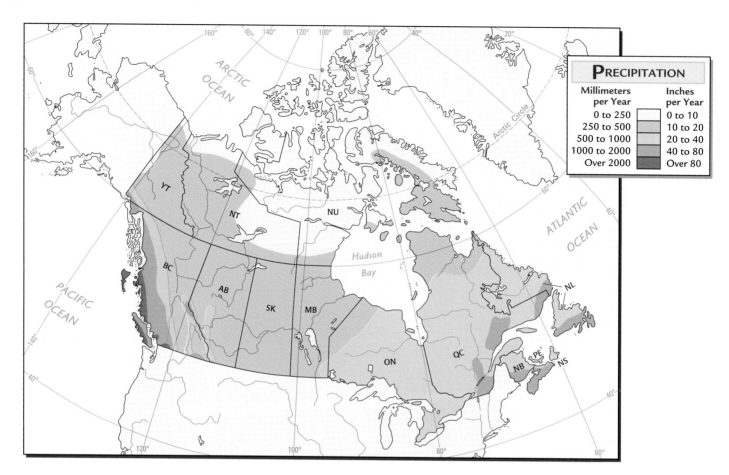

PRECIPITATION

Millimeters per Year	Inches per Year
0 to 250	0 to 10
250 to 500	10 to 20
500 to 1000	20 to 40
1000 to 2000	40 to 80
Over 2000	Over 80

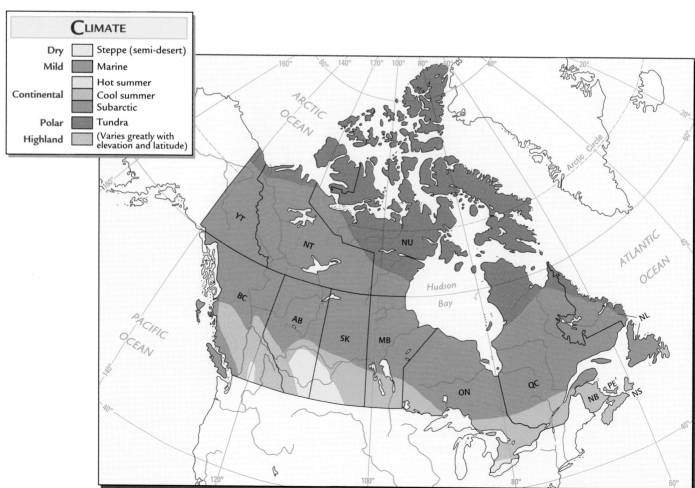

CLIMATE

Dry	Steppe (semi-desert)
Mild	Marine
Continental	Hot summer
	Cool summer
	Subarctic
Polar	Tundra
Highland	(Varies greatly with elevation and latitude)

CANADIAN AGRICULTURE

Canadian agriculture travels worldwide. Canada exports crops to the United States, Japan, and Mexico. Canola—used in cooking oil, cosmetics, and biodiesel fuel—generates over US$2 billion in export income a year.

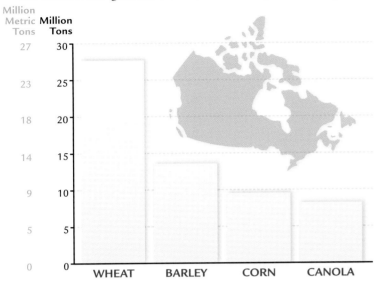

Canada exports nearly US$3 billion worth of fish and fish products. These fisherman are unloading their day's catch of cod in Petty Harbour, Newfoundland and Labrador. Overfishing in Canadian waters has critically endangered several species of fish.

Forests—Canada's Surplus Crop

Short growing seasons throughout much of Canada make farming difficult, but not forestry. Forests cover nearly 40 percent of the country. Two-thirds of British Columbia is forested. The forest industry is Canada's single largest net exporter, contributing approximately US$35 billion to the country's trade surplus.

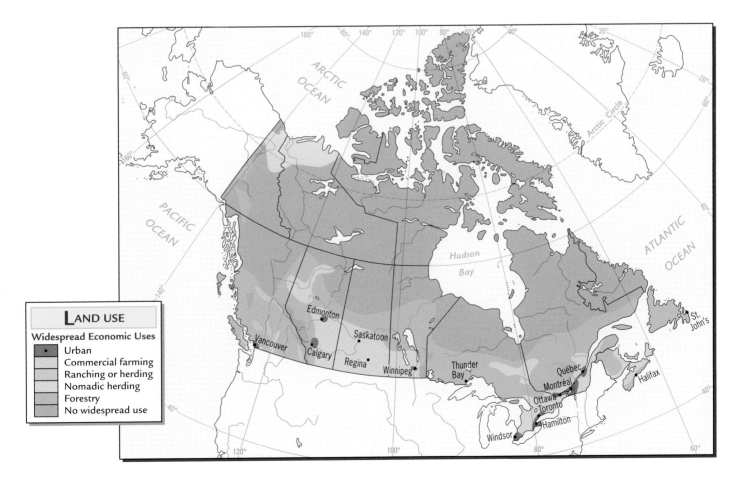

LAND USE

Widespread Economic Uses
- Urban
- Commercial farming
- Ranching or herding
- Nomadic herding
- Forestry
- No widespread use

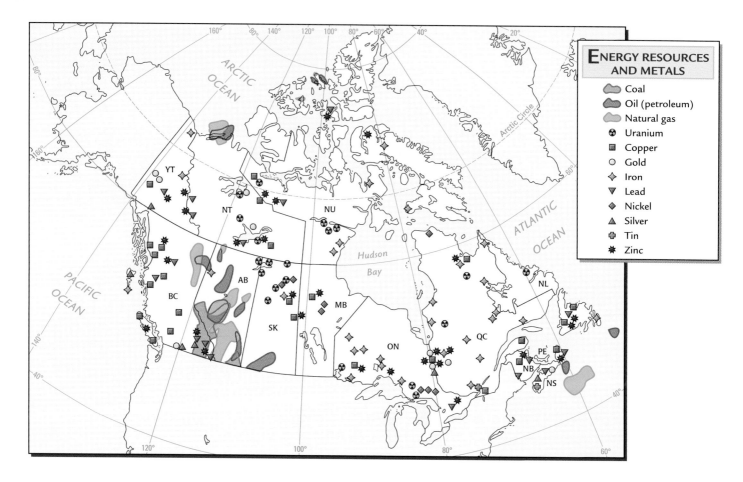

ENERGY RESOURCES AND METALS

- Coal
- Oil (petroleum)
- Natural gas
- ⊕ Uranium
- ▪ Copper
- ○ Gold
- ◇ Iron
- ▽ Lead
- ◆ Nickel
- ▲ Silver
- ✚ Tin
- ✳ Zinc

MAJOR HIGHWAYS AND AIRPORTS

Canada has more than 300 airports and over 850,000 miles (1.4 million kilometers) of road. The Trans-Canada Highway is the world's longest highway. It connects all 10 Canadian provinces.

Airline Passengers per Year

- ✈ 20 to 35 million
- ✈ 10 to 20 million
- ✈ 2 to 10 million
- • Other airport
- ～ Trans-Canada and other major highways

Located on the St. Lawrence River, Québec is the oldest city in Canada. Québec is a World Heritage City that hosts over 9 million visitors a year.

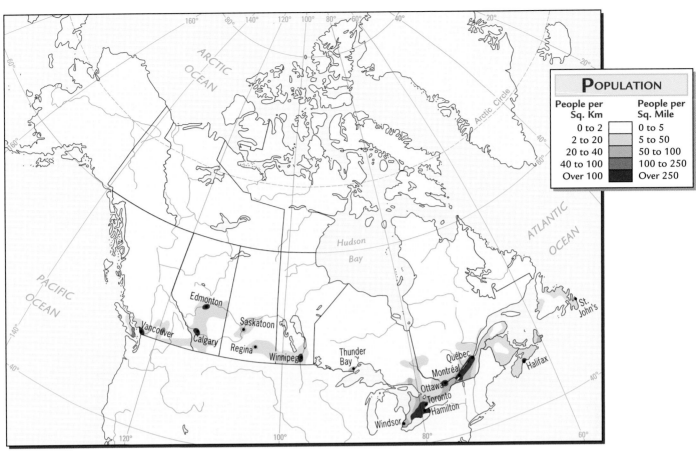

POPULATION

People per Sq. Km	People per Sq. Mile
0 to 2	0 to 5
2 to 20	5 to 50
20 to 40	50 to 100
40 to 100	100 to 250
Over 100	Over 250

ETHNIC COMPOSITION CANADA

- British 12.0%
- All Others 47.5%
- French 6.4%
- German 4.0%
- Italian 4.0%
- Irish 2.8%
- Ukrainian 1.8%
- Dutch 1.8%
- Polish 1.4%
- Portuguese 1.4%
- Chinese 5.3%
- Indo-Pakistani 4.3%
- Arab 1.2%
- Filipino 1.5%
- Amerindian (First Nation, Inuit, Métis) 3.1%
- West Indian 1.5%

more at NDAtlas.com

LANGUAGES OF CANADA

- Chinese 2.9%
- Other single languages 14.7%
- Multiple languages 1.3%
- English 58.5%
- French 22.6%

Canada has two official languages: English and French. However, recent immigrants also diversify the country's mix of languages. Compare this graph with the ethnic composition graph above. *more at NDAtlas.com*

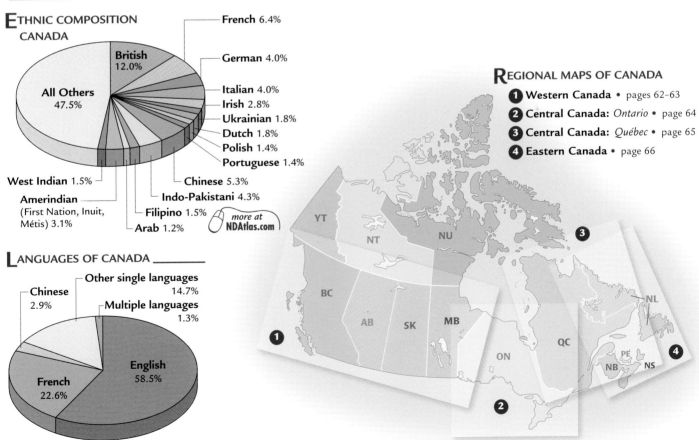

REGIONAL MAPS OF CANADA

1. **Western Canada** • pages 62–63
2. **Central Canada:** *Ontario* • page 64
3. **Central Canada:** *Québec* • page 65
4. **Eastern Canada** • page 66

Continues on pages 54–55

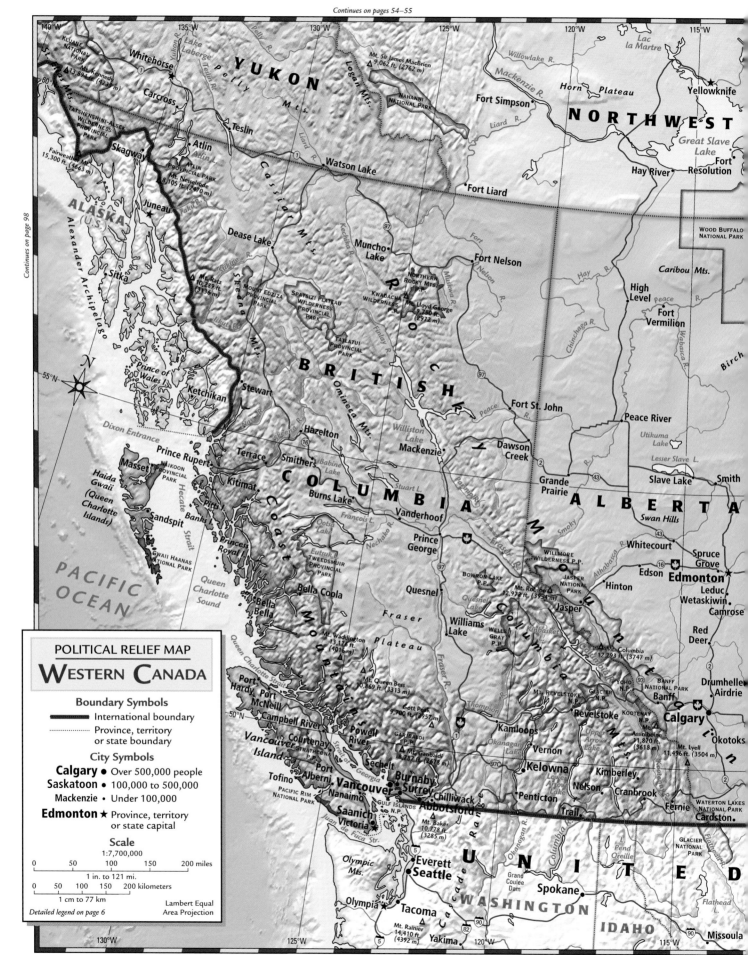

Continues on page 98

POLITICAL RELIEF MAP

WESTERN CANADA

Boundary Symbols

━━━━ International boundary

.... Province, territory
or state boundary

City Symbols

Calgary ● Over 500,000 people

Saskatoon ● 100,000 to 500,000

Mackenzie • Under 100,000

Edmonton ★ Province, territory
or state capital

Scale

1:7,700,000

| 0 | 50 | 100 | 150 | 200 miles |

1 in. to 121 mi.

| 0 | 50 | 100 | 150 | 200 kilometers |

1 cm to 77 km

Detailed legend on page 6   Lambert Equal
Area Projection

Continues on pages 94–95

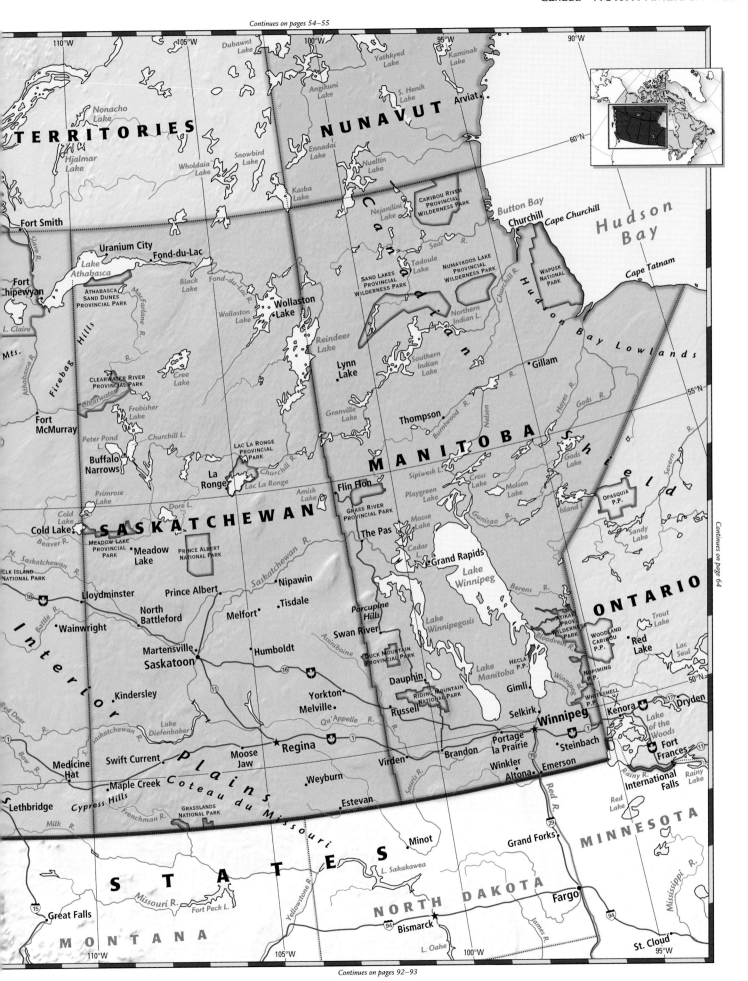

Continues on pages 54–55

Continues on page 64

Continues on pages 92–93

Continues on pages 54–55

POLITICAL RELIEF MAP

CENTRAL CANADA

ONTARIO

Boundary Symbols
━━━━━ International boundary

············· Province or state boundary

City Symbols
Mississauga ● Over 500,000 people

Sudbury ● 100,000 to 500,000

Nipigon • Under 100,000

Ottawa ⊗ National capital

Toronto ★ Province or state capital

Scale
1:9,000,000

0   50   100   150   200 miles

1 in. to 142 mi.

0   50   100   150   200 kilometers

1 cm to 90 km

Detailed legend on page 6   Albers Equal Area Projection

Continues on pages 62–63

Continues on page 65

Continues on pages 92–93

Continues on pages 82–83

Continues on pages 54–55
Continues on page 64
Continues on page 66
Continues on pages 82–83

POLITICAL RELIEF MAP
CENTRAL CANADA
QUÉBEC

Boundary Symbols
International boundary
Province or state boundary

City Symbols
Montréal ● Over 500,000 people
Saguenay ● 100,000 to 500,000
Kuujjuaq · Under 100,000
Ottawa ⊛ National capital
Québec ★ Province, territory, or state capital

Scale
1:10,000,000
0 50 100 150 200 miles
1 in. to 158 mi.
0 50 100 150 200 kilometers
1 cm to 100 km

Detailed legend on page 6   Lambert Equal Area Projection

Continues on pages 54–55

POLITICAL RELIEF MAP
EASTERN CANADA

Boundary Symbols
—— International boundary
········· Province or state boundary

City Symbols
Halifax ● Over 100,000 people
Moncton ● 25,000 to 100,000
Makkovik • Under 25,000
St. John's ★ Province capital

Scale
1:8,000,000
0   50   100   150   200 miles
1 in. to 126 mi.
0   50 100 150 200 kilometers
1 cm to 80 km

Detailed legend on page 6   Lambert Equal Area Projection

65°W
Killiniq Island
(Nunavut)
Cape Chidley
60°W

Ungava Bay

TORNGAT MOUNTAINS
NATIONAL PARK RESERVE

Torngat Mts.

Mont D'Iberville
△ 5,420 ft. (1652 m)

R. aux Feuilles
Kuujjuaq
R. aux Mélèzes
R. George
R. de la Baleine
R. Caniapiscau
Fraser R.

Nain

Labrador Sea

Labrador Peninsula
QUÉBEC

Continues on page 65

55°N

Schefferville
Makkovik

Adlatok R.
Kanairiktok R.
Naskaupi R.
Rigolet
Hamilton Inlet

Réservoir de Caniapiscau
Menihek Lakes
Smallwood Res.
Lake Melville

C a n a d i a n

Churchill Falls
Churchill Falls
Mealy Mts.
Cartwright

Lac Opiscotéo
Ross Bay Junction
Twin Falls
Churchill R.
Happy Valley-Goose Bay
Eagle R.

ATLANTIC
OCEAN

Labrador City
Little Mecatina
L. Brûlé
Alexis R.

S h i e l d
Otish Mts.
Lake Ashuanipi
R. Ste-Marguerite
R. aux Outardes
R. Moisie
Port Hope Simpson

**NEWFOUNDLAND
AND
LABRADOR**

Réservoir Manicouagan
R. Romaine
R. Natashquan
R. du Petit Mécatina
R. St. Augustin
R. St. Paul
Strait of Belle Isle

St. Anthony

Sept-Îles

50°N

Havre-Saint-Pierre
MINGAN ARCHIPELAGO
NATIONAL PARK RESERVE

Long Range Mts.
White Bay

Baie-Comeau

Pointe des Monts

Anticosti Island

GROS MORNE
NATIONAL PARK

Notre Dame Bay

Chic-Chocs Mts.
Mts. Matane
GASPÉSIE P.P.
Gaspé
FORILLON N.P.
Windsor
Gander
Bonavista Bay

St. Lawrence River
(138)
Notre Dame Mts.
Rimouski
Gaspé Peninsula
Bay of Islands
Corner Brook
Grand Lake
Grand Falls
TERRA NOVA N.P.

Gulf of
St. Lawrence
Stephenville
Lloyds R.
Newfoundland
Trinity Bay

(132)
Chandler
St. George's Bay
Long Range Mts.
Clarenville
Conception Bay
Cape Spear

Campbellton
Chaleur Bay
Magdalen Islands
(Québec)
Cabot Strait

(185)
Edmundston
Bathurst
MOUNT CARLETON P.P.
Placentia
Avalon Peninsula
Cape Race

St. John R.
Grand Falls
NEW
Miramichi
KOUCHIBOUGUAC N.P.
(11)
Miramichi R.
**PRINCE
EDWARD
ISLAND**
CAPE BRETON
HIGHLANDS
N.P.
PRINCE EDWARD ISLAND N.P.
Channel-Port aux Basques
Fortune Bay
St.-Pierre and Miquelon
(France)
Placentia Bay
St. Mary's Bay

MAINE
(U.S.)
(95)
(2)
BRUNSWICK
Fredericton
Summerside
Northumberland Str.
(1)
Charlottetown
(105)
Sydney
Glace Bay
St. John's

Saint John
FUNDY N.P.
Amherst
(104)
New Glasgow
Truro
Port Hawkesbury
Louisburg
Cape Breton I.
St. Ann's Bay
Bras d'Or L.

(101)
NOVA
Sherbrooke
Canso
ATLANTIC

Digby
Grand Manan Island
KEJIMKUJIK NATIONAL PARK
(102)
(103)
SCOTIA
Halifax
Lunenburg

Gulf of
Maine
Yarmouth
L. Rossignol
Shelburne
Sable I.
(Nova Scotia)

OCEAN

Cape Sable
65°W
60°W
55°W

45°N

N

Continues on pages 82–83

70°W
65°W
60°N
55°N
50°N
55°W
50°W
55°N
50°N
45°N

How does mining affect the economy?

Canada produces more than 70 minerals and metals. Its petroleum industry is growing rapidly. The mining industry makes important contributions to Canada's economy. However, do the economic benefits of mining outweigh its toll on the environment? There are many perspectives on this issue. Here are two of them.

MINING IN CANADA
Value of Mining (US$)
- More than 5 billion
- 3 to 5 billion
- 1 to 3 billion
- Less than 1 billion

Community dependent on mining

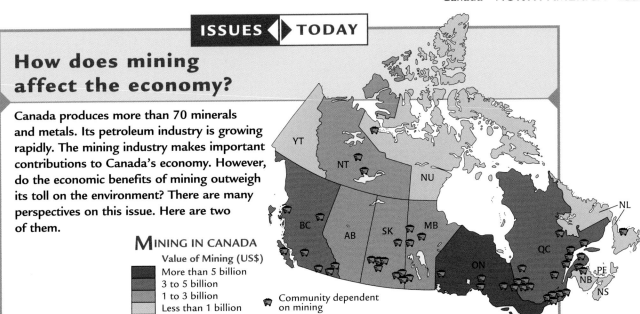

Mining causes profound damage to the environment.

- Mining is very disruptive to the environment. Roughly 125 tons of ore are excavated to extract just one ton of copper.

- Mining not only affects the environment at the site of the mine, but also harms the surrounding area. For example, an open-pit mine near Jasper National Park in Alberta has threatened the habitat of grizzly bears and contaminated the park's ground water.

- Canada has over 10,000 abandoned mines. The government must pay for their rehabilitation to minimize their impact on the environment.

- The mining and processing of resources pollute more than just the land and water. Processing oil sands in Canada produces three times the greenhouse gas emissions of conventional oil production.

In 1950 there was nothing at this Québec site but forest. A town soon grew up around a copper mine. When the mine closed in 1999, it left hundreds of unemployed workers and a huge hole in the ground.

The benefits of mining outweigh its costs.

- The mining and mineral processing industries are major employers in Canada. These industries employ about 369,000 full-time workers.

- The minerals and metals industry pay some of the highest wages in the Canadian economy, averaging over US$880 per week. In comparison, the average weekly wages in Canada are about US$620.

- The thriving mining industry has helped push Canada's unemployment rate to record lows. Oil-rich Alberta and British Columbia recently accounted for almost half of all job gains in Canada.

- Mining yields a host of minerals that are essential in many other industries. For example, the energy industry uses 29 different minerals to generate and deliver the energy we depend on every day.

GDP BY SECTOR

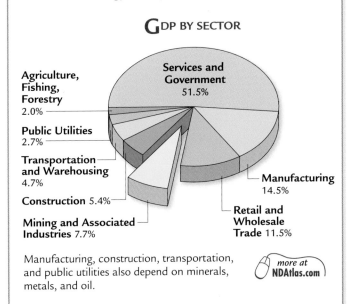

- Agriculture, Fishing, Forestry 2.0%
- Public Utilities 2.7%
- Transportation and Warehousing 4.7%
- Construction 5.4%
- Mining and Associated Industries 7.7%
- Services and Government 51.5%
- Manufacturing 14.5%
- Retail and Wholesale Trade 11.5%

Manufacturing, construction, transportation, and public utilities also depend on minerals, metals, and oil.

more at NDAtlas.com

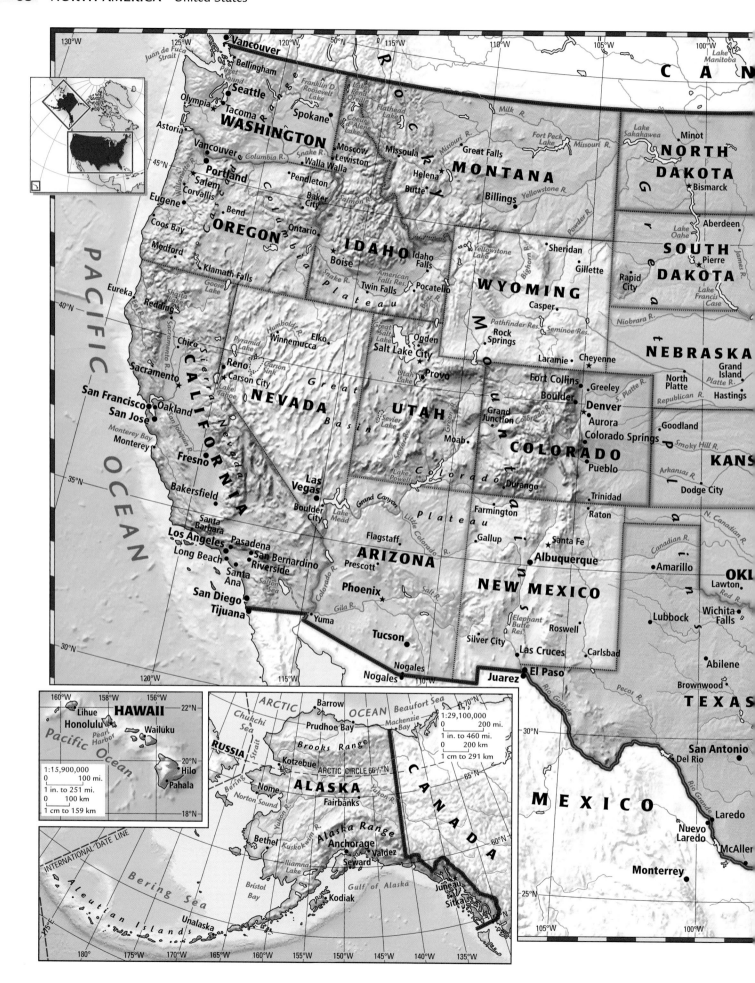

A D A

Lake Winnipeg
Winnipeg
Lake of the Woods
Lake Nipigon
Québec
Moosehead Lake
MAINE
Bangor
St. Lawrence R.
Bay of Fundy

Thunder Bay
Montréal
VERMONT
Augusta
Red R.
Red Lake
Ottawa
Ogdensburg
Burlington
NEW HAMPSHIRE
Portland
Grand Forks
Duluth
Marquette
Sault Ste. Marie
Lake Champlain
Montpelier
Concord
Manchester
Fargo
Lake Superior
Sault Ste. Marie
Watertown
Boston
MASSACHUSETTS
MINNESOTA
MICHIGAN
Alpena
Lake Huron
Toronto
Lake Ontario
Rochester
Utica
Syracuse
Albany
Springfield
Providence
RHODE ISLAND
CONNECTICUT

WISCONSIN
Wausau
Traverse City
Georgian Bay
Buffalo
NEW YORK
Binghamton
Hartford
St. Cloud
St. Paul
Eau Claire
Green Bay
Lake Michigan
Saginaw
Flint
Lake Erie
Erie
Oil City
Scranton
Newark
New York City
Minneapolis
Grand Rapids
Lansing
Detroit
Cleveland
Youngstown
PENNSYLVANIA
Allentown
Trenton
NEW JERSEY
Sioux Falls
Rochester
La Crosse
Madison
Milwaukee
Kenosha
Ann Arbor
Akron
Canton
Harrisburg
Philadelphia
Wilmington
Atlantic City
Mason City
Waterloo
Dubuque
Rockford
Chicago
Gary
Toledo
Lima
OHIO
Columbus
Pittsburgh
Baltimore
Dover
DELAWARE
Sioux City
IOWA
Cedar Rapids
Aurora
South Bend
Fort Wayne
Dayton
Clarksburg
Annapolis
MARYLAND
Des Moines
Davenport
Moline
Rock Island
Hammond
INDIANA
Indianapolis
Cincinnati
WEST VIRGINIA
Arlington
Washington, D.C.
Omaha
Council Bluffs
Burlington
Peoria
Champaign
Springfield
Terre Haute
Charleston
Charlottesville
Lincoln
ILLINOIS
Frankfort
Huntington
VIRGINIA
Richmond
Norfolk
Virginia Beach
St. Joseph
Hannibal
Evansville
Louisville
Lexington
Roanoke
Portsmouth
Elizabeth City
Kansas City
Independence
St. Louis
Owensboro
KENTUCKY
Bristol
Johnson City
Greensboro
NORTH
Raleigh
Albemarle Sound
Salina
Topeka
Lawrence
Jefferson City
Carbondale
Paducah
Bowling Green
Winston-Salem
Durham
CAROLINA
Pamlico Sound
Wichita
MISSOURI
Nashville
Knoxville
Asheville
Charlotte
Pittsburg
Joplin
Springfield
Lake of the Ozarks
Lake O' The Cherokees
Table Rock L.
Fayetteville
Jonesboro
Blytheville
TENNESSEE
Chattanooga
Greenville
SOUTH
Columbia
Wilmington
Tulsa
Oklahoma City
ARKANSAS
Memphis
Huntsville
Rome
Atlanta
CAROLINA
Charleston
AHOMA
Fort Smith
Little Rock
Birmingham
Augusta
Hot Springs
Pine Bluff
MISSISSIPPI
Tuscaloosa
GEORGIA
Macon
Savannah
Lake Texoma
Greenville
ALABAMA
Columbus
Texarkana
Monroe
Vicksburg
Meridian
Montgomery
Dallas
Jackson
Dothan
Albany
Valdosta
Fort Worth
Hattiesburg
Jacksonville
Waco
LOUISIANA
Shreveport
Alexandria
Mobile
Tallahassee
FLORIDA
Daytona Beach
Austin
Beaumont
Lake Charles
Lafayette
Baton Rouge
New Orleans
Gulfport
Biloxi
Pensacola
Mobile Bay
Orlando
Houston
Galveston
Delta of the Mississippi River
Apalachee Bay
Corpus Christi
Gulf of Mexico
Tampa
St. Petersburg
Tampa Bay
Lake Okeechobee
Padre I.
Ft. Lauderdale
Hialeah
Miami
Brownsville
Matamoros
Key West
Straits of Florida
TROPIC OF CANCER 23½°N
CUBA

ATLANTIC OCEAN

POLITICAL RELIEF MAP

UNITED STATES

Boundary Symbols
International boundary
State boundary

City Symbols
Los Angeles ● Over 500,000 people
Anchorage ● 100,000 to 500,000
Marquette • Under 100,000
Washington, D.C. ⊗ National capital
Honolulu ★ State capital

Scale
1:12,700,000
0   100   200   300 miles
1 in. to 200 mi.
0   100   200   300 kilometers
1 cm to 127 km

Detailed legend on page 6   Albers Equal Area Projection

CANADA

Lake Winnipeg
Lake Nipigon
Lake of the Woods
Red Lake
MINNESOTA
Mesabi Range
St. Paul
Minneapolis
Mississippi River
Isle Royale
Lake Superior
WISCONSIN
Wisconsin R.
Upper Peninsula
MICHIGAN
Lower Peninsula
Lake Michigan
Lake Huron
Georgian Bay
Lake Ontario
Toronto
Niagara Falls
Lake Erie
Cleveland
Detroit
IOWA
Des Moines R.
Rock R.
Chicago
ILLINOIS
INDIANA
OHIO
Ohio River
Scioto R.
White R.
Wabash
Mississippi River
Missouri River
Kansas R.
Kansas City
Lake of the Ozarks
MISSOURI
Ozark Plateau
Flint Hills
Lake O' the Cherokees
Boston Mts.
Table Rock Lake
Arkansas R.
OKLAHOMA
ARKANSAS
Ouachita Mts.
KENTUCKY
TENNESSEE
Tennessee R.
Cumberland R.
Memphis
MISSISSIPPI
Yazoo R.
ALABAMA
Pearl R.
Tombigbee R.
Alabama R.

Central Lowland

Appalachian Mountains
Cumberland Plateau
Mt. Mitchell 6,684 ft. (2037 m)
Blue Ridge
Piedmont
WEST VIRGINIA
VIRGINIA
Washington D.C.
MARYLAND
Potomac R.
James R.
Roanoke R.
Great Dismal Swamp
Albemarle Sound
NORTH CAROLINA
Pamlico Sound
Cape Hatteras
Cape Fear
Pee Dee R.
SOUTH CAROLINA
Saluda R.
Savannah R.
Atlanta
J. Strom Thurmond Res. (Clarks Hill L.)
GEORGIA
Chattahoochee R.
Charleston
Sea Islands
Altamaha R.
Okefenokee Swamp
St. Johns R.
Cape Canaveral
FLORIDA
Florida Peninsula
Tampa Bay
Lake Okeechobee
Everglades
Miami
Cape Sable
Dry Tortugas
Florida Keys
Straits of Florida
CUBA

Atlantic Coastal Plain
ATLANTIC OCEAN

Montréal
Ottawa
St. Lawrence River
Moosehead Lake
MAINE
Bay of Fundy
Lake Champlain
Adirondack Mts.
Mohawk R.
Green Mts.
VERMONT
White Mts.
Mt. Washington 6,288 ft. (1917 m)
NEW HAMPSHIRE
Boston
MASSACHUSETTS
Cape Cod
RHODE ISLAND
CONNECTICUT
NEW YORK
Catskill Mts.
Hudson R.
Long Island
New York City
NEW JERSEY
PENNSYLVANIA
Allegheny Plateau
Susquehanna R.
DELAWARE
Delaware Bay
Chesapeake Bay

Mississippi River
LOUISIANA
Red R.
Toledo Bend Res.
Sam Rayburn Res.
Dallas
Brazos R.
Houston
Galveston Bay
Atchafalaya Bay
New Orleans
Delta of the Mississippi River
Mobile Bay
Cape San Blas
Apalachee Bay
Gulf Coastal Plain
Padre I.

Gulf of Mexico

TROPIC OF CANCER 23½°N

N

LAND COVER MAP
UNITED STATES

Cropland	Grassland	Tundra	Glacier
Semi-desert & desert	Tropical rain forest	Broadleaf forest	Needleleaf forest

Boundary Symbols
——— International boundary
——— State boundary

Scale
1:12,700,000

0   100   200   300 miles
1 in. to 200 mi.

0   100   200   300 kilometers
1 cm to 127 km

Detailed legend on page 6   Albers Equal Area Projection

ELEVATION MAP
UNITED STATES

Meters Above Sea Level	Feet Above Sea Level
Over 3000	Over 10,000
1500 to 3000	5,000 to 10,000
600 to 1500	2,000 to 5,000
300 to 600	1,000 to 2,000
150 to 300	500 to 1,000
0 to 150	0 to 500
Below sea level	Below sea level

Boundary Symbols

International boundary
State boundary

Scale
1:13,900,000

0   100   200   300 miles
1 in. to 220 mi.

0   100   200   300 kilometers
1 cm to 139 km

Detailed legend on page 6   Bonne Projection

CROSS SECTION
Vertical exaggeration 41 to 1
Scale at 36°N: 1 in. to 240 mi., 1 cm to 150 km

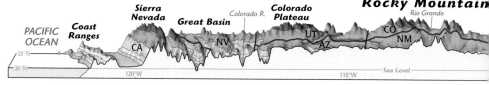

Great Plains

Ozark Plateau

Central Lowland

Appalachian Mountains

Atlantic Coastal Plain

ATLANTIC OCEAN

KS

OK

MO

Mississippi R.

Tennessee R.

KY

VA

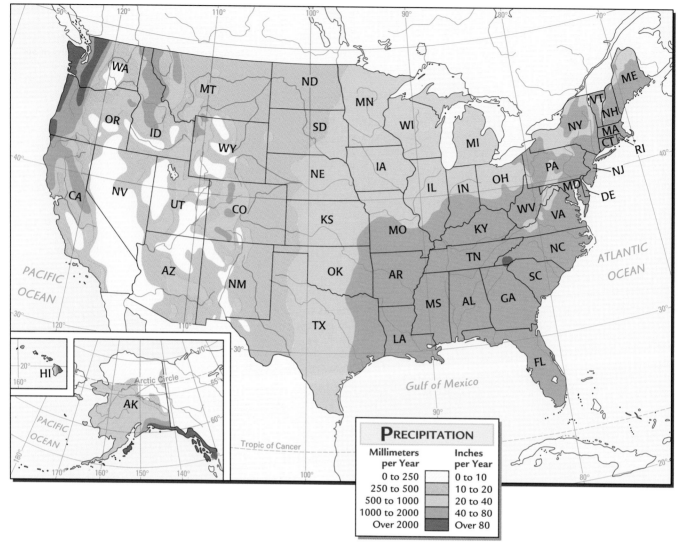

PRECIPITATION

Millimeters per Year	Inches per Year
0 to 250	0 to 10
250 to 500	10 to 20
500 to 1000	20 to 40
1000 to 2000	40 to 80
Over 2000	Over 80

WETLANDS

Wetlands play a key role in watershed protection. They provide a barrier against floods and serve as natural filters by trapping pollutants stored in water. They also provide habitat for wildlife.

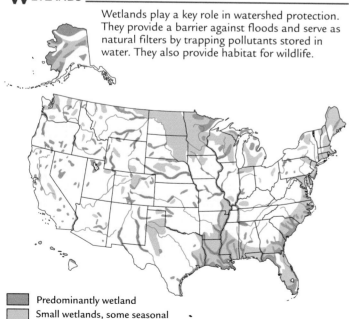

■ Predominantly wetland
▢ Small wetlands, some seasonal

During the past 200 years, more than half the wetlands in the United States have been drained, filled, or paved to develop agricultural land or to expand cities, towns, and resorts. Part of this coastal marsh in South Carolina was destroyed to make room for housing.

California has the most extreme fire weather in the United States. Strong desert winds and frequent drought combine to produce major wildfires. Valleys and canyons create natural paths for wildfires.

TORNADOES AND HURRICANES

Hurricanes are powerful storms that form over tropical ocean waters and often strike the Atlantic and Gulf coasts. **Tornadoes** are quickly rotating columns of air that form under a thundercloud. Tornadoes can strike in any state, but frequently touch down in a belt known as "Tornado Alley."

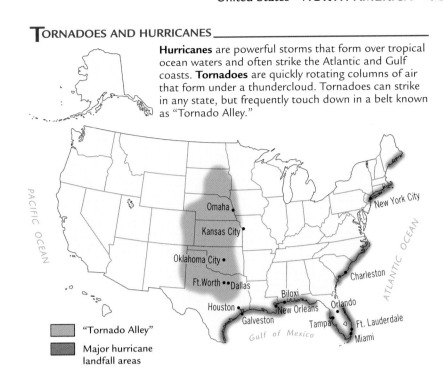

"Tornado Alley"

Major hurricane landfall areas

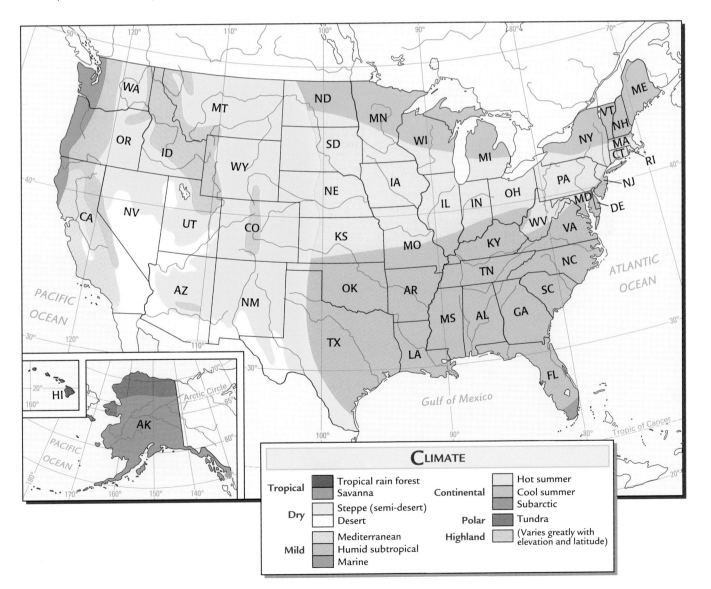

CLIMATE

Tropical
- Tropical rain forest
- Savanna

Dry
- Steppe (semi-desert)
- Desert

Mild
- Mediterranean
- Humid subtropical
- Marine

Continental
- Hot summer
- Cool summer
- Subarctic

Polar
- Tundra

Highland
- (Varies greatly with elevation and latitude)

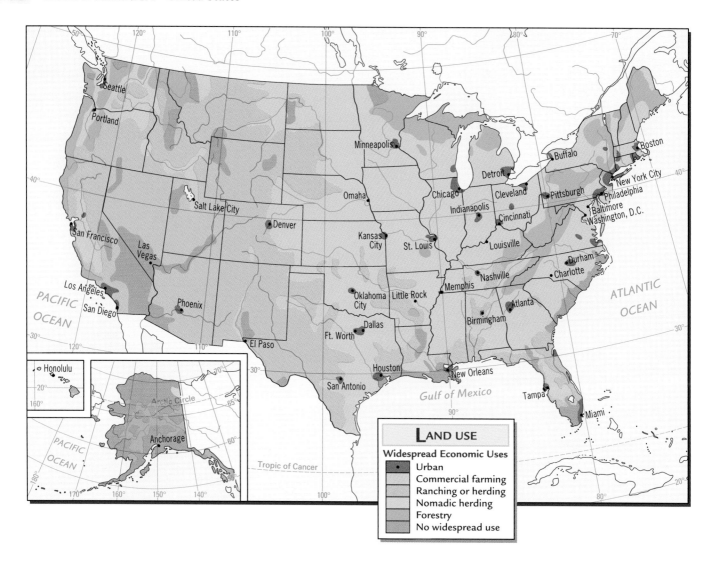

LAND USE

Widespread Economic Uses
- Urban
- Commercial farming
- Ranching or herding
- Nomadic herding
- Forestry
- No widespread use

CHANGE IN U.S. FARMS

	1900	1950	2002
Percentage of U.S. population working on farms (farm population)	41.9%	15.3%	1.1%
Number of farms (=1 million farms)	5.7 million	5.4 million	2.1 million
Average farm size (=100 acres)	147 acres	216 acres	441 acres

Most farms in the United States are commercial farms, like this chicken farm. Some poultry breeders raise more than a million birds at a time on their farms.

Since the turn of the twentieth century, the United States has moved toward fewer, but much larger, farms. The percentage of people directly engaged in farming has also dropped dramatically.

AGRICULTURAL EXPORTS

The United States is a leading exporter of corn, wheat, poultry, and other crops. However, agriculture accounts for only one percent of our country's gross domestic product.

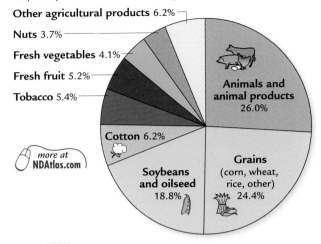

- Other agricultural products 6.2%
- Nuts 3.7%
- Fresh vegetables 4.1%
- Fresh fruit 5.2%
- Tobacco 5.4%
- Cotton 6.2%
- Soybeans and oilseed 18.8%
- Animals and animal products 26.0%
- Grains (corn, wheat, rice, other) 24.4%

more at NDAtlas.com

Iowa and Illinois are the leading producers of corn and soybeans in the United States. Both crops are used to feed people and animals, and are also used to make many nonfood items.

Still a Nation of Farmers

Agribusiness *is one of the most rapidly growing industries in the United States. It includes farms and businesses that produce, process, distribute, transport, and sell farm products. Nearly one out of every four workers in the United States is employed in agribusiness.*

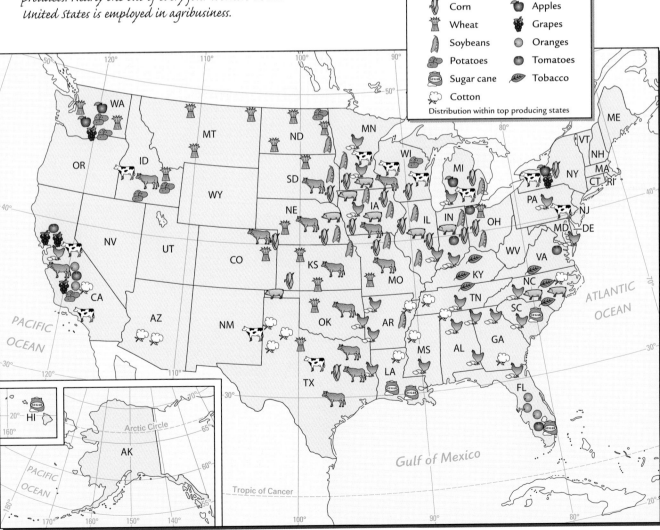

AGRICULTURAL PRODUCTS

Livestock
- Beef
- Dairy
- Hogs
- Poultry

Crops
- Corn
- Wheat
- Soybeans
- Potatoes
- Sugar cane
- Cotton
- Apples
- Grapes
- Oranges
- Tomatoes
- Tobacco

Distribution within top producing states

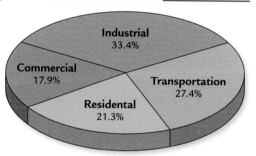

Wind power is a clean energy source that is inexhaustible. However, it is only commercially useful in areas that have strong, steady winds. Only about 0.12 percent of electric power in the United States is produced by wind.

Times Square in New York City serves as a snapshot of different energy resources and how they are used. Oil is used for transportation, electricity provides power for lights, and heating oil or natural gas supplies heat.

Sources of Consumed Energy

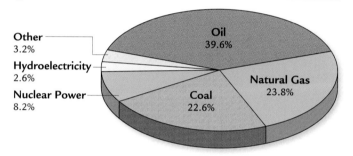

Other
3.2%

Hydroelectricity
2.6%

Nuclear Power
8.2%

Oil
39.6%

Natural Gas
23.8%

Coal
22.6%

Uses of Consumed Energy

Industrial
33.4%

Commercial
17.9%

Transportation
27.4%

Residental
21.3%

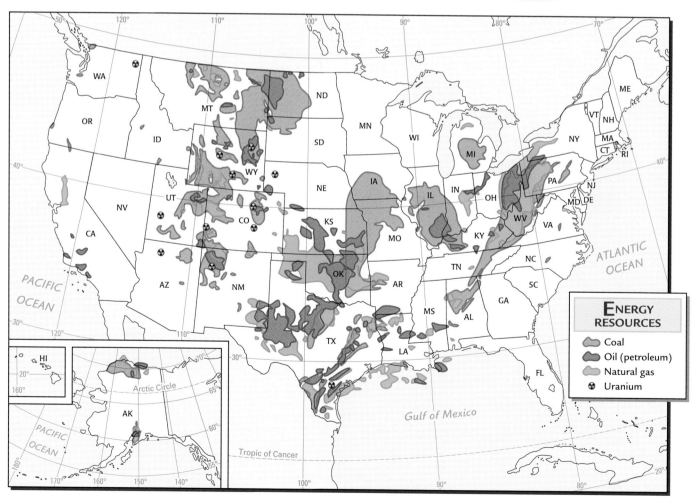

Energy Resources

- Coal
- Oil (petroleum)
- Natural gas
- Uranium

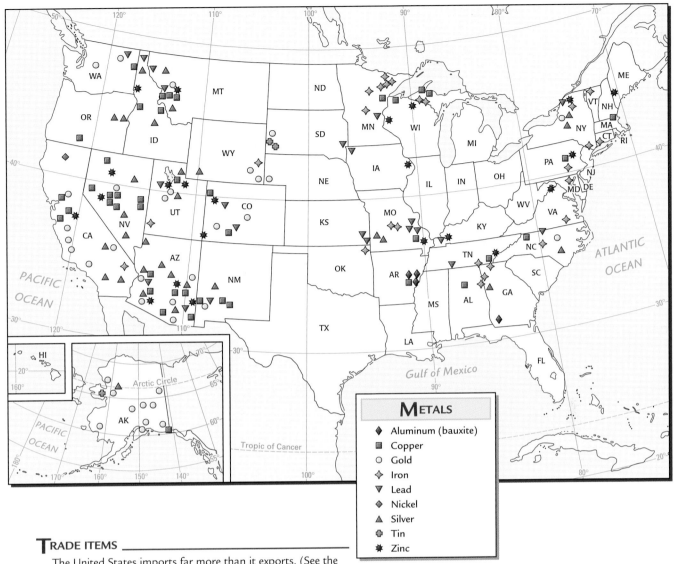

METALS

◆ Aluminum (bauxite)
■ Copper
○ Gold
✦ Iron
▼ Lead
◆ Nickel
▲ Silver
✛ Tin
✳ Zinc

TRADE ITEMS

The United States imports far more than it exports. (See the Balance of Trade graph on page 40.) As a result, 17.5 percent of all imports is a much higher amount than 17.9 percent of all exports.

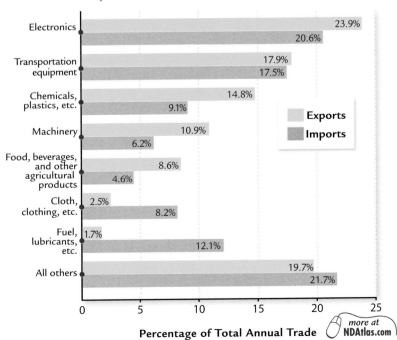

Electronics 23.9% / 20.6%
Transportation equipment 17.9% / 17.5%
Chemicals, plastics, etc. 14.8% / 9.1%
Machinery 10.9% / 6.2%
Food, beverages, and other agricultural products 8.6% / 4.6%
Cloth, clothing, etc. 2.5% / 8.2%
Fuel, lubricants, etc. 1.7% / 12.1%
All others 19.7% / 21.7%

Exports
Imports

Percentage of Total Annual Trade
more at NDAtlas.com

GROSS DOMESTIC PRODUCT BY STATE

- Florida 5.1%
- Illinois 4.6%
- Pennsylvania 4.1%
- Ohio 3.6%
- New Jersey 3.6%
- Michigan 3.3%

New York 7.7%
Texas 7.5%
California 13.2%
All Other States 47.3%

more at NDAtlas.com

Nine states in the United States produce more than half of the country's GDP. The GDP of California alone is larger than the GDP of Canada.

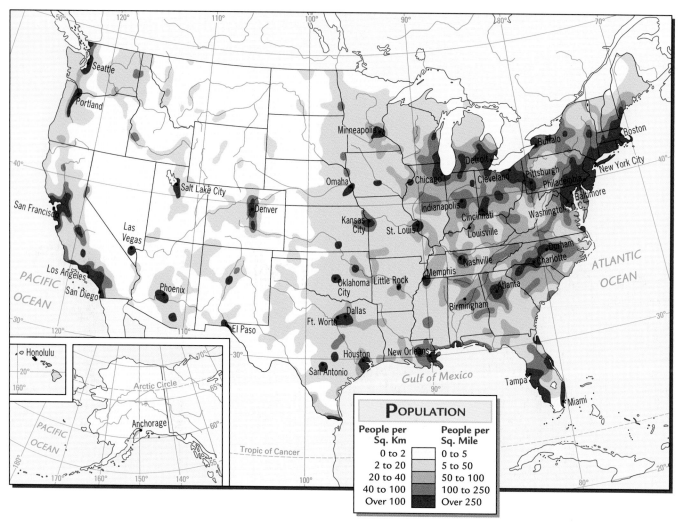

POPULATION

People per Sq. Km	People per Sq. Mile
0 to 2	0 to 5
2 to 20	5 to 50
20 to 40	50 to 100
40 to 100	100 to 250
Over 100	Over 250

Major highways and airports

The U.S. highway network consists of 4 million miles (6.4 million kilometers) of streets and roads. Air travel is the fastest-growing means of transportation in the United States. In 1975 less than 50 percent of all Americans had flown, while today that number has climbed to 80 percent.

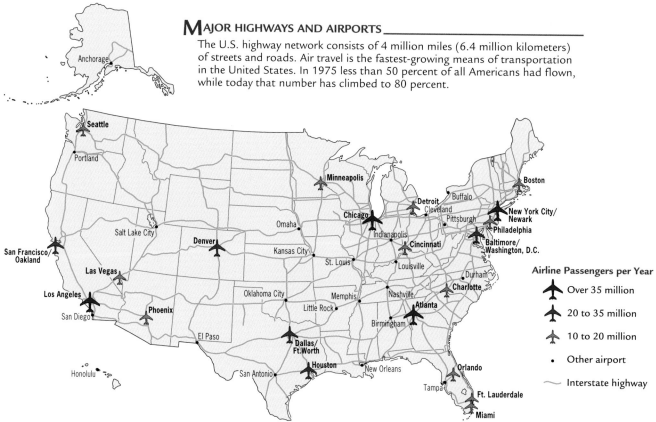

Airline Passengers per Year

- Over 35 million
- 20 to 35 million
- 10 to 20 million
- Other airport
- Interstate highway

Population in Motion

Domestic migration refers to the movement of people within a country. In the past, the United States' population moved westward. Today the population is shifting from north to south. Between 2000 and 2004, New York experienced the highest out-migration in the country, while Florida was the primary destination for migrants.

more at NDAtlas.com

ALASKA AREA COMPARISON

Alaska
589,194 sq. mi.
(1 526 006 sq. km)

Contiguous
United States
3,021,295 sq. mi.
(7 825 112 sq. km)

ETHNIC COMPOSITION UNITED STATES

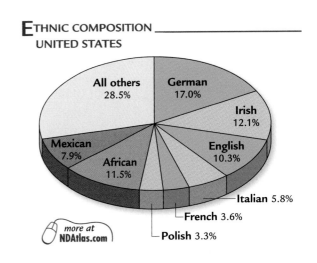

- All others 28.5%
- German 17.0%
- Irish 12.1%
- English 10.3%
- Italian 5.8%
- French 3.6%
- Polish 3.3%
- African 11.5%
- Mexican 7.9%

more at NDAtlas.com

REGIONAL MAPS OF THE UNITED STATES

1 Northeastern U.S.
pages 82–83
Connecticut, Maine, Massachusetts, New Hampshire, New Jersey, New York, Pennsylvania, Rhode Island, Vermont

2 East Central U.S. • pages 84–85
Delaware, Indiana, Kentucky, Maryland, Ohio, North Carolina, Tennessee, Virginia, West Virginia

3 Southeastern U.S. • pages 86–87
Alabama, Florida, Georgia, Mississippi, South Carolina

4 South Central U.S. • pages 88–89
Arkansas, Louisiana, Oklahoma, Texas

5 Central U.S. • pages 90–91
Illinois, Iowa, Kansas, Missouri, Nebraska

6 North Central U.S. • pages 92–93
Michigan, Minnesota, North Dakota, South Dakota, Wisconsin

7 Northwestern U.S. • pages 94–95
Idaho, Montana, Oregon, Washington, Wyoming

8 Southwestern U.S. • pages 96–97
Arizona, California, Colorado, Nevada, New Mexico, Utah

9 Alaska • page 98

10 Hawaii • page 98

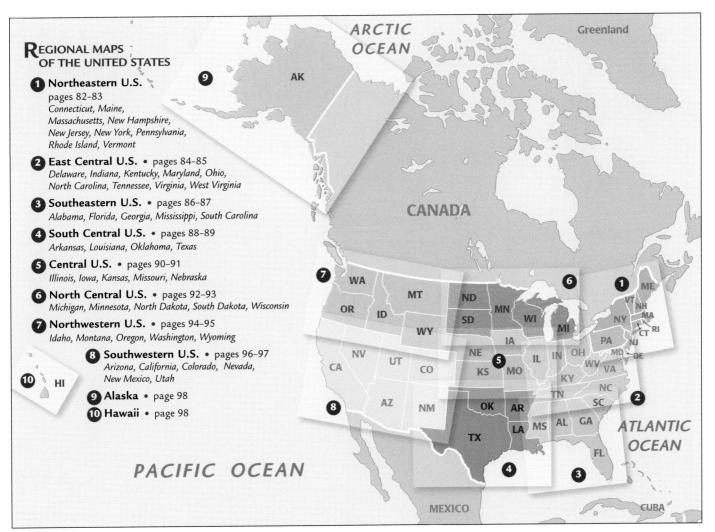

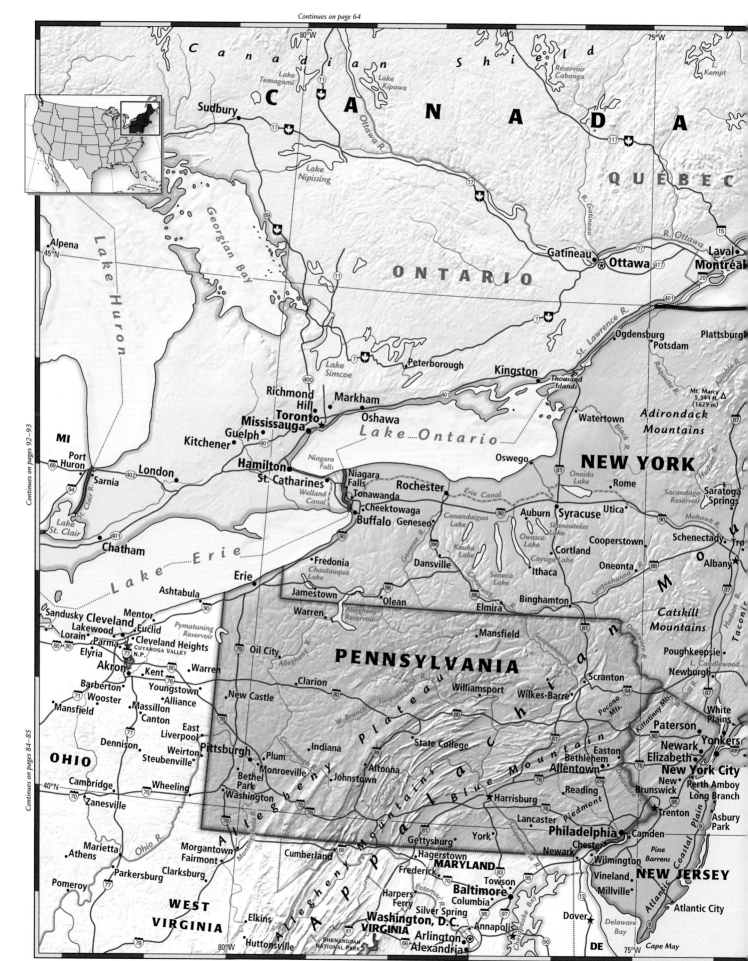

Continues on page 64

80°W
75°W

Canadian Shield

L. Kempt

L. Temagami
Lake Kipawa
Réservoir Cabonga

C **A** **N** **A** **D** **A**

Sudbury

11

QUÉBEC

17

117

Lake Nipissing

R. Ottawa
R. Gatineau

Ottawa R.

15

Alpena

Lake Huron

45°N

Gatineau
Ottawa
417

Laval
Montréal
20

O N T A R I O

11

401

7

Georgian Bay

Lake Simcoe

Peterborough

Kingston

Thousand Islands

Ogdensburg
Potsdam
Plattsburg

Raquette R.

Mt. Marcy 5,344 ft. (1629 m)

400

Richmond Hill
Markham
Oshawa

401

Adirondack Mountains

MI

Toronto
Mississauga

Lake Ontario

Watertown

Black R.

Guelph
Kitchener

401

Niagara Falls

Oswego

NEW YORK

81

Oneida Lake

Rome

Sacandaga Reservoir

87

Saratoga Springs

Port Huron
69

Sarnia
402
London

Hamilton
St. Catharines

Welland Canal

Niagara Falls
Tonawanda
Cheektowaga
Buffalo
Geneseo

Rochester

Erie Canal

90

Auburn
Syracuse

Utica

Mohawk R.

Schenectady
Tr

Albany

94

Lake St. Clair

401

Chatham

Lake Erie

90

Genesee R.

Canandaigua Lake

Skaneateles Lake
Owasco Lake

Cortland

Cooperstown

Oneonta

Susquehanna R.

87

Hudson R.

Catskill Mountains

Taconic

M

Fredonia
Chautauqua Lake

Keuka Lake

Dansville

Seneca Lake
Cayuga Lake

Ithaca

Chemung R.

Erie

Ashtabula

90

Jamestown
Olean
Warren

Allegheny Reservoir

Binghamton

Elmira

Poughkeepsie

L. Candlewood

Newburgh

87

Mentor

Sandusky Cleveland
Lakewood Euclid
Lorain Cleveland Heights
Parma

Pymatuning Reservoir

Mansfield

81

Delaware R.

White Plains

Wallkill R.

Kittatinny Mts.

Paterson

84

Elyria
80
CUYAHOGA VALLEY N.P.
77

79

Oil City

PENNSYLVANIA

Scranton

Pocono Mts.

Newark
Yonkers

80

Akron

Barberton
71 Wooster
Mansfield

Kent
Warren

Youngstown
Alliance
Massillon
Canton

76

New Castle

Clarion

80

Williamsport

Wilkes-Barre

81

78

Easton
Bethlehem
Allentown

Elizabeth

495

New York City

Allegheny R.

Susquehanna R.

W. Branch

State College

99

Indiana

Altoona
Johnstown

Blue Mountain

78

Reading

476

New Brunswick
Perth Amboy
Long Branch

East Liverpool
Dennison

Weirton
Steubenville

Pittsburgh
Plum
Monroeville

Conemaugh R.

Juniata R.

81

Harrisburg

Delaware R.

Piedmont

Trenton

Asbury Park

OHIO

Cambridge

Wheeling

40°N

70

Bethel Park
Washington

79

76

70

Lancaster

Reading

Philadelphia
Camden

Monongahela R.

65

Gettysburg
York

81

Newark
Chester

Pine Barrens

Zanesville

Morgantown
Fairmont

Cumberland
68

Hagerstown

83

Wilmington
Vineland
Millville

NEW JERSEY

Marietta
Athens

Parkersburg

Clarksburg

Frederick

MARYLAND

Towson
Baltimore
Columbia

95

Atlantic Coastal Plain

Atlantic City

Pomeroy

77

Ohio R.

WEST VIRGINIA

Elkins

Harpers Ferry
Silver Spring

Potomac R.

Annapolis
97
95

Chesapeake Bay

Dover

13

Delaware Bay

9

Cape May

DE

Huttonsville

79

SHENANDOAH NATIONAL PARK

Washington, D.C.
VIRGINIA
Arlington
Alexandria

66

50

80°W
75°W

Continues on pages 92–93
Continues on pages 84–85

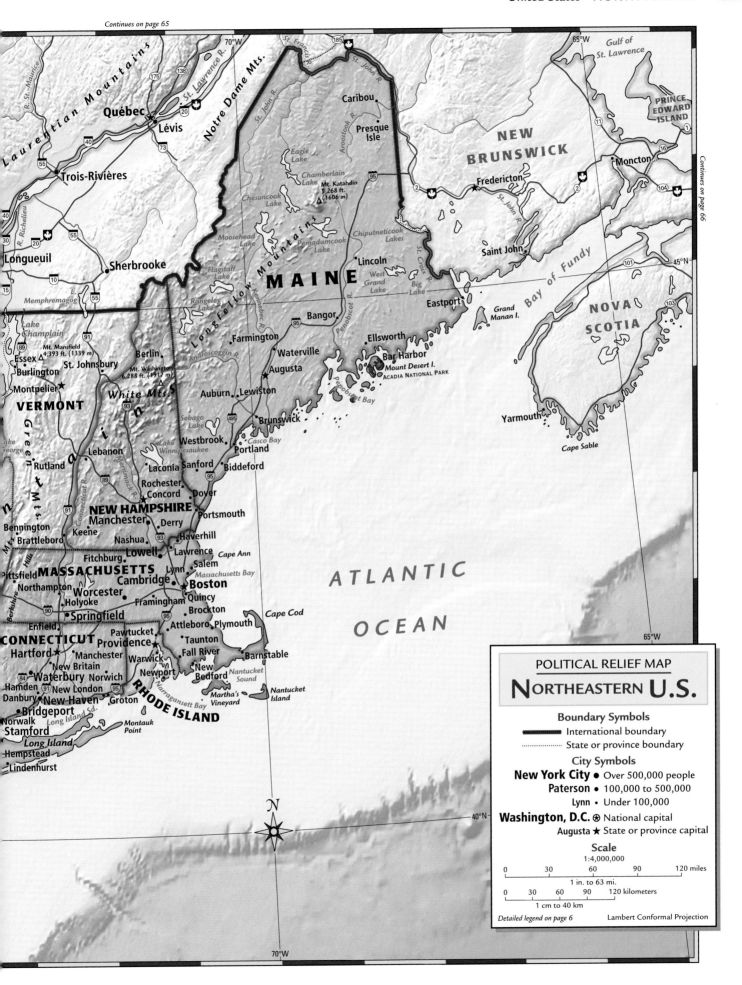

Continues on page 65

Continues on page 66

Laurentian Mountains

R. St-Maurice

Québec
Lévis

Trois-Rivières

Notre Dame Mts.

St. Lawrence R.

St. Francis R.

St. John R.

Caribou

Presque Isle

NEW BRUNSWICK

PRINCE EDWARD ISLAND

Gulf of St. Lawrence

Moncton

Fredericton

Saint John

Eagle Lake

Chamberlain Lake

Chesuncook Lake

Mt. Katahdin 5,268 ft. (1606 m)

Aroostook R.

St. John R.

Longueuil

R. Richelieu

Sherbrooke

Flagstaff Lake

Moosehead Lake

Pemadumcook Lake

Chiputneticook Lakes

St. Croix R.

Bay of Fundy

NOVA SCOTIA

L. Memphremagog

Lake Champlain

Mt. Mansfield 4,393 ft. (1339 m)

Rangeley Lake

Longfellow Mountains

MAINE

Lincoln

West Grand Lake

Big Lake

Eastport

Grand Manan I.

Essex

Burlington

St. Johnsbury

Berlin

Mt. Washington 6,288 ft. (1917 m)

Farmington

Bangor

Penobscot R.

Ellsworth

Bar Harbor

Mount Desert I.

ACADIA NATIONAL PARK

Montpelier

VERMONT

White Mts.

Waterville

Augusta

Kennebec R.

Penobscot Bay

Green Mts.

Androscoggin R.

Auburn

Lewiston

Brunswick

Yarmouth

Cape Sable

Lake George

Rutland

Lebanon

Sebago Lake

Westbrook

Casco Bay

Portland

Merrimack R.

Lake Winnipesaukee

Laconia

Sanford

Biddeford

Rochester

Concord

Dover

Portsmouth

Bennington

NEW HAMPSHIRE

Manchester

Derry

Connecticut R.

Keene

Nashua

Haverhill

Lawrence

Cape Ann

Brattleboro

Fitchburg

Lowell

Salem

ATLANTIC OCEAN

Pittsfield

MASSACHUSETTS

Lynn

Massachusetts Bay

Northampton

Worcester

Cambridge

Berkshire Hills

Holyoke

Framingham

Quincy

Boston

Springfield

Brockton

Cape Cod

Enfield

Attleboro

Plymouth

CONNECTICUT

Pawtucket

Providence

Taunton

Barnstable

Hartford

Manchester

Warwick

Fall River

New Bedford

Nantucket Sound

Nantucket Island

New Britain

Newport

Waterbury

Norwich

Hamden

New London

RHODE ISLAND

Martha's Vineyard

Danbury

New Haven

Groton

Narragansett Bay

Bridgeport

Norwalk

Long Island Sd.

Montauk Point

Stamford

Long Island

Hempstead

Lindenhurst

POLITICAL RELIEF MAP
Northeastern U.S.

Boundary Symbols
International boundary
State or province boundary

City Symbols
New York City ● Over 500,000 people
Paterson ● 100,000 to 500,000
Lynn • Under 100,000

Washington, D.C. ⊕ National capital
Augusta ★ State or province capital

Scale
1:4,000,000

0   30   60   90   120 miles
1 in. to 63 mi.

0   30   60   90   120 kilometers
1 cm to 40 km

Detailed legend on page 6   Lambert Conformal Projection

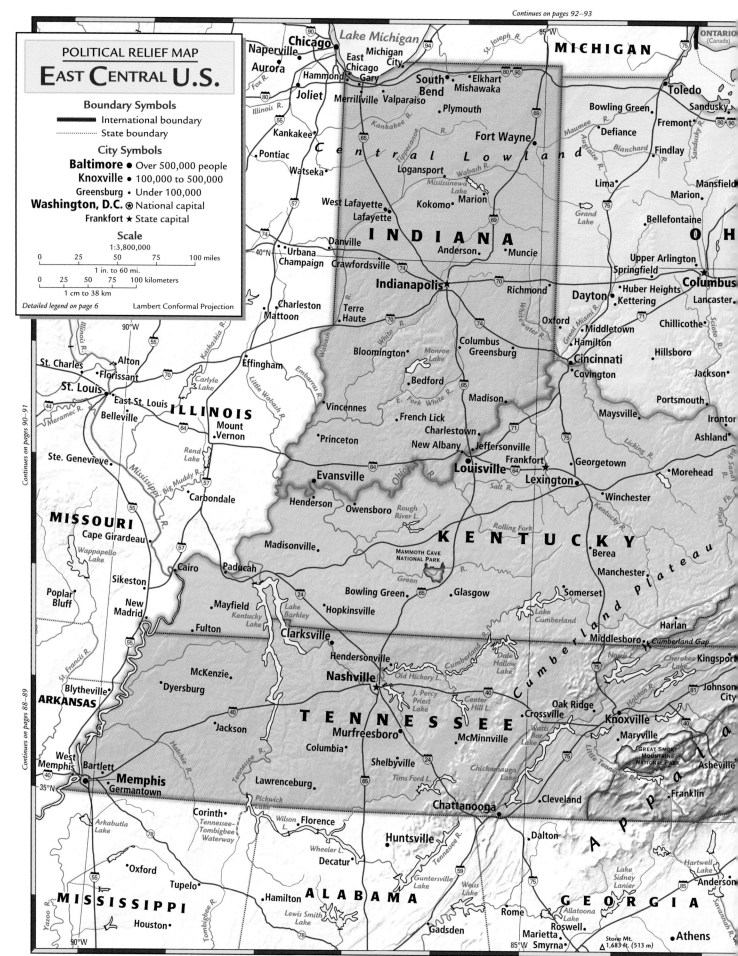

Continues on pages 92–93

POLITICAL RELIEF MAP
EAST CENTRAL U.S.

Boundary Symbols
━━━━━ International boundary
.... State boundary

City Symbols
Baltimore ● Over 500,000 people
Knoxville ● 100,000 to 500,000
Greensburg • Under 100,000
Washington, D.C. ⊗ National capital
Frankfort ★ State capital

Scale
1:3,800,000

0 ─ 25 ─ 50 ─ 75 ─ 100 miles
1 in. to 60 mi.

0 ─ 25 ─ 50 ─ 75 ─ 100 kilometers
1 cm to 38 km

Detailed legend on page 6   Lambert Conformal Projection

Continues on pages 90–91

Continues on pages 88–89

Continues on pages 86–87

Continues on pages 82–83

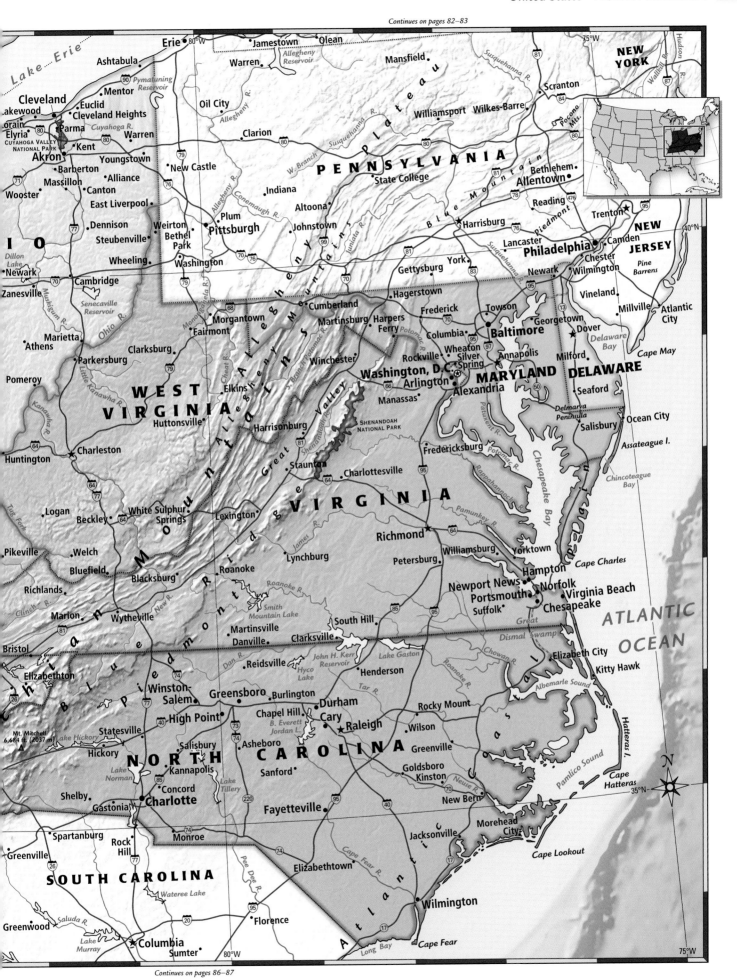

Continues on pages 86–87

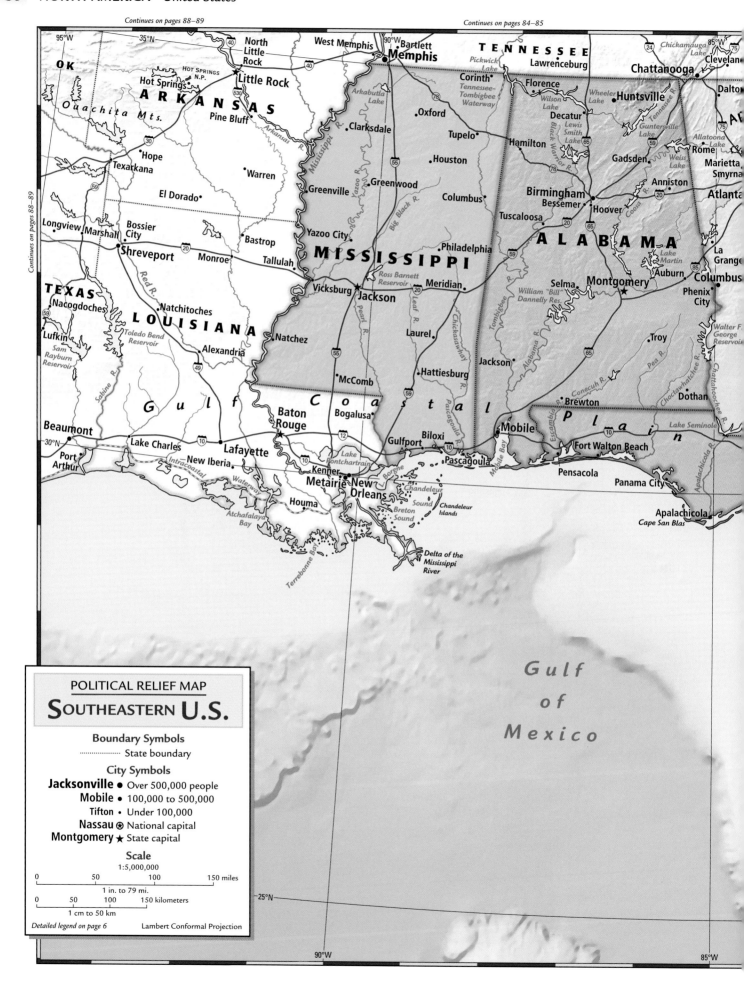

Continues on pages 88–89

Continues on pages 84–85

Continues on pages 88–89

POLITICAL RELIEF MAP

SOUTHEASTERN U.S.

Boundary Symbols

·················· State boundary

City Symbols

Jacksonville ● Over 500,000 people
Mobile ● 100,000 to 500,000
Tifton • Under 100,000
Nassau ⊕ National capital
Montgomery ★ State capital

Scale

1:5,000,000

0   50   150 miles

1 in. to 79 mi.

0   50   100   150 kilometers

1 cm to 50 km

Detailed legend on page 6   Lambert Conformal Projection

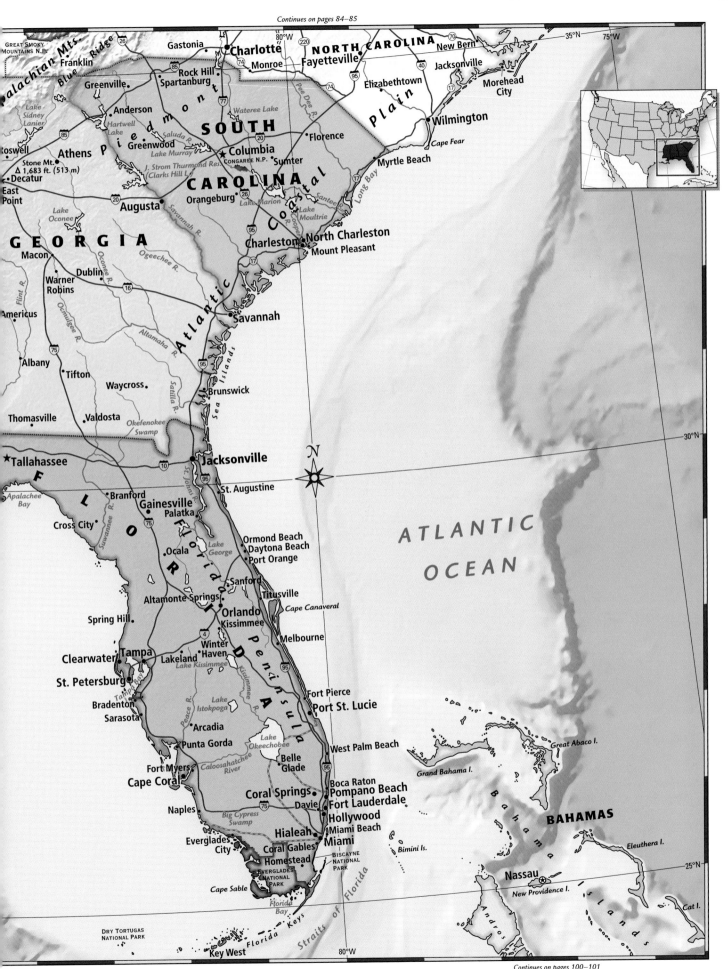

Continues on pages 84–85

GREAT SMOKY
MOUNTAINS N.P.
Franklin
Gastonia •Charlotte **NORTH CAROLINA** •New Bern
Fayetteville
Monroe
Jacksonville
Rock Hill Elizabethtown
Greenville. Spartanburg Morehead
City
Anderson **SOUTH** Florence •Wilmington
Athens Greenwood *Cape Fear*
Stone Mt. •Columbia
△ 1,683 ft. (513 m) CONGAREE N.P. Sumter **CAROLINA** Myrtle Beach
East Decatur
Point
Augusta Orangeburg Charleston •North Charleston
GEORGIA Mount Pleasant
Macon
Dublin
Warner
Robins
Americus
Savannah
Albany
Tifton
Waycross. Brunswick
Thomasville
Valdosta Okefenokee
Swamp

★**Tallahassee** Jacksonville **ATLANTIC**
Branford St. Augustine
Apalachee **OCEAN**
Bay Gainesville
Cross City Palatka

F Ormond Beach
L Ocala Daytona Beach
O Port Orange
R Sanford
Altamonte Springs Titusville
Spring Hill **I** Orlando *Cape Canaveral*
Kissimmee
D Melbourne
Clearwater Tampa Winter
Lakeland Haven
St. Petersburg **A**
Bradenton Fort Pierce
Sarasota Port St. Lucie
Arcadia
Punta Gorda
West Palm Beach
Fort Myers Belle
Cape Coral Glade Boca Raton
Coral Springs Pompano Beach
Naples Davie Fort Lauderdale
Hollywood
Hialeah Miami Beach
Everglades Miami
City Coral Gables
Homestead BISCAYNE
EVERGLADES NATIONAL
NATIONAL PARK
PARK
Cape Sable

BAHAMAS
Great Abaco I.
Grand Bahama I.
Nassau
New Providence I.
Bimini Is. *Eleuthera I.*
Andros *Cat I.*

DRY TORTUGAS
NATIONAL PARK
Key West *Florida Keys* *Straits of Florida*

Continues on pages 100–101

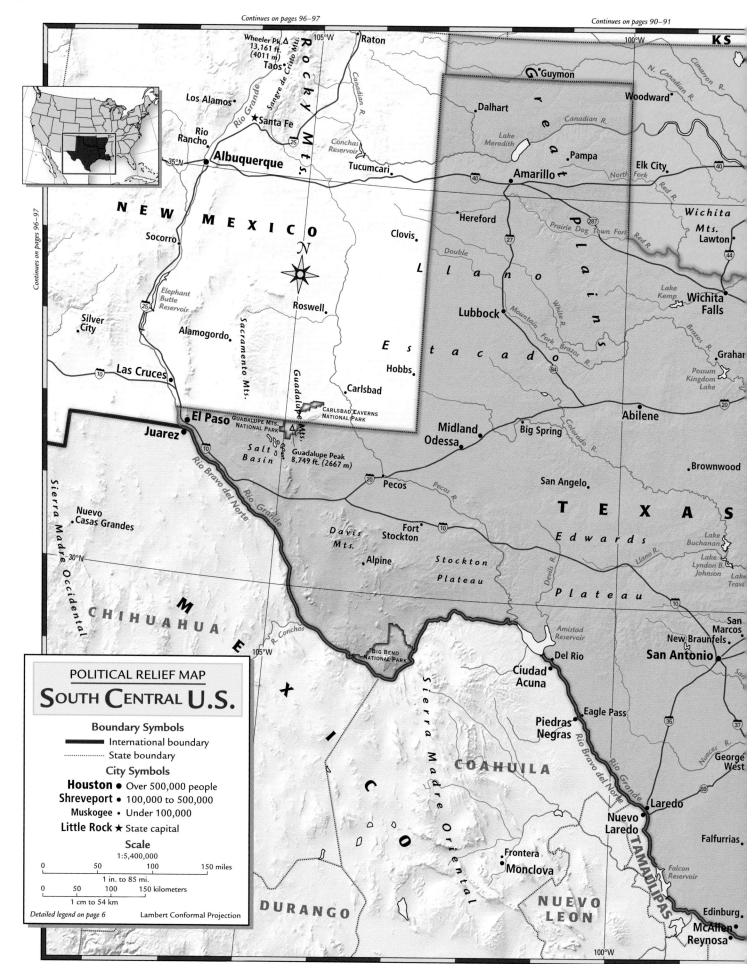

Continues on pages 96–97
Continues on pages 90–91

KS

Wheeler Pk. △
13,161 ft.
(4011 m)

•Raton

105°W

•Guymon

•Woodward

•Dalhart

N. Canadian R.

Cimarron R.

Taos•

Los Alamos•

Rio Grande

Sangre de Cristo Mts.

Canadian R.

★Santa Fe

Rio
Rancho•

35°N

•Albuquerque

Conchas
Reservoir

Lake
Meredith

•Pampa

Canadian R.

Elk City•

North Fork

40

R o c k y   M t s.

N E W   M E X I C O

Socorro•

•Hereford

27

•Amarillo

287

Red R.

Wichita
Mts.
•Lawton

44

Clovis•

Prairie Dog Town Fork

G r e a t   P l a i n s

Double

Red R.

Elephant
Butte
Reservoir

25

Roswell•

L l a n o

Silver
City•

Alamogordo•

Sacramento Mts.

Mountain Fork Brazos

White R.

Lake
Kemp

•Wichita
Falls

Las Cruces•

10

Lubbock•

84

•Graham

E s t a c a d o

Possum
Kingdom
Lake

Hobbs•

Guadalupe Mts.

Carlsbad•

CARLSBAD CAVERNS
NATIONAL PARK

•Abilene

20

El Paso•

GUADALUPE MTS.
NATIONAL PARK

△

•Midland
Odessa•

Big Spring•

Colorado R.

Juarez•

10

Salt
Basin

Guadalupe Peak
8,749 ft. (2667 m)

Rio Bravo del Norte

Rio Grande

20

Pecos•

Pecas R.

San Angelo•

•Brownwood

T E X A S

Sierra Madre Occidental

Nuevo
Casas Grandes•

30°N

Davis
Mts.

•Fort
Stockton

10

E d w a r d s

Lake
Buchanan

Alpine•

Stockton
Plateau

P l a t e a u

Llano R.

Lake
Lyndon B.
Johnson

Lake
Travi

C H I H U A H U A

R. Conchos

Big Bend
NATIONAL PARK

Devils R.

Amistad
Reservoir

10

•San
Marcos

•New Braunfels

M

105°W

Del Rio•

Ciudad
Acuna•

San Antonio

E

Sierra Madre Oriental

Eagle Pass•

35

37

X

Piedras
Negras•

Rio Bravo del Norte

Nueces R.

•George
West

I

C

COAHUILA

69

•Laredo

O

Nuevo
Laredo•

TAMAULIPAS

•Falfurrias

Frontera•

Monclova

Falcon
Reservoir

**N U E V O
L E O N**

•Edinburg

DURANGO

100°W

•McAllen
Reynosa•

POLITICAL RELIEF MAP
South **C**entral **U.S.**

Boundary Symbols
International boundary
.... State boundary

City Symbols
Houston • Over 500,000 people
Shreveport • 100,000 to 500,000
Muskogee • Under 100,000
Little Rock ★ State capital

Scale
1:5,400,000

0   50   100   150 miles

1 in. to 85 mi.

0   50   100   150 kilometers

1 cm to 54 km

Detailed legend on page 6   Lambert Conformal Projection

Continues on pages 90–91

Continues on pages 84–85

Continues on pages 86–87

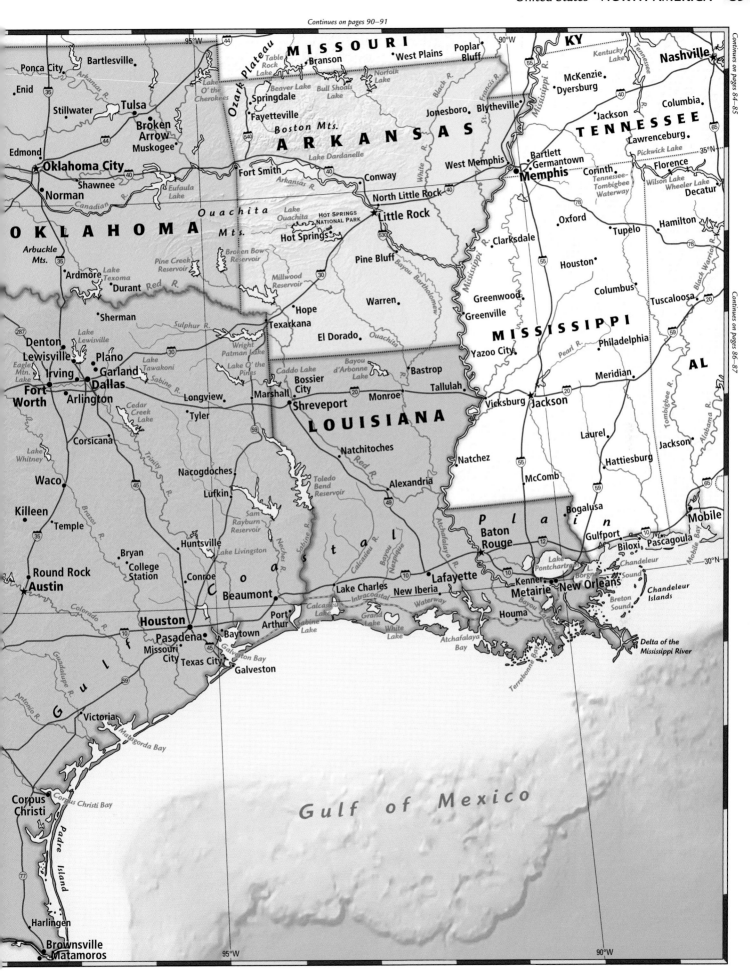

Ponca City
Bartlesville
Enid
Stillwater
Tulsa
Broken Arrow
Muskogee
Edmond
Oklahoma City
Shawnee
Norman
OKLAHOMA
Arbuckle Mts.
Ardmore
Lake Texoma
Durant
Sherman
Red R.
Denton
Lewisville
Lake Lewisville
Plano
Garland
Eagle Mtn. Lake
Irving
Fort Worth
Dallas
Arlington
Lake Tawakoni
Corsicana
Cedar Creek Lake
Lake Whitney
Waco
Killeen
Temple
Round Rock
Austin
Bryan
College Station
Brazos R.
Guadalupe R.
Colorado R.
Victoria
Corpus Christi
Corpus Christi Bay
Padre Island
Harlingen
Brownsville
Matamoros

MISSOURI
Ozark Plateau
Table Rock Lake
Branson
Beaver Lake
Bull Shoals Lake
Springdale
Fayetteville
Boston Mts.
Lake Dardanelle
ARKANSAS
Fort Smith
Eufaula Lake
Canadian R.
Arkansas R.
Conway
North Little Rock
Ouachita Mts.
Lake Ouachita
HOT SPRINGS NATIONAL PARK
Little Rock
Hot Springs
Pine Creek Reservoir
Broken Bow Reservoir
Millwood Reservoir
Sulphur R.
Hope
Texarkana
Warren
Wright Patman Lake
El Dorado
Lake O' the Pines
Caddo Lake
Bossier City
Bayou d'Arbonne Lake
Bastrop
Longview
Marshall
Shreveport
Monroe
Tallulah
Sabine R.
Tyler
LOUISIANA
Natchitoches
Nacogdoches
Red R.
Toledo Bend Reservoir
Alexandria
Lufkin
Sam Rayburn Reservoir
Huntsville
Lake Livingston
Conroe
Neches R.
Sabine R.
Calcasieu R.
Bayou Nezpique
Atchafalaya R.
Baton Rouge
Beaumont
Lake Charles
Lafayette
New Iberia
Houston
Port Arthur
Pasadena
Baytown
Galveston Bay
Missouri City
Texas City
Galveston
Calcasieu Lake
Sabine Lake
Intracoastal Waterway
Grand Lake
White Lake
Atchafalaya Bay
Houma
Terrebonne Bay
Gulf Coastal Plain
Matagorda Bay

West Plains
Poplar Bluff
Norfolk Lake
Black R.
Jonesboro
Blytheville
West Memphis
Francis R.
Mississippi R.
White R.
Memphis
Bartlett
Germantown
Corinth
Pine Bluff
Bayou Bartholomew
Greenwood
Greenville
Yazoo City
Mississippi R.
Vicksburg
Jackson
MISSISSIPPI
Pearl R.
Philadelphia
Meridian
Laurel
Natchez
McComb
Bogalusa
Gulfport
Biloxi
Pascagoula
Lake Pontchartrain
Kenner
Metairie
New Orleans
Breton Sound
Chandeleur Sound
Chandeleur Islands
Delta of the Mississippi River
Bayou Lafourche

KY
Kentucky Lake
Nashville
McKenzie
Dyersburg
Jackson
Columbia
TENNESSEE
Lawrenceburg
Pickwick Lake
Florence
Tennessee-Tombigbee Waterway
Wilson Lake
Wheeler Lake
Decatur
Oxford
Tupelo
Hamilton
Houston
Columbus
Tuscaloosa
Black Warrior R.
AL
Tombigbee R.
Alabama R.
Jackson
Hattiesburg
Mobile
Mobile Bay

Gulf of Mexico

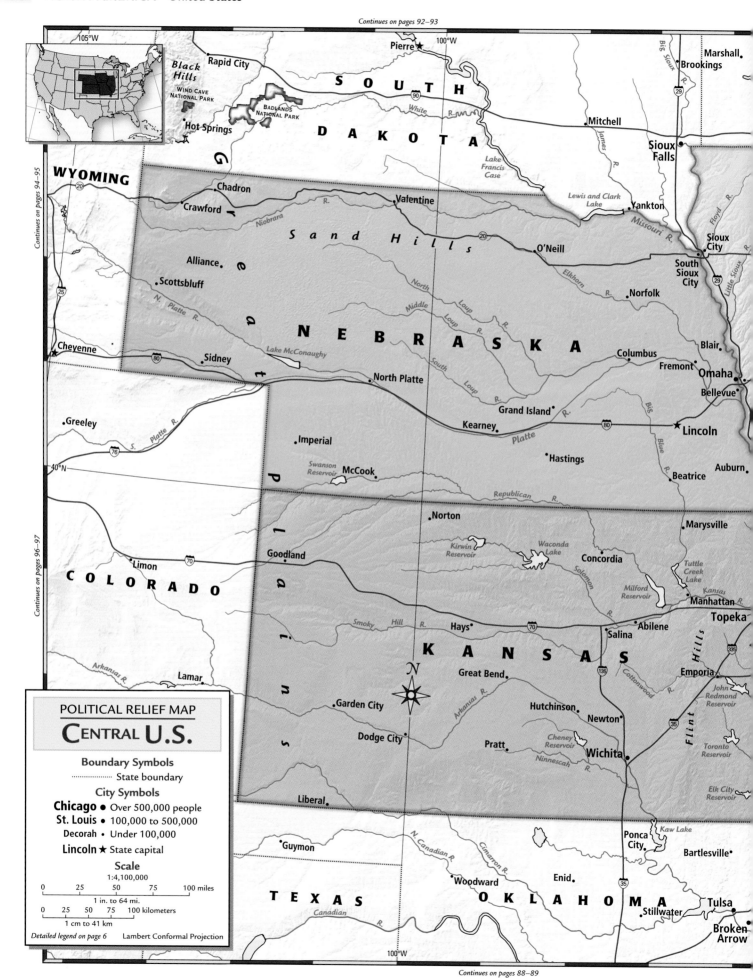

Continues on pages 92–93

105°W

100°W

WYOMING

Continues on pages 94–95

Continues on pages 96–97

Pierre ★

Rapid City

Black Hills

WIND CAVE NATIONAL PARK

Hot Springs

BADLANDS NATIONAL PARK

S O U T H

White R.

D A K O T A

James R.

Lake Francis Case

Lewis and Clark Lake

Marshall

Brookings

Mitchell

Sioux Falls

Big Sioux

Floyd R.

29

Chadron

Crawford

Niobrara R.

Valentine

S a n d   H i l l s

O'Neill

Yankton

Missouri R.

Sioux City

South Sioux City

29

Little Sioux R.

Alliance

Scottsbluff

North Platte R.

North Loup R.

Middle Loup R.

Loup R.

Elkhorn R.

N E B R A S K A

Norfolk

Columbus

Blair

Fremont

Omaha

Cheyenne

80

Sidney

Lake McConaughy

South Loup R.

Kearney

Grand Island

Platte R.

Big Blue R.

80

Lincoln ★

Bellevue

Greeley

S. Platte R.

76

Imperial

Hastings

Blue R.

Auburn

40°N

Swanson Reservoir

McCook

Republican R.

Beatrice

Norton

Marysville

Limon

70

Goodland

Kirwin Reservoir

Waconda Lake

Concordia

Solomon R.

Milford Reservoir

Tuttle Creek Lake

C O L O R A D O

G r e a t   P l a i n s

Smoky Hill R.

Hays

70

Salina

Abilene

Kansas R.

Manhattan

Topeka

335

Arkansas R.

Lamar

K A N S A S

Great Bend

Arkansas R.

Hutchinson

Newton

135

Cottonwood

Flint Hills

Emporia

John Redmond Reservoir

Garden City

Dodge City

Pratt

Cheney Reservoir

Ninnescah R.

Wichita

Toronto Reservoir

35

Liberal

Elk City Reservoir

Kaw Lake

Ponca City

Bartlesville

Guymon

N. Canadian R.

Cimarron R.

Woodward

Enid

35

Tulsa

T E X A S

Canadian R.

O K L A H O M A

Stillwater

Broken Arrow

100°W

POLITICAL RELIEF MAP

Central U.S.

Boundary Symbols

············· State boundary

City Symbols

Chicago ● Over 500,000 people

St. Louis ● 100,000 to 500,000

Decorah • Under 100,000

Lincoln ★ State capital

Scale

1:4,100,000

0   25   50   75   100 miles

1 in. to 64 mi.

0   25   50   75   100 kilometers

1 cm to 41 km

Detailed legend on page 6   Lambert Conformal Projection

Continues on pages 88–89

Continues on pages 92–93

MINNESOTA

MI

Mankato
Rochester
Winona

Spencer

Forest City
Mason City
Decorah
Fayette

Storm Lake

Fort Dodge
Cedar Falls
Waterloo

IOWA

Denison
Ames
Marshalltown
Cedar Rapids

Council Bluffs

Des Moines
Saylorville Reservoir
Grinnell
Iowa City
Bettendorf
Davenport
Moline

Osceola
Ottumwa
Rock Island

Rathbun Reservoir
Burlington
Galesburg

Keokuk
Macomb

ILLINOIS

Bethany
Kirksville

Central

Quincy
Springfield
Jacksonville
Decatur
Charleston

St. Joseph
Chillicothe
Hannibal

Atchison
Holt

Leavenworth

Kansas City
Independence
Kansas City
Columbia
St. Peters
St. Charles
Alton
Florissant
University City

Overland
Lees Summit
Lawrence Park
Olathe

Sedalia
Jefferson City

MISSOURI

Lake of the Ozarks
Rolla

Fort Scott
Pomme de Terre Reservoir

Stockton Lake
Ste. Genevieve
Carbondale

Pittsburg

Springfield
Joplin
West Plains
Poplar Bluff

Coffeyville
Branson
Bull Shoals Lake

Table Rock Lake
Beaver Lake
Norfolk Lake

Lake O' the Cherokees

Springdale

Muskogee
Fayetteville

ARKANSAS

Boston Mts.

Jonesboro

WISCONSIN

Appleton
Oshkosh
Fond du Lac
Sheboygan
Lake Winnebago

Wisconsin Dells

La Crosse

Austin

Madison

Milwaukee

Janesville
Racine
Kenosha
Waukegan

Muskegon

Holland

Benton Harbor

Dubuque
Galena
Freeport
Rockford
Arlington Heights
Evanston
St. Joseph

Chicago
Michigan City

Clinton
Sterling
DeKalb
Elgin
Elmhurst
Naperville
Aurora
Hammond
Gary

South Bend

Joliet
Calumet City
Valparaiso

La Salle

Kankakee
Pontiac
Watseka

Logansport

Peoria

Normal
Bloomington

West Lafayette
Lafayette

Champaign
Urbana
Crawfordsville
Danville

INDIANA

Taylorville
Mattoon
Terre Haute

Lake Shelbyville

Effingham
Bloomington

Lowland

Vincennes

Belleville
Mount Vernon

Evansville
Henderson
Owensboro

Carlyle Lake

St. Louis
East St. Louis
Kirkwood

Rend Lake

Cape Girardeau

Wappello Lake

Sikeston

New Madrid

Cairo

Paducah

Madisonville
Hopkinsville

KENTUCKY

Mayfield
Clarksville

Lake Barkley

Kentucky Lake

Dyersburg

Blytheville

TENNESSEE

Columbia

Jackson

Ozark Plateau

Continues on pages 84–85

Continues on pages 62–63

Moose Jaw

105°W

Regina

Qu'Appelle R.

100°W

Lake Manitoba

Lake Winnipeg

95°W

C A N A

50°N

SASKATCHEWAN

Brandon

Assiniboine R.

Winnipeg

M A N I T O B A

Kenora

Lake of the Woods

Continues on pages 94–95

Wolf Point

Missouri R.

Williston

Stanley

Minot

Turtle Mts.

Rugby

Devils Lake

Souris R.

Pembina

Red Red R.

Grafton

Thief River Falls

Rainy R.

International Falls

Upper Red Lake

Lower Red Lake

Glendive

Yellowstone R.

94

G r e a t

Lake Sakakawea

THEODORE ROOSEVELT NATIONAL PARK

Knife R.

Garrison Dam

Missouri R.

NORTH DAKOTA

Sheyenne R.

Grand Forks

29

Red River Valley

Bemidji

Lake Itasca

Leech Lake

MONTANA

Little Missouri Badlands

Medora

Dickinson

Mandan

Bismarck

94

Jamestown

Heart R.

Cannonball R.

Valley City

Fargo

Moorhead

M I N N E S O T

Wahpeton

Fergus Falls

Mississippi R.

Brainerd

Mille Lacs Lake

45°N

Buffalo

Grand R.

Moreau R.

Mobridge

Aberdeen

Lake Oahe

Sisseton

Lake Traverse

Big Stone Lake

Alexandria

St. Cloud

90

Belle Fourche R.

S O U T H   D A K O T A

James R.

Watertown

Big Sioux R.

29

Willmar

Lake Shetak

Minneapolis

Black Hills

Harney Peak 7,242 ft. (2207 m)

Rapid City

Mt. Rushmore

Oahe Dam

Pierre

Bad R.

Lake Sharpe

Huron

Brookings

Marshall

Minnesota R.

Mankato

WY

WIND CAVE NATIONAL PARK

Cheyenne R.

Murdo

90

Big Bend Dam

White R.

Mitchell

Worthington

90

Fairmont

Hot Springs

Badlands

BADLANDS NATIONAL PARK

Wounded Knee

P l a i n s

Lake Francis Case

Sioux Falls

Spencer

Des Moines R.

Chadron

Pine Ridge

Valentine

20

Fort Randall Dam

Yankton

Vermillion

Sioux City

Fort Dodge

20

Niobrara R.

Lewis and Clark Lake

Gavins Point Dam

South Sioux City

Norfolk

I O W A

Ames

Scottsbluff

S a n d   H i l l s

North Platte R.

N E B R A S K A

Missouri R.

Fremont

Omaha

Council Bluffs

35

CO

80

North Platte

Grand Island

Kearney

Platte R.

80

Lincoln

29

South Platte R.

76

100°W

95°W

Continues on pages 90–91

Continues on page 64

90°W

85°W

50°N

POLITICAL RELIEF MAP

NORTH CENTRAL U.S.

Boundary Symbols
━━━━ International boundary
.... State or province boundary

City Symbols
Detroit ● Over 500,000 people
Green Bay ● 100,000 to 500,000
Bemidji • Under 100,000

Bismarck ★ State or province capital

Scale
1:4,700,000

| 0 | 35 | 70 | 105 | 140 miles |

1 in. to 75 mi.

| 0 | 35 | 70 | 105 | 140 kilometers |

1 cm to 47 km

Detailed legend on page 6   Lambert Conformal Projection

D A

O N T A R I O

Lake Nipigon

11

17

11

Rainy L.

VOYAGEURS NATIONAL PARK

Vermillion Lake

Ely

Mesabi Range

Hibbing

St. Louis R.

Duluth

Superior

Ashland

Apostle Islands

Gogebic Range

Ironwood

Hayward

Park Falls

Flambeau R.

Rice Lake

W I S C O N S I N

Thunder Bay

ISLE ROYALE NATIONAL PARK

Isle Royale

Lake   S u p e r i o r

Houghton

Keweenaw Peninsula

Keweenaw Bay

Marquette

Grand Island

Munising

Iron River

Menominee Range

Escanaba

Rhinelander

Whitefish Bay

Sault Ste. Marie

Sault Ste. Marie

75

M   Upper Peninsula

I

Straits

Beaver Island

Drummond Island

of Mackinac

North Channel

Manitoulin Island

17

C

Charlevoix

Alpena

Lake Huron

45°N

H

Grand Traverse Bay

Manitou Islands

St. Paul

Bloomington

94

Eau Claire

Marshfield

Wausau

Stevens Point

Northfield

Lake City

Rochester

Winona

Tomah

90

94

La Crosse

Austin

90

Mason City

Driftless Area

Prairie du Chien

Madison

Janesville

Beloit

Waterloo

Dubuque

Cedar Rapids

Cedar R.

380

Iowa City

Davenport

Rock Island

Moline

80

I L L I N O I S

74

Ottumwa

Wisconsin Dells

Wisconsin R.

39

Chippewa R.

Wisconsin R.

Mississippi R.

St. Croix R.

Green Bay

Appleton

Menasha

Neenah

Oshkosh

Lake Winnebago

Fond du Lac

Fox R.

43

Sheboygan

Manitowoc

Door Peninsula

Green Bay

Wauwatosa

West Allis

Milwaukee

Racine

Kenosha

Waukegan

Evanston

Chicago

Elgin

Naperville

Aurora

Gary

Hammond

Joliet

57

55

Kankakee

Peoria

Illinois R.

20

90

39

Rockford

88

Rock R.

Mississippi R.

Lake Michigan

A

N

Traverse City

Cadillac

131

Ludington

Manistee R.

Lower Peninsula

Midland

127

Bay City

Saginaw

Shiawassee R.

Muskegon

Muskegon R.

Grand Rapids

96

Grand R.

Flint

69

Sarnia

Port Huron

St. Clair R.

75

94

Grand Haven

Holland

Wyoming

Lansing

East Lansing

Pontiac

96

Warren

Detroit

Dearborn

Windsor

Lake St. Clair

Battle Creek

Kalamazoo

Portage

Jackson

Ann Arbor

94

St. Joseph R.

South Bend

Elkhart

Fort Wayne

69

INDIANA

Wabash R.

65

Benton Harbor

St. Joseph

Au Sable R.

Saginaw Bay

Lake Erie

Toledo

90

80

Lima

Findlay

75

OHIO

71

Continues on pages 90–91

Continues on pages 84–85

Continues on page 64

Continues on page 64

C e n t r a l   L o w l a n d

A

35

35

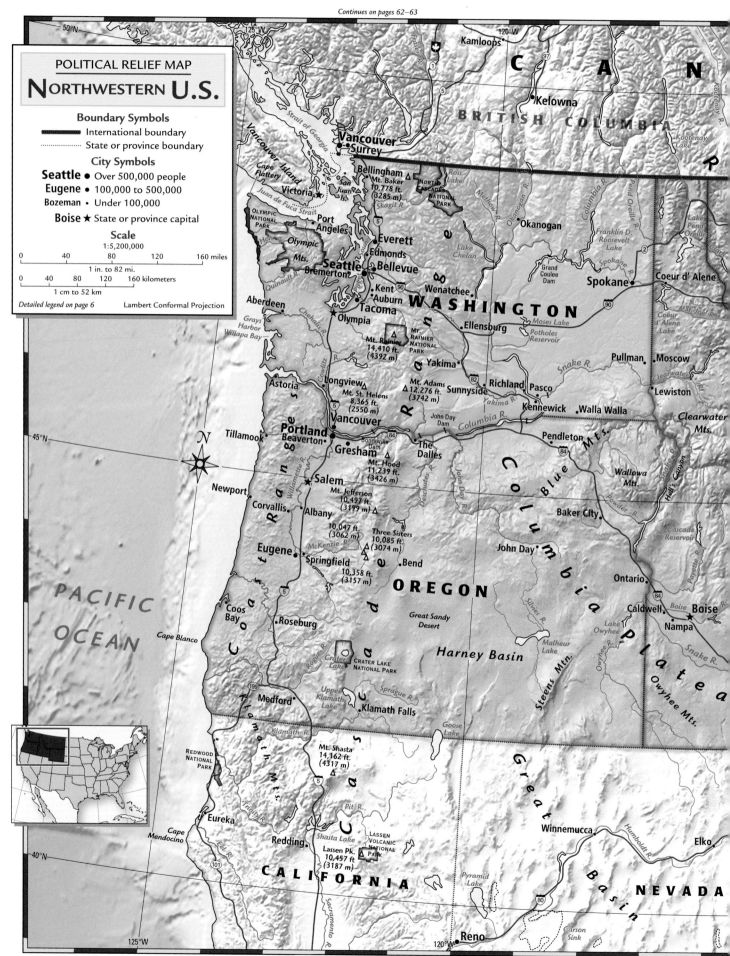

Continues on pages 62–63

POLITICAL RELIEF MAP
NORTHWESTERN U.S.

Boundary Symbols
—————— International boundary
···················· State or province boundary

City Symbols
Seattle ● Over 500,000 people
Eugene ● 100,000 to 500,000
Bozeman • Under 100,000

Boise ★ State or province capital

Scale
1:5,200,000

0   40   80   120   160 miles

1 in. to 82 mi.

0   40   80   120   160 kilometers

1 cm to 52 km

Detailed legend on page 6   Lambert Conformal Projection

Continues on pages 96–97

Continues on pages 62–63

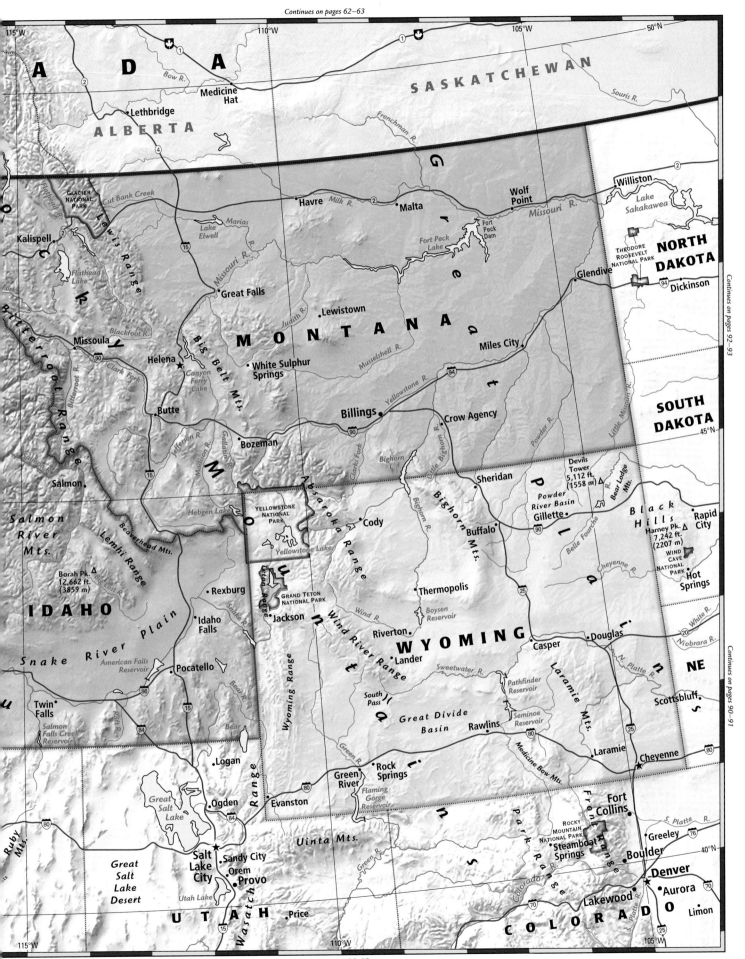

Continues on pages 92–93
Continues on pages 90–91
Continues on pages 96–97

CANADA

SASKATCHEWAN

Souris R.

ALBERTA

Medicine Hat

Lethbridge

Bow R.

Williston

Lake Sakakawea

THEODORE ROOSEVELT NATIONAL PARK

NORTH DAKOTA

Dickinson

SOUTH DAKOTA

GLACIER NATIONAL PARK

Cut Bank Creek

Flathead R.

Kalispell

Lewis Range

Flathead Lake

Lake Elwell

Marias R.

Havre

Milk R.

Malta

Missouri R.

Wolf Point

Fort Peck Lake

Fort Peck Dam

Glendive

Great Falls

Missouri R.

Blackfoot R.

Missoula

Big Belt Mts.

MONTANA

Judith R.

Lewistown

Musselshell R.

Miles City

Bitterroot Range

Bitterroot R.

Helena

Clark Fork

Canyon Ferry Lake

Butte

Jefferson R.

Madison R.

Gallatin R.

Bozeman

White Sulphur Springs

Billings

Yellowstone R.

Crow Agency

Salmon

Salmon River Mts.

Lemhi Range

Beaverhead Mts.

Big Lost R.

Borah Pk. △ 12,662 ft. (3859 m)

Hebgen Lake

YELLOWSTONE NATIONAL PARK

Yellowstone Lake

Absaroka Range

Clarks Fork

Bighorn

Cody

Sheridan

Little Bighorn R.

Bighorn Mts.

Powder R.

Devils Tower 5,112 ft. (1558 m) △

Bear Lodge Mts.

Powder River Basin

Gillette

Belle Fourche R.

Black Hills

Harney Pk. △ 7,242 ft. (2207 m)

Rapid City

WIND CAVE NATIONAL PARK

Hot Springs

IDAHO

Rexburg

Idaho Falls

Snake River Plain

American Falls Reservoir

Pocatello

GRAND TETON NATIONAL PARK

Jackson

Snake R.

Wind River Range

Buffalo

Thermopolis

Boysen Reservoir

Wind R.

Riverton

WYOMING

Lander

Casper

Douglas

N. Platte R.

White R.

Niobrara R.

NE

Twin Falls

Salmon Falls Creek Reservoir

Raft R.

Bear R.

Sweetwater R.

South Pass

Great Divide Basin

Rawlins

Pathfinder Reservoir

Seminoe Reservoir

Laramie Mts.

Scottsbluff

Logan

Wasatch Range

Green R.

Green River

Rock Springs

Flaming Gorge Reservoir

Medicine Bow Mts.

Laramie

Cheyenne

Ruby Mts.

Ogden

Evanston

Uinta Mts.

Park Range

Front Range

ROCKY MOUNTAIN NATIONAL PARK

Fort Collins

S. Platte R.

Greeley

Great Salt Lake

Salt Lake City

Sandy City

Orem

Provo

Utah Lake

Great Salt Lake Desert

Colorado R.

Steamboat Springs

Boulder

Denver

Aurora

Price

Lakewood

Limon

S. Platte R.

UTAH

COLORADO

WYOMING

Continues on pages 94–95

POLITICAL RELIEF MAP
SOUTHWESTERN U.S.

Boundary Symbols
━━━ International boundary
··········· State boundary

City Symbols
Los Angeles ● Over 500,000 people
Tempe ● 100,000 to 500,000
Greeley • Under 100,000

Santa Fe ★ State capital

Scale
1:5,400,000

0 — 50 — 100 — 150 miles
1 in. to 85 mi.

0 — 50 — 100 — 150 kilometers
1 cm to 54 km

Detailed legend on page 6   Lambert Conformal Projection

Continues on page 108

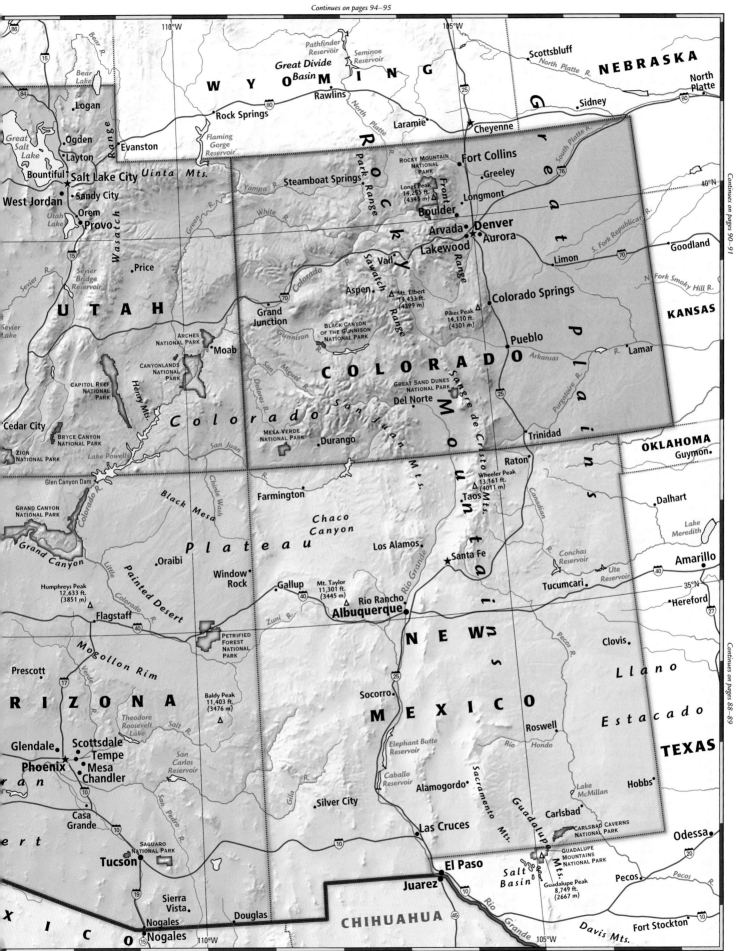

Continues on pages 94–95

Continues on pages 90–91

Continues on pages 88–89

WYOMING

Great Divide Basin

Pathfinder Reservoir

Seminoe Reservoir

Scottsbluff

NEBRASKA

North Platte R.

North Platte

Rawlins

Rock Springs

Sidney

80

Laramie

Cheyenne

25

ROCKY MOUNTAIN NATIONAL PARK

Fort Collins

Greeley

Longs Peak 14,255 ft. (4345 m)

Longmont

Boulder

Arvada   Denver

Lakewood   Aurora

Limon

70

Goodland

Great Plains

KANSAS

Logan

Ogden

Layton

Bountiful   Salt Lake City

West Jordan   Sandy City

Orem   Provo

Great Salt Lake

Bear Lake

Bear R.

86

15

84

Evanston

Flaming Gorge Reservoir

Range

Uinta Mts.

Yampa R.

White R.

Steamboat Springs

Park Range

Vail

Sawatch Range

Aspen

△ Mt. Elbert 14,433 ft. (4399 m)

Pikes Peak △ 14,110 ft. (4301 m)

Colorado Springs

Pueblo

S. Platte R.

S. Fork Republican R.

N. Fork Smoky Hill R.

Limon

Lamar

Price

Sevier R.

Sevier Bridge Reservoir

Sevier Lake

UTAH

Wasatch Range

15

Grand Junction

70

Colorado R.

Gunnison R.

BLACK CANYON OF THE GUNNISON NATIONAL PARK

COLORADO

Arkansas R.

Purgatoire R.

Cedar City

ZION NATIONAL PARK

BRYCE CANYON NATIONAL PARK

CAPITOL REEF NATIONAL PARK

Henry Mts.

ARCHES NATIONAL PARK

Moab

CANYONLANDS NATIONAL PARK

Lake Powell

Colorado Plateau

San Juan R.

Dolores R.

San Miguel R.

San Juan Mts.

MESA VERDE NATIONAL PARK

GREAT SAND DUNES NATIONAL PARK

Del Norte

Durango

Trinidad

Raton

Wheeler Peak △ 13,161 ft. (4011 m)

Sangre de Cristo Mts.

OKLAHOMA

Guymon

Dalhart

Glen Canyon Dam

GRAND CANYON NATIONAL PARK

Grand Canyon

Colorado R.

Little Colorado R.

Black Mesa

Chinle Wash

Farmington

Chaco Canyon

Los Alamos

Santa Fe ★

Taos

Canadian R.

Conchas Reservoir

Ute Reservoir

Lake Meredith

Amarillo

40

Oraibi

Window Rock

Gallup

40

Mt. Taylor 11,301 ft. (3445 m) △

Rio Rancho

Albuquerque △

Zuni R.

Rio Grande

Tucumcari

35°N

Hereford

27

Humphreys Peak 12,633 ft. (3851 m) △

Flagstaff

40

Painted Desert

PETRIFIED FOREST NATIONAL PARK

Prescott

17

Mogollon Rim

Verde R.

Baldy Peak 11,403 ft. (3476 m) △

ARIZONA

Theodore Roosevelt Lake

Salt R.

San Carlos Reservoir

NEW MEXICO

Sacramento Mts.

Guadalupe Mts.

Socorro

25

Roswell

Clovis

Llano Estacado

TEXAS

Glendale

Scottsdale

Phoenix   Tempe

Mesa

Chandler

10

Casa Grande

10

SAGUARO NATIONAL PARK

Tucson

19

Sierra Vista

Nogales

Nogales

15

Douglas

San Carlos R.

Gila R.

San Pedro R.

Silver City

Las Cruces

Elephant Butte Reservoir

Caballo Reservoir

Rio Grande

Alamogordo

Rio Hondo

Pecos R.

Carlsbad

Lake McMillan

CARLSBAD CAVERNS NATIONAL PARK

Hobbs

Odessa

Pecos R.

Pecos

20

El Paso

Juarez

45

CHIHUAHUA

Salt Basin

GUADALUPE MOUNTAINS NATIONAL PARK

Guadalupe Peak △ 8,749 ft. (2667 m)

Rio Grande

Davis Mts.

Fort Stockton

10

110°W

105°W

40°N

35°N

Continues on page 108

Continues on pages 88–89

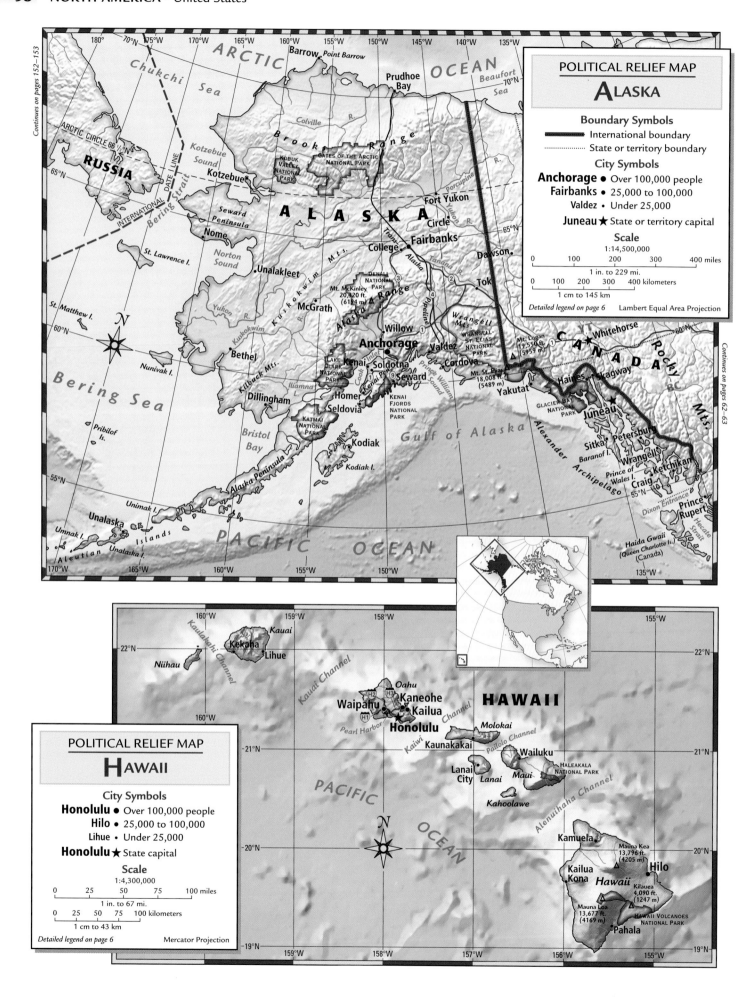

Continues on pages 152–153

POLITICAL RELIEF MAP
ALASKA

Boundary Symbols
━━━ International boundary
┈┈┈ State or territory boundary

City Symbols
Anchorage ● Over 100,000 people
Fairbanks ● 25,000 to 100,000
Valdez • Under 25,000
Juneau ★ State or territory capital

Scale
1:14,500,000
0   100   200   300   400 miles
1 in. to 229 mi.
0   100   200   300   400 kilometers
1 cm to 145 km

Detailed legend on page 6   Lambert Equal Area Projection

ARCTIC OCEAN
Chukchi Sea
Barrow Point Barrow
Prudhoe Bay
Beaufort Sea
ARCTIC CIRCLE 66½°N
RUSSIA
Colville R.
Brooks Range
KOBUK VALLEY NATIONAL PARK
GATES OF THE ARCTIC NATIONAL PARK
Kotzebue Sound
Kotzebue
Seward Peninsula
Porcupine
Fort Yukon
Yukon R.
Nome
Circle
Fairbanks
College
Dawson
Norton Sound
Unalakleet
St. Lawrence I.
Kuskokwim Mts.
DENALI NATIONAL PARK
Mt. McKinley 20,320 ft. (6194 m)
Tanana R.
Alaska Range
Tok
Trans Alaska Pipeline
McGrath
Yukon R.
Willow
Wrangell Mts.
WRANGELL–St. ELIAS NATIONAL PARK
Whitehorse
Mt. Logan 19,550 ft. (5959 m)
CANADA
Anchorage
Valdez
Cordova
Bethel
Kilbuck Mts.
LAKE CLARK NATIONAL PARK
Kenai
Cook Inlet
Soldotna
Kenai Pen.
Seward
Prince William Sound
Mt. St. Elias 18,008 ft. (5489 m)
Yakutat
Rocky Mts.
BC
Iliamna
Dillingham
Homer
Seldovia
KENAI FJORDS NATIONAL PARK
GLACIER BAY NATIONAL PARK
Haines
Skagway
Juneau
Kukchuk
Nunivak I.
St. Matthew I.
Bering Sea
Bristol Bay
KATMAI NATIONAL PARK
Alaska Peninsula
Kodiak
Kodiak I.
Gulf of Alaska
Alexander Archipelago
Sitka
Petersburg
Baranof I.
Wrangell
Prince of Wales I.
Craig
Ketchikan
Dixon Entrance
Prince Rupert
Haida Gwaii (Queen Charlotte Is.) (Canada)
Hecate Strait
Pribilof Is.
Umnak I.
Unalaska
Unalaska I.
Aleutian Islands
Unimak I.
PACIFIC OCEAN

Continues on pages 62–63

POLITICAL RELIEF MAP
HAWAII

City Symbols
Honolulu ● Over 100,000 people
Hilo ● 25,000 to 100,000
Lihue • Under 25,000
Honolulu ★ State capital

Scale
1:4,300,000
0   25   50   75   100 miles
1 in. to 67 mi.
0   25   50   75   100 kilometers
1 cm to 43 km

Detailed legend on page 6   Mercator Projection

Kauai
Kekaha
Lihue
Niihau
Kaulakahi Channel
Kauai Channel
HAWAII
Oahu
Kaneohe
Waipahu
Kailua
Honolulu
Pearl Harbor
Molokai
Kaunakakai
Kaiwi Channel
Pailolo Channel
Wailuku
HALEAKALA NATIONAL PARK
Lanai City
Lanai
Maui
Kahoolawe
Alenuihaha Channel
Kamuela
Mauna Kea 13,796 ft. (4205 m)
Kailua Kona
Hawaii
Kilauea 4,090 ft. (1247 m)
Hilo
Mauna Loa 13,677 ft. (4169 m)
HAWAII VOLCANOES NATIONAL PARK
Pahala
PACIFIC OCEAN

ISSUES ◀▶ TODAY

How should a country exercise power beyond its borders?

The U.S. military has ground, sea, and air forces spread across the globe to defend its allies and its own interests. As the world's only superpower, the United States often acts alone—*unilateralism*. Some argue that it should work with other countries—*multilateralism*. How should a country respond to world problems? There are many perspectives on this issue. Here are two of them.

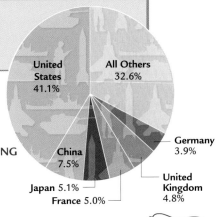

WORLD MILITARY SPENDING
The United States spends over US$370 billion dollars a year on its military.

United States 41.1%
All Others 32.6%
Germany 3.9%
United Kingdom 4.8%
France 5.0%
Japan 5.1%
China 7.5%

more at NDAtlas.com

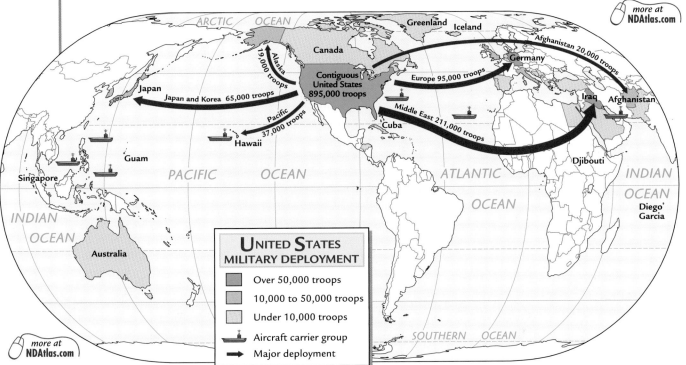

UNITED STATES MILITARY DEPLOYMENT

- Over 50,000 troops
- 10,000 to 50,000 troops
- Under 10,000 troops
- ⛴ Aircraft carrier group
- → Major deployment

more at NDAtlas.com

A country must protect its interests and act alone.

- The attacks on September 11, 2001, proved that Americans are not safe on their own soil. To ensure the safety of American citizens, the United States needs to be able to make decisions swiftly and take action on its own.

- The United States has the largest economy and leads the world in military spending. No other country or group of countries has the resources needed to maintain order on a global scale.

- Coalitions and multilateral organizations take a long time to reach a consensus. By the time everyone agrees on a course of action, the situation is often more difficult to resolve.

- Turmoil in Kosovo and Sudan illustrate the ineffectiveness of multilateral organizations, such as the United Nations (UN). The UN has tried unsuccessfully to implement peace agreements in both areas.

A country should work cooperatively with other countries.

- Important issues confronting the United States, such as terrorism, are the same issues facing the rest of the world. Only multilateral action can achieve meaningful solutions.

- The United States would benefit from allies sharing the human and financial costs of military action in global conflicts.

- The multilateral peacekeeping efforts of the United Nations cost less annually than what New York City spends on its fire and police departments.

- A "going it alone" attitude isolates the United States from its global neighbors. In the future, when the United States needs help, it may find the world community uncooperative.

- No country or organization is infallible. The built-in checks and balances of multilateral decisions protect the United States and the world.

UNITED STATES

Los Angeles
San Diego
Tijuana
Mexicali
Nogales
Phoenix
Memphis
Dallas
Nogales
Juarez
El Paso
Rio Grande
Houston
New Orleans

NORTH

AMERICA

Angel de la
Guarda I.
Hermosillo
Tiburon I.
Alvaro
Obregon Res.
Cedros I.
Point
Eugenia
Ciudad Obregon
Chihuahua
Conchos R.
Rio Bravo del Norte
Amistad
Res.

Baja California
Gulf of California (Sea of Cortes)
Sierra Madre Occidental
Sierra Madre Oriental

Sebastian
Vizcaino Bay
San Jose I.
Santa
Margarita I.
La Paz
Torreon
Saltillo
Monterrey
Matamoros
Brownsville
Nuevo Laredo
Laredo

Gulf of Mexico

TROPIC OF CANCER 23½°N
Cape San Lucas
Mazatlan

MEXICO

Ciudad Victoria
Madre
Lagoon

Tres Marias Is.
Plateau of Mexico
San Luis Potosi
Tampico
Cape Rojo
Tepic
Leon
Puerto Vallarta
Cape Corrientes
L. Chapala
Guadalajara
Morelia
Cancun
Merida
Campeche
Yucatan Peninsula

Revillagigedo Is.
(Mex.)

PACIFIC

OCEAN

Paricutin
Volcano
9,213 ft.
(2808 m)
Mexico City
Nezahualcoyotl
Puebla
Veracruz
Popocatepetl
17,887 ft.
(5452 m)
Pico de Orizaba
18,405 ft. (5610 m)
Villahermosa
Bay of
Campeche
Terminos
Lagoon
Hondo R.
Chetumal
Bay

Sierra Madre del Sur
Balsas R.
El Chichon
3,478 ft. (1060 m)
BELIZE
Belmopan

Acapulco
Oaxaca
Sierra Madre
Angostura
Res.
L. Izabal
Gulf of
Tehuantepec
Tajumulco
13,845 ft.
(4220 m)
GUATEMALA
San Pedro Sula
Gulf of

Guatemala City
Tegucigalpa
San Salvador
EL SALVADOR
Gulf of
Fonseca

Mississippi R.

Colorado R.
Yaqui R.
Fuerte R.
Panuco R.
Coastal Plain

N

POLITICAL RELIEF MAP
MIDDLE AMERICA

Boundary Symbols
.... International boundary

City Symbols
Monterrey ● Over 500,000 people
Veracruz ● 100,000 to 500,000
Limon • Under 100,000

Mexico City ⊗ National capital

Scale
1:15,300,000

0   100   200   300 miles

1 in. to 242 mi.

0   100   200   300 kilometers

1 cm to 153 km

Detailed legend on page 6   Albers Equal Area Projection

10°N

100°W

90°W

110°W

Cocos I.
(Costa Rica)

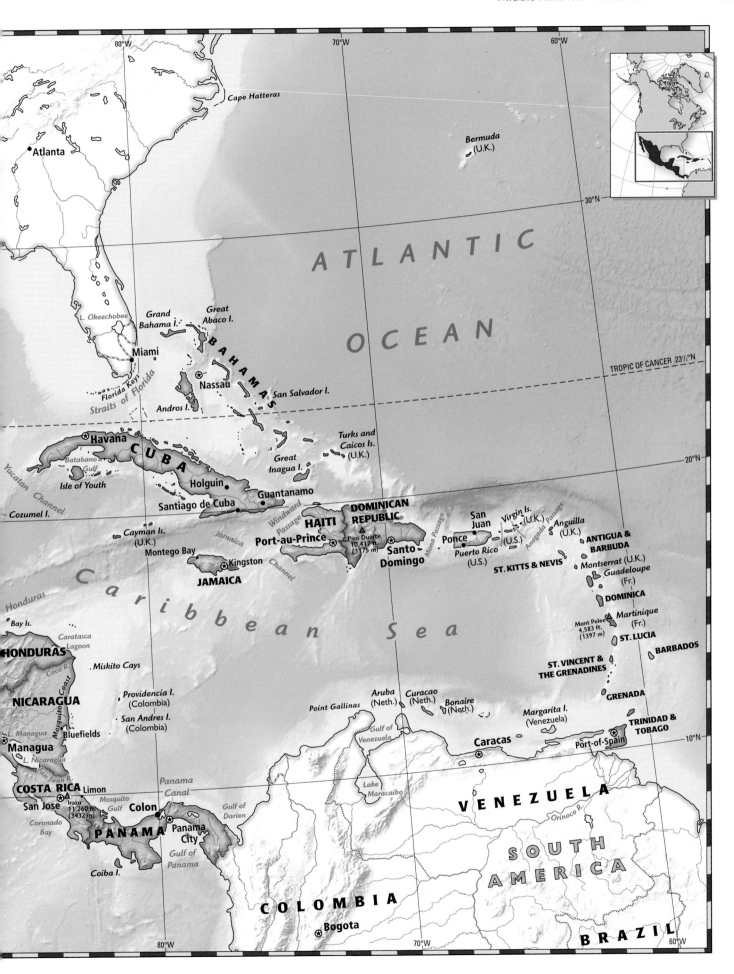

80°W · 70°W · 60°W

Atlanta

Bermuda
(U.K.)

30°N

A T L A N T I C

O C E A N

L. Okeechobee

Grand
Bahama I.

Great
Abaco I.

Miami

B A H A M A S

Nassau

San Salvador I.

Florida Keys

Straits of Florida

Andros I.

TROPIC OF CANCER 23½°N

Havana

C U B A

Batabano
Gulf

Yucatan Channel

Isle of Youth

Holguin

Great
Inagua I.

Turks and
Caicos Is.
(U.K.)

20°N

Cozumel I.

Santiago de Cuba

Guantanamo

Windward Passage

**DOMINICAN
REPUBLIC**

San
Juan

Virgin Is. (U.K.)

Anguilla
(U.K.)

**ANTIGUA &
BARBUDA**

Cayman Is.
(U.K.)

Jamaica

HAITI

Pico Duarte
10,417 ft.
(3175 m)

Ponce

Puerto Rico
(U.S.)

Anegada Passage

Virgin Is.
(U.S.)

Montserrat (U.K.)

Mona Passage

Montego Bay

Port-au-Prince

Santo
Domingo

ST. KITTS & NEVIS

Guadeloupe
(Fr.)

Kingston

Jamaica Channel

DOMINICA

JAMAICA

Mont Pelee
4,583 ft.
(1397 m)

Martinique
(Fr.)

ST. LUCIA

Honduras

C a r i b b e a n   S e a

BARBADOS

Bay Is.

Caratasca
Lagoon

**ST. VINCENT &
THE GRENADINES**

HONDURAS

Coco R.

Miskito Cays

GRENADA

Mosquito Coast

NICARAGUA

Providencia I.
(Colombia)

Aruba
(Neth.)

Curacao
(Neth.)

Bonaire
(Neth.)

Margarita I.
(Venezuela)

**TRINIDAD &
TOBAGO**

L. Managua

Bluefields

San Andres I.
(Colombia)

Point Gallinas

Managua

L. Nicaragua

Gulf of
Venezuela

Caracas

Port-of-Spain

10°N

San Juan R.

Panama
Canal

COSTA RICA

Limon

Lake
Maracaibo

V E N E Z U E L A

Mosquito
Gulf

Irazu
11,260 ft.
(3432 m)

Colon

Gulf of
Darien

San Jose

Coronado
Bay

PANAMA

Panama
City

Orinoco R.

S O U T H

Gulf of
Panama

A M E R I C A

Coiba I.

C O L O M B I A

Bogota

B R A Z I L

80°W · 70°W · 60°W

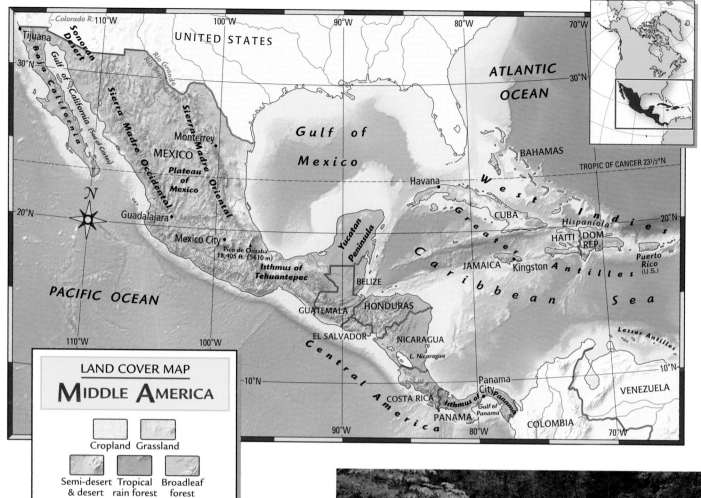

LAND COVER MAP
MIDDLE AMERICA

Cropland Grassland

Semi-desert Tropical Broadleaf
& desert rain forest forest

Boundary Symbols

International boundary

Scale
1:28,000,000

| 0 | 150 | 300 | 450 | 600 miles |

1 in. to 442 mi.

| 0 | 150 | 300 | 450 | 600 kilometers |

1 cm to 280 km

Detailed legend on page 6   Albers Equal Area Projection

Ecotourism helps protect approximately two-thirds of Costa Rica's undisturbed tropical rain forests. Hanging bridges, like the one above, are used to protect the rain forest floors while tourists admire the landscape. (For more on tropical rain forests, see pages 30 and 120.)

The Sonoran Desert is wetter than most deserts, receiving up to 12 inches (300 millimeters) of rain each year. Its summer rainy season sustains a variety of plants and animals—over 20 percent of Mexico's plant species.

Trickle Down

The Colorado River is the main river in the southwestern United States and northwestern Mexico. Much of the river's water is diverted to Los Angeles. Hydroelectric dams and irrigation for agriculture have also reduced the amount of water reaching the river's delta. Some years the river never reaches its mouth at the Gulf of California.

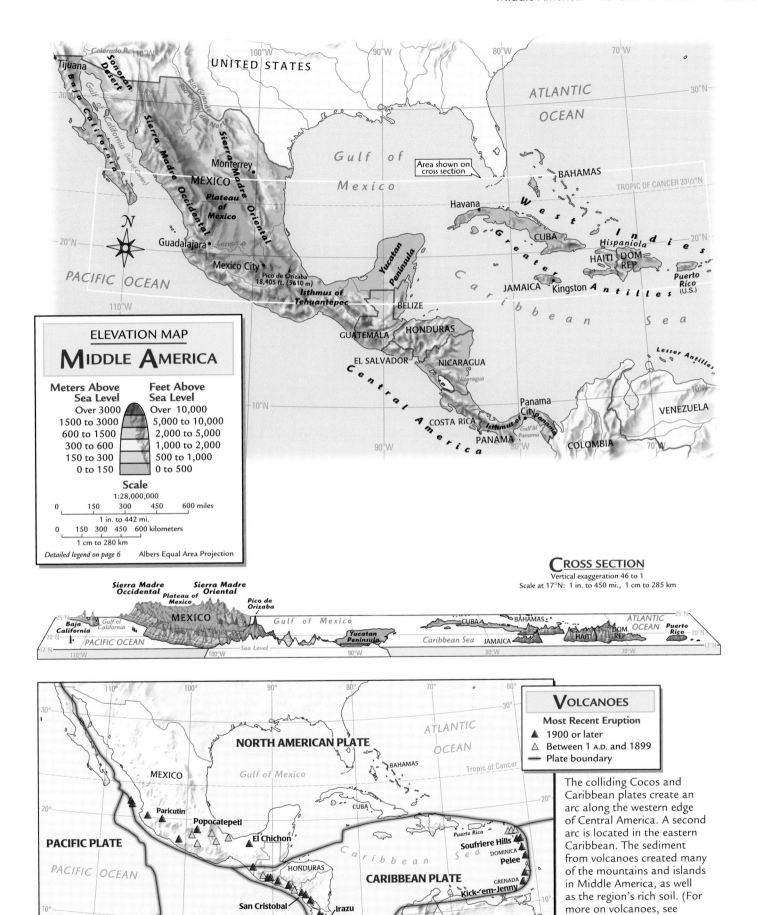

ELEVATION MAP
MIDDLE AMERICA

Meters Above Sea Level	Feet Above Sea Level
Over 3000	Over 10,000
1500 to 3000	5,000 to 10,000
600 to 1500	2,000 to 5,000
300 to 600	1,000 to 2,000
150 to 300	500 to 1,000
0 to 150	0 to 500

Scale
1:28,000,000

0   150   300   450   600 miles
1 in. to 442 mi.

0   150   300   450   600 kilometers
1 cm to 280 km

Detailed legend on page 6   Albers Equal Area Projection

CROSS SECTION
Vertical exaggeration 46 to 1
Scale at 17°N: 1 in. to 450 mi., 1 cm to 285 km

VOLCANOES
Most Recent Eruption
▲ 1900 or later
△ Between 1 A.D. and 1899
— Plate boundary

The colliding Cocos and Caribbean plates create an arc along the western edge of Central America. A second arc is located in the eastern Caribbean. The sediment from volcanoes created many of the mountains and islands in Middle America, as well as the region's rich soil. (For more on volcanoes, see pages 16–17.)

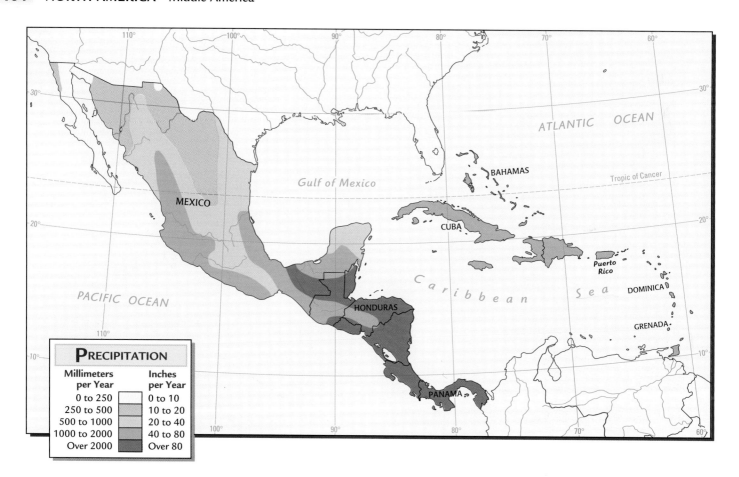

PRECIPITATION

Millimeters per Year	Inches per Year
0 to 250	0 to 10
250 to 500	10 to 20
500 to 1000	20 to 40
1000 to 2000	40 to 80
Over 2000	Over 80

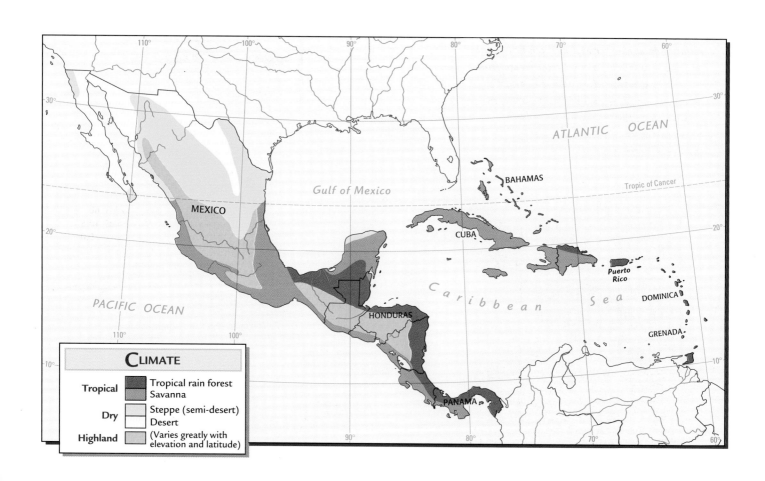

CLIMATE

Tropical	Tropical rain forest
	Savanna
Dry	Steppe (semi-desert)
	Desert
Highland	(Varies greatly with elevation and latitude)

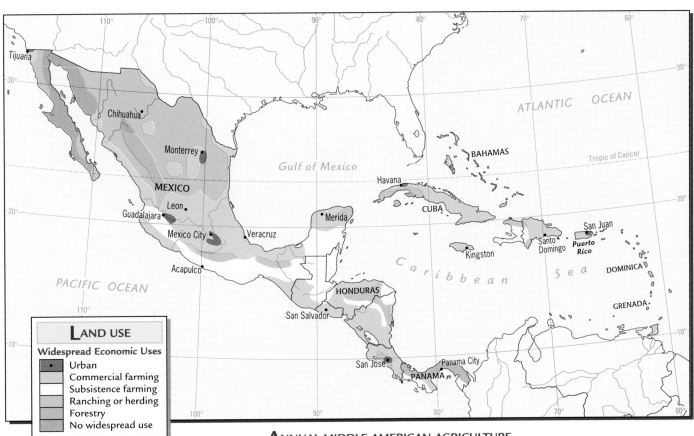

LAND USE

Widespread Economic Uses
- Urban
- Commercial farming
- Subsistence farming
- Ranching or herding
- Forestry
- No widespread use

From Bananas to Beaches

Middle American countries were once called **banana republics** because of their heavy reliance on one major export, such as bananas or coffee. Large land owners and foreign fruit companies dominated both politics and the economy. Now tourism provides much of the economic growth for this region. About 43 percent of the GDP in the Bahamas is from tourism.

more at NDAtlas.com

Many Caribbean farmers sell fresh produce, such as plantains, mangoes, and coconuts, at open-air markets like this one in Grenada.

ANNUAL MIDDLE AMERICAN AGRICULTURE

Agriculture remains important to Middle America. Fruit and sugar cane are key exports for Mexico and Cuba. Costa Rica exports approximately 2 million tons of bananas to the United States and other countries each year.

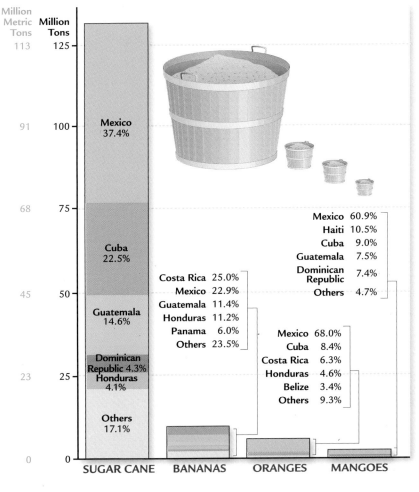

Million Metric Tons	Million Tons
113	125
91	100
68	75
45	50
23	25
0	0

SUGAR CANE
- Mexico 37.4%
- Cuba 22.5%
- Guatemala 14.6%
- Dominican Republic 4.3%
- Honduras 4.1%
- Others 17.1%

BANANAS
- Costa Rica 25.0%
- Mexico 22.9%
- Guatemala 11.4%
- Honduras 11.2%
- Panama 6.0%
- Others 23.5%

ORANGES
- Mexico 60.9%
- Haiti 10.5%
- Cuba 9.0%
- Guatemala 7.5%
- Dominican Republic 7.4%
- Others 4.7%

MANGOES
- Mexico 68.0%
- Cuba 8.4%
- Costa Rica 6.3%
- Honduras 4.6%
- Belize 3.4%
- Others 9.3%

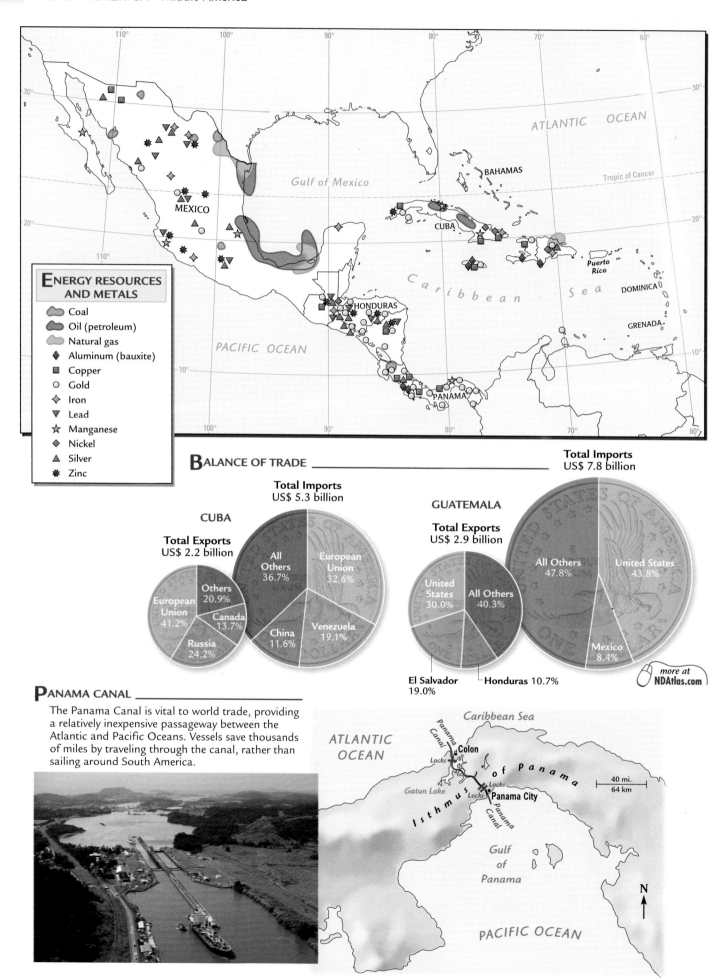

ENERGY RESOURCES AND METALS

- Coal
- Oil (petroleum)
- Natural gas
- ◆ Aluminum (bauxite)
- ■ Copper
- ○ Gold
- ◇ Iron
- ▽ Lead
- ☆ Manganese
- ◆ Nickel
- ▲ Silver
- ✳ Zinc

BALANCE OF TRADE

CUBA

Total Exports
US$ 2.2 billion

European Union 41.2%
Others 20.9%
Canada 13.7%
Russia 24.2%

Total Imports
US$ 5.3 billion

All Others 36.7%
European Union 32.6%
China 11.6%
Venezuela 19.1%

GUATEMALA

Total Exports
US$ 2.9 billion

United States 30.0%
All Others 40.3%
El Salvador 19.0%
Honduras 10.7%

Total Imports
US$ 7.8 billion

All Others 47.8%
United States 43.8%
Mexico 8.4%

more at NDAtlas.com

PANAMA CANAL

The Panama Canal is vital to world trade, providing a relatively inexpensive passageway between the Atlantic and Pacific Oceans. Vessels save thousands of miles by traveling through the canal, rather than sailing around South America.

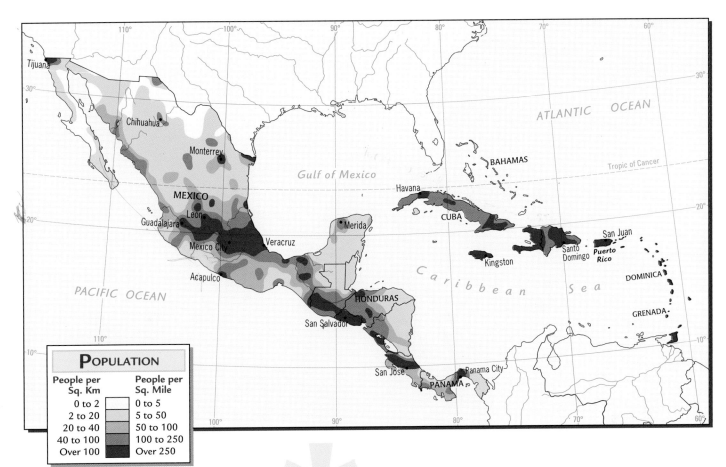

POPULATION

People per Sq. Km	People per Sq. Mile
0 to 2	0 to 5
2 to 20	5 to 50
20 to 40	50 to 100
40 to 100	100 to 250
Over 100	Over 250

The Caribbean Difference

Indigenous West Indians did not survive contact with Europeans. Plantation owners replaced them with African slaves. As a result, the Caribbean is very different from the rest of Middle America. Most West Indians today have African ancestors and many speak French, English, Dutch, or local dialects called patois or creole. In contrast, most people in Mexico and Central America have indigenous ancestors and speak Spanish.

more at NDAtlas.com

REGIONAL MAPS OF MIDDLE AMERICA

1 **Mexico** • page 108
2 **Puerto Rico and the Lesser Antilles** • page 109
3 **Central America** • page 109

LATIN AMERICA

- Spanish
- Portuguese
- French
- Other (non-Latin)

Latin America includes Middle America and South America. This region is called "Latin America" because most of its people speak Spanish, Portuguese, or French—all Latin-based languages. (See page 43.)

Continues on pages 68–69

POLITICAL RELIEF MAP
MEXICO

Boundary Symbols
▬▬▬▬▬ International boundary
············· State boundary

City Symbols
Leon ● Over 1,000,000 people
Guadalupe • 500,000 to 1,000,000
Nogales • Under 500,000
Mexico City ⊗ National capital
Villahermosa ★ State capital

Scale
1:17,700,000

0   125   250   375   500 miles

1 in. to 280 mi.

0   125   250   375   500 kilometers

1 cm to 177 km

Detailed legend on page 6   Albers Equal Area Projection

Mexican States Not Named Above
❶ AGUASCALIENTES ❻ FEDERAL DISTRICT
❷ GUANAJUATO ❼ MEXICO
❸ QUERETARO ❽ MORELOS
❹ HIDALGO ❾ PUEBLA
❺ TLAXCALA ❿ TABASCO

Continues on page 109

A *quinceañera* is a traditional celebration for 15-year-old girls in Mexico and other Latin American countries, marking their passage into womanhood. The day of the quinceañera often begins with a mass and concludes with a formal dinner and dance.

MEXICO AREA COMPARISON

■ **Mexico**
758,449 sq. mi.
(1 964 375 sq. km)

□ **Contiguous
United States**
3,021,295 sq. mi.
(7 825 112 sq. km)

Not Quite Equal

Puerto Rico is a self-governing commonwealth of the United States. Puerto Ricans are U.S. citizens and are subject to most federal laws. Puerto Rico has its own constitution, elects its own governor, and handles its own local affairs like a state. However, Puerto Ricans cannot vote in presidential or congressional elections and do not pay federal taxes.

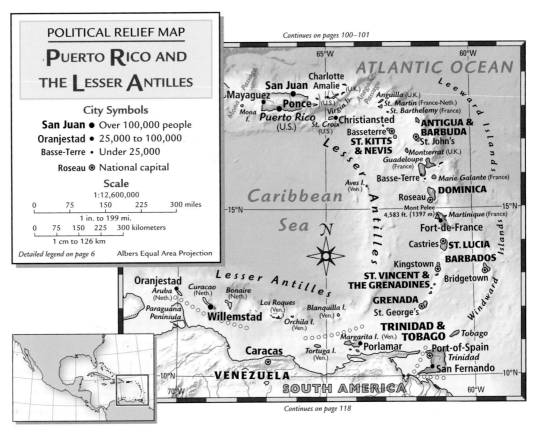

POLITICAL RELIEF MAP
PUERTO RICO AND THE LESSER ANTILLES

City Symbols
San Juan ● Over 100,000 people
Oranjestad ● 25,000 to 100,000
Basse-Terre • Under 25,000
Roseau ⊕ National capital

Scale
1:12,600,000

0   75   150   225   300 miles

1 in. to 199 mi.

0   75   150   225   300 kilometers

1 cm to 126 km

Detailed legend on page 6   Albers Equal Area Projection

Continues on pages 100–101

Continues on page 118

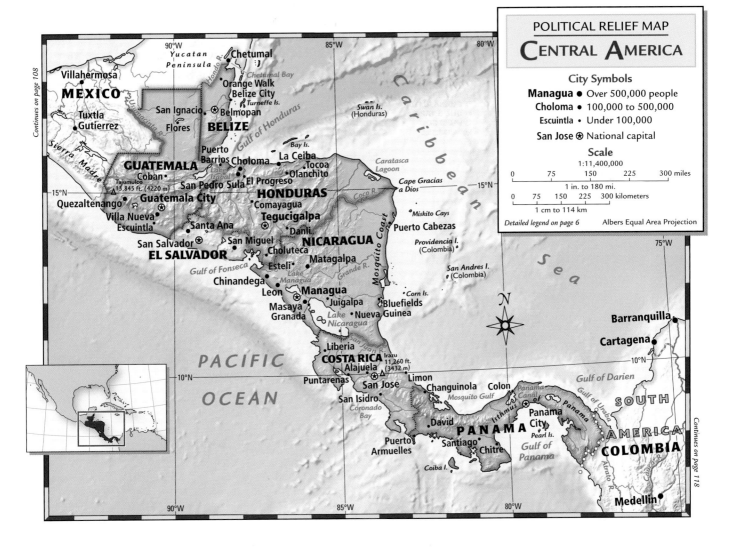

POLITICAL RELIEF MAP
CENTRAL AMERICA

City Symbols
Managua ● Over 500,000 people
Choloma ● 100,000 to 500,000
Escuintla • Under 100,000
San Jose ⊕ National capital

Scale
1:11,400,000

0   75   150   225   300 miles

1 in. to 180 mi.

0   75   150   225   300 kilometers

1 cm to 114 km

Detailed legend on page 6   Albers Equal Area Projection

Continues on page 108

Continues on page 118

ISSUES ◆ TODAY

What rights do indigenous people have?

INDIGENOUS PEOPLE OF TROPICAL NORTH AMERICA

Yukateko (Maya)

MEXICO
Tzotzil   Tzeltal   BELIZE
GUATEMALA
Q'eqche
Mam
Maya K'iche
Kaqchikel   HONDURAS
Pipil Lenca   Miskito
EL SALVADOR   NICARAGUA

COSTA RICA

Ngöbe
PANAMA

▪ Mainly indigenous population

Mam Large indigenous group today

By the mid-1500's, most of Middle America had fallen under Spanish rule. Agreements between the Spanish king and natives guaranteed indigenous groups ownership of their ancestral lands. Most of these agreements have been ignored. Should indigenous people own this land? There are many perspectives on this issue. Here are two of them.

Indigenous people are entitled to their ancestral land.

- Indigenous people of the past were exploited by colonizing powers. They have a legal claim to ancestral lands that were guaranteed to them in treaties or other binding agreements with Spain and their successor governments.

- Indigenous communities consider their land to be sacred. The dispossession of land would lead to the extinction of indigenous communities, their cultures, and their traditions.

- Indigenous knowledge of plants and their medicinal properties, sustainable agriculture practices, land conservation, and other expertise would disappear along with the people.

- The traditional economy of indigenous people is less destructive to the environment and to natural resources than that of the commercial economy.

Indigenous protesters in Panama demonstrate against proposals to enlarge the Panama Canal and build more roads—which would result in the loss of land.

It is impractical to enforce indigenous claims.

- It would be nearly impossible to examine and interpret hundreds of years' worth of incomplete historical documents to determine who has rightful ownership of the land.

- The original treaties were feudal and assumed that all land belonged to the king. Adapting these treaties to modern property laws, which focus on individuals, is almost impossible.

- Few people today live a traditional indigenous lifestyle. However, most people in Central America have descended, at least partly, from indigenous groups. Deciding who receives "ancestral" land would create new conflicts.

- Current land owners should not be punished by having land taken from them for crimes that may or may not have been committed by their ancestors.

ETHNIC COMPOSITION GUATEMALA

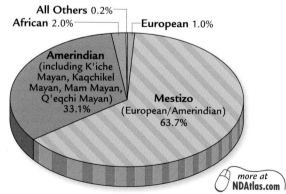

All Others 0.2%
African 2.0%
European 1.0%

Amerindian (including K'iche Mayan, Kaqchikel Mayan, Mam Mayan, Q'eqchi Mayan) 33.1%

Mestizo (European/Amerindian) 63.7%

more at NDAtlas.com

Mestizos in Central America are the result of intermarriage between indigenous people and the Spanish long ago. Over 90 percent of the people in Guatemala, Honduras, and El Salvador have indigenous ancestry.

SOUTH AMERICA

South America is known for its lively and diverse cities, the towering Andes Mountains, and the Amazon Rain Forest—the largest rain forest in the world.

PHYSICAL FEATURES

Mountains
Highest peak: Aconcagua 22,831 ft. (6 959 m)

Longest range: Andes Mountains 4,500 mi. (7 200 km)

Largest Island
Tierra del Fuego 19,280 sq. mi. (49 935 sq. km)

Lakes
Largest: Lake Maracaibo 5,217 sq. mi. (13 512 sq. km) ★

Highest large lake: Lake Titicaca elev. 12,507 ft. (3 812 km)

Longest Rivers
Amazon 4,000 mi. (6 437 km) ★

Parana 3,032 mi. (4 880 km) ★

Other Key Physical Features
Amazon Basin
Pampas
Patagonia
Guiana Highlands
Brazilian Highlands

CULTURAL FEATURES

Population 375,700,000

Largest Countries
By area: Brazil 3,287,612 sq. mi. (8 514 877 sq. km) ★

Argentina 1,073,400 sq. mi. (2 780 092 sq. km) ★

By population: Brazil 188,078,227

Population Density
Most densely populated: Ecuador 129.0 people per sq. mi. (49.8 per sq. km)

Least densely populated: French Guiana 6.2 people per sq. mi. (2.4 per sq. km)

Largest Urban Areas
Sao Paulo, Brazil 20,262,000 ★

Buenos Aires, Argentina 13,074,000 ★

Rio de Janeiro, Brazil 11,950,000 ★

★ Among the world's largest. See the inside front cover.

more at NDAtlas.com
For more maps, graphs, and photos of South America, go to NystromDeskAtlas.com.

AREA COMPARISON

■ South America
6,885,000 sq. mi. (17 832 000 sq. km)

Contiguous United States
3,021,295 sq. mi. (7 825 112 sq. km)

World Extreme Angel Falls, the highest waterfall in the world, drops 3,212 ft. (979 m) in southeast Venezuela.

REGIONAL MAPS OF SOUTH AMERICA

❶ Northwestern South America • page 118

❷ Southern South America • page 118

❸ Brazil and Its Neighbors • page 119

111

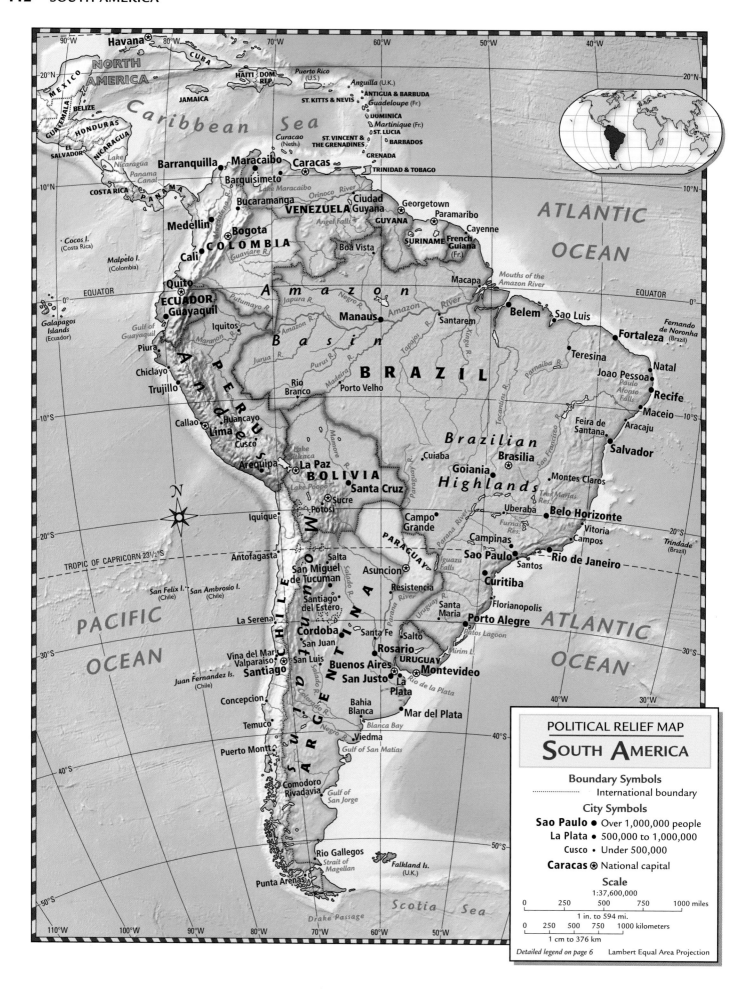

POLITICAL RELIEF MAP

SOUTH AMERICA

Boundary Symbols

.... International boundary

City Symbols

Sao Paulo ● Over 1,000,000 people

La Plata ● 500,000 to 1,000,000

Cusco · Under 500,000

Caracas ⊗ National capital

Scale

1:37,600,000

| 0 | 250 | 500 | 750 | 1000 miles |

1 in. to 594 mi.

| 0 | 250 | 500 | 750 | 1000 kilometers |

1 cm to 376 km

Detailed legend on page 6   Lambert Equal Area Projection

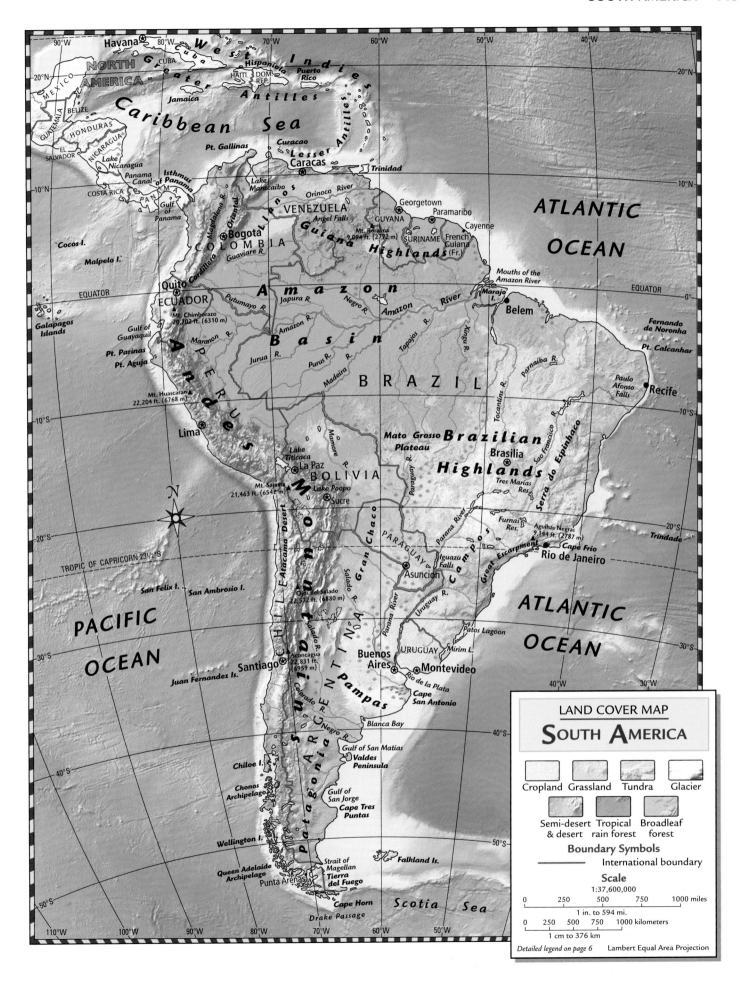

90°W Havana ⊛ 80°W 70°W 60°W 50°W 40°W 20°N

West Indies
NORTH Greater CUBA
AMERICA Hispaniola
Jamaica HAITI DOM. Puerto
MEXICO REP. Rico Antilles

Caribbean   Sea

GUATEMALA BELIZE Pt. Gallinas Curacao Lesser
EL HONDURAS Caracas ⊛ Antilles
SALVADOR NICARAGUA Trinidad

Lake Llanos VENEZUELA Georgetown Paramaribo **ATLANTIC**
Nicaragua Angel Falls GUYANA Cayenne
Isthmus Bogota ⊛ Mt. Roraima SURINAME French **OCEAN**
Panama COLOMBIA 9,094 ft. (2772 m) Guiana
Canal Gulf Oriental Guiana Highlands (Fr.)
of Cordillera
Panama Guaviare R.

COSTA RICA Mouths of the
PANAMA A m a z o n Amazon River
Cocos I. Quito ⊛ Marajo Fernando
EQUATOR ECUADOR Japura R. Amazon River I. de Noronha
Mt. Chimborazo Putumayo R. Negro R. Belem Pt. Calcanhar
Galapagos 20,702 ft. (6310 m) B a s i n
Islands Gulf of Amazon R. Tapajos R.
Guayaquil Maranon R. Purus R. R. Madeira Xingu R. Parnaiba R. Paulo
Pt. Parinas Jurua R. R. Afonso Recife
Pt. Aguja A B R A Z I L Falls

Mt. Huascaran Mato Grosso **Brazilian** Serra
22,204 ft. (6768 m) Plateau do
Lima ⊛ Mamore **Highlands** Espinhaco

Lake Brasilia ⊛
Titicaca La Paz ⊛ Tres Marias
BOLIVIA Res.
Mt. Sajama Lake Poopo Sucre ⊛
21,463 ft. (6542 m) Furnas Agulhas Negras
Ojos del Salado Paraguay R. Res. 9,144 ft. (2787 m) Trindade
TROPIC OF CAPRICORN 23½°S 22,572 ft. (6880 m) Gran Chaco Cape Frio
San Felix I. San Ambrosio I. Great Escarpment Rio de Janeiro
Iguazu Parana River Campos
Falls Asuncion ⊛ **ATLANTIC**
PARAGUAY
Salado R. Uruguay R. **OCEAN**
PACIFIC Aconcagua Salado R.
22,831 ft. Patos Lagoon
OCEAN (6959 m) Santiago ⊛ **Pampas** URUGUAY Mirim L.
Juan Fernandez Is. Colorado R. Buenos Montevideo ⊛
Aires Rio de la Plata
Negro R. Cape
San Antonio
Blanca Bay

Gulf of San Matias
Chiloe I. Valdes
Chonos Peninsula
Archipelago
Gulf of
San Jorge Cape Tres
Puntas
Wellington I. Strait of
Queen Adelaide Magellan Falkland Is.
Archipelago Tierra
Punta Arenas del Fuego **Scotia   Sea**
Cape Horn
Drake Passage

110°W 100°W 90°W 80°W 70°W 60°W 50°W

LAND COVER MAP
SOUTH AMERICA

Cropland Grassland Tundra Glacier

Semi-desert Tropical Broadleaf
& desert rain forest forest

Boundary Symbols
————— International boundary

Scale
1:37,600,000
0 250 500 750 1000 miles
1 in. to 594 mi.
0 250 500 750 1000 kilometers
1 cm to 376 km

Detailed legend on page 6 Lambert Equal Area Projection

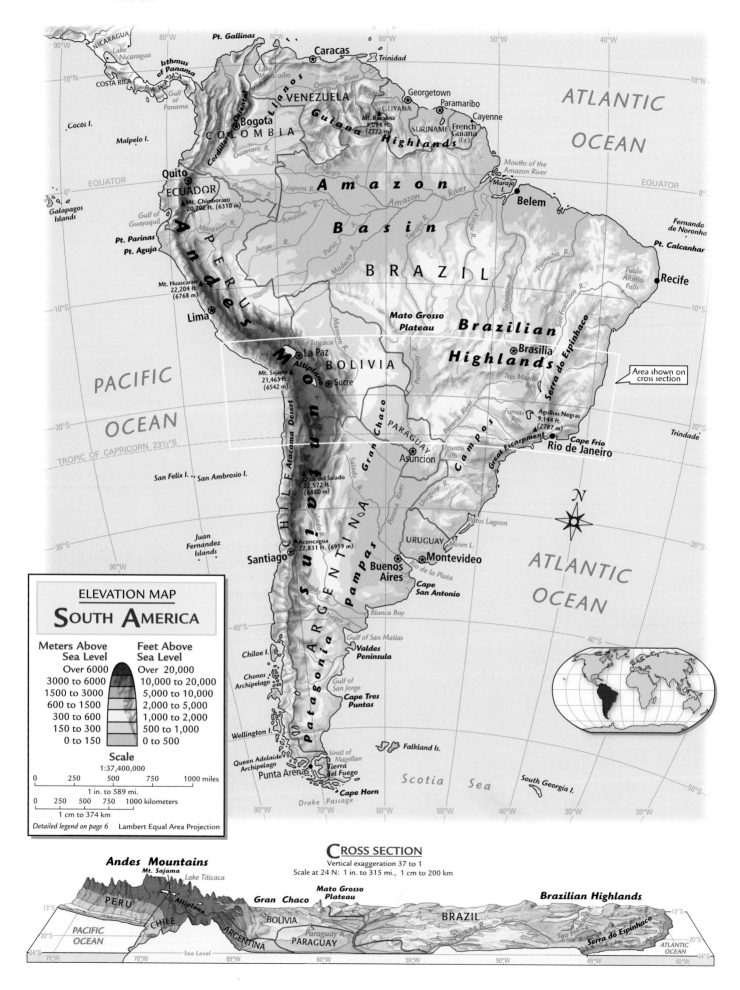

NICARAGUA
Lake Nicaragua
Pt. Gallinas
80°W
70°W
60°W
50°W
40°W
90°W
Caracas
Trinidad
ATLANTIC
OCEAN
Isthmus of Panama
COSTA RICA
10°N
PANAMA
Gulf of Panama
Llanos
VENEZUELA
Orinoco River
Georgetown
Paramaribo
10°N
Cocos I.
Cordillera Oriental
Bogota
Guiana
GUYANA
Cayenne
Malpelo I.
COLOMBIA
Highlands
Mt. Roraima
9,094 ft. (2772 m)
SURINAME
French Guiana (Fr.)
Mouths of the Amazon River
EQUATOR
Quito
ECUADOR
Guaviare R.
Negro
Japura R.
A m a z o n
River
Marajo
EQUATOR
Galapagos Islands
Mt. Chimborazo 20,702 ft. (6310 m)
Putumayo R.
Amazon
Belem
Fernando de Noronha
Maranon R.
Amazon
B a s i n
Pt. Parinas
Jurua R.
Purus R.
Madeira R.
Xingu R.
Tapajos R.
Pt. Calcanhar
Pt. Aguja
B R A Z I L
Paulo Afonso Falls
Recife
Mt. Huascaran 22,204 ft. (6768 m)
Mamore R.
Parnaiba R.
10°S
Lima
Mato Grosso Plateau
Sao Francisco R.
10°S
A n d e s
P E R U
Lake Titicaca
La Paz
Brazilian
Serra do Espinhaco
La Paz
BOLIVIA
Highlands
Brasilia
Altiplano
M o u n t a i n s
Mt. Sajama 21,463 ft. (6542 m)
Sucre
Tres Marias Res.
PACIFIC
20°S
Paraguay R.
Parana River
Furnas Res.
Agulhas Negras 9,144 ft. (2787 m)
Area shown on cross section
Atacama Desert
Gran Chaco
PARAGUAY
Campos
Great Escarpment
Cape Frio
Trindade
OCEAN
Ojos del Salado 22,572 ft. (6880 m)
Iguazu Falls
Rio de Janeiro
TROPIC OF CAPRICORN 23½°S
San Felix I.
San Ambrosio I.
Salado R.
Asuncion
Uruguay R.
C H I L E
S u r i v u t u n
Santiago
Aconcagua 22,831 ft. (6959 m)
A R G E N T I N A
P a m p a s
Patos Lagoon
N
Juan Fernandez Islands
URUGUAY
Montevideo
ATLANTIC
30°S
Buenos Aires
Rio de la Plata
30°S
90°W
Negro R.
Colorado R.
Cape San Antonio
OCEAN
Blanca Bay
Chiloe I.
Valdes Peninsula
Gulf of San Matias
40°S
P a t a g o n i a
Chonos Archipelago
Gulf of San Jorge
Cape Tres Puntas
40°S
Wellington I.
Queen Adelaide Archipelago
Strait of Magellan
Falkland Is.
South Georgia I.
Punta Arenas
Tierra del Fuego
S c o t i a
S e a
50°S
Cape Horn
Drake Passage
80°W
70°W
60°W
50°W
40°W
30°W
20°W

ELEVATION MAP
SOUTH AMERICA

Meters Above Sea Level	Feet Above Sea Level
Over 6000	Over 20,000
3000 to 6000	10,000 to 20,000
1500 to 3000	5,000 to 10,000
600 to 1500	2,000 to 5,000
300 to 600	1,000 to 2,000
150 to 300	500 to 1,000
0 to 150	0 to 500

Scale
1:37,400,000

0 250 500 750 1000 miles
1 in. to 589 mi.

0 250 500 750 1000 kilometers
1 cm to 374 km

Detailed legend on page 6   Lambert Equal Area Projection

CROSS SECTION
Vertical exaggeration 37 to 1
Scale at 24 N: 1 in. to 315 mi., 1 cm to 200 km

Andes Mountains
Mt. Sajama
Lake Titicaca
13°S
PERU
Altiplano
Gran Chaco
Mato Grosso Plateau
Brazilian Highlands
CHILE
BOLIVIA
20°S
PACIFIC OCEAN
ARGENTINA
PARAGUAY
Paraguay R.
B R A Z I L
Parana R.
Sao Francisco R.
Serra do Espinhaco
ATLANTIC OCEAN
Sea Level
24°S
75°W
70°W
65°W
60°W
55°W
50°W
45°W
40°W
13°S
20°S
24°S

ALTITUDE ZONES IN THE ANDES

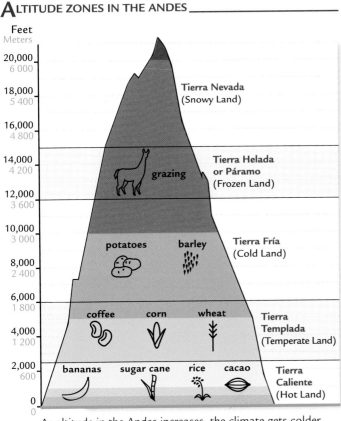

Feet
Meters

- 20,000 / 6 000
- 18,000 / 5 400 — **Tierra Nevada** (Snowy Land)
- 16,000 / 4 800
- 14,000 / 4 200 — **Tierra Helada or Páramo** (Frozen Land)

grazing

- 12,000 / 3 600 — **Tierra Fría** (Cold Land)
- 10,000 / 3 000

potatoes   barley

- 8,000 / 2 400
- 6,000 / 1 800 — **Tierra Templada** (Temperate Land)

coffee   corn   wheat

- 4,000 / 1 200
- 2,000 / 600 — **Tierra Caliente** (Hot Land)

bananas   sugar cane   rice   cacao

- 0 / 0

As altitude in the Andes increases, the climate gets colder and drier. For centuries, indigenous people in the region have cultivated crops that grow well at each elevation zone and climate.

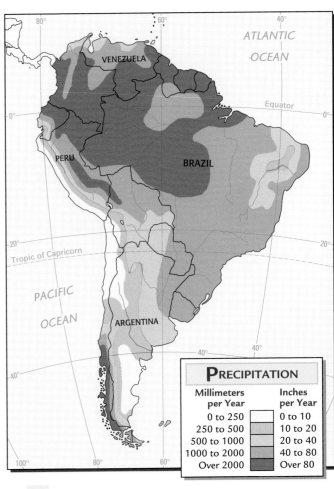

PRECIPITATION

Millimeters per Year	Inches per Year
0 to 250	0 to 10
250 to 500	10 to 20
500 to 1000	20 to 40
1000 to 2000	40 to 80
Over 2000	Over 80

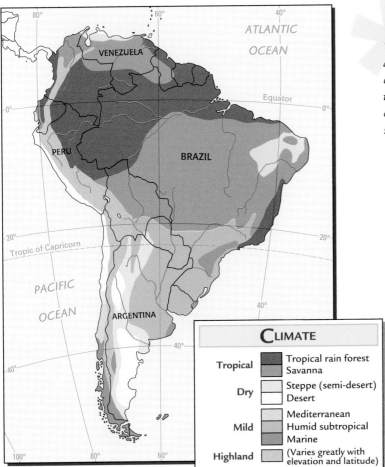

CLIMATE

Tropical	Tropical rain forest
	Savanna
Dry	Steppe (semi-desert)
	Desert
Mild	Mediterranean
	Humid subtropical
	Marine
Highland	(Varies greatly with elevation and latitude)

Desert by the Sea

The Atacama Desert along coastal Peru and Chile is among the driest places on Earth. Its dry conditions are caused by the cold Peru Current, which flows north along the western coast of the continent. This surface current cools the air, preventing it from holding much moisture, so very little rain falls in this region.

CLIMOGRAPHS

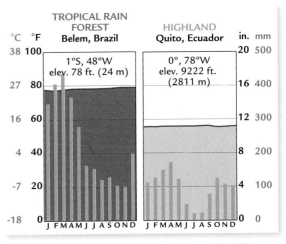

Both Quito and Belem are near the Equator. The difference in their elevations explains why Quito is colder and drier. Air temperature drops about 3.5°F for each rise of 1000 feet (6.5°C for each 1000 meters). *more at* NDAtlas.com

LAND USE

Widespread Economic Uses

- Urban
- Commercial farming
- Subsistence farming
- Ranching or herding
- Forestry
- No widespread use

Fuel for Thought

During an oil crisis, Brazil found an alternative to gasoline—the biofuel **ethanol**. Made from sugar cane, ethanol today accounts for 40 percent of all vehicle fuel in Brazil. It is cleaner and cheaper to produce than gasoline.

These derricks and pumps are in oil-rich Lake Maracaibo in northwestern Venezuela. Venezuela, a founding member of OPEC (see page 160), has the largest oil reserves in the Western Hemisphere and is the fifth largest exporter of oil in the world.

BALANCE OF TRADE
CHILE

Total Exports
US$ 32 billion

- European Union 25.0%
- All Others 37.8%
- United States 14.8%
- Japan 12.0%
- China 10.4%

Total Imports
US$ 25 billion

- Argentina 18.5%
- All Others 38.0%
- European Union 16.0%
- United States 15.1%
- Brazil 12.4%

more at NDAtlas.com

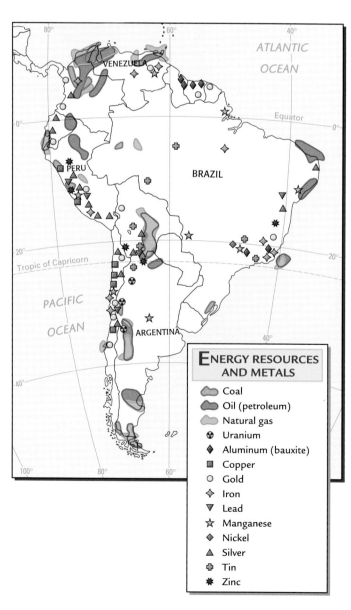

ENERGY RESOURCES AND METALS

- Coal
- Oil (petroleum)
- Natural gas
- ⊛ Uranium
- ◆ Aluminum (bauxite)
- ■ Copper
- ○ Gold
- ◈ Iron
- ▽ Lead
- ☆ Manganese
- ◆ Nickel
- ▲ Silver
- ✚ Tin
- ✳ Zinc

NATURAL POPULATION GROWTH
SOUTH AMERICA

Bolivia
1.6%
24
8

Brazil
1.1%
17
6

Peru
1.5%
21
6

World
1.1%
20
9

Legend:
- Births
- Deaths

Annual Birth and Death Rates
(per 1,000 people)

0 10 20 30 40 50

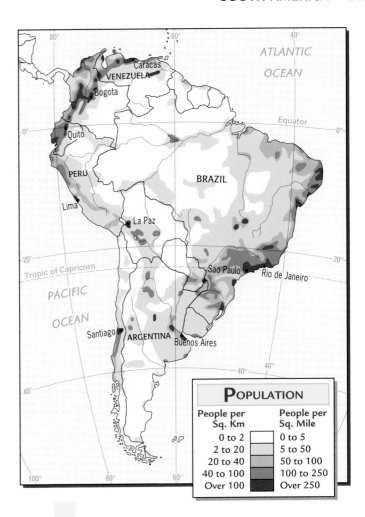

POPULATION

People per Sq. Km	People per Sq. Mile
0 to 2	0 to 5
2 to 20	5 to 50
20 to 40	50 to 100
40 to 100	100 to 250
Over 100	Over 250

Mixed Roots

Mestizo is Spanish for mixed. In Latin America, the term is used to describe a person of mixed European and American Indian parentage. **Mulatto** describes a person of mixed European and African parentage. Over 85 percent of the people in Paraguay are mestizo, while over 35 percent of those in French Guiana are mulatto.

more at
NDAtlas.com

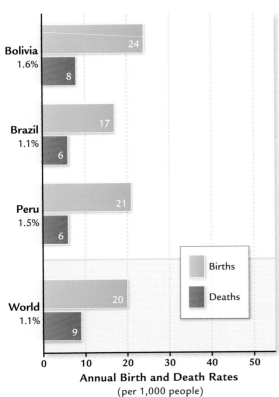

DESCENDANTS OF INDIGENOUS SOUTH AMERICANS*

Percentage of Population
- 85 to 100
- 70 to 85
- 50 to 70
- Under 10

Aymara Large indigenous group today

*Includes mestizo

Peru has one of the larger indigenous populations in South America. (For more information, see page 119.) Many Quechua and Aymara still farm and bring goods to market in the highlands.

Continues on pages 100–101

Caribbean Sea

DOMINICA
Martinique
(France)
ST. LUCIA
ST. VINCENT &
THE GRENADINES
GRENADA
BARBADOS
Margarita I.
(Ven.)
TRINIDAD & TOBAGO

NICARAGUA

Point Gallinas
Aruba *Curacao*
(Neth.) *(Neth.)*
Bonaire
(Neth.)

Santa Marta
Cristobal Colon
18,947 ft.
(5775 m)
Cartagena
Barranquilla
Maracaibo
Caracas
Cumana

COSTA RICA
San Jose
PANAMA
Panama Canal
Panama City
Gulf of Panama

Soledad
Lake Maracaibo
Barquisimeto
Valencia
Maracay
Barcelona
Maturin

NORTH AMERICA

Bello
Medellin
Cucuta
San Cristobal
Bucaramanga
Pico Bolivar
16,427 ft. (5007 m)
VENEZUELA
Ciudad Bolivar
Ciudad Guayana

Malpelo I.
(Colombia)
Pereira
Ibague
Buenaventura
Cali
Neiva
Bogota
Villavicencio
COLOMBIA
Meta R.
Georgetown
GUYANA
Mt. Roraima
9,094 ft.
(2772 m)
Angel Falls
Guiana Highlands
Kaieteur Falls

Pasto
EQUATOR
Orinoco R.
Guaviare R.
Boa Vista
Branco R.

Santo Domingo
Manta
Quito
ECUADOR
Mt. Chimborazo
20,702 ft. (6310 m)
Caqueta R.
Napo R.
Putumayo R.
Amazon R.
Negro R.

Guayaquil
Gulf of Guayaquil
Cuenca
Machala
Iquitos
Maranon R.
Javari R.
Ucayali R.
Jurua R.
Purus R.
BRAZIL

Talara
Punta Parinas
Paita
Aguja Point
Piura
Chiclayo
Trujillo
Chimbote
Mt. Huascaran
22,204 ft. (6768 m)
Pucallpa
Rio Branco
Madre de Dios R.

PACIFIC OCEAN
Callao
Lima
Huanuco
Huancayo
Ayacucho
Cusco
Ica
Juliaca
Lake Titicaca
Arequipa
La Paz
BOLIVIA
Andes Mountains
Altiplano
Tacna

Continues on page 119

Continues on page 119

POLITICAL RELIEF MAP
NORTHWESTERN SOUTH AMERICA

City Symbols
Guayaquil ● Over 1,000,000 people
Cuiaba ● 500,000 to 1,000,000
Huanuco • Under 500,000

Caracas ⊗ National capital

Scale
1:26,300,000

0   150   300   450   600 miles
1 in. to 415 mi.

0   150 300 450 600 kilometers
1 cm to 263 km

Detailed legend on page 6   Lambert Equal Area Projection

PERU
Cochabamba
Arica
Mt. Sajama
21,463 ft. (6542 m)
Iquique
Lake Poopo
Sucre
Santa Cruz
BOLIVIA
Tarija
Atacama Desert
Altiplano

TROPIC OF CAPRICORN 23½°S
Antofagasta
San Salvador de Jujuy
Salta
San Miguel de Tucuman
Formosa
Gran Chaco
Pilcomayo R.
Bermejo R.
PARAGUAY
Asuncion

PACIFIC OCEAN
Copiapo
Ojos del Salado
22,572 ft. (6880 m)
Santiago del Estero
Resistencia
Salado R.
Corrientes
Posadas
Iguazu Falls
Parana R.
BRAZIL
Santa Maria

La Serena
Coquimbo
Aconcagua
22,831 ft. (6959 m)
Cordoba
San Juan
Santa Fe
Parana
Rosario
URUGUAY
Concordia
Uruguay R.
Mirim Lake

CHILE
Vina del Mar
Valparaiso
Santiago
Rancagua
Talca
Mendoza
San Luis
Uspallata Pass
Rio Cuarto
Buenos Aires
San Justo
La Plata
Montevideo
Rio de la Plata

Talcahuano
Concepcion
Central Valley
Temuco
Neuquen
ARGENTINA
Pampas
Colorado R.
Bahia Blanca
Mar del Plata
Blanca Bay
Negro R.

Andes Mountains
Puerto Montt
Chiloe I.
Valdes Peninsula
-131 ft. (-40 m)
Gulf of San Matias
ATLANTIC OCEAN

Corcovado Gulf
Chonos Archipelago
Chubut R.
Comodoro Rivadavia
Gulf of San Jorge
Cape Tres Puntas

Gulf of Penas
Patagonia
Laguna del Carbon
-344 ft. (-105 m)
Grande Bay
Falkland Islands
(U.K.)

Queen Adelaide Archipelago
Strait of Magellan
Punta Arenas
Tierra del Fuego
Staten I.
Beagle Channel
Cape Horn
Strait of Magellan

POLITICAL RELIEF MAP
SOUTHERN SOUTH AMERICA

City Symbols
Cordoba ● Over 1,000,000 people
Rosario ● 500,000 to 100,000
Temuco • Under 500,000

Santiago ⊗ National capital

Scale
1:27,600,000

0   150   300   450   600 miles
1 in. to 436 mi.

0   150 300 450 600 kilometers
1 cm to 276 km

Detailed legend on page 6   Lambert Equal Area Projection

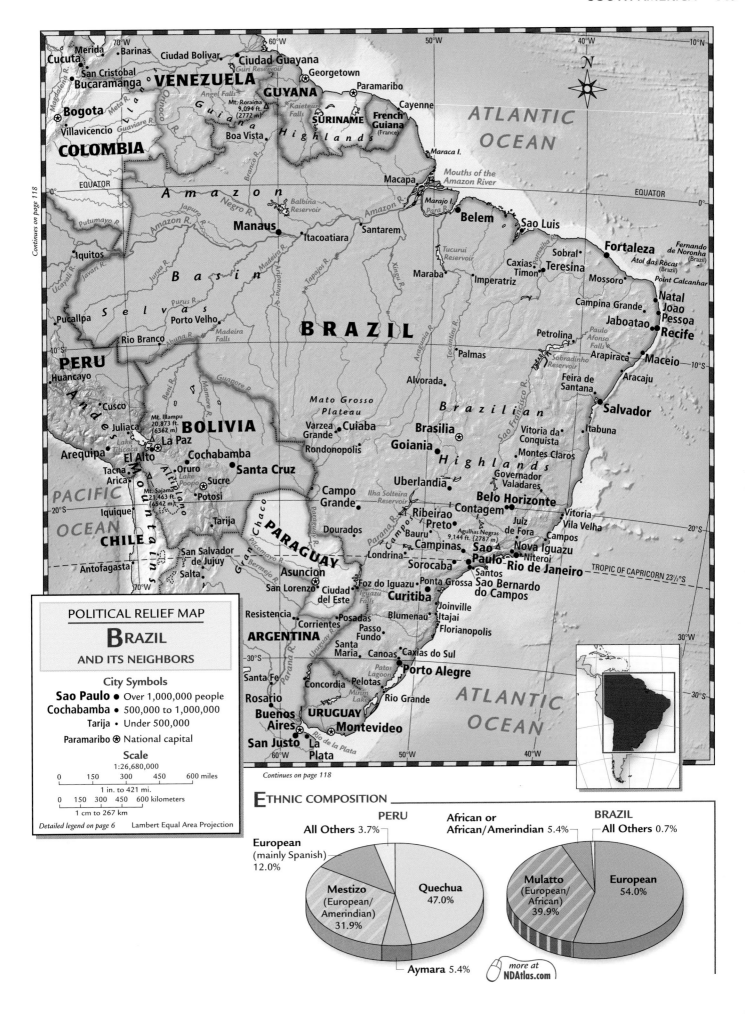

ATLANTIC OCEAN

PACIFIC OCEAN

ATLANTIC OCEAN

COLOMBIA

VENEZUELA
Merida • Barinas
Cucuta • San Cristobal • Ciudad Bolivar • Ciudad Guayana
Bucaramanga ⊗ Georgetown
Bogota • Villavicencio
GUYANA Paramaribo
SURINAME Cayenne
French Guiana (France)
Boa Vista

Mt. Roraima
9,094 ft.
(2772 m) △

Guri Reservoir
Angel Falls
Kaieteur Falls
Orinoco
Guiana Highlands
Maraca I.

EQUATOR

Amazon Negro R.
Balbina Reservoir
Mouths of the Amazon River
Macapa
Marajo I.
Para R.
Belem
Sao Luis

Manaus • Itacoatiara • Santarem
Amazon R.

Fortaleza
Fernando de Noronha (Brazil)
Atol das Rocas (Brazil)
Point Calcanhar

Iquitos
Basin
Selvas
Javari R.
Ucayali R.
Purus R.
Jurua R.
Madeira R.
Tapajos R.
Xingu R.
Tucurui Reservoir
Sobral
Caxias • Timon • Teresina
Maraba • Imperatriz
Mossoro
Campina Grande
Natal
Joao Pessoa
Jaboatao
Recife

Pucallpa
Porto Velho
Madeira Falls
Rio Branco
Abuna R.
BRAZIL
Araguaia R.
Tocantins R.
Petrolina
Paulo Afonso Falls
Arapiraca
Maceio

PERU
Huancayo
Cusco
Juliaca
Mt. Illampu
20,873 ft.
(6362 m) △
BOLIVIA
La Paz
El Alto
Cochabamba
Palmas
Alvorada
Sobradinho Reservoir
Feira de Santana
Aracaju
Salvador
Itabuna

Arequipa
Tacna
Arica
Oruro
Lake Poopo
Sucre
Mt. Sajama
21,463 ft.
(6542 m) △
Potosi
Santa Cruz
Altiplano
Mato Grosso Plateau
Varzea Grande • Cuiaba
Rondonopolis
Goiania
Brasilia ⊗
Brazilian Highlands
Vitoria da Conquista
Montes Claros
Governador Valadares

Iquique
Tarija
Campo Grande
Ilha Solteira Reservoir
Uberlandia
Contagem
Belo Horizonte
Vitoria

Antofagasta
CHILE
Andes Mountains
PARAGUAY
Dourados
Gran Chaco
Pilcomayo R.
Bermejo R.
Paraguay R.
Parana R.
Campos R.
Ribeirao Preto
Bauru
Agulhas Negras
9,144 ft. (2787 m) △
Juiz de Fora
Campos
Vila Velha
Nova Iguazu
Niteroi
Sao Paulo
Rio de Janeiro
Santos
TROPIC OF CAPRICORN 23½°S

San Salvador de Jujuy
Salta
Asuncion ⊗
San Lorenzo
Ciudad del Este
Iguazu Falls
Foz do Iguazu
Ponta Grossa
Londrina
Campinas
Sorocaba
Sao Bernardo do Campos

ARGENTINA
Resistencia
Corrientes
Posadas
Passo Fundo
Blumenau
Itajai
Joinville
Florianopolis
Curitiba

Santa Maria
Canoas
Caxias do Sul
Uruguay R.

Santa Fe
Concordia
Pelotas
Patos Lagoon
Porto Alegre

Rosario
Mirim Lake
Rio Grande

Buenos Aires
URUGUAY
San Justo
La Plata
Rio de la Plata
Montevideo

Continues on page 118

Continues on page 118

POLITICAL RELIEF MAP

BRAZIL

AND ITS NEIGHBORS

City Symbols

Sao Paulo • Over 1,000,000 people
Cochabamba • 500,000 to 1,000,000
Tarija • Under 500,000

Paramaribo ⊗ National capital

Scale

1:26,680,000

0 — 150 — 300 — 450 — 600 miles
1 in. to 421 mi.

0 — 150 — 300 — 450 — 600 kilometers
1 cm to 267 km

Detailed legend on page 6   Lambert Equal Area Projection

ETHNIC COMPOSITION

PERU

All Others 3.7%
European (mainly Spanish) 12.0%
Mestizo (European/Amerindian) 31.9%
Quechua 47.0%
Aymara 5.4%

BRAZIL

African or African/Amerindian 5.4%
All Others 0.7%
Mulatto (European/African) 39.9%
European 54.0%

more at NDAtlas.com

ISSUES ▶ TODAY

What should be done about the rain forest?

The Amazon Rain Forest, the largest in the world, is shrinking. It contains the widest variety of plant and animal life on Earth and is important to the continent's economy.

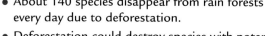

VENEZUELA

Amazon Rain Forest

PERU

BRAZIL

ARGENTINA

TROPICAL RAIN FOREST

- Rain forest today
- Deforested area

In recent years about 10,000 square miles (26 000 square kilometers) of forest in Brazil have been deforested annually. Should deforestation be allowed to continue? There are many perspectives on this issue. Here are two of them.

Deforestation has a disastrous impact on the environment.

- Trees and plants in the rain forest absorb greenhouse gases. Deforestation, on the other hand, contributes to global warming. Brazil emits more greenhouse gases than any other country in South America.

- About 140 species disappear from rain forests every day due to deforestation.

- Deforestation could destroy species with potential cures for diseases. About 25 percent of modern medicines were developed from rain forest plants. Less than 1 percent of rain forest species, however, have been tested for medical value.

- Deforestation displaces the indigenous people who have lived in the rain forest for centuries. Today about 350,000 indigenous people live in Brazil.

- Harvesting products—including fruits, nuts, and medicinal plants—often earns 40 times as much money per acre as deforested cattle ranches do.

Deforestation is necessary for the economy.

- About 60 percent of all arable land in Brazil is unused. Deforestation allows the country to utilize more of its land.

- Deforestation is an indicator of Brazil's economy. When the economy is growing, ranchers expand their pastures, the government builds highways, and deforestation increases.

- Brazil has an external debt of over US$200 billion. Money generated from major exports such as timber and coffee provides a fast way for Brazil to repay foreign governments and banks.

- Subsistence farmers depend on forest products for their livelihoods.

- Attempts to "save the earth" place an unfair burden on South Americans who could be prohibited from using about two-fifths of their own land. Other countries, such as the United States, have already cleared 90 percent of their original forests.

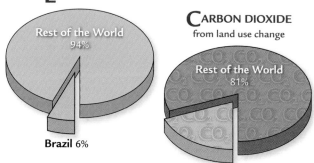

LAND AREA

Rest of the World 94%

Brazil 6%

CARBON DIOXIDE
from land use change

Rest of the World 81%

Brazil 19%

When land is deforested, carbon dioxide levels rise. Brazil contributes a disproportionate share of this pollutant. Carbon dioxide, ozone, and methane are all greenhouse gases that contribute to global warming.

more at **NDAtlas.com**

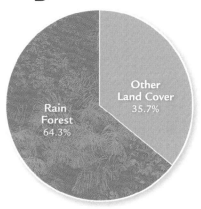

BRAZIL'S LAND COVER

Other Land Cover 35.7%

Rain Forest 64.3%

Rain forest in Brazil occupies over 2 million square miles (5.5 million square kilometers). This rain forest is roughly eight times the size of Texas.

AFRICA

Africa, located mainly within the tropics, has 53 countries—more than any other continent on Earth. A land of many cultures, Africa is home to hundreds of ethnic groups. The people of Africa speak more than 1,000 languages.

PHYSICAL FEATURES

Mountains
Highest peak: Mt. Kilimanjaro 19,340 ft. (5 895 m)

Longest range: Atlas Mountains 1,500 mi. (2 410 km)

Largest Island
Madagascar 226,658 sq. mi. (587 041 sq. km)

Largest Lakes
Lake Victoria 26,600 sq. mi. (68 900 sq. km)★

Lake Tanganyika 12,600 sq. mi. (32 600 km)★

Longest Rivers
Nile 4,132 mi. (6 650 km)★

Congo 2,900 mi. (4 700 km)★

Other Key Physical Features
Sahara
Sahel
Congo Basin
Great Rift Valley
Katanga Plateau
Bie Plateau
Somali Peninsula
Ethiopian Highlands

CULTURAL FEATURES

Population 915,700,000

Largest Countries
By area: Algeria 919,595 sq. mi. (2 381 741 sq km)★

Dem. Rep. of the Congo 905,354 sq. mi. (2 345 858 sq. km)

Sudan 718,723 sq. mi. (1 861 484 sq. km)

By population: Nigeria 131,859,731

Population Density
Most densely populated: Mauritius 1,574.7 people per sq. mi. (608.2 per sq. km)

Least densely populated: Western Sahara 2.7 people per sq. mi. (1.0 per sq. km)

Largest Urban Areas
Cairo, Egypt 11,001,000★

Lagos, Nigeria 10,578,000★

★Among the world's largest. See the inside front cover.

more at NDAtlas.com
For more maps, graphs, and photos of Africa, go to NystromDeskAtlas.com.

AREA COMPARISON

■ Africa
11,680,000 sq. mi. (30 251 000 sq. km)

Contiguous United States
3,021,295 sq. mi. (7 825 112 sq. km)

World Extreme The Sahara is the largest desert in the world, covering approximately 3.5 million sq. mi. (9 million sq. km). About 2 million people live in the Sahara despite its dry climate. Ninety large oases scattered throughout the Sahara provide water, shelter, and arable land for growing food.

REGIONAL MAPS OF AFRICA

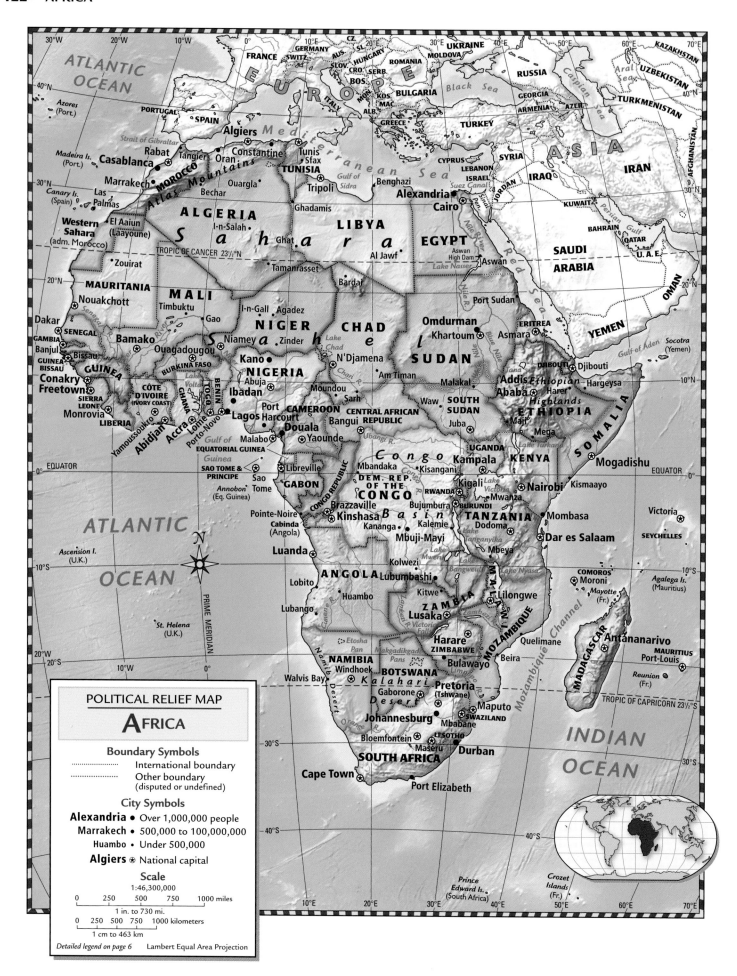

POLITICAL RELIEF MAP

AFRICA

Boundary Symbols

.... International boundary

.... Other boundary
(disputed or undefined)

City Symbols

Alexandria • Over 1,000,000 people

Marrakech • 500,000 to 100,000,000

Huambo • Under 500,000

Algiers ⊛ National capital

Scale

1:46,300,000

0   250   500   750   1000 miles

1 in. to 730 mi.

0   250   500   750   1000 kilometers

1 cm to 463 km

Detailed legend on page 6   Lambert Equal Area Projection

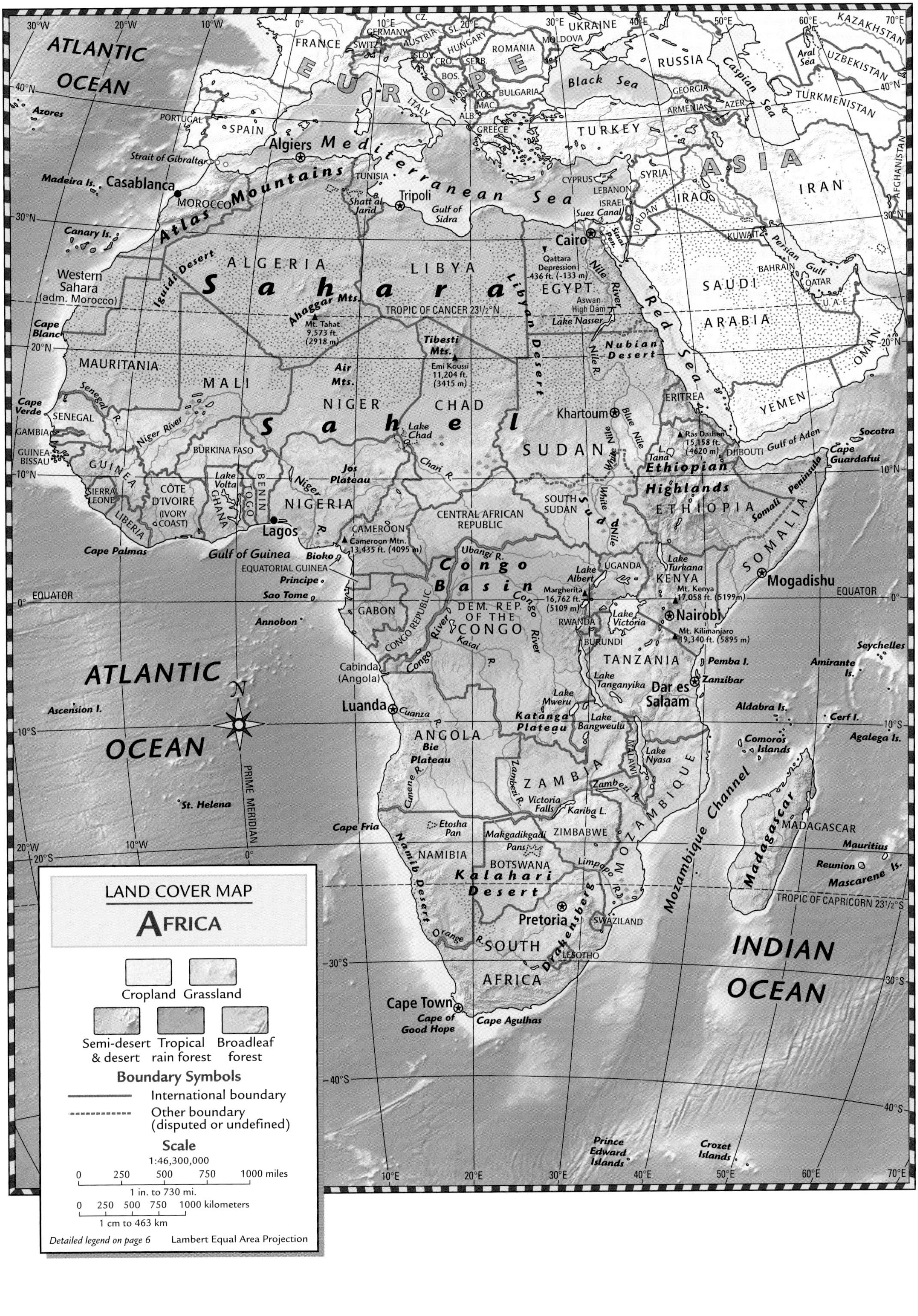

ATLANTIC OCEAN
Azores
PORTUGAL
SPAIN
FRANCE
SWITZ.
GERMANY
CZ.
AUSTRIA
SLOV.
SL.
HUNGARY
CRO.
SERB.
BOS.
MON.
KOS.
MAC.
ALB.
ITALY
ROMANIA
BULGARIA
GREECE
MOLDOVA
UKRAINE
RUSSIA
E U R O P E
Black Sea
GEORGIA
ARMENIA
AZER.
Caspian Sea
KAZAKHSTAN
Aral Sea
UZBEKISTAN
TURKMENISTAN
AFGHANISTAN
TURKEY
CYPRUS
SYRIA
LEBANON
ISRAEL
JORDAN
IRAQ
IRAN
A S I A
KUWAIT
BAHRAIN
QATAR
U.A.E.
Persian Gulf
SAUDI ARABIA
OMAN
YEMEN
Suez Canal
Sinai Pen.
Strait of Gibraltar
Algiers
Mediterranean Sea
Madeira Is.
Casablanca
MOROCCO
Atlas Mountains
TUNISIA
Shatt al Jarid
Tripoli
Gulf of Sidra
Canary Is.
Cairo
Qattara Depression -436 ft. (-133 m)
Western Sahara (adm. Morocco)
Iguidi Desert
ALGERIA
LIBYA
EGYPT
Libyan Desert
Sahara
Ahaggar Mts.
TROPIC OF CANCER 23½°N
Aswan High Dam
Lake Nasser
Nile River
Red Sea
Cape Blanc
Mt. Tahat 9,573 ft. (2918 m)
Tibesti Mts.
Emi Koussi 11,204 ft. (3415 m)
Nubian Desert
Nile R.
MAURITANIA
MALI
Air Mts.
NIGER
CHAD
ERITREA
Cape Verde
Senegal R.
SENEGAL
GAMBIA
GUINEA-BISSAU
GUINEA
Niger River
BURKINA FASO
Sahel
Lake Chad
Khartoum
Blue Nile
White Nile
SUDAN
Ras Dashen 15,158 ft. (4620 m)
L. Tana
DJIBOUTI
Gulf of Aden
Socotra
Cape Guardafui
Ethiopian Highlands
Somali Peninsula
SIERRA LEONE
LIBERIA
CÔTE D'IVOIRE (IVORY COAST)
Lake Volta
GHANA
TOGO
BENIN
Jos Plateau
Niger R.
NIGERIA
Lagos
Chari R.
SOUTH SUDAN
Sudd
CENTRAL AFRICAN REPUBLIC
ETHIOPIA
SOMALIA
Cape Palmas
Gulf of Guinea
Bioko
CAMEROON
Cameroon Mtn. 13,435 ft. (4095 m)
EQUATORIAL GUINEA
Principe
Sao Tome
Annobon
Ubangi R.
Congo Basin
Congo River
Lake Albert
UGANDA
Lake Turkana
KENYA
Mogadishu
Margherita 16,762 ft. (5109 m)
Mt. Kenya 17,058 ft. (5199 m)
EQUATOR
GABON
CONGO REPUBLIC
DEM. REP. OF THE CONGO
RWANDA
BURUNDI
Lake Victoria
Nairobi
Mt. Kilimanjaro 19,340 ft. (5895 m)
Kasai R.
TANZANIA
Pemba I.
Zanzibar
Seychelles
Amirante Is.
Cabinda (Angola)
Lake Tanganyika
Dar es Salaam
Lake Mweru
Ascension I.
Luanda
Cuanza R.
Katanga Plateau
Lake Bangweulu
Aldabra Is.
Cerf I.
Agalega Is.
Comoros Islands
ANGOLA
Bie Plateau
MALAWI
Lake Nyasa
Cunene R.
Zambezi R.
ZAMBIA
Zambezi R.
Victoria Falls
Kariba L.
MOZAMBIQUE
Mozambique Channel
St. Helena
PRIME MERIDIAN
Cape Fria
Etosha Pan
Makgadikgadi Pans
ZIMBABWE
MADAGASCAR
Madagascar
Mauritius
Reunion
Mascarene Is.
NAMIBIA
Namib Desert
BOTSWANA
Kalahari Desert
Limpopo R.
TROPIC OF CAPRICORN 23½°S
Pretoria
SWAZILAND
Drakensberg
Orange R.
SOUTH AFRICA
LESOTHO
INDIAN OCEAN
Cape Town
Cape of Good Hope
Cape Agulhas
Prince Edward Islands
Crozet Islands
30°W
20°W
10°W
0°
10°E
20°E
30°E
40°E
50°E
60°E
70°E
40°N
30°N
20°N
10°N
10°S
20°S
30°S
40°S
LAND COVER MAP
AFRICA
Cropland
Grassland
Semi-desert & desert
Tropical rain forest
Broadleaf forest
Boundary Symbols
International boundary
Other boundary (disputed or undefined)
Scale
1:46,300,000
0 250 500 750 1000 miles
1 in. to 730 mi.
0 250 500 750 1000 kilometers
1 cm to 463 km
Detailed legend on page 6
Lambert Equal Area Projection

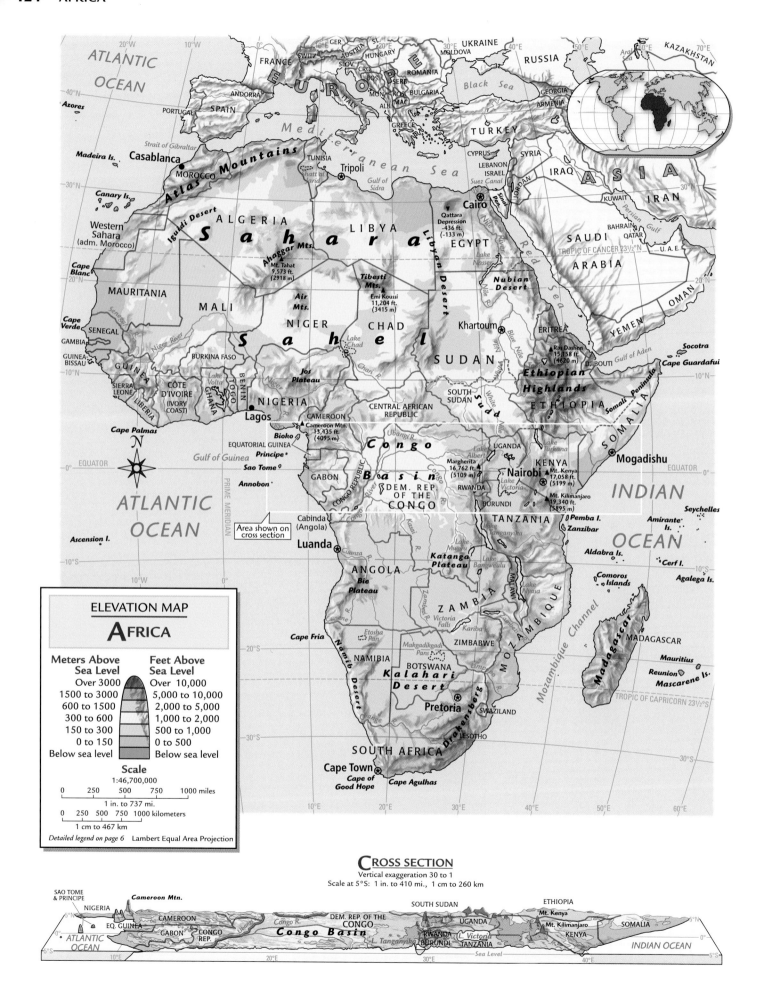

ATLANTIC OCEAN

Azores

Madeira Is.
Casablanca
MOROCCO
Atlas Mountains

Canary Is.

Western Sahara (adm. Morocco)

Cape Blanc

MAURITANIA

Cape Verde

SENEGAL

GAMBIA

GUINEA-BISSAU

GUINEA

SIERRA LEONE

LIBERIA

CÔTE D'IVOIRE (IVORY COAST)

Cape Palmas

ATLANTIC OCEAN

Ascension I.

EUROPE

PORTUGAL
SPAIN

ANDORRA

FRANCE
SWITZ.
GER.
AUSTRIA
HUNGARY
SLOV.
CRO.
BOS.
SERB.
MON.
KOS.
MAC.
ALB.
ITALY
GREECE

UKRAINE
MOLDOVA
ROMANIA
BULGARIA

RUSSIA

GEORGIA
ARMENIA

Black Sea

TURKEY

CYPRUS
SYRIA
LEBANON
ISRAEL

IRAQ

ASIA

KAZAKHSTAN

Aral Sea

Strait of Gibraltar

Mediterranean Sea

TUNISIA
Tripoli
Chott el Jerid

Gulf of Sidra

Suez Canal
Sinai Pen.

Cairo
Qattara Depression -436 ft. (-133 m)

JORDAN

KUWAIT

IRAN

BAHRAIN

SAUDI ARABIA

QATAR
U.A.E.

Iguidi Desert

ALGERIA
Sahara
LIBYA

EGYPT
Lake Nasser

Libyan Desert

Red Sea

OMAN

Ahaggar Mts.
Mt. Tahat 9,573 ft. (2918 m)

Tibesti Mts.
Emi Koussi 11,204 ft. (3415 m)

Nubian Desert

TROPIC OF CANCER 23½°N

Cape Verde

MALI
Sahel

NIGER

Air Mts.

CHAD

SUDAN

Khartoum

ERITREA
Ras Dashen 15,158 ft. (4620 m)
DJIBOUTI

Gulf of Aden

Socotra

Cape Guardafui

Senegal River
Niger River

BURKINA FASO

Lake Volta

TOGO
BENIN
GHANA

Jos Plateau

Lake Chad

Chari R.

NIGERIA

Lagos

CAMEROON
Cameroon Mtn. 13,435 ft. (4095 m)
Bioko

SOUTH SUDAN

Sudd

White Nile

Blue Nile

Ethiopian Highlands

ETHIOPIA

Somali Peninsula

CENTRAL AFRICAN REPUBLIC

EQUATORIAL GUINEA
Principe
Sao Tome

Gulf of Guinea

PRIME MERIDIAN

Area shown on cross section

Congo
Basin

Ubangi R.

UGANDA

Lake Albert

Lake Turkana

SOMALIA

EQUATOR

GABON

Annobon

CONGO REPUBLIC

Congo River

DEM. REP. OF THE CONGO

Margherita 16,762 ft. (5109 m)

RWANDA
BURUNDI

KENYA
Nairobi
Mt. Kenya 17,058 ft. (5199 m)

Mt. Kilimanjaro 19,340 ft. (5895 m)

Mogadishu

INDIAN OCEAN

Seychelles

Cabinda (Angola)

Luanda

TANZANIA

Lake Tanganyika

Pemba I.
Zanzibar

Amirante Is.

Aldabra Is.

Cerf I.

Kasai R.
Cuanza R.

ANGOLA

Bie Plateau

Katanga Plateau

Lake Mweru

Lake Bangweulu

Lake Nyasa

Comoros Islands

Agalega Is.

Cape Fria

Cunene R.

ZAMBIA
Zambezi R.

MALAWI

MADAGASCAR

Mauritius
Reunion
Mascarene Is.

Etosha Pan

Victoria Falls

Kariba L.

ZIMBABWE

Mozambique Channel

Cape Fria

Makgadikgadi Pans

Limpopo R.

MOZAMBIQUE

TROPIC OF CAPRICORN 23½°S

NAMIBIA

Namib Desert

Kalahari Desert

BOTSWANA

Orange River

SOUTH AFRICA

Pretoria
SWAZILAND

Drakensberg
LESOTHO

Cape Town
Cape of Good Hope
Cape Agulhas

ELEVATION MAP
AFRICA

Meters Above Sea Level	Feet Above Sea Level
Over 3000	Over 10,000
1500 to 3000	5,000 to 10,000
600 to 1500	2,000 to 5,000
300 to 600	1,000 to 2,000
150 to 300	500 to 1,000
0 to 150	0 to 500
Below sea level	Below sea level

Scale
1:46,700,000

0 250 500 750 1000 miles

1 in. to 737 mi.

0 250 500 750 1000 kilometers

1 cm to 467 km

Detailed legend on page 6   Lambert Equal Area Projection

CROSS SECTION
Vertical exaggeration 30 to 1
Scale at 5°S: 1 in. to 410 mi., 1 cm to 260 km

SAO TOME & PRINCIPE
NIGERIA
Cameroon Mtn.
EQ. GUINEA
CAMEROON
GABON
CONGO REP.
ATLANTIC OCEAN
Congo R.
Congo Basin
DEM. REP. OF THE CONGO
RWANDA
BURUNDI
L. Tanganyika
SOUTH SUDAN
UGANDA
L. Victoria
TANZANIA
Mt. Kenya
Mt. Kilimanjaro
ETHIOPIA
KENYA
SOMALIA
INDIAN OCEAN
Sea Level

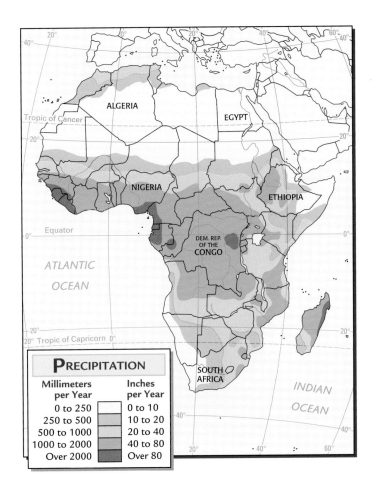

PRECIPITATION

Millimeters per Year	Inches per Year
0 to 250	0 to 10
250 to 500	10 to 20
500 to 1000	20 to 40
1000 to 2000	40 to 80
Over 2000	Over 80

Niger is one of the world's poorest countries, with 60 percent of its population living on less than US$1 a day. Ninety percent of its labor force is involved in agriculture. Unsophisticated farming methods and cycles of drought, however, result in shortages of food. Here, a woman in Niger threshes millet by hand.

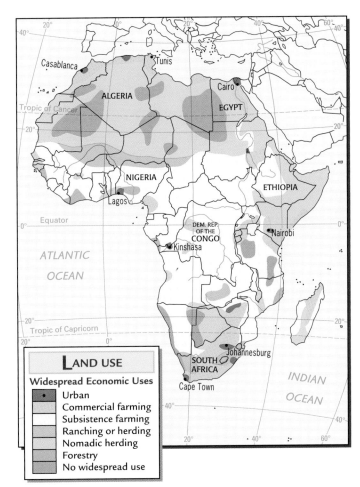

LAND USE

Widespread Economic Uses

- Urban
- Commercial farming
- Subsistence farming
- Ranching or herding
- Nomadic herding
- Forestry
- No widespread use

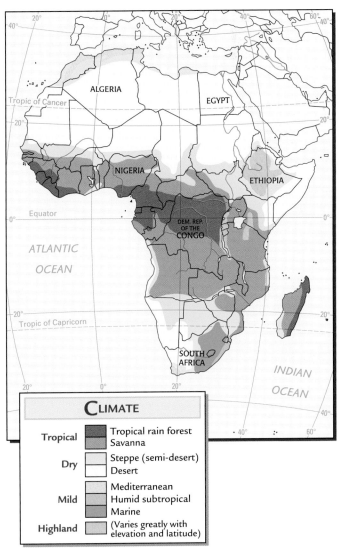

CLIMATE

Tropical	Tropical rain forest
	Savanna
Dry	Steppe (semi-desert)
	Desert
Mild	Mediterranean
	Humid subtropical
	Marine
Highland	(Varies greatly with elevation and latitude)

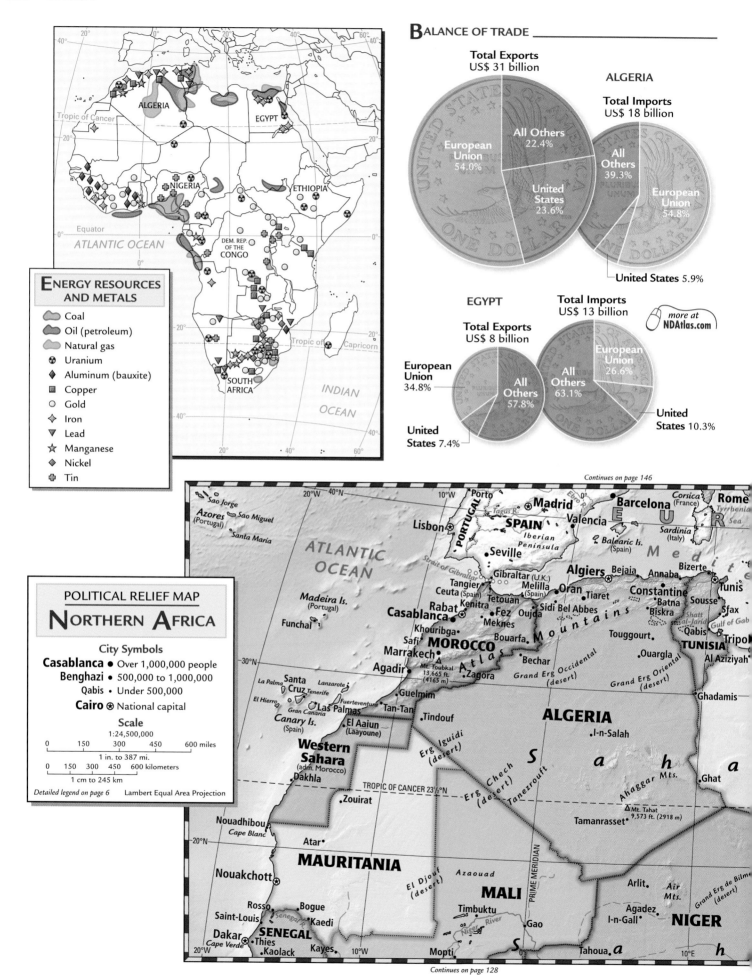

ENERGY RESOURCES AND METALS

- Coal
- Oil (petroleum)
- Natural gas
- Uranium
- Aluminum (bauxite)
- Copper
- Gold
- Iron
- Lead
- Manganese
- Nickel
- Tin

BALANCE OF TRADE

Total Exports US$ 31 billion

ALGERIA

Total Imports US$ 18 billion

European Union 54.0%
All Others 22.4%
United States 23.6%

All Others 39.3%
European Union 54.8%
United States 5.9%

EGYPT

Total Imports US$ 13 billion

Total Exports US$ 8 billion

European Union 34.8%
All Others 57.8%
United States 7.4%

All Others 63.1%
European Union 26.6%
United States 10.3%

more at NDAtlas.com

Continues on page 146

POLITICAL RELIEF MAP
NORTHERN AFRICA

City Symbols

Casablanca ● Over 1,000,000 people
Benghazi • 500,000 to 1,000,000
Qabis • Under 500,000
Cairo ⊛ National capital

Scale
1:24,500,000

| 0 | 150 | 300 | 450 | 600 miles |

1 in. to 387 mi.

| 0 | 150 | 300 | 450 | 600 kilometers |

1 cm to 245 km

Detailed legend on page 6   Lambert Equal Area Projection

Continues on page 128

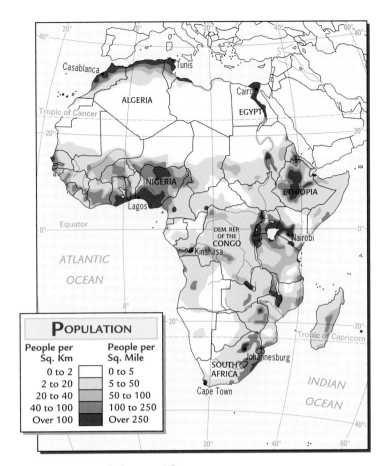

POPULATION

People per Sq. Km	People per Sq. Mile
0 to 2	0 to 5
2 to 20	5 to 50
20 to 40	50 to 100
40 to 100	100 to 250
Over 100	Over 250

Continues on page 147

NATURAL POPULATION GROWTH
AFRICA

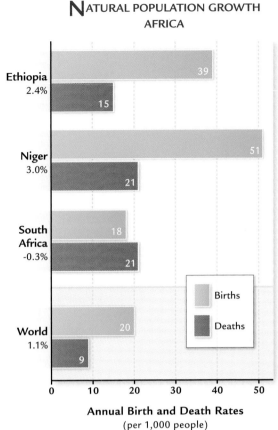

Ethiopia 2.4% — Births 39, Deaths 15

Niger 3.0% — Births 51, Deaths 21

South Africa -0.3% — Births 18, Deaths 21

World 1.1% — Births 20, Deaths 9

Annual Birth and Death Rates
(per 1,000 people)

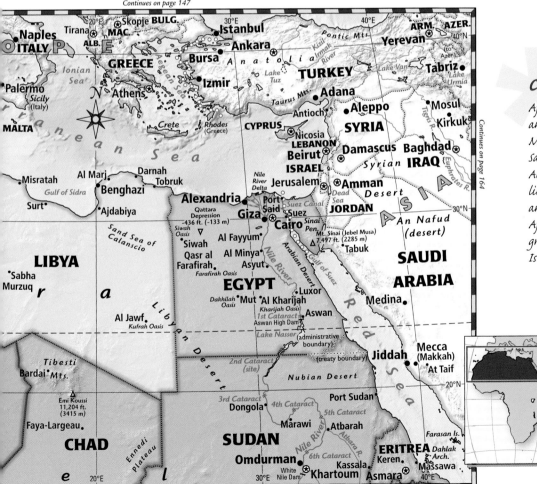

Continental Divide

Africa is divided both physically and culturally by the Sahara. Most Africans living north of the Sahara are Arab and Muslim. About 75 percent of all Africans live south of the Sahara. They are more diverse than northern Africans. They belong to 800 ethnic groups and follow Christianity, Islam, or traditional religions.

Continues on page 129

Continues on page 130

Continues on page 164

Continues on pages 126–127

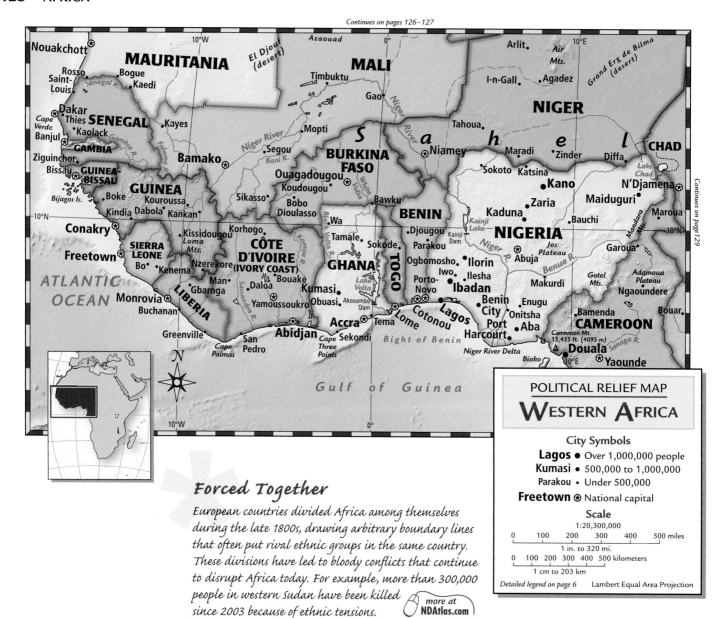

Continues on page 129

POLITICAL RELIEF MAP
WESTERN AFRICA

City Symbols

Lagos ● Over 1,000,000 people
Kumasi ● 500,000 to 1,000,000
Parakou • Under 500,000

Freetown ⊗ National capital

Scale
1:20,300,000

0   100   200   300   400   500 miles
1 in. to 320 mi.
0 100 200 300 400 500 kilometers
1 cm to 203 km

Detailed legend on page 6   Lambert Equal Area Projection

Forced Together

European countries divided Africa among themselves during the late 1800s, drawing arbitrary boundary lines that often put rival ethnic groups in the same country. These divisions have led to bloody conflicts that continue to disrupt Africa today. For example, more than 300,000 people in western Sudan have been killed since 2003 because of ethnic tensions.

more at
NDAtlas.com

ETHNIC COMPOSITION

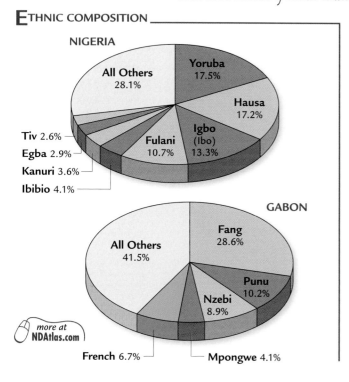

NIGERIA

- Yoruba 17.5%
- Hausa 17.2%
- Igbo (Ibo) 13.3%
- Fulani 10.7%
- All Others 28.1%
- Tiv 2.6%
- Egba 2.9%
- Kanuri 3.6%
- Ibibio 4.1%

GABON

- Fang 28.6%
- All Others 41.5%
- Punu 10.2%
- Nzebi 8.9%
- French 6.7%
- Mpongwe 4.1%

more at
NDAtlas.com

Education is important to economic development, yet 40 million African children—most of them girls—do not attend school. Here a Nigerian student completes a math assignment. Only 76 percent of all men and 61 percent of all women in Nigeria can read and write.

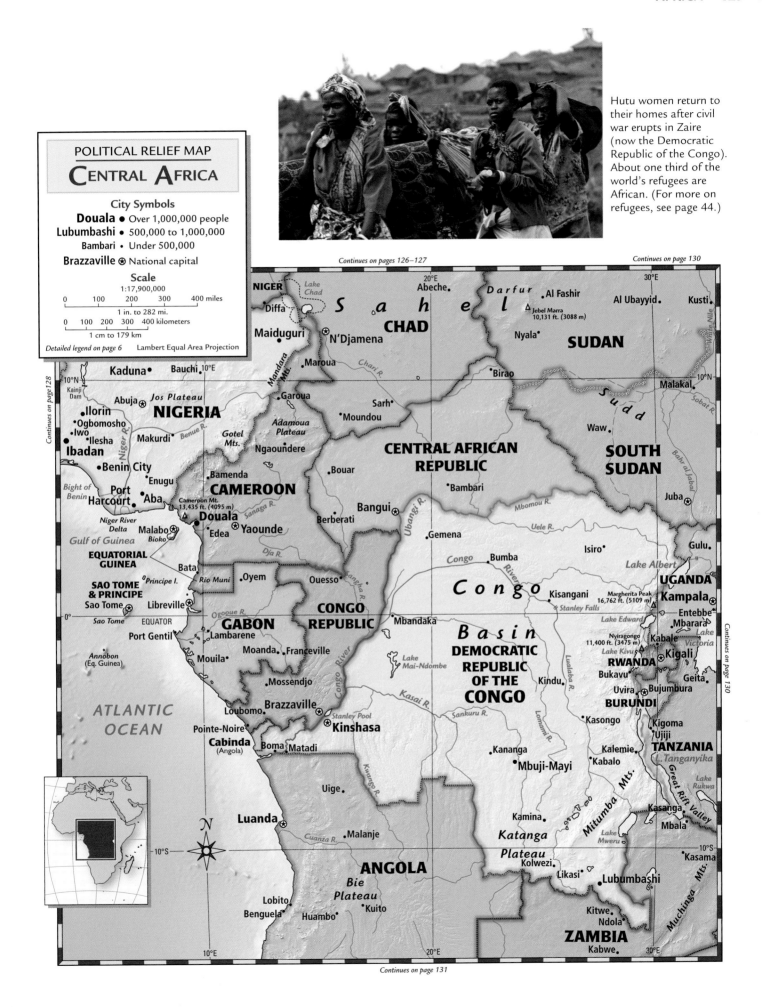

Hutu women return to their homes after civil war erupts in Zaire (now the Democratic Republic of the Congo). About one third of the world's refugees are African. (For more on refugees, see page 44.)

POLITICAL RELIEF MAP
CENTRAL AFRICA

City Symbols
Douala ● Over 1,000,000 people
Lubumbashi • 500,000 to 1,000,000
Bambari • Under 500,000
Brazzaville ⊛ National capital

Scale
1:17,900,000

| | | | | |
0 100 200 300 400 miles
1 in. to 282 mi.
0 100 200 300 400 kilometers
1 cm to 179 km

Detailed legend on page 6   Lambert Equal Area Projection

Continues on pages 126–127

Continues on page 130

Continues on page 128

Continues on page 130

NIGER
Lake Chad
20°E
Abeche
Darfur
Al Fashir
30°E
Al Ubayyid
Kusti
Diffa
△ Jebel Marra 10,131 ft. (3088 m)
White Nile
Maiduguri
N'Djamena
CHAD
Nyala
SUDAN
Maroua
Chari R.
Birao
10°N
Malakal
Sobat R.
Kaduna
Bauchi
10°E
10°N
Garoua
Sudd
Kainji Dam
Abuja
Jos Plateau
Sarh
Moundou
Waw
Bahr al Jabal
Ilorin
Ogbomosho
Iwo
Ilesha
NIGERIA
Makurdi
Benue R.
Adamoua Plateau
Gotel Mts.
Ngaoundere
Bouar
CENTRAL AFRICAN REPUBLIC
Bambari
SOUTH SUDAN
Juba
Ibadan
Benin City
Enugu
Bamenda
CAMEROON
Bangui
Berberati
Ubangi R.
Mbomou R.
Uele R.
Isiro
Gulu
Port Harcourt
Aba
Cameroon Mt. 13,435 ft. (4095 m)
Doula
Sanaga R.
Yaounde
Gemena
Congo
Bumba
Lake Albert
UGANDA
Kampala
Bight of Benin
Niger River Delta
Malabo
Bioko
Edea
Dja R.
Congo River
Kisangani
Margherita Peak 16,762 ft. (5109 m)
Entebbe
Mbarara
EQUATORIAL GUINEA
Bata
Stanley Falls
Lake Edward
Kabale
Lake Victoria
Gulf of Guinea
SAO TOME & PRINCIPE
Principe I.
Rio Muni
Oyem
Ouesso
Sangha R.
Congo Basin
Nyiragongo 11,400 ft. (3475 m)
Lake Kivu
Kigali
Sao Tome
Libreville
Ogooue R.
CONGO REPUBLIC
Mbandaka
DEMOCRATIC
Bukavu
RWANDA
Geita
Sao Tome
EQUATOR
GABON
Mbandaka
Uvira
Bujumbura
Port Gentil
Lambarene
Lake Mai-Ndombe
REPUBLIC
Kindu
BURUNDI
Annobon (Eq. Guinea)
Moanda
Franceville
OF THE
Lualaba R.
Kigoma
Ujiji
Mossendjo
Congo River
CONGO
Kasongo
Kalemie
TANZANIA
L. Tanganyika
Loubomo
Brazzaville
Kasai R.
Sankuru R.
Kabalo
ATLANTIC OCEAN
Stanley Pool
Kananga
Lomami R.
Lake Rukwa
Pointe-Noire
Kinshasa
Mbuji-Mayi
Kamina
Kasanga
Cabinda (Angola)
Boma
Matadi
Kwango R.
Mbala
Uige
Kamina
Mitumba Mts.
Lake Mweru
Great Rift Valley
Luanda
Katanga
Kasama
Malanje
Cuanza R.
Plateau
Kolwezi
10°S
ANGOLA
Bie Plateau
Likasi
Lubumbashi
Muchinga Mts.
Lobito
Benguela
Huambo
Kuito
Kitwe
Ndola
ZAMBIA
Kabwe

Continues on page 131

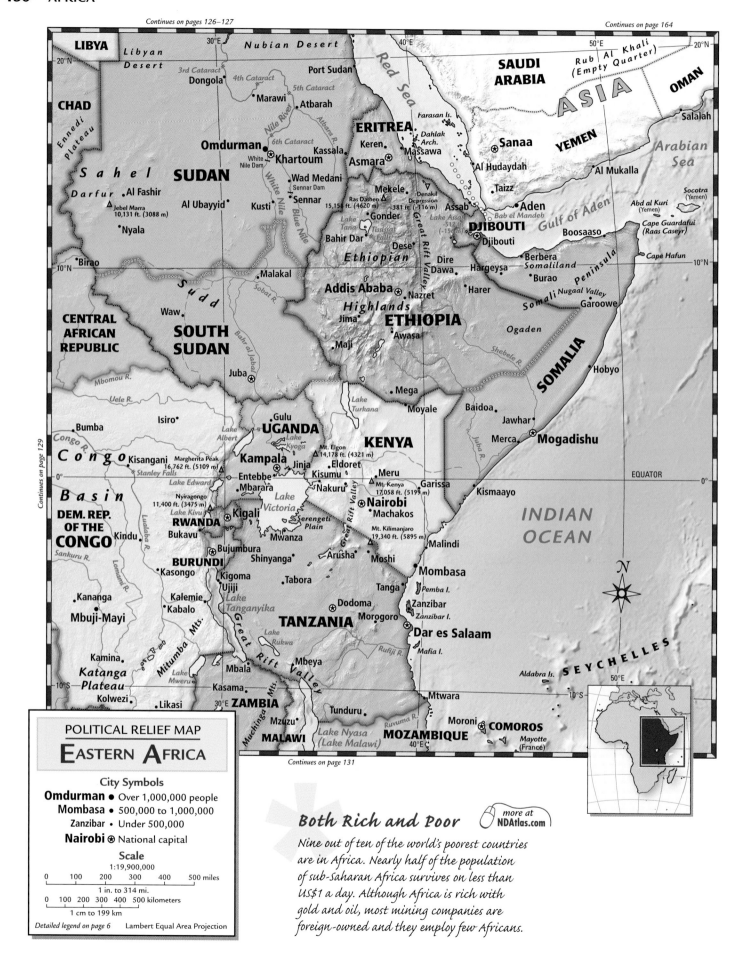

Continues on pages 126–127

Continues on page 164

LIBYA

Libyan Desert

30°E   *Nubian Desert*   40°E   50°E   20°N

SAUDI ARABIA

Rub' Al Khali (Empty Quarter)

ASIA

OMAN

CHAD

Ennedi Plateau

3rd Cataract

Dongola

4th Cataract

Port Sudan

Marawi

5th Cataract

Atbarah

6th Cataract

Omdurman

White Nile Dam

Khartoum

Kassala

ERITREA

Keren

Dahlak Arch.

Massawa

Farasan Is.

Sanaa

YEMEN

Salalah

Arabian Sea

Sahel

SUDAN

Darfur Al Fashir

△ *Jebel Marra 10,131 ft. (3088 m)*

Al Ubayyid•

Nyala

Wad Medani

Sennar Dam

Sennar

Asmara ⊛

Mekele

Denakil Depression -381 ft. (-116 m)

Al Hudaydah

Taizz

Al Mukalla

Socotra (Yemen)

Kusti•

△ *Ras Dashen 15,158 ft. (4620 m)*

Gonder

Lake Assal -512 ft. (-156 m)

Assab

Bab el Mandeb

Aden

Gulf of Aden

Boosaaso

DJIBOUTI

Djibouti ⊛

Abd al Kuri (Yemen)

Cape Guardafui (Raas Caseyr)

Birao•

Sudd

Malakal

Sobat R.

Lake Tana

Tississat Falls

Bahir Dar

Dese•

Ethiopian

Dire Dawa

Hargeysa

Berbera

Burao

Somaliland

Somali Peninsula

Nugaal Valley

Cape Hafun

10°N

CENTRAL AFRICAN REPUBLIC

Waw•

SOUTH SUDAN

Bahr al Jabal

Juba ⊛

Addis Ababa ⊛

Highlands

Jima•

Maji•

Nazret

ETHIOPIA

Awasa•

Harer

Ogaden

Garoowe

Shebele R.

Continues on page 129

Bumba•

Congo R.

Isiro•

Lake Albert

Gulu•

UGANDA

Lake Kyoga

Lake Turkana

Mega•

Moyale•

Baidoa•

SOMALIA

Hobyo•

Kisangani•

Margherita Peak 16,762 ft. (5109 m)

Stanley Falls

Kampala ⊛

Lake Edward

Entebbe•

△ *Mt. Elgon 14,178 ft. (4321 m)*

Jinja•

Eldoret•

KENYA

Meru•

Jawhar•

Merca•

Mogadishu ⊛

Congo Basin

Nyiragongo 11,400 ft. (3475 m)

Lake Kivu

Mbarara•

Kisumu•

Nakuru•

△ *Mt. Kenya 17,058 ft. (5199 m)*

Garissa•

EQUATOR

0°

Kindu•

DEM. REP. OF THE CONGO

Lualaba R.

Sankuru R.

Kigali ⊛

RWANDA

Bukavu•

Lake Victoria

Nairobi ⊛

Machakos•

Kismaayo•

INDIAN OCEAN

Kananga•

Mbuji-Mayi•

Kasongo•

Bujumbura ⊛

BURUNDI

Kigoma•

Ujiji•

Serengeti Plain

Mwanza•

Shinyanga•

Arusha•

Great Rift Valley

△ *Mt. Kilimanjaro 19,340 ft. (5895 m)*

Moshi•

Malindi•

Kamina•

Kalemie•

Kabalo•

Lake Tanganyika

Dodoma ⊛

Tabora•

Morogoro•

Tanga•

Mombasa•

Pemba I.

Zanzibar•

Zanzibar I.

Katanga Plateau

Kolwezi•

Likasi•

Mitumba Mts.

Lake Mweru

Mbala•

Kasama•

Lake Rukwa

TANZANIA

Rufiji R.

Dar es Salaam ⊛

Mafia I.

SEYCHELLES

10°S

30°E

ZAMBIA

Mzuzu•

MALAWI

Mbeya•

Muchinga Mts.

Great Rift Valley

Tunduru•

Ruvuma R.

Mtwara•

Moroni ⊛

COMOROS

Mayotte (France)

Aldabra Is.

50°E

10°S

Lake Nyasa (Lake Malawi)

MOZAMBIQUE

40°E

Continues on page 131

POLITICAL RELIEF MAP
EASTERN AFRICA

City Symbols
Omdurman ● Over 1,000,000 people
Mombasa ● 500,000 to 1,000,000
Zanzibar • Under 500,000
Nairobi ⊛ National capital

Scale
1:19,900,000

0   100   200   300   400   500 miles
1 in. to 314 mi.

0 100 200 300 400 500 kilometers
1 cm to 199 km

Detailed legend on page 6   Lambert Equal Area Projection

more at
NDAtlas.com

Both Rich and Poor

Nine out of ten of the world's poorest countries are in Africa. Nearly half of the population of sub-Saharan Africa survives on less than US$1 a day. Although Africa is rich with gold and oil, most mining companies are foreign-owned and they employ few Africans.

GREAT RIFT VALLEY

The Great Rift Valley stretches 4500 miles (7200 kilometers) from Syria in western Asia to Mozambique in southern Africa. The valley is being formed along a fault zone that is developing into a divergent plate boundary (see pages 16–17). In places, it has stretched Africa by up to 60 miles. Lake Tanganyika and Lake Nyasa are just two of the many lakes formed by the rift.

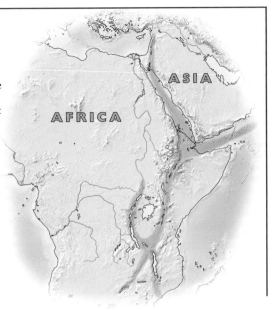

🝔 Great Rift Valley

In a dry, mountainous region of northwestern Namibia, the Himba people maintain most of their traditional ways of life. These herders, once threatened by war and drought, now profit from ecotourism.

Continues on page 129   Continues on page 130

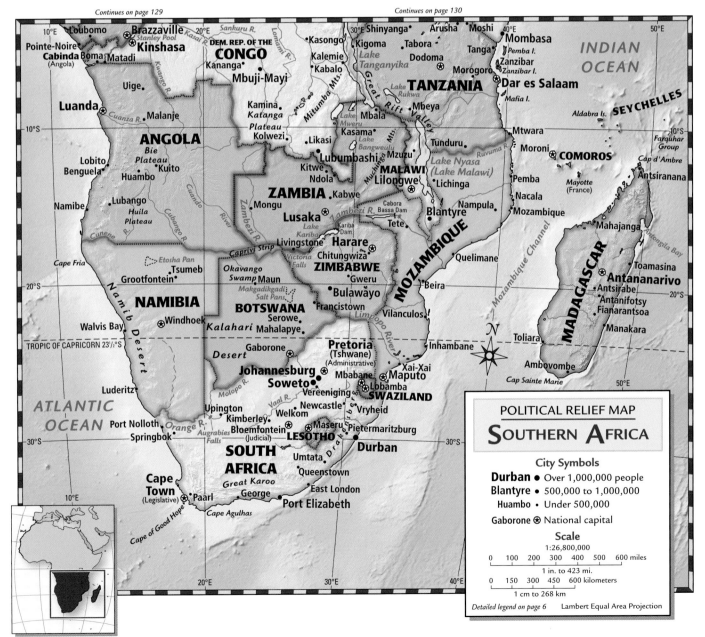

POLITICAL RELIEF MAP
SOUTHERN AFRICA

City Symbols

Durban ● Over 1,000,000 people
Blantyre • 500,000 to 1,000,000
Huambo • Under 500,000

Gaborone ⊗ National capital

Scale
1:26,800,000

0 100 200 300 400 500 600 miles
1 in. to 423 mi.

0 150 300 450 600 kilometers
1 cm to 268 km

Detailed legend on page 6   Lambert Equal Area Projection

How should the AIDS pandemic be controlled?

AIDS (acquired immune deficiency syndrome) is the leading cause of death in Africa. Reaching worldwide pandemic status in the early 1980s, AIDS now kills about 6,600 Africans every day. Currently more than 20 million Africans have HIV (human immunodeficiency virus), the virus that causes AIDS. Approximately 1.9 million of them are children. What is the best way to prevent HIV/AIDS? There are many perspectives on this issue. Here are two of them.

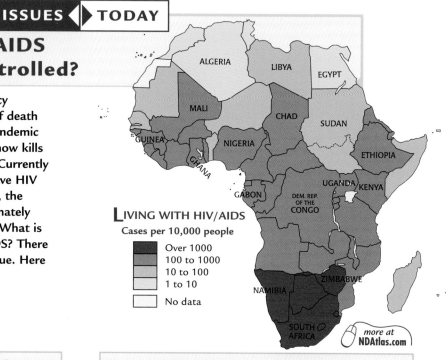

LIVING WITH HIV/AIDS
Cases per 10,000 people

■	Over 1000
■	100 to 1000
■	10 to 100
■	1 to 10
□	No data

more at NDAtlas.com

Education will help control the AIDS pandemic.

- Medical treatment only helps those already infected with HIV. Even with treatment, people can still spread the disease.

- Some people have misconceptions about HIV/AIDS transmission and cures. Once they have a genuine understanding of HIV/AIDS, they can take effective steps to protect themselves, their partners, and their children.

- Education programs for children in South Africa, Zimbabwe, and Malawi teach HIV/AIDS awareness. They enable children and young adults to make more informed decisions.

- Although talk of AIDS in African cultures was once considered taboo, increased public awareness about HIV/AIDS prevention has led to safer lifestyles for many Africans. A government campaign for AIDS education in Uganda resulted in a 70 percent drop in HIV cases during the 1990s.

South African marchers, both with and without HIV, reduce the stigma of the disease and increase public awareness of treatment options.

Affordable treatment will help AIDS patients.

- Combating the spread of the disease with affordable treatment will benefit over 60 percent of all people living with HIV.

- Generic AIDS drugs have been made available for as little as US$140 per person annually.

- The stigma of HIV/AIDS results in a population that fears finding out if they have the disease. Of those with HIV, 90 percent are unaware they are infected. With treatment available, people are often more willing to be tested.

- Without affordable treatment, AIDS will cripple Africa's already weakened economy. Six million 15- to 24-year-old Africans are currently infected with HIV.

- Free antiretroviral drugs reduced AIDS deaths for Brazilians by almost 50 percent. Such a policy could also prolong the lives of most African AIDS patients.

POPULATION PYRAMID ZIMBABWE

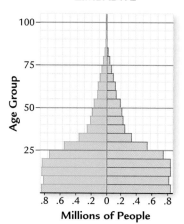

About 1.8 million people in Zimbabwe are living with HIV/AIDS. Zimbabwe has one of the shortest life expectancies in the world—an average of just 39 years.

more at NDAtlas.com

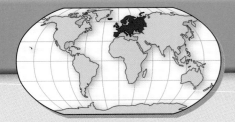

EUROPE

Europe, which shares a landmass with Asia, is the second most densely populated continent. It is the birthplace of modern industry.

PHYSICAL FEATURES

Mountains
Highest peak:	Mt. Elbrus 18,510 ft. (5 642 m)
Longest range:	Ural Mountains* 1,500 mi. (2 400 km)

Largest Island
Great Britain 88,764 sq. mi. (229 898 sq. km)

Largest Lakes
Caspian Sea* 143,300 sq. mi. (371 000 sq. km)★
Lake Ladoga 6,835 sq. mi. (17 703 sq. km)★

Longest Rivers
Volga 2,193 mi. (3 530 km)★
Danube 1,770 mi. (2 850 km)

Other Key Physical Features
Caucasus Mountains*
Alps
Apennines
Carpathian Mountains
Pyrennes
Northern European Plain
Central Russian Upland
Scandinavian Peninsula
Iberian Peninsula
Balkan Peninsula

CULTURAL FEATURES

Population 727,700,000

Largest Country
By area: Russia* 6,592,800 sq. mi. (17 075 400 sq. km)★
By population: Russia* 142,893,540

Population Density
Most densely populated: Monaco 43,390.7 people per sq. mi. (16 688.7 per sq. km)
Least densely populated: Iceland 7.5 people per sq. mi. (2.9 per sq. km)

Largest Urban Areas
Moscow, Russia 10,550,000★
Istanbul, Turkey* 10,525,000★

★ Among the world's largest. See the inside front cover.

* Located in both Europe and Asia.

AREA COMPARISON

■ Europe
4,033,000 sq. mi.
(10 445 000 sq. km)

Contiguous United States
3,021,295 sq. mi.
(7 825 112 sq. km)

World Extreme Vatican City is the world's smallest independent country, with only 109 acres (44 hectares) and a population of less than 1,000. The Vatican is located entirely within Rome, Italy. It is the headquarters of the Roman Catholic Church.

REGIONAL MAPS OF EUROPE

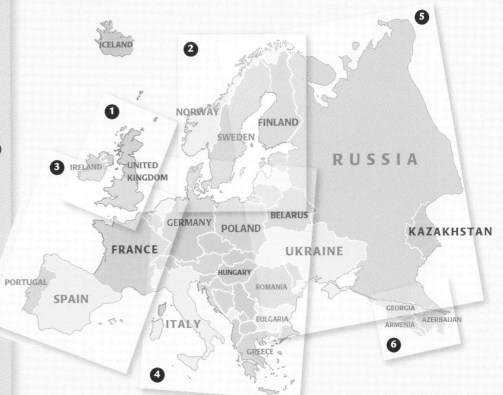

more at NDAtlas.com
For more maps, graphs, and photos of Europe, go to NystromDeskAtlas.com.

POLITICAL RELIEF MAP
EUROPE

Boundary Symbols
.... International boundary
.... Other boundary
(disputed or undefined)
▫ Small country

City Symbols
Hamburg ● Over 1,000,000 people
Seville ● 500,000 to 1,000,000
Orel • Under 500,000
Prague ⊛ National capital

Scale
1:17,400,000

0   100   200   300   400 miles

1 in. to 275 mi.

0   100 200 300 400 kilometers

1 cm to 174 km

Detailed legend on page 6   Bonne Projection

TIC OCEAN

Hammerfest
Vardo
Narvik
Kiruna
Murmansk
Kola Pen.
Barents Sea
Novaya Zemlya
Kolguyev I.
Pechora R.

Lapland
L. Inarijarvi
White Sea
Arkhangelsk
Syktyvkar

FINLAND
Oulu
Bothnia
Gulf of
Vaasa
Lake Onega
Northern Dvina R.
Sukhona R.
Onega R.

RUSSIA

Ural Mountains

Ob River

60°N

Tampere
L. Saimaa
Turku
Helsinki
Lake Ladoga
Kirov
Perm
Yekaterinburg
Chelyabinsk

Gulf of Finland
St. Petersburg
Kamskoye Res.
Kama R.
Izhevsk
Vyatka R.

ESTONIA
Tallinn
L. Peipus
Pskov
Rybinsk Res.
Volga River
Yaroslavl
Gorki Res.
Kazan
Ufa

70°E

LATVIA
Riga
Tver
Moscow
Nizhniy Novgorod
Oka R.
Kuybyshev Res.

LITHUANIA
Neman R.
Vilnius
(to Russia)
Smolensk
Tula
Penza
Samara

BELARUS
Warsaw
Orel
Orenburg
Ural River
Oral

50°N

Bryansk
Kursk
Voronezh
Saratov
Volgograd Res.
KAZAKHSTAN

ASIA

European Plain

Pripyat R.
Chernobyl
Kiev
Kharkiv
Ural River
Aral Sea
Syr Darya

Lviv
Dnieper R.
Donets R.
Volgograd
Volga River
Astrakhan

UKRAINE
Dniester R.
Dnipropetrovsk
Donetsk
Don R.
Steppe

MOLDOVA
Chisinau
Rostov-na-Donu
Volga R. Delta
UZBEKISTAN
Amu Darya

Cluj-Napoca
Mures R.
Prut R.
Odessa
Kerch
Krasnodar

ROMANIA
Crimean Pen.
Sea of Azov
Caspian Sea

Transylvanian Alps
Sevastopol
Yalta
Novorossiysk
Groznyy
TURKMENISTAN

Bucharest
Constanta
Caucasus Mountains
Ashgabat

Danube River
Black Sea
GEORGIA
Tbilisi
AZERBAIJAN
Baku

BULGARIA
Varna
ARMENIA
Yerevan

Sofia
Balkan
Plovdiv
Bosporus
TURKEY

DONIA
Peninsula
Istanbul
Sea of Marmara
Ankara
Lake Tuz
Lake Van
Lake Urmia
Tehran

Thessaloniki
Dardanelles
GREECE
Euboea
Aegean Sea
Athens
Cyclades

IRAN

Rhodes
Crete (Greece)
Sea
CYPRUS
Nicosia
Cyprus
LEBANON
SYRIA
IRAQ

20°E
30°E
40°E
50°E
60°E
70°N
70°E
80°E
60°N
50°N
40°N
30°E
40°E
50°E

LAND COVER MAP

EUROPE

Cropland Grassland Tundra Glacier

Semi-desert Broadleaf Needleleaf
& desert forest forest

Boundary Symbols

— International boundary

----- Other boundary
(disputed or undefined)

⊡ Small country

Scale

1:17,400,000

0 100 200 300 400 miles

1 in. to 275 mi.

0 100 200 300 400 kilometers

1 cm to 174 km

Detailed legend on page 6   Bonne Projection

ARC

Reykjavik

Iceland
Hekla
4,892 ft.
(1491 m)

Surtsey I.

ICELAND

ARCTIC CIRCLE 66½°N

PRIME MERIDIAN

Lofoten
Is.

Norwegian

Sea

Trondheims Fiord

Faroe
Islands

NORWAY

Scandinavian

Peninsula

SWEDEN

Rockall

Shetland
Islands

Sogne Fiord

Hardanger Fiord

Bokna Fiord

Oslo

L. Malaren

L.
Vanern

Stockholm

Hebrides

Orkney
Islands

North

Skagerrak

L.
Vattern

Gotaland

British

Isles

Grampian Mts.

Sea

DENMARK

Copenhagen

Kattegat

Jutland

Baltic

Ireland

IRELAND

Irish Sea

Great
Britain

UNITED
KINGDOM

Bornholm

A T L A N T I C

Celtic

Sea

Cambrian
Mts.

London
Thames

Frisian Is.

Ijsselmeer

NETHERLANDS

Elbe R.

Berlin

Oder
R.

Vistula R.

N o r t h e r n

O C E A N

English Channel

Channel Is.

BELGIUM

Rhine

GERMANY

Ore Mts.

POLA

Seine

Paris
River

LUXEMBOURG

Elbe R.

CZECH REPUBLIC

Carpa

Bay of
Biscay

Cape Finisterre

Loire
R.

Paris Basin

F R A N C E

Danube
River

Munich

SLOVAKIA

Cantabrian Mts.

Aquitaine
Basin

Massif
Central

Pyrenees

SWITZERLAND

L. Geneva

LIECH.

AUSTRIA

HUNGARY

Douro R.

Iberian

Duero R.

Ebro R.

ANDORRA

Mt. Blanc
15,771 ft.
(4807 m)

A l p s

Rhone

Po R.

SLOVENIA

Drava R.

Great
Hungaria

Lisbon

PORTUGAL

Madrid

SPAIN

Tagus R.

Guadiana
R.

MONACO

Gulf of
Lion

Ligurian
Sea

SAN
MARINO

Tiber R.

CROATIA

BOSNIA

Dinaric Alps

SERBIA

Cape St. Vincent

Peninsula

Guadalquivir R.

Balearic Sea

Corsica

VATICAN CITY

Rome

A p e n n i n e s

Adriatic
Sea

MONTENEGRO

KOSOVO

Balearic Islands

Sardinia

I T A L Y

MACEDONIA

Strait of
Gibraltar

Gibraltar (U.K.)

Mt. Vesuvius
4,190 ft.
(1277 m)

M e d i t e r r a n e a n

Tyrrhenian
Sea

Gulf of
Taranto

ALBANIA

Pindus Mts.

Algiers

Sicily

Ionian
Sea

Ionian
Islands

Peloponnesus

MOROCCO

A F R I C A

A L G E R I A

TUNISIA

Tunis

MALTA
Maltese Is.

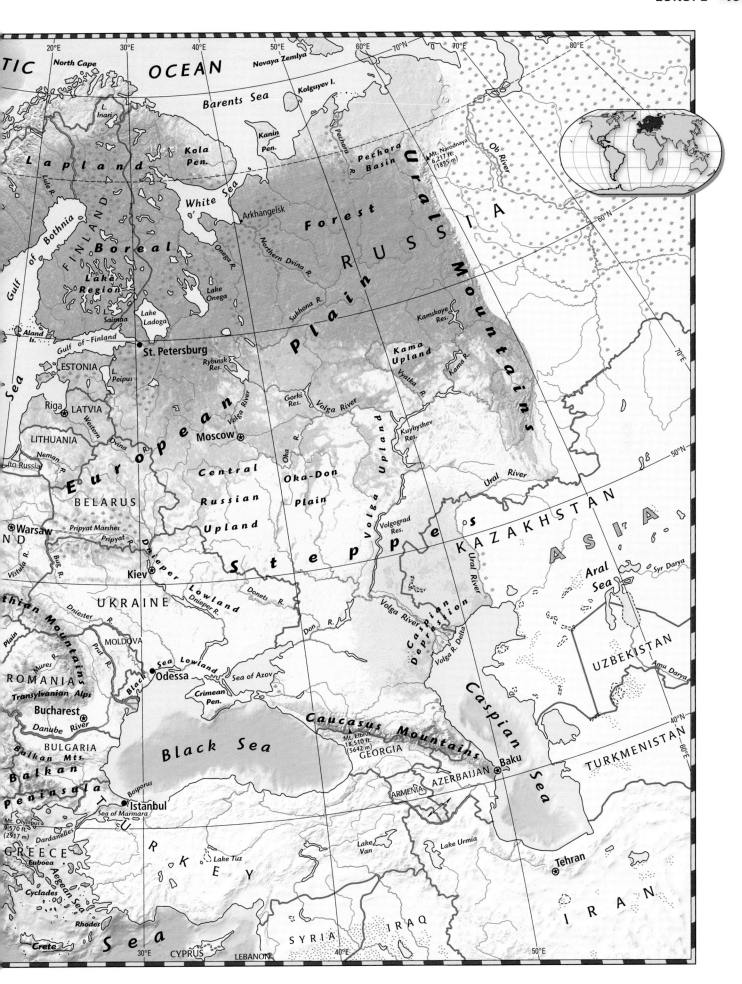

TIC

North Cape

OCEAN

20°E   30°E   40°E   50°E   60°E   70°N   70°N   80°E

Novaya Zemlya

Barents Sea

Kolguyev I.

L. Inari

Kanin Pen.

Pechora

Pechora Basin

Mt. Narodnaya 6,217 ft. (1895 m)

Ob River

Kola Pen.

L a p l a n d

White Sea

Forest

Arkhangelsk

60°E

Gulf of Bothnia

FINLAND

B o r e a l

Onega R.

Northern Dvina R.

R U S S I A

A S I A

Lake Region

L. Saimaa

Lake Onega

Sukhona R.

Kamskoye Res.

Lake Ladoga

U r a l s   M o u n t a i n s

Aland Is.

Gulf of Finland

St. Petersburg

P l a i n

Kama Upland

Kama R.

ESTONIA

Rybinsk Res.

Vyatka R.

L. Peipus

Gorki Res.

Volga River

Kuybyshev Res.

50°N

Riga   LATVIA

Volga River

E u r o p e a n

Moscow

LITHUANIA

Western Dvina

Oka R.

Volga Upland

Neman R.

Central

Oka-Don

(to Russia)

BELARUS

Russian

plain

Volgograd Res.

Ural River

70°E

K A Z A K H S T A N

Warsaw

Pripyat Marshes

Upland

ND

Pripyat R.

Dnieper R.

Aral Sea

Syr Darya

Bug R.

S   t   e   p   p   e   s

Ural River

Vistula R.

Kiev

Lowland

Volga River

50°N

Dnieper R.

Donets R.

Caspian Depression

60°E

U K R A I N E

Dniester R.

Don R.

Volga R. Delta

thian

MOLDOVA

Prut R.

U Z B E K I S T A N

Mountains

Mures

ROMANIA

Black Sea Lowland

Odessa

Sea of Azov

Amu Darya

Plain

Transylvanian Alps

Crimean Pen.

40°N

Bucharest

C a u c a s u s   M o u n t a i n s

Danube River

Mt. Elbrus 18,510 ft. (5642 m)

BULGARIA

C a s p i a n

GEORGIA

Balkan Mts.

B a l k a n

B l a c k   S e a

AZERBAIJAN   Baku

S e a

TURKMENISTAN

Peninsula

Bosporus

ARMENIA

60°E

Mt. Olympus 9,570 ft. (2917 m)

Istanbul

Sea of Marmara

Dardanelles

GREECE

T

Euboea

Lake Van

Lake Urmia

U

I R A N

Aegean Sea

R

Lake Tuz

Cyclades

K

Tehran

E

Rhodes

Y

Crete

S e a

IRAQ

SYRIA

30°E

CYPRUS   LEBANON

40°E

50°E

ELEVATION MAP
EUROPE

Meters Above Sea Level	Feet Above Sea Level
Over 3000	Over 10,000
1500 to 3000	5,000 to 10,000
600 to 1500	2,000 to 5,000
300 to 600	1,000 to 2,000
150 to 300	500 to 1,000
0 to 150	0 to 500
Below sea level	Below sea level

Scale
1:20,800,000

0   125   250   375   500 miles
1 in. to 328 mi.

0   125   250   375   500 kilometers
1 cm to 208 km

Detailed legend on page 6   Lambert Equal Area Projection

CROSS SECTION
Vertical exaggeration 40 to 1
Scale at 42°N: 1 in. to 291 mi., 1 cm to 184 km

RECLAIMED LAND IN THE NETHERLANDS

Polder (reclaimed land)

Dam   Canal

Elevation

Land above sea level — sea level
Land below sea level — ocean

About 27 percent of the Netherlands is below sea level. **Polders**, land that has been reclaimed from the sea or marsh, now cover much of this lowland.

Life Beneath the Sea

For centuries the Dutch have reclaimed land from the North Sea. Dikes hold the sea back, while canals and pumps drain the water. Windmills once powered the pumps, but today they run on diesel and electricity. In 1986 the most recent Dutch province, Flevoland, was created entirely from reclaimed land.

In the central Swiss Alps, green Lauterbrunnen Valley sits 11,000 feet (3353 meters) below the mountain Jungfrau. Jungfrau has an elevation of 13,641 feet (4158 meters) and is snow-capped year-round.

Caucasus Mountains

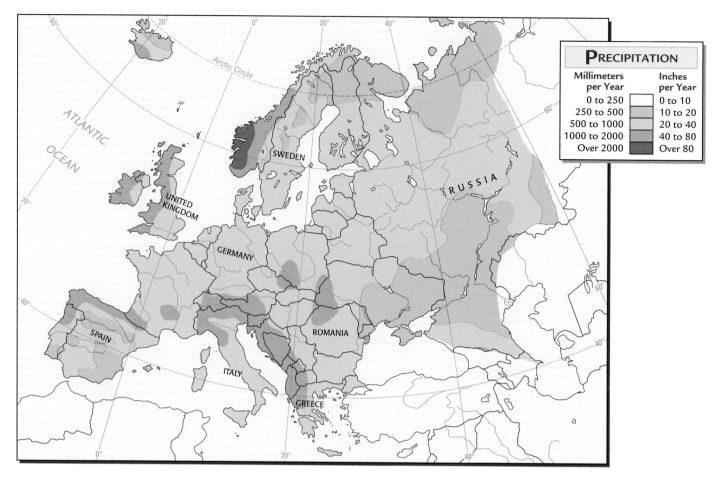

PRECIPITATION

Millimeters per Year	Inches per Year
0 to 250	0 to 10
250 to 500	10 to 20
500 to 1000	20 to 40
1000 to 2000	40 to 80
Over 2000	Over 80

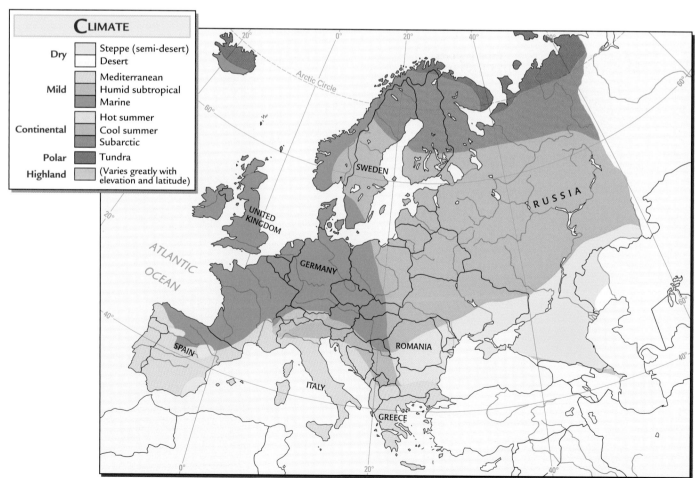

CLIMATE

Dry		Steppe (semi-desert)
		Desert
Mild		Mediterranean
		Humid subtropical
		Marine
Continental		Hot summer
		Cool summer
		Subarctic
Polar		Tundra
Highland		(Varies greatly with elevation and latitude)

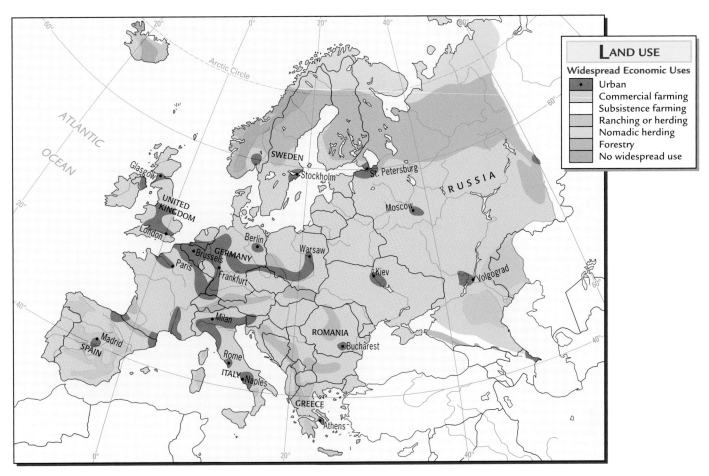

LAND USE

Widespread Economic Uses

- Urban
- Commercial farming
- Subsistence farming
- Ranching or herding
- Nomadic herding
- Forestry
- No widespread use

BALANCE OF TRADE
EUROPEAN UNION

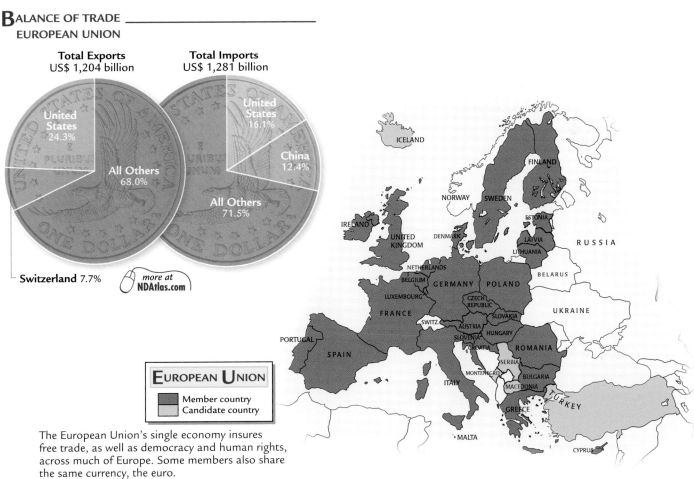

Total Exports
US$ 1,204 billion

Total Imports
US$ 1,281 billion

United States 24.3%

All Others 68.0%

Switzerland 7.7%

more at NDAtlas.com

United States 16.1%

China 12.4%

All Others 71.5%

EUROPEAN UNION

- Member country
- Candidate country

The European Union's single economy insures free trade, as well as democracy and human rights, across much of Europe. Some members also share the same currency, the euro.

ENERGY RESOURCES AND METALS

- Coal
- Oil (petroleum)
- Natural gas
- ⊕ Uranium
- ◆ Aluminum (bauxite)
- ■ Copper
- ○ Gold
- ✦ Iron
- ▼ Lead
- ★ Manganese
- ◆ Nickel
- ▲ Silver
- ✚ Tin
- ✳ Zinc

Geothermal power, energy from the earth's heat, can generate electricity with little pollution. This geothermal power plant in Iceland is located on a plate boundary, near a volcano. About half of Iceland's energy is geothermal.

SOURCES OF EUROPEAN ELECTRICITY

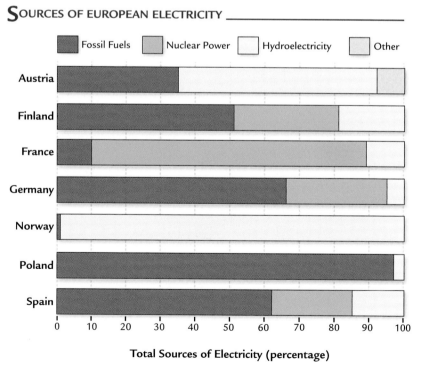

Legend: Fossil Fuels · Nuclear Power · Hydroelectricity · Other

Countries: Austria, Finland, France, Germany, Norway, Poland, Spain

Total Sources of Electricity (percentage)

Due to local resources and government priorities, European countries stress different methods of meeting their energy needs. Even so, most European countries make use of more than one energy source.

NATURAL POPULATION GROWTH EUROPE

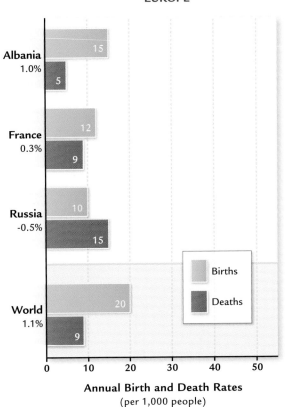

Albania
1.0%
- 15 (Births)
- 5 (Deaths)

France
0.3%
- 12 (Births)
- 9 (Deaths)

Russia
-0.5%
- 10 (Births)
- 15 (Deaths)

World
1.1%
- 20 (Births)
- 9 (Deaths)

Births
Deaths

0 10 20 30 40 50

Annual Birth and Death Rates
(per 1,000 people)

MAJOR HIGHWAYS AND AIRPORTS

Europe's highways and airports are concentrated in western Europe, where the population density and wealth are highest. Compare this map with similar maps on pages 60 and 80.

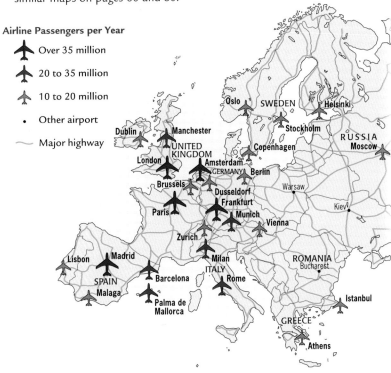

Airline Passengers per Year

✈ Over 35 million

✈ 20 to 35 million

✈ 10 to 20 million

• Other airport

〜 Major highway

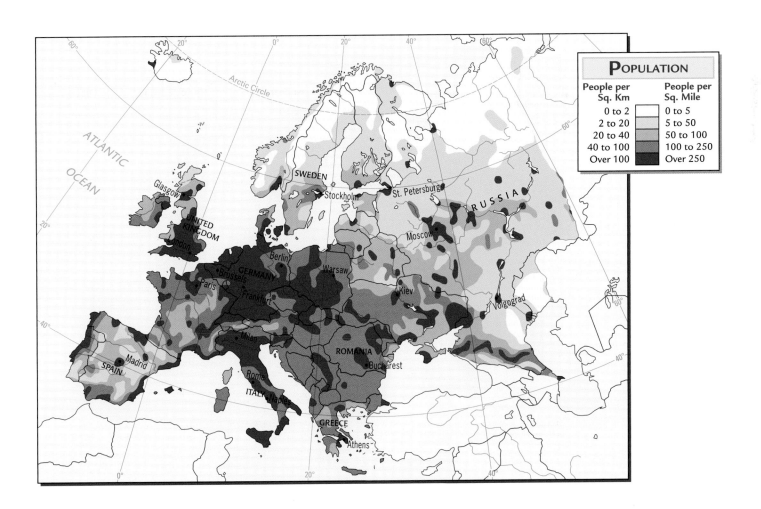

POPULATION

People per Sq. Km	People per Sq. Mile
0 to 2	0 to 5
2 to 20	5 to 50
20 to 40	50 to 100
40 to 100	100 to 250
Over 100	Over 250

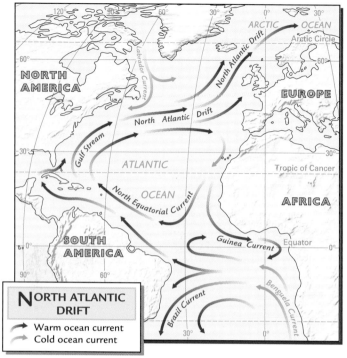

NORTH ATLANTIC DRIFT

→ Warm ocean current
→ Cold ocean current

The North Atlantic Drift is responsible for the mild climate of western and northern Europe. It relays the warm currents and winds of the Gulf Stream to the continent. Increasing amounts of cold meltwater from Greenland's ice cap, though, could block its eastward flow.

CLIMOGRAPHS

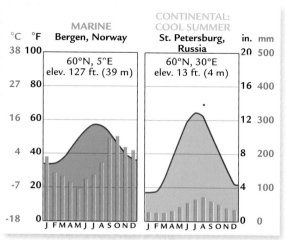

Bergen and St. Petersburg share the same latitude. However, the North Atlantic Drift keeps Bergen, on the Atlantic, warmer overall than St. Petersburg, which is much farther from the ocean.

more at NDAtlas.com

POLITICAL RELIEF MAP
BRITISH ISLES

City Symbols

London ● Over 1,000,000 people
Sheffield ● 500,000 to 1,000,000
Limerick • Under 500,000

Dublin ⊛ National capital

Scale
1:9,690,000

0   50   100   150   200 miles
1 in. to 153 mi.
0 50 100 150 200 kilometers
1 cm to 97 km

Detailed legend on page 6   Bonne Projection

Ireland, one of the British Isles, is divided between the country of Ireland and the land of Northern Ireland, which is part of the United Kingdom. These parade-goers are celebrating St. Patrick's Day in Belfast, Northern Ireland.

Continues on page 146

POLITICAL RELIEF MAP
NORTHERN EUROPE

City Symbols

Hamburg ● Over 1,000,000 people
Stockholm ● 500,000 to 1,000,000
Bergen • Under 500,000
Helsinki ⊛ National capital

Scale
1:9,640,000

| 0 | 50 | 100 | 150 | 200 miles |

1 in. to 152 mi.

| 0 | 50 | 100 | 150 | 200 kilometers |

1 cm to 96 km

Detailed legend on page 6   Bonne Projection

Continues on page 148
Continues on page 147

ARCTIC OCEAN
Barents Sea
Hammerfest
North Cape
Vadso
Varanger Fiord
70°N
Tromso
Pechenga
Severomorsk
Murmansk
Harstad
Lapland
Monchegorsk
Apatity
Kirovsk
Kola Peninsula
Narvik
Kiruna
Lofoten Is.
Torne R.
Muonio R.
Bodo
Lake Inari
ARCTIC CIRCLE 66½°N
Mo i Rana
Lule R.
Rovaniemi
65°N
Trondheim Fiord
Kjolen Mts.
Lulea
Kem
65°N
Omega Bay
Norwegian Sea
Skelleftea
Oulu
White Sea
Molde
Alesund
Trondheim
Ume R.
Umea
Kajaani
FINLAND
Peninsula
Indals R.
Ornskoldsvik
Kokkola
Joensuu
Ostersund
NORWAY
Galdhopiggen
8,100 ft (2469 m) △
Scandinavian
Sundsvall
Vaasa
Lake Region
Petrozavodsk
Sogne Fiord
Lillehammer
Hamar
SWEDEN
Osterdal R.
Jyvaskyla
L. Saimaa
Bergen
Gjovik
Gavle
Tampere
Pori
Imatra
Lake Ladoga
60°N
Hardanger Fiord
Klar R.
Hameenlinna
Lahti
Lappeenranta
Vyborg
Svir R.
Oslo
Drammen
Moss
Turku
Kotka
St. Petersburg
60°N
Stavanger
Sandnes
Skien
Fredrikstad
Uppsala
Espoo
Helsinki
Kolpino
Bohna Fiord
Arendal
Larvik
Vasteras
Aland Is. (Finland)
Gulf of Finland
Narva
RUSSIA
Cape Lindesnes (The Naze)
Kristiansand
Karlstad
Orebro
Eskilstuna
Stockholm
Tallinn
Kohtla-Jarve
Velikiy Novgorod
Skagerrak
L. Malaren
Hiiumaa
ESTONIA
Lake Peipus
Lake Ilmen
Valdai Hills
North Sea
Goteborg
Gota Canal
Norrkoping
Parnu
Viljandi
Pskov
Lake Vanern
Linkoping
Saaremaa
Tartu
Alborg
Boras
Jonkoping
Visby
Gulf of Riga
Randers
Jutland
Gotaland
Kungsbacka
Halmstad
Vaxjo
Gotland
Ventspils
LATVIA
Arhus
Kattegat
Kalmar
Oland
Riga
W. Dvina R.
Velikiye Luki
DENMARK
Helsingborg
Lund
Liepaja
Jelgava
Esbjerg
Kolding
Copenhagen
Rezekne
Odense
Fyn
Sjaelland
Malmo
Klaipeda
Siauliai
Daugavpils
European Plain
Kiel Canal
Bornholm (Denmark)
Panevezys
Vitsyebsk
Baltic Sea
LITHUANIA
Hamburg
Lubeck
Kiel
Rugen
Gdynia
Gulf of Gdansk
Kaliningrad *(to Russia)*
Kaunas
Vilnius
BELARUS
Smolensk
Bremen
Rostock
Neman R.
Chernyakhovsk
Alytus
Dnieper R.
Orsha
GERMANY
Szczecin
POLAND
Northern
Olsztyn
Hrodna
Lida
Minsk
Mahilyow
Elbe R.

The Center of Things

The Prime Meridian is the line of longitude at 0°. Unlike the Equator, the Prime Meridian could be located anywhere. An international conference in 1884 decided that the Prime Meridian should pass through the Royal Greenwich Observatory in London (see map at left).

Continues on page 144
Continues on page 145
Continues on page 147

15°W
10°W
5°W
0°
5°E

Galway • Dublin
Leeds •
North Sea
Frisian Is.
Groningen

Tralee •
IRELAND
Liverpool • Sheffield •
The Wash
NETHERLANDS
Bremen

Limerick •
UNITED
Birmingham • Leicester Coventry •
Norwich •
Amsterdam
Ijsselmeer
Bielefeld

Waterford •
KINGDOM
The Hague •
Utrecht •
Arnhem •
Dortmund

Cork •
British
Cardiff • Bristol •
London
Rotterdam •
Essen •
Dusseldorf •

Isles
Bristol Channel
Thames R.
Dover •
Antwerp •
Cologne •

St. George's Channel
Celtic Sea
Southampton • Portsmouth •
Calais •
Ghent •
Brussels
Liege •
GERMANY

Plymouth •
Strait of Dover
Lille •
BELGIUM
Frankfurt •

Land's End
English Channel
Amiens •
St. Quentin •
LUXEMBOURG
Luxembourg
Mannheim •

Cherbourg •
Le Havre •
Rouen •
Reims •
Metz •
Nancy •
Strasbourg •

50°N
Channel Is. (U.K.)
Gulf of St. Malo
Caen •
Seine
Paris
Paris Basin
Marne River
Meuse R.
Rhine River
Black Forest

Brest •
Normandy
St. Malo •
Versailles •
Chartres •
Le Mans •
Dijon •
Saône R.
Vosges Mts.
Basel •
SWITZ.

Brittany
Rennes •
Orleans •
Besancon •
Jura Mts.
Bern •
Lake Geneva

Angers •
Loire River
Tours •
FRANCE
Mulhouse •

Nantes •
Geneva •

Bay of Biscay
La Rochelle •
Vichy •
Lyon •
Mt. Blanc 15,771 ft. (4807 m)
Turin •
ALPS

45°N
Limoges •
Clermont-Ferrand •
Allier R.
St. Etienne •
Grenoble •
45°N

Bordeaux •
Aquitaine
Garonne R.
Massif Central
ITALY

Basin
Dordogne R.
Rhone River
Nimes •
Avignon •
MONACO
Riviera

Cevennes
Toulouse •
Montpellier •
Aix-en-Provence •
Nice •

A Coruna •
Gijon • Santander •
San Sebastian •
Pau •
Carcassonne •
Narbonne •
Marseille •
Toulon •

Cape Finisterre
Oviedo •
Cantabrian Mts.
Bilbao •
Pyrenees
ANDORRA
Gulf of Lion

Vigo •
Mino R.
Leon •
Vitoria-Gasteiz •
Andorra la Vella
Perpignan •

ATLANTIC OCEAN
Ourense •
Valladolid •
Zaragoza •
Ebro River
Catalonia
Barcelona

Braga •
PORTUGAL
Salamanca •
Sierra de Guadarrama
Tarragona •

40°N
Porto •
Douro R.
Duero River
Sierra de Gredos
Madrid
Balearic Sea
Minorca •
N
40°N

Coimbra •
Tagus R.
Palma • Majorca
Balearic Is. (Spain)

Lisbon
Setubal •
Cacares •
SPAIN
Valencia •

Badajoz •
Guadiana R.
Jucar R.
Ibiza •

Iberian
Albacete •

Peninsula
Elche •
Mediterranean Sea

Sierra Morena
Murcia •
Alicante •

Cape St. Vincent
Huelva •
Cordoba •

Guadalquivir R.
Granada •
Cartagena •

Seville
Sierra Nevada
Almeria •
Algiers •
Bejaia •

Cadiz •
Malaga •
Gibraltar (U.K.)
Oran •
ALGERIA
Constantine •

Strait of Gibraltar
Ceuta (Spain)
AFRICA

35°N
Tangier •
Tetouan •
Melilla (Spain)
Batna •
35°N

MOROCCO
Oran •

10°W
0°
5°E

Continues on page 126

POLITICAL RELIEF MAP
WESTERN EUROPE

City Symbols
Barcelona ● Over 1,000,000 people
Marseille ● 500,000 to 1,000,000
Porto ● Under 500,000
Paris ⊛ National capital

Scale
1:10,400,000

0 50 100 150 200 miles
1 in. to 164 mi.

0 50 100 150 200 kilometers
1 cm to 104 km

Detailed legend on page 6
Bonne Projection

ETHNIC COMPOSITION

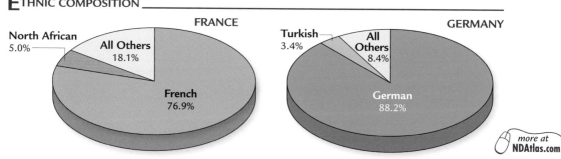

FRANCE

North African 5.0%
All Others 18.1%
French 76.9%

GERMANY

Turkish 3.4%
All Others 8.4%
German 88.2%

more at NDAtlas.com

Continues on page 145

POLITICAL RELIEF MAP
CENTRAL EUROPE

City Symbols
Milan • Over 1,000,000 people
Bremen • 500,000 to 1,000,000
Salzburg • Under 500,000
Warsaw ⊛ National capital

Scale
1:10,900,000
0   75   150   225   300 miles
1 in. to 173 mi.
0   75   150   225   300 kilometers
1 cm to 109 km

Detailed legend on page 6   Bonne Projection

5°E 10°E 15°E 20°E 25°E 30°E

North Sea

Skagerrak

Goteborg Jonkoping Visby Gotland EST.

SWEDEN Gotaland LATVIA

Alborg Kalmar Oland Riga W. Dvina R.

Randers Arhus Kattegat Liepaja Daugavpils

Jutland Helsingborg Lund Siauliai

DENMARK Copenhagen Malmo Klaipeda LITHUANIA

Esbjerg Odense Fyn Sjaelland Bornholm (Denmark) Kaunas Vilnius

Kiel Canal Rugen Neman R. (to Russia) BELARUS

Frisian Is. Hamburg Kiel Lubeck Rostock Gdynia Gulf of Gdansk Kaliningrad

NETH. Bremerhaven Szczecin Gdansk Elblag

Amsterdam Bremen Hannover Brandenburg Bydgoszcz Torun Olsztyin Bialystok

Ijsselmeer The Hague Bielefeld Braunschweig Berlin Warta R. Vistula R.

Rotterdam Munster Magdeburg Potsdam Poznan Wloclawek POLAND Warsaw

Essen Dortmund Halle Leipzig Oder R. Kalisz Lodz Radom Lublin

Aachen Dusseldorf Kassel Erfurt Dresden Wroclaw Kielce Ostrowiec

Brussels Bonn Cologne Chemitz Czestochowa Bug R.

BELGIUM Wiesbaden GERMANY Ore Mts. Katowice Rzeszow

LUXEMBOURG Frankfurt Prague Vistula R. Krakow

Luxembourg Bayreuth Plzen CZECH Ostrava 50°N Carpathian

Mannheim Nuremberg Bohemia REPUBLIC Brno Moravia Kosice

Metz Strasbourg Stuttgart Danube R. SLOVAKIA UKRAINE

FRANCE Vosges Mts. Black Forest Bavaria Augsburg Linz Bratislava Miskolc Debrecen Satu Mare Iasi Chisinau

Saone R. Rhine River Ulm Munich Salzburg Vienna Gyor Oradea Cluj-Napoca MOL.

Basel Zurich AUSTRIA Budapest HUNGARY Targu Mures

SWITZERLAND Bern LIECHTENSTEIN Innsbruck Klagenfurt Graz Great Hungarian Plain Arad ROMANIA

Geneva Jura Mts. Bolzano ALPS Lake Balaton Szeged Timisoara Mures R.

Mt. Blanc Trento Ljubljana Maribor Pecs Subotica Brasov Galati

15,771 ft. (4807 m) Brescia SLOVENIA Drava R. Novi Sad Transylvanian Alps Braila

Grenoble Verona Trieste Zagreb Osijek Belgrade Drobeta-Turnu Severin Ploiesti

Milan Turin Padua Venice Rijeka Sava R. CROATIA SERBIA Pitesti Bucharest

Genoa Parma Ferrara Dinaric Banja Luka Craiova Olt R. Ruse Dobrich

La Spezia Modena Bologna BOSNIA- Kragujevac Morava R. Constanta

Nice Carrara Pisa Rimini Zadar HERZEGOVINA Cacak BULGARIA Varna

MONACO Livorno Florence Sarajevo Nis Sofia Sliven Burgas

Corsica (France) Perugia Ancona Split Mostar MONTENEGRO Pristina Balkan Mts. Stara Zagora Black Sea

Bastia Elba (Italy) Pescara Dubrovnik KOSOVO Peninsula Plovdiv Maritsa R. Edirne

Ajaccio VATICAN CITY Podgorica Tetovo Skopje Rhodope Mts. Istanbul

Rome ITALY Foggia ALBANIA MACEDONIA Serrai Kavala Thrace TURKEY Bursa

Sassari Bari Durres Tirana Bitola Thessaloniki Thasos Balikesir

Mt. Vesuvius 4,190 ft. (1277 m) Brindisi Korce Florina Samothrace ASIA

Naples Salerno Taranto Vlore Katerini Gokceada Limnos Manisa

Sardinia (Italy) Gulf of Taranto Mt. Olympus 9,570 ft. (2917 m) Larisa Volos Aegean Sea Izmir

Cagliari Cosenza Corfu Ioannina Northern Sporades Lesbos

Tyrrhenian Sea Catanzaro Ionian Is. Agrinion GREECE Euboea Sea Chios

Palermo Lipari Is. Khalkis Samos Cyclades

Messina Reggio di Calabria Patrai Athens Dodecanese

Mt. Etna 10,902 ft. (3323 m) Catania Piraeus Rhodes

Annaba Pantelleria (Italy) Sicily (Italy) Peloponnesus Rhodes (Greece)

Tunis MALTA Valletta Kalamai Khania Iraklion

ALGERIA AFRICA Lampedusa (Italy) Ionian Sea Crete (Greece)

Susah TUNISIA Mediterranean Sea

Sfax

Continues on page 146

Continues on page 148

Continues on page 164

POLITICAL RELIEF MAP
EASTERN EUROPE

City Symbols

Kazan ● Over 1,000,000 people
Lviv ● 500,000 to 1,000,000
Vologda • Under 500,000
Minsk ⊛ National capital

Scale
1:14,600,000

0   75   150   225   300 miles

1 in. to 230 mi.

0   75 150 225 300 kilometers

1 cm to 146 km

Detailed legend on page 6   Bonne Projection

Continues on page 145
Continues on page 147
Continues on pages 152–153
Continues on page 165

30°E   35°E   40°E   45°E   50°E   55°E

Vadso
Varanger Fiord
70°N
Pechenga
Barents   *Sea*
Kolguyev I.
Vaigach I.
Murmansk
Kanin
Pen.
Salekhard
Monchegorsk
Chesha
Bay
70°E
Apatity Kirovsk **Kola**
Peninsula
ARCTIC CIRCLE 66½°N
Pechora Basin
Inta
65°E
Kem
Pechora R.
A S I A
Ob River
Mt. Narodnaya
6,217 ft. (1895 m)
Severodvinsk
Arkhangelsk
Ukhta
White
Sea
Onega Bay
Mezen R.
Zheleznodorozhny
Syktyvkar
60°N
Kokkola
Onega R.
Northern Dvina R.
Konzakovski Kamen
5148 ft. (1569 m)
60°E
FINLAND
Kuopio
Lake
Region
Petrozavodsk
Kotlas
Vychegda R.
Serov
Jyvaskyla   Pori
Tampere
Lake
Onega
Northern Uvals
Berezniki
55°E
Aland Is.
(Finland)
Lahti
Lake
Ladoga
R U S S I A
Kamskoye
Reservoir
Nizhniy
Tagil
Turku Espoo Helsinki
Vyborg
Kirov
Kama
Upland
Perm
Stockholm
Gulf of Finland
Narva
St. Petersburg
Vologda
Cherepovets
Izhevsk
Yekaterinburg
Hiiumaa Tallinn
Velikiy
Novgorod
Rybinsk
Reservoir
Kostroma
Kazan
Naberezhnyye
Chelny
ESTONIA Tartu
Lake
Peipus
Lake
Ilmen
Yaroslavl
Gorki
Reservoir
Nizhniy
Novgorod
55°N
Saaremaa
Parnu
Pskov
Tver
Ivanovo
Cheboksary
Volga R.
Ufa
Gulf of
Riga
Riga
Valdai Hills
Vladimir Dzerzhinsk
Magnitogorsk
60°E
Liepaja
LATVIA
Velikiye
Luki
Volga R.
⊛ **Moscow**
Saransk
Ulyanovsk
Kuybyshev
Reservoir
Salavat
Klaipeda
Siauliai
W. Dvina R.
Daugavpils
Ryazan
Ural Mts.
LITHUANIA
Smolensk
Tula
Penza
Samara
Neman R.
Kaunas
Vitsyebsk
Kaluga
Oka-Don
Tolyatti
(to Russia)
Kaliningrad
⊛ **Vilnius**
Dnieper R.
Mahilyow
Central
Orel
Lowland
Tambov
Plain
Orenburg
Hrodna
⊛ **Minsk**
Bryansk
Russian
Lipetsk
Volga Upland
Saratov
Oral
Orsk
POLAND
Bialystok
Baranavichy Babruysk
Homyel
Upland
Kursk
Voronezh
Volga River
Volga Upland
KAZAKHSTAN
⊛ **Warsaw**
Brest
Pripyat
Marshes
Chernihiv
Belgorod
S   *t*
Volgograd
Reservoir
Aqtobe
Lublin
Pinsk
Pripyat
Desna
Kiev
Kiev
Reservoir
Kharkiv
e   *p*   *p*   *e*   *s*
Ural River
50°N
Bug R.
Rivne
Zhytomyr
Dnieper R.
Poltava
Don River
Tsimlyansk
Reservoir
Atyrau
Lviv
Ternopil
UKRAINE
Kremenchuk
Reservoir
Kremenchuk
Donets R.
Don R.
Depression
Uzhhorod
Vinnytsya
Cherkasy
Lowland
Pivdennyy Buh R.
Dniprohes Dam
Dnieper R.
Dnipropetrovsk
Volgograd
Chernivtsi
Kirovohrad
Donetsk
Luhansk
Astrakhan
Carpathian
Dniester River
Prut R.
Kryvyy Rih
Volga River
MOLDOVA
Chisinau
Mykolayiv
Zaporizhzhya Taganrog
KAZAKHSTAN
Mountains
Cluj-
Napoca
Iasi
Tiraspol
Black Sea Lowland
Kakhovka
Reservoir
Mariupol
Rostov-na-Donu
45°N
ROMANIA
Brasov
Transylvanian Alps
Galati
Odessa
Kherson
Sea of Azov
Astrakhan
Caspian
A S I A
Ploiesti
Braila
Crimean
Peninsula
Kerch
Kuban R.
Stavropol
Pitesti Craiova
Danube
River
Delta
Simferopol
Sevastopol
Strait of Kerch
Krasnodar
Maykop
Aqtau
⊛ **Bucharest**
Yalta
Novorossiysk
Caucasus
Olt R.
Danube R.
Ruse
Constanta
Sochi
Mt. Elbrus
18,510 ft. (5642 m)
Terek R.
Groznyy
Makhachkala
55°E
BULGARIA
Varna
Black
Sea
Vladikavkaz
Chechnya
Derbent
Balkan Mts.
Stara Zagora
Burgas
N
Abkhazia
Mountains
Garabogazkol
Aylagy
Marista R.
Plovdiv
South
Ossetia
Caspian
Sea
Rhodope Mts.
Batumi
GEORGIA
Kur R.
TURKMENISTAN
Istanbul
Thrace
Zonguldak
Samsun
Tbilisi
40°N
GREECE
Izmit
Trabzon
Pontic Mountains
ARMENIA **AZERBAIJAN** ⊛ **Baku**
25°E
40°N
Bursa
30°E
TURKEY
35°E
40°E
Yerevan
50°E

Continues on page 164   Continues on page 149

Russia is the world's largest country—nearly twice the size of Canada. Russia stretches across Europe and Asia from the Baltic Sea to the Pacific Ocean and from the Arctic Ocean to the Black and Caspian Seas. Asian Russia is often called "Siberia."

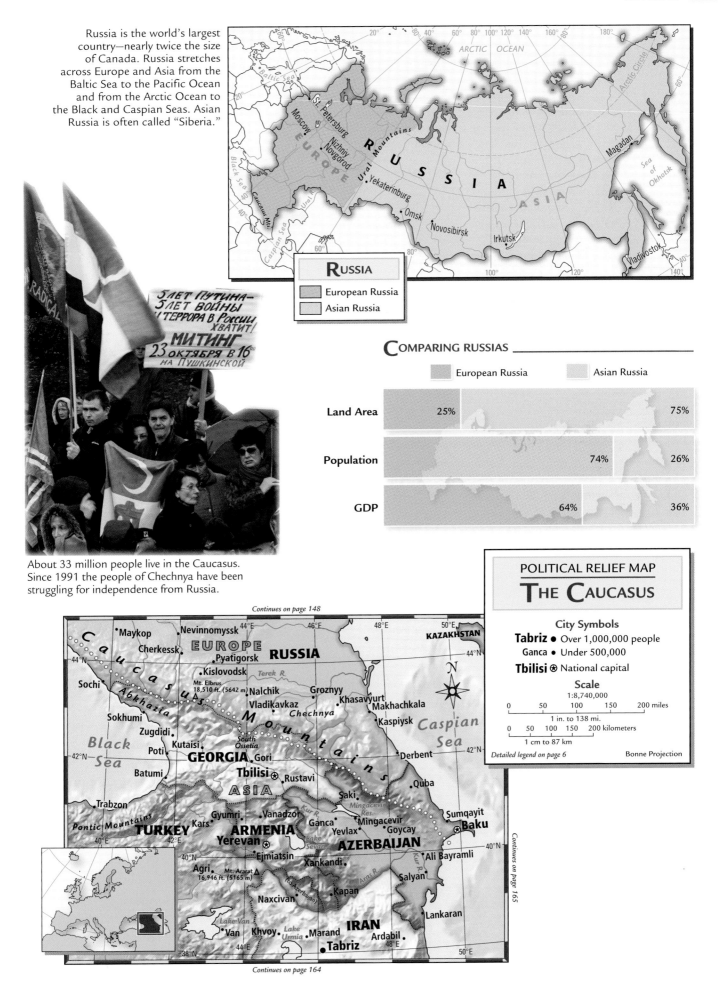

RUSSIA

- European Russia
- Asian Russia

COMPARING RUSSIAS

- European Russia
- Asian Russia

	European Russia	Asian Russia
Land Area	25%	75%
Population	74%	26%
GDP	64%	36%

About 33 million people live in the Caucasus. Since 1991 the people of Chechnya have been struggling for independence from Russia.

POLITICAL RELIEF MAP
THE CAUCASUS

City Symbols

Tabriz ● Over 1,000,000 people

Ganca ● Under 500,000

Tbilisi ⊗ National capital

Scale

1:8,740,000

| 0 | 50 | 100 | 150 | 200 miles |

1 in. to 138 mi.

| 0 | 50 | 100 | 150 | 200 kilometers |

1 cm to 87 km

Detailed legend on page 6   Bonne Projection

Continues on page 148

Continues on page 165

Continues on page 164

ISSUES ◀▶ TODAY

What should be done about industrial pollution?

Europe has been the home of modern industry since the 1700s. One of Europe's primary concerns is the harm to forests, buildings, and health caused by industrial pollution.

However, measures that reduce industry's environmental impact are often costly and disruptive. How can governments deal with the problem? There are many perspectives on this issue. Here are two of them.

DAMAGED FORESTS
Percentage of Trees Damaged

- 40 or more
- 30 to 40
- 20 to 30
- 10 to 20
- Under 10
- No data

Industry must be regulated to protect the environment.

- Europe is responsible for one-third of the world's greenhouse gas emissions. At least 20 percent of Europe's emissions are caused by industry.

- In prosperous years, the manufacturing industry in Europe increases the amount of greenhouse gases in the atmosphere by over 17 million tons.

- Environmental policies have improved air quality throughout Europe. Emissions of sulphur dioxide have decreased by 50 percent, of nitrogen oxide by 19 percent, and of ozone-producing gases by 14 percent.

- In 1952 London smog of soot, sulfur dioxide, and nitrous oxides killed over 4,000 people in just four days. Pollution controls have reduced this danger, but about 37 million Europeans are still exposed to dangerous levels of pollution at least once a year.

- A cleaner environment not only benefits future generations, it also improves our current quality of life.

An estimated 57 percent of the trees in forests in the Czech Republic have been damaged by acid rain. Yet the Czech Republic produces even more acid rain than it receives from prevailing winds.

Environmental laws must not suppress economic growth.

- If environmental laws force companies to purchase expensive environmental technology, goods become more expensive. This gives goods produced in countries with weaker environmental regulations an advantage.

- Major shifts in environmental policy can seriously disrupt the economy and society. Eastern Europe has suffered serious unemployment as governments have tried to adopt EU environmental standards.

- Europe's steel industry, a major source of industrial pollution, employs about 300,000 people. It produces 160 million tons of steel each year, valued at more than 70 billion euros (US$ 88 billion).

- Industry is no longer the major contributor to air pollution in Europe. Agriculture produces more than twice the amount of acid rain pollutants, while employing less than one-sixth as many people as industry does.

SOURCES OF ACID RAIN POLLUTION

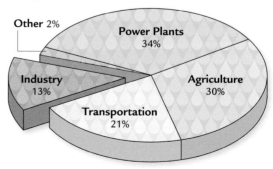

- Other 2%
- Power Plants 34%
- Industry 13%
- Agriculture 30%
- Transportation 21%

Acid rain pollutants, such as sulfur oxides and nitrogen oxides, come primarily from the burning of gasoline, oil, and coal.

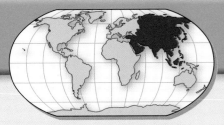

ASIA

Asia, which shares a landmass with Europe, is the largest and most populous continent. It is home to over half of the world's population.

PHYSICAL FEATURES

Mountains
Highest peak: Mt. Everest 29,035 ft. (8 850 m) ★

Longest ranges: Himalayas 1,500 mi. (2 400 km)

Ural Mountains* 1,500 mi. (2 400 km)

Largest Island
Borneo 287,000 sq. mi. (743 330 sq. km)

Lakes
Largest: Caspian Sea* 143,300 sq. mi. (371 000 sq. km) ★

Lake Baikal 12,200 sq. mi. (31 500 sq. km) ★

Deepest: Lake Baikal 5,315 ft. deep (1 620 m)

Longest Rivers
Yangtze 3,915 mi. (6 300 km) ★

Yenisey 3,442 mi. (5 540 km) ★

Other Key Physical Features
West Siberian Plain Plateau of Iran
Plateau of Tibet Arabian Peninsula
Central Siberian Plateau Indochina Peninsula

CULTURAL FEATURES

Population 3,957,700,000

Largest Countries
By area: Russia* 6,592,800 sq. mi. (17 075 400 sq. km) ★

China 3,696,100 sq. mi. (9 572 900 sq. km) ★

By population: China 1,313,973,713
India 1,095,351,995

Population Density
Most densely populated: Singapore 16,699.4 people per sq. mi. (6 455.0 per sq. km)

Least densely populated: Mongolia 4.7 people per sq. mi. (1.8 per sq. km)

Largest Urban Areas
Tokyo, Japan 36,669,000 ★

Delhi, India 22,157,000 ★

★ Among the world's largest. See the inside front cover.

* Located in both Europe and Asia.

more at NDAtlas.com
For more maps, graphs, and photos of Asia, go to **NystromDeskAtlas.com**.

AREA COMPARISON

Asia
16,992,000 sq. mi.
(44 009 000 sq. km)

Contiguous United States
3,021,295 sq. mi.
(7 825 112 sq. km)

 World Extreme The Dead Sea is located in southwestern Asia between Israel and Jordan. At 1,365 feet (416 meters) below sea level, the Dead Sea coast is the lowest land on Earth. The sea itself is also the world's saltiest body of water, about nine times saltier than the oceans.

REGIONAL MAPS OF ASIA

① **Southwestern Asia** • page 164

② **Central Asia** • page 165

③ **Southern Asia** • page 166

④ **Southeastern Asia** • page 167

⑤ **Eastern Asia:** *China, Mongolia, and Taiwan* • page 168

⑥ **Eastern Asia:** *Japan and the Koreas* • page 169

RUSSIA

TURKEY

KAZAKHSTAN

MONGOLIA

JAPAN

IRAN

CHINA

SAUDI ARABIA

INDIA

PHILIPPINES

INDONESIA

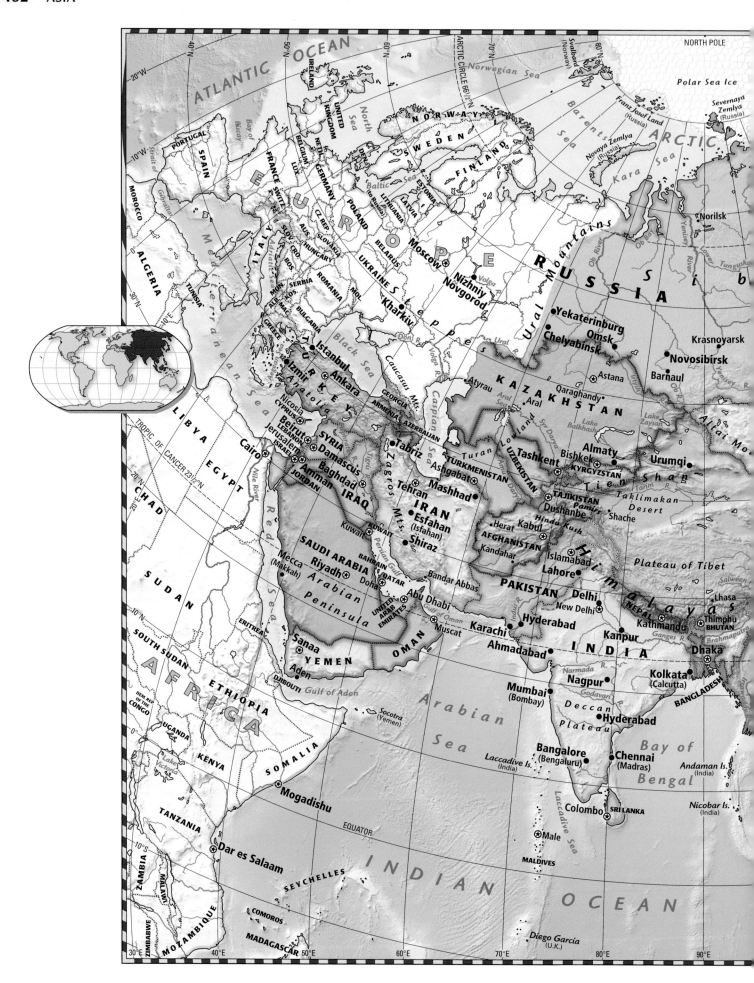

POLITICAL RELIEF MAP

ASIA

Boundary Symbols

.... International boundary

.... Other boundary
(disputed or undefined)

▣ Small country

City Symbols

Karachi ● Over 1,000,000 people

Vladivostok ● 500,000 to 1,000,000

Aral • Under 500,000

Tokyo ⊗ National capital

Scale

1:43,100,000

| 0 | 250 | 500 | 750 | 1000 miles |

1 in. to 680 mi.

| 0 | 250 | 500 | 750 | 1000 kilometers |

1 cm to 431 km

Detailed legend on page 6   Lambert Equal Area Projection

OCEAN

Laptev
Sea

New Siberian Is.
(Russia)

East
Siberian
Sea

Wrangel I.
(Russia)

ARCTIC CIRCLE 66½°N

Gulf of
Anadyr

Bering
Sea

Aleutian Is.
(U.S.)

INTERNATIONAL DATE LINE

Tiksi

Verkhoyansk

Indigirka R.

Kolyma R.

Magadan

Petropavlovsk-
Kamchatskiy

Kamchatka

Commander Is.

Olenek R.

Lena R.

Yakutsk

Siberia

Sea of
Okhotsk

Sakhalin I.

Bratsk Res.

Lake
Baikal

Irkutsk

Chita

Amur River

Khabarovsk

Sapporo

Kuril Islands
(Russia)

PACIFIC

MONGOLIA

⊗ Ulaanbaatar

Gobi

Qiqihar

Harbin

Jilin

Songhua R.

Changchun

Fushun

Vladivostok

Sea of
Japan
(East Sea)

JAPAN

● Sendai

OCEAN

Mountains

Shenyang

NORTH KOREA

Pyongyang

Tokyo

Beijing ⊗

Huang He

Bo Hai

Dalian

SOUTH KOREA

Seoul

Kyoto

Osaka Yokohama

20°N

Tianjin

Qingdao

Yellow R.

Pusan

Korea Strait

Fukuoka

Hiroshima

TROPIC OF CANCER 23½°N

MARSHALL
ISLANDS

Taiyuan

Yellow
Sea

Grand

Bonin Is.
(Japan)

170°E

Qinghai
Lake

Lanzhou

Xian

Nanjing

Canal

Shanghai

East
China
Sea

Volcano Is.
(Japan)

10°N

CHINA

Chengdu

Yangtze R.

Wuhan

Hangzhou

Dongting L.

Poyang
Lake

Fuzhou

Ryukyu Islands (Japan)

Northern
Mariana
Islands
(U.S.)

Chongqing

Taipei

Guam
(U.S.)

Kunming

Xi Jiang

Guangzhou

TAIWAN

Taiwan Strait

Luzon
Strait

Mekong R.

Mandalay

Hanoi

Macau

Hong
Kong

Philippine

**MYANMAR
(BURMA)**

LAOS

Gulf of
Tonkin

Sea

FEDERATED STATES OF MICRONESIA

Nay Pyi Taw

Vientiane (Viangchan)

VIETNAM

Quezon City

Yangon
(Rangoon)

Salween R.

Da Nang

Manila

PHILIPPINES

EQUATOR

0°

THAILAND

Indochina

Spratly Is.
(disputed)

Cebu

PALAU

Peninsula

Andaman
Sea

Bangkok

CAMBODIA

Phnom Penh ⊗

Davao

SOLOMON
ISLANDS

Ho Chi
Minh
City

Sulu
Sea

Gulf of
Thailand

Bandar Seri
Begawan

Celebes
Sea

Songkhla

Str. of Malacca

BRUNEI ⊗

Manado

Jayapura

PAPUA NEW GUINEA

Solomon
Sea

South China Sea

M A L A Y S I A

Sibu

Coral
Sea

Medan

⊗ Kuala Lumpur

SINGAPORE

10°S

Pontianak

Padang

Banjarmasin

I N D O N E S I A

Arafura
Sea

Gulf of
Carpentaria

AUSTRALIA

AUSTRALIA

Palembang

Jakarta

Java Sea

Makassar

Banda Sea

Semarang

**EAST
TIMOR**

Dili

20°S

Bandung ⊗

Surabaya

Kupang

Timor Sea

100°E   110°E   120°E   130°E   140°E   150°E   160°E

NORTH POLE

ATLANTIC OCEAN

Polar Sea Ice

ARCTIC OCEAN

ARCTIC

Norwegian Sea

Svalbard

Franz Josef Land

Severnaya Zemlya

North Cape

Barents Sea

Novaya Zemlya

Kolguyev I.

Kara Sea

Taymyr Peninsula

Gydan Pen.

Yamal Pen.

Yenisey River

Central Siberian Plateau

Lower Tunguska

North Sea

SWEDEN

FINLAND

NORWAY

IRELAND

UNITED KINGDOM

Baltic Sea

ESTONIA

LATVIA

LITHUANIA

DENMARK

NETH.

BELGIUM

GERMANY

FRANCE

LUX.

SWITZ.

CZ. REP.

SLOVAKIA

HUNGARY

POLAND

BELARUS

UKRAINE

AUS.

SLOVENIA

ROMANIA

BOS. SERBIA

BULGARIA

MONT. MAC.

ALB.

GREECE

ITALY

Adriatic Sea

PORTUGAL

SPAIN

Bay of Biscay

Strait of Gibraltar

MOROCCO

ALGERIA

TUNISIA

Mediterranean Sea

EUROPE

Volga

Steppes

Don R.

Volga R.

RUSSIA

Ural R.

Ural Mountains

West Siberian Plain

Ob River

Ob Bay

Ob R.

Irtysh

SIBERIA

Boreal

Novosibirsk

Sayan

Yenisey R.

Caspian Depression

Black Sea

Caucasus Mts.

GEORGIA

ARMENIA

AZERBAIJAN

Caspian Sea

Aral Sea

KAZAKHSTAN

Kazakh Uplands

Lake Zaysan

Lake Balkhash

Dzungarian Basin

Altai Mts.

TURKEY

Ankara

Anatolia

CYPRUS

LEBANON

ISRAEL

SYRIA

Jerusalem

JORDAN

Euphrates R.

Tigris R.

IRAQ

Zagros Mts.

Turan Lowland

Syr Darya

TURKMENISTAN

Amu Darya

UZBEKISTAN

Tashkent

Almaty

KYRGYZSTAN

Tien Shan

Elburz Mts.

Tehran

IRAN

Plateau of Iran

Kara Kum (desert)

TAJIKISTAN

Pamirs

Tarim R.

Taklimakan Desert

LIBYA

EGYPT

Nile River

Sinai Pen.

Red Sea

An Nafud (desert)

SAUDI ARABIA

Arabian Peninsula

Mecca (Makkah)

Empty Quarter

KUWAIT

BAHRAIN

QATAR

Persian Gulf

UNITED ARAB EMIRATES

OMAN

Gulf of Oman

AFGHANISTAN

Hindu Kush

Mt. Godwin Austen (K2) 28,250 ft (8611 m)

Kunlun Mountains

Plateau of Tibet

Mt. Everest 29,035 ft (8850 m)

Salween R.

PAKISTAN

Indus R.

Great Indian Desert

Karachi

Himalayas

NEPAL

BHUTAN

Ganges Plain

INDIA

Ganges R.

Brahmaputra R.

BANGLADESH

Irrawaddy R.

CHAD

SUDAN

SOUTH SUDAN

ERITREA

YEMEN

Gulf of Aden

DJIBOUTI

ETHIOPIA

DEM. REP. OF THE CONGO

UGANDA

KENYA

Lake Victoria

SOMALIA

AFRICA

Socotra

Narmada R.

Mumbai (Bombay)

Godavari

Deccan Plateau

Western Ghats

Eastern Ghats

Kolkata (Calcutta)

Arabian Sea

Laccadive Islands

Laccadive Sea

Bay of Bengal

Andaman Islands

TANZANIA

ZAMBIA

MALAWI

ZIMBABWE

MOZAMBIQUE

MADAGASCAR

Comoros Is.

Amirante Isles

Seychelles

EQUATOR

INDIAN OCEAN

Maldive Islands

Sri Lanka

SRI LANKA

Nicobar Islands

Diego Garcia

20°W

10°W

0°

10°E

20°E

30°E

40°E

50°E

60°E

70°E

80°E

90°E

40°N

50°N

60°N

ARCTIC CIRCLE 66½°N

TROPIC OF CANCER 23½°N

30°N

20°N

10°N

0°

10°S

LAND COVER MAP
ASIA

Cropland Grassland Tundra Glacier

Semi-desert & desert Tropical rain forest Broadleaf forest Needleleaf forest

Boundary Symbols

—————— International boundary

---------- Other boundary (disputed or undefined)

▣ Small country

Scale
1:43,100,000

0 250 500 750 1000 miles

1 in. to 680 mi.

0 250 500 750 1000 kilometers

1 cm to 431 km

Detailed legend on page 6 Lambert Equal Area Projection

OCEAN

Laptev Sea

East Siberian Sea

New Siberian Is.

Wrangel I.

Gulf of Anadyr

Bering Sea

Olenek R.

Lena R.

Indigirka R.

East Siberian Uplands

Kolyma R.

Kolyma Range

ARCTIC CIRCLE 66½°N

Commander Is.

Aleutian Is.

Siberia

Forest

Dzhugdzhur Ra.

Sea of Okhotsk

Kamchatka Pen.

Lake Baikal

Bratsk Res.

Stanovoy Mts.

Yablonovyy Mts.

Amur River

Amur R.

Sakhalin I.

Kuril Islands

Mts.

Greater Khingan Range

Songhua R.

Manchurian Plain

Sikhote-Alin Mts.

Hokkaido

PACIFIC

MONGOLIA

Gobi

Vladivostok

Sea of Japan (East Sea)

JAPAN

Honshu

OCEAN

ntains

Huang He

Beijing

Yellow R.

Yalu R.

NORTH KOREA

SOUTH KOREA

Korean Pen.

Tokyo

Izu Islands

TROPIC OF CANCER 23½°N

Qilian Shan

Qinghai

Grand Canal

Bo Gulf

Yellow Sea

Korea Strait

Kyushu

Shikoku

Ryukyu Islands

Okinawa

Bonin Is.

Volcano Is.

Iwo To (Iwo Jima)

Marshall Islands

CHINA

North China Plain

Shanghai

East China Sea

Mariana Islands

Sichuan Basin

Yangtze R.

Yangtze R.

Poyang Lake

Dongting Lake

Taiwan Strait

TAIWAN

Taiwan

Guam

Chongqing

Yangtze R.

Danba Shan

Yunnan Plateau

Nan Range

Xi Jiang

Hong Kong

Luzon Strait

Philippine Sea

Caroline Islands

MYANMAR (BURMA)

Red R.

Gulf of Tonkin

Hainan

Philippine Sea

Palau Is.

LAOS

Mekong R.

VIETNAM

Luzon

PHILIPPINES

EQUATOR

THAILAND

Mt. Pinatubo 4,875 ft. (1486 m)

Manila

Admiralty Is.

New Ireland

Indochina Peninsula

Tonle Sap

Spratly Is.

Mindanao

New Britain

Andaman Sea

CAMBODIA

Ho Chi Minh City

Palawan

Sulu Sea

PAPUA NEW GUINEA

Solomon Sea

Malay Pen.

Gulf of Thailand

South China Sea

Celebes Sea

Halmahera

New Guinea

Str. of Malacca

MALAYSIA

BRUNEI

Sibu

Borneo

Sulawesi (Celebes)

Ceram

INDONESIA

Arafura Sea

Coral Sea

Sumatra

Java Sea

Banda Sea

Gulf of Carpentaria

AUSTRALIA

Jakarta

Java

Bali

Sumbawa

Flores

Sumba

EAST TIMOR

Timor

Timor Sea

AUSTRALIA

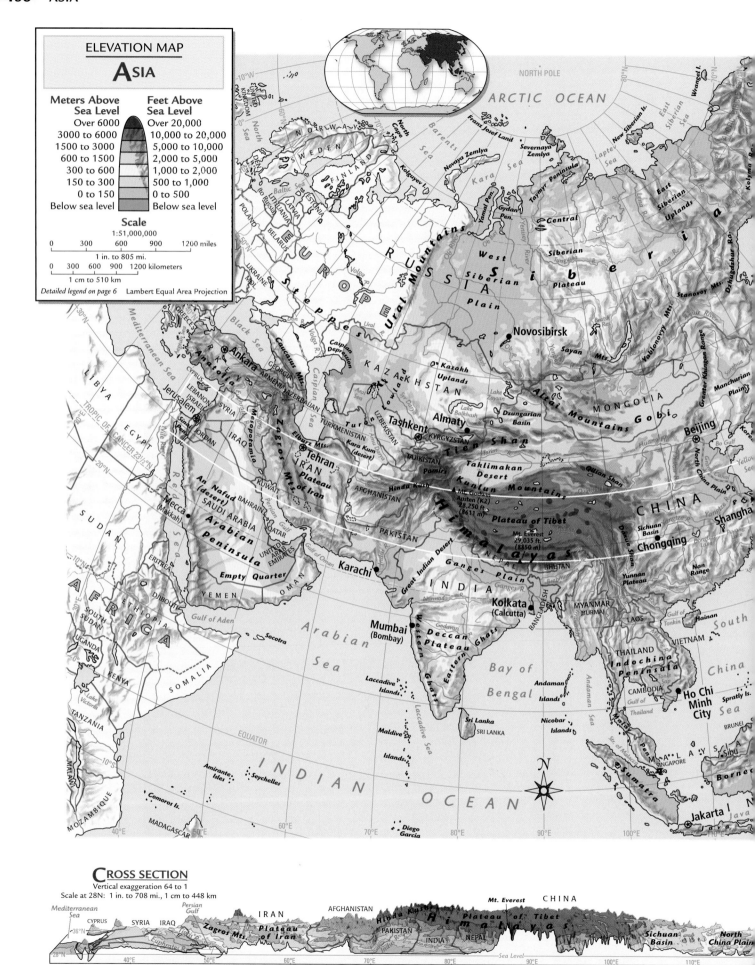

ELEVATION MAP
ASIA

Meters Above Sea Level	Feet Above Sea Level
Over 6000	Over 20,000
3000 to 6000	10,000 to 20,000
1500 to 3000	5,000 to 10,000
600 to 1500	2,000 to 5,000
300 to 600	1,000 to 2,000
150 to 300	500 to 1,000
0 to 150	0 to 500
Below sea level	Below sea level

Scale
1:51,000,000

0   300   600   900   1200 miles
1 in. to 805 mi.

0   300   600   900   1200 kilometers
1 cm to 510 km

Detailed legend on page 6   Lambert Equal Area Projection

NORTH POLE
ARCTIC OCEAN

CROSS SECTION
Vertical exaggeration 64 to 1
Scale at 28N: 1 in. to 708 mi., 1 cm to 448 km

The Himalayas are the highest mountain range in the world. At an elevation of about 11,300 feet (3400 meters), this village in Nepal is surrounded by many of the world's highest peaks.

PLATE MOVEMENT AND THE HIMALAYAS

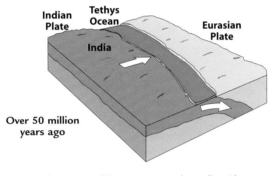

Indian Plate **Tethys Ocean** **Eurasian Plate**

India

Over 50 million years ago

Indian Plate **Himalayas** **Eurasian Plate**

India

Today

About 50 million years ago, the Indian Plate collided with the Eurasian Plate, resulting in in the formation of the Himalayas. The range continues to grow today, with Mount Everest rising about 0.2 inches (5 millimeters) per year. (See pages 16–17.)

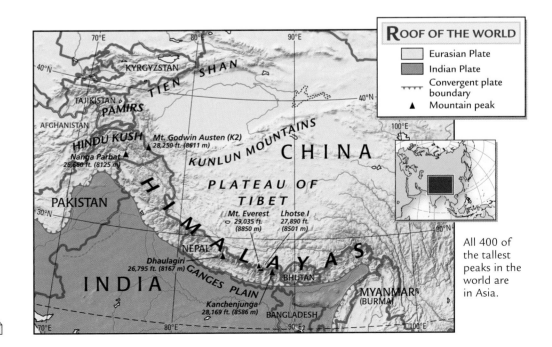

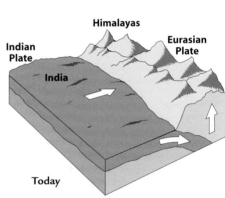

ROOF OF THE WORLD

- Eurasian Plate
- Indian Plate
- ⊥⊥⊥ Convergent plate boundary
- ▲ Mountain peak

KYRGYZSTAN

TIEN SHAN

TAJIKISTAN

PAMIRS

AFGHANISTAN

HINDU KUSH

Nanga Parbat
26,660 ft. (8125 m)

Mt. Godwin Austen (K2)
▲ 28,250 ft. (8611 m)

KUNLUN MOUNTAINS

CHINA

PLATEAU OF TIBET

Mt. Everest
29,035 ft.
(8850 m)

Lhotse I
27,890 ft.
(8501 m)

PAKISTAN

HIMALAYAS

NEPAL

Dhaulagiri
26,795 ft. (8167 m)

GANGES PLAIN

BHUTAN

INDIA

Kanchenjunga
28,169 ft. (8586 m)

BANGLADESH

MYANMAR (BURMA)

All 400 of the tallest peaks in the world are in Asia.

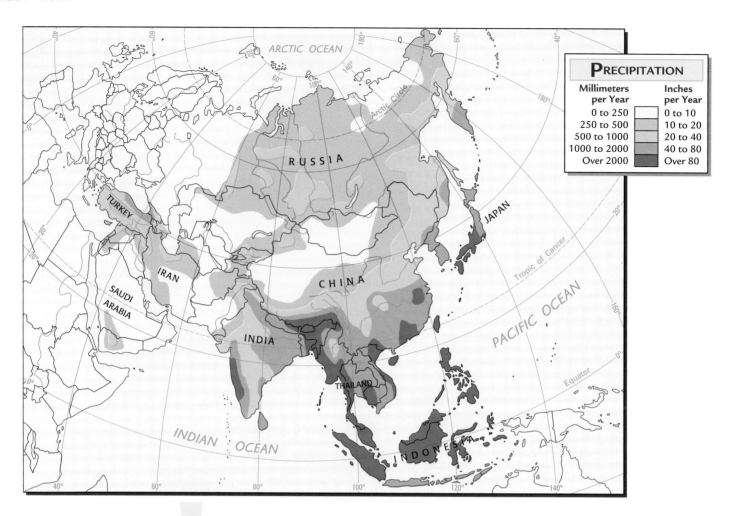

PRECIPITATION

Millimeters per Year	Inches per Year
0 to 250	0 to 10
250 to 500	10 to 20
500 to 1000	20 to 40
1000 to 2000	40 to 80
Over 2000	Over 80

The Dry Continent

More than half of Asia receives 20 inches (500 millimeters) or less of precipitation per year. Asian deserts include the An Nafud and Empty Quarter on the Arabian Peninsula, as well as the Kara Kum Desert, Great Indian Desert, Taklimakan Desert, and Gobi. Even Siberia's tundra has been called the "cold desert."

DRY MONSOON

→ Cold, dry wind

The climate of southeastern Asia and India is greatly influenced by large-scale seasonal wind systems called **monsoons**. In winter, dry winds generated over the cold surface of the land blow toward the warmer oceans and keep clouds away.

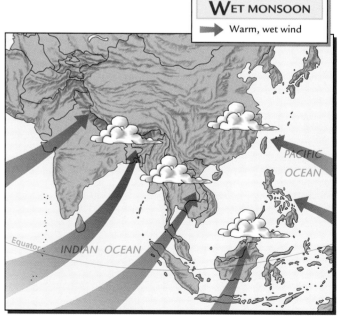

WET MONSOON

→ Warm, wet wind

In summer, the monsoon changes from dry to wet as the winds reverse direction. Cooler air over the oceans rushes toward warm land, bringing massive amounts of moisture that produce rain. The region's growing season occurs with the wet monsoon.

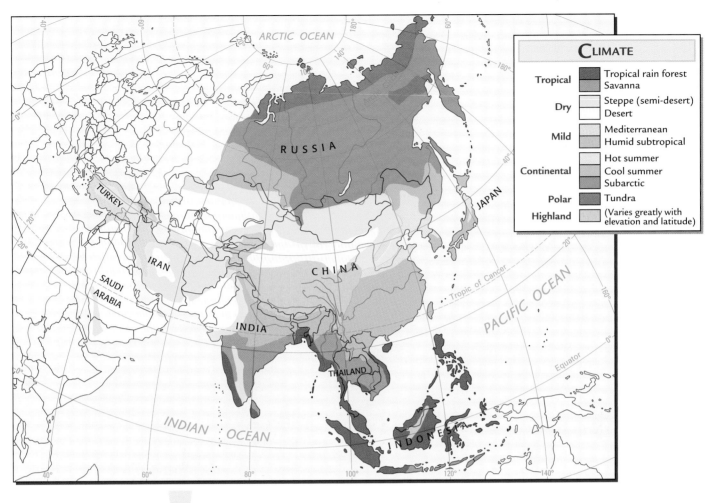

CLIMATE

Tropical		Tropical rain forest
		Savanna
Dry		Steppe (semi-desert)
		Desert
Mild		Mediterranean
		Humid subtropical
Continental		Hot summer
		Cool summer
		Subarctic
Polar		Tundra
Highland		(Varies greatly with elevation and latitude)

Si-brrr-ia

In Russia, snow and ice cover Siberia for half the year, and the temperature can drop as low as −90°F (−68°C). Verkhoyansk, a town in northeastern Siberia near the Arctic Circle, is the world's coldest continuously inhabited settlement. Without a nearby ocean to moderate its climate, Verkhoyansk can have annual high and low temperatures 140°F (80°C) apart.

During the wet monsoons, intense rainfall can flood city streets, as it has here in India. In July of 2005, 37 inches (940 millimeters) of rain fell on Mumbai in just 24 hours.

CLIMOGRAPHS

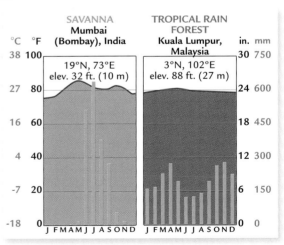

| | SAVANNA Mumbai (Bombay), India | TROPICAL RAIN FOREST Kuala Lumpur, Malaysia | |
| °C °F | 19°N, 73°E elev. 32 ft. (10 m) | 3°N, 102°E elev. 88 ft. (27 m) | in. mm |

While Mumbai and Kuala Lumpur each receive over 80 inches (2000 millimeters) of precipitation per year, their rain patterns are very different. Kuala Lumpur receives significant amounts of rain each month, while Mumbai receives most of its rain during the summer monsoon.

more at NDAtlas.com

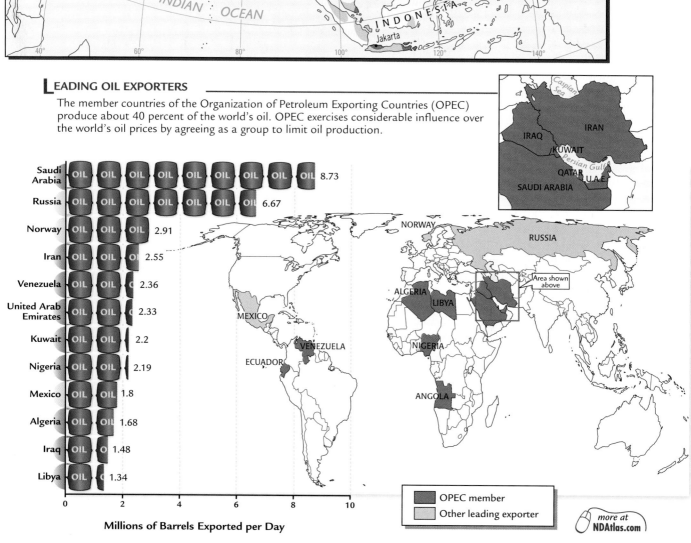

LAND USE

Widespread Economic Uses
- Urban
- Commercial farming
- Subsistence farming
- Ranching or herding
- Nomadic herding
- Forestry
- No widespread use

LEADING OIL EXPORTERS

The member countries of the Organization of Petroleum Exporting Countries (OPEC) produce about 40 percent of the world's oil. OPEC exercises considerable influence over the world's oil prices by agreeing as a group to limit oil production.

Country	Millions of Barrels Exported per Day
Saudi Arabia	8.73
Russia	6.67
Norway	2.91
Iran	2.55
Venezuela	2.36
United Arab Emirates	2.33
Kuwait	2.2
Nigeria	2.19
Mexico	1.8
Algeria	1.68
Iraq	1.48
Libya	1.34

Millions of Barrels Exported per Day

- OPEC member
- Other leading exporter

more at **NDAtlas.com**

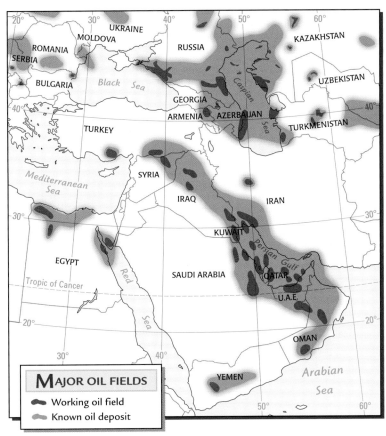

MAJOR OIL FIELDS

🔵 Working oil field
🔵 Known oil deposit

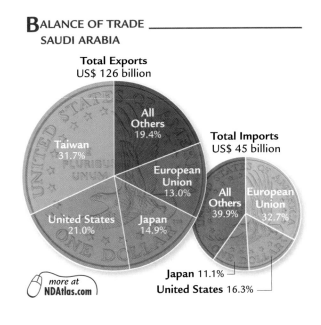

BALANCE OF TRADE
SAUDI ARABIA

Total Exports
US$ 126 billion

Taiwan 31.7%
All Others 19.4%
United States 21.0%
Japan 14.9%
European Union 13.0%

Total Imports
US$ 45 billion

All Others 39.9%
European Union 32.7%
Japan 11.1%
United States 16.3%

more at
NDAtlas.com

Over half of the world's proven oil reserves are located in southwestern Asia. As global oil resources continue to be depleted, southwestern Asia is becoming increasingly important for meeting the world's energy needs.

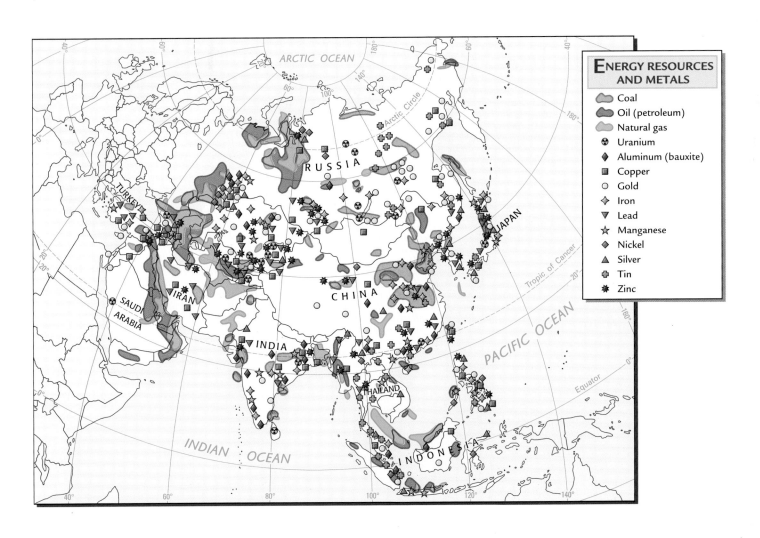

ENERGY RESOURCES AND METALS

🔵 Coal
🔵 Oil (petroleum)
🔵 Natural gas
⊛ Uranium
◆ Aluminum (bauxite)
◼ Copper
○ Gold
◇ Iron
▽ Lead
✦ Manganese
◆ Nickel
▲ Silver
✚ Tin
✳ Zinc

POPULATION

People per Sq. Km	People per Sq. Mile
0 to 2	0 to 5
2 to 20	5 to 50
20 to 40	50 to 100
40 to 100	100 to 250
Over 100	Over 250

Map labels: ARCTIC OCEAN · Arctic Circle · RUSSIA · TURKEY · Tashkent · Baghdad · IRAN · Tehran · SAUDI ARABIA · Delhi · INDIA · Dhaka · Mumbai · CHINA · Beijing · Shanghai · JAPAN · Tokyo · Tropic of Cancer · PACIFIC OCEAN · Hong Kong · THAILAND · Manila · INDIAN OCEAN · INDONESIA · Jakarta · Equator

Say It in Mandarin

Ni hao is a Mandarin greeting spoken by over 850 million people in China, Taiwan, and other countries. Mandarin, one of the most spoken languages in the world, is a Sino-Tibetan language. (See page 43.)

more at NDAtlas.com

With a population of over 16 million people, Shanghai is the largest city in China. These shoppers in crowded Shanghai are enjoying the week-long Lunar New Year holiday.

NATURAL POPULATION GROWTH ASIA

China
0.6%
Births: 13
Deaths: 7

India
1.4%
Births: 22
Deaths: 8

Laos
2.4%
Births: 36
Deaths: 12

World
1.1%
Births: 20
Deaths: 9

Legend: Births / Deaths

0 10 20 30 40 50

Annual Birth and Death Rates
(per 1,000 people)

WORLD POPULATION

Six countries in Asia—China, India, Indonesia, Pakistan, Bangladesh, and Japan—are home to about half of the world's population. The nearly three billion people living in these countries, however, occupy less than 11 percent of the world's land area.

□ Represents 1 million people

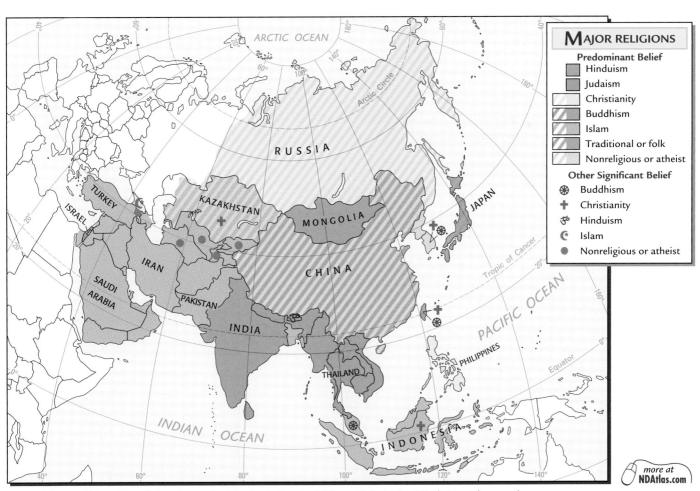

MAJOR RELIGIONS

Predominant Belief
- Hinduism
- Judaism
- Christianity
- Buddhism
- Islam
- Traditional or folk
- Nonreligious or atheist

Other Significant Belief
- ⊛ Buddhism
- ✝ Christianity
- ॐ Hinduism
- ☪ Islam
- ● Nonreligious or atheist

more at NDAtlas.com

Most of the world's major religions began in Asia, including Buddhism, Christianity, Hinduism, Islam, and Judaism. These religions are practiced by over 70 percent of the world's population. (See page 42.)

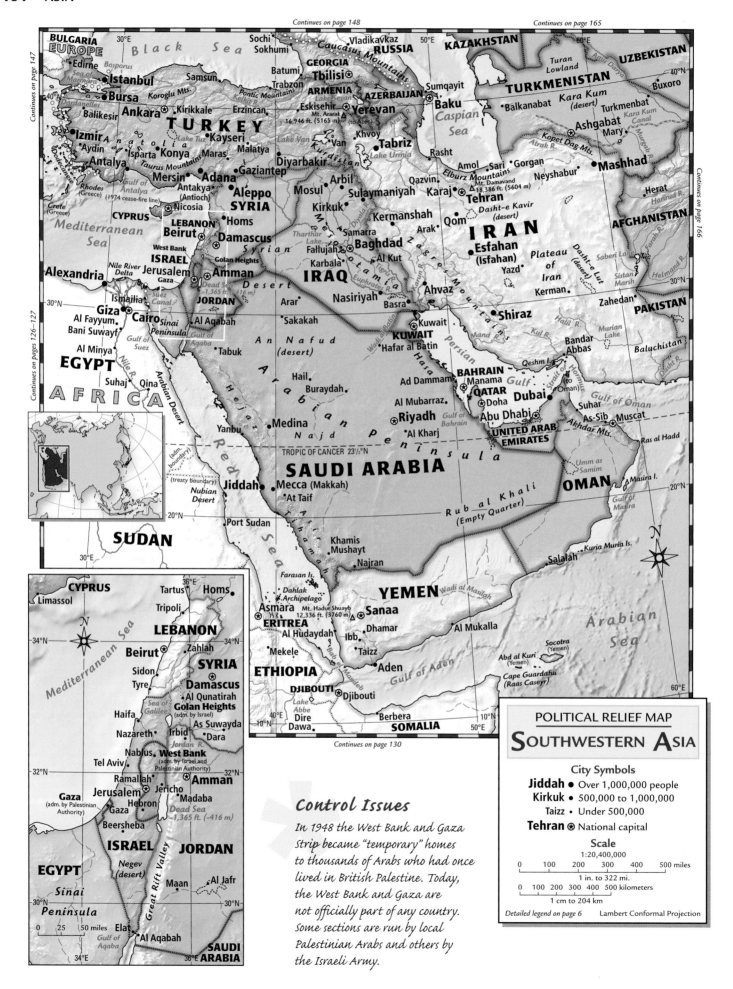

Continues on page 148

Continues on page 165

Continues on page 147

Continues on page 166

Continues on pages 126–127

Continues on page 130

Control Issues

In 1948 the West Bank and Gaza Strip became "temporary" homes to thousands of Arabs who had once lived in British Palestine. Today, the West Bank and Gaza are not officially part of any country. Some sections are run by local Palestinian Arabs and others by the Israeli Army.

POLITICAL RELIEF MAP

SOUTHWESTERN ASIA

City Symbols

Jiddah ● Over 1,000,000 people
Kirkuk ● 500,000 to 1,000,000
Taizz • Under 500,000
Tehran ⊛ National capital

Scale

1:20,400,000

0   100   200   300   400   500 miles
1 in. to 322 mi.

0 100 200 300 400 500 kilometers
1 cm to 204 km

Detailed legend on page 6   Lambert Conformal Projection

Continues on page 148

Continues on pages 152–153

Continues on page 148

Continues on page 168

Continues on page 149

Continues on page 164

Continues on page 166

POLITICAL RELIEF MAP

CENTRAL ASIA

City Symbols

Almaty • Over 1,000,000 people
Barnaul • 500,000 to 1,000,000
Atyrau • Under 500,000

Tashkent ⊗ National capital

Scale

1:17,700,000

| 0 | 100 | 200 | 300 | 400 miles |

1 in. to 280 mi.

| 0 | 100 | 200 | 300 | 400 kilometers |

1 cm to 177 km

Detailed legend on page 6   Lambert Equal Area Projection

ARAL SEA

The Amu Darya drains into the Aral Sea. Beginning in 1956, water from the river was diverted to irrigate cotton fields in the desert of what now is Turkmenistan. Once the fourth largest lake in the world, the Aral Sea is now one-quarter of its former size. Today the port of Muynak is 90 miles (150 kilometers) from the shore of the Aral Sea.

1976

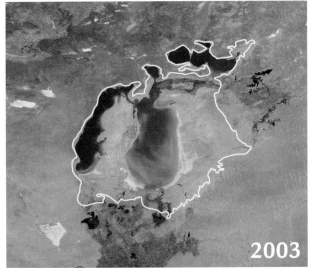

2003

Teenagers in India celebrate Bhai Tika with music and dancing. Bhai Tika is a Hindu festival that honors brothers and sisters. It is part of Diwali, a festival of lights usually held in October or November.

Uniquely Indian

The Indian subcontinent is separated from the rest of Asia by the Himalayas. While the subcontinent was not completely cut off from the rest of the continent, it did develop its own unique culture. The subcontinent includes Pakistan, India, Nepal, Bhutan, Bangladesh, and Sri Lanka.

Continues on page 165

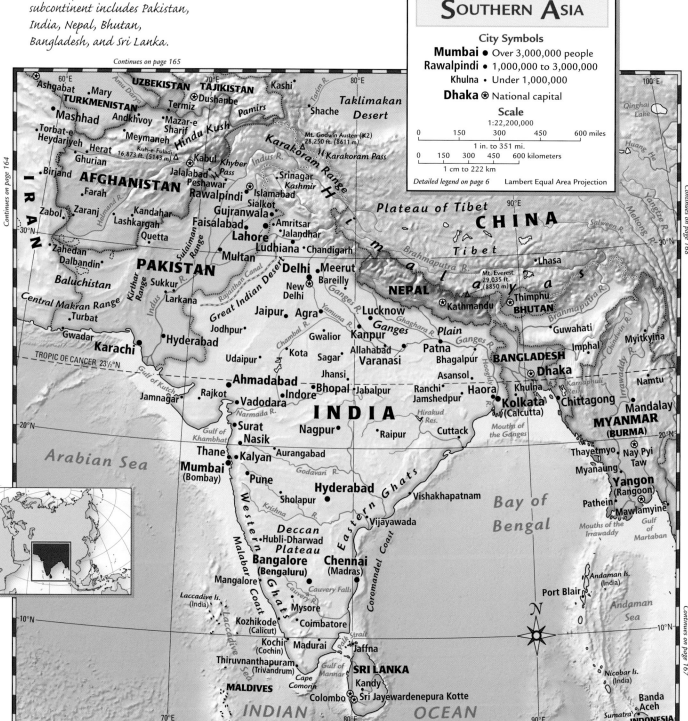

POLITICAL RELIEF MAP

SOUTHERN ASIA

City Symbols

Mumbai ● Over 3,000,000 people
Rawalpindi ● 1,000,000 to 3,000,000
Khulna • Under 1,000,000

Dhaka ⊛ National capital

Scale

1:22,200,000

| 0 | 150 | 300 | 450 | 600 miles |

1 in. to 351 mi.

| 0 | 150 | 300 | 450 | 600 kilometers |

1 cm to 222 km

Detailed legend on page 6   Lambert Equal Area Projection

Continues on page 164

Continues on page 168

Continues on page 167

Continues on page 168

POLITICAL RELIEF MAP
SOUTHEASTERN ASIA

City Symbols
Guangzhou ● Over 3,000,000 people
Medan ● 1,000,000 to 3,000,000
Ipoh • Under 1,000,000
Bangkok ⊗ National capital

Scale
1:21,100,000

| 0 | 100 | 200 | 300 | 400 | 500 miles |

1 in. to 335 mi.

| 0 | 100 | 200 | 300 | 400 | 500 kilometers |

1 cm to 211 km

Detailed legend on page 6   Lambert Equal Area Projection

Himalayas
BHUTAN
Brahmaputra R.
Guwahati
INDIA
Imphal
Myitkyina
Panzhihua
Yunnan Plateau
Guiyang
Guangzhou
Nanchang
CHINA
110°E
Kunming
Chindwin R.
Irrawaddy R.
Salween R.
Mekong R.
Black R.
Hongshui R.
Wuzhou
Shantou
Xi Jiang
TROPIC OF CANCER 23½°N
Chittagong
Namtu
Mandalay
Nanning
Macau
Hong Kong
MYANMAR
(BURMA)
Dien Bien Phu
Hanoi
Haiphong
Haikou
20°N
Nay Pyi Taw
Louangphrabang
Nam Dinh
20°N
Thayetmyo
Chiang Rai
LAOS
Gulf of Tonkin
Hainan
120°E
Myanaung
Chiang Mai
Vientiane (Viangchan)
Vinh
Escarpada Point
Yangon (Rangoon)
Bago
Udon Thani
Annamite Mts.
Luzon
Philippine Sea
Pathein
Mawlamyine
THAILAND
Khon Kaen
Chi R.
Savannakhet
Hue
Da Nang
Mt. Pinatubo 4,875 ft. (1486 m)
Quezon City
Pagoda Point
Gulf of Martaban
Chao Phraya R.
Mun R.
Indochina Peninsula
VIETNAM
South China Sea
Manila
Andaman Is. (India)
Nakhon Ratchasima
Thon Buri
Khone Falls
Plateau of Kontum
Qui Nhon
Mindoro
Samar
Port Blair
Andaman Sea
Mergui
Bangkok
CAMBODIA
Kracheh
Tonle Sap
Nha Trang
PHILIPPINES
Panay
Iloilo
Bacolod
Cebu
Archipelago
Phnom Penh
Bien Hoa
Negros
10°N
Nicobar Is. (India)
Gulf of Thailand
Long Xuyen
Ho Chi Minh City
N
Puerto Princesa
Butuan
Surat Thani
Isthmus of Kra
Can Tho
Mouths of the Mekong
Spratly Is. (disputed)
Palawan
Sulu Sea
Pagadian
Mindanao
Davao
Songkhla
Point Bai Bung
Con Son Is.
General Santos
Kuala Terengganu
Kinabalu 13,455 ft. (4101 m)
Balabac Strait
Sandakan
Banda Aceh
George Town
Kuantan
Natuna Besar Is. (Indonesia)
Kota Kinabalu
Bandar Seri Begawan
BRUNEI
Celebes Sea
Tarakan
Ipoh
M A L A Y S I A
Serasun Strait
INDONESIA
Manado
INDONESIA
Medan
Kiang
Kuala Lumpur
Putrajaya
Strait of Malacca
Kuching
Sibu
Sarawak
Rajang R.
Kayan R.
Borneo
Sulawesi (Celebes)
Molucca Sea
Pematangsiantar
Simeulue
Strait of Makassar
Kapuas R.
INDIAN OCEAN
Nias
Sumatra
Johor Baharu
SINGAPORE
Pekanbaru
110°E
120°E
0° EQUATOR

(inset map — Scale at Equator)
Scale at Equator
1:31,800,000

| 0 | | 250 mi. |

1 in. to 502 mi.

| 0 | | 250 km |

1 cm to 318 km

Miller Projection

Banda Aceh
Ipoh
Kota Kinabalu
Bandar Seri Begawan
Sandakan
PHILIPPINES
Talaud Is. (Indonesia)
Medan
Kuala Lumpur
Natuna Besar Is. (Indonesia)
BRUNEI
Celebes Sea
Morotai I.
M A L A Y S I A
Tarakan
Simeulue I.
Pekanbaru
SINGAPORE
Sibu
Manado
Halmahera
Waigeo I.
Nias
EQUATOR
Kuching
Borneo
Pontianak
Molucca Sea
Waigeo I.
Batu Is.
Padang
Samarinda
Palu
Sula Is.
Sorong
Manokwari
Biak I.
Jambi
Bangka
Balikpapan
Ceram Sea
Fakfak
Jayapura
Mentawai Is.
Sumatra
Karimata Strait
Sulawesi (Celebes)
Buru I.
Ceram
Dempo 10,364 ft. (3159 m)
Palembang
Belitung
Banjarmasin
Ambon
Jaya Peak 16,503 ft. (5030 m)
New Guinea
PAPUA NEW GUINEA
Enggano I.
I N D O N E S I A
Greater Sunda Is.
Java Sea
Makassar
Banda Sea
Aru Is.
Jakarta
Semarang
Flores Sea
Wetar
Moa
Tanimbar Is.
Dolak I.
INDIAN OCEAN
Bandung
Java
Malang
Mt. Tambora 9,350 ft. (2850 m)
Bali
Sumbawa
Lombok
Flores
Lesser Sunda Is.
Dili
EAST TIMOR
Merauke
Slamet 11,247 ft. (3428 m)
Semeru 12,060 ft. (3676 m)
Sumba
Timor
Kupang
Arafura Sea
Christmas I. (Australia)
Sunda Strait
Timor Sea
10°S
100°E
110°E
120°E
130°E
140°E

Continues on page 166

Continues on pages 172–173

Continues on page 179

BALANCE OF TRADE
CHINA

Total Exports
US$ 593 billion

- United States 21.1%
- All Others 31.4%
- European Union 18.1%
- Japan 12.4%
- Hong Kong, China 17.0%

Total Imports
US$ 561 billion

- Japan 16.8%
- All Others 48.1%
- European Union 12.5%
- Taiwan 11.5%
- South Korea 11.1%

more at NDAtlas.com

TOP ASIAN GDPs

	GDP (US$ millions)
China	$8,158,000
Japan	$3,867,000
India	$3,678,000
South Korea	$983,300
Indonesia	$899,000

GDP (US$ millions)

Many of the world's largest economies are located in Asia. Some—such as South Korea and Japan—are **mature** with high standards of living and moderate growth, while others—such as India and China—are **emerging** with moderate to low standards of living and high growth.

more at NDAtlas.com

POLITICAL RELIEF MAP
EASTERN ASIA
CHINA, MONGOLIA, and TAIWAN

City Symbols

Shenyang ● Over 3,000,000 people
Kaohsiung ● 1,000,000 to 3,000,000
Uliastay ● Under 1,000,000

Beijing ⊛ National capital

Scale
1:30,700,000

0   200   400   600   800 miles
1 in. to 489 mi.
0   200   400   600   800 kilometers
1 cm to 307 km

Detailed legend on page 6   Lambert Equal Area Projection

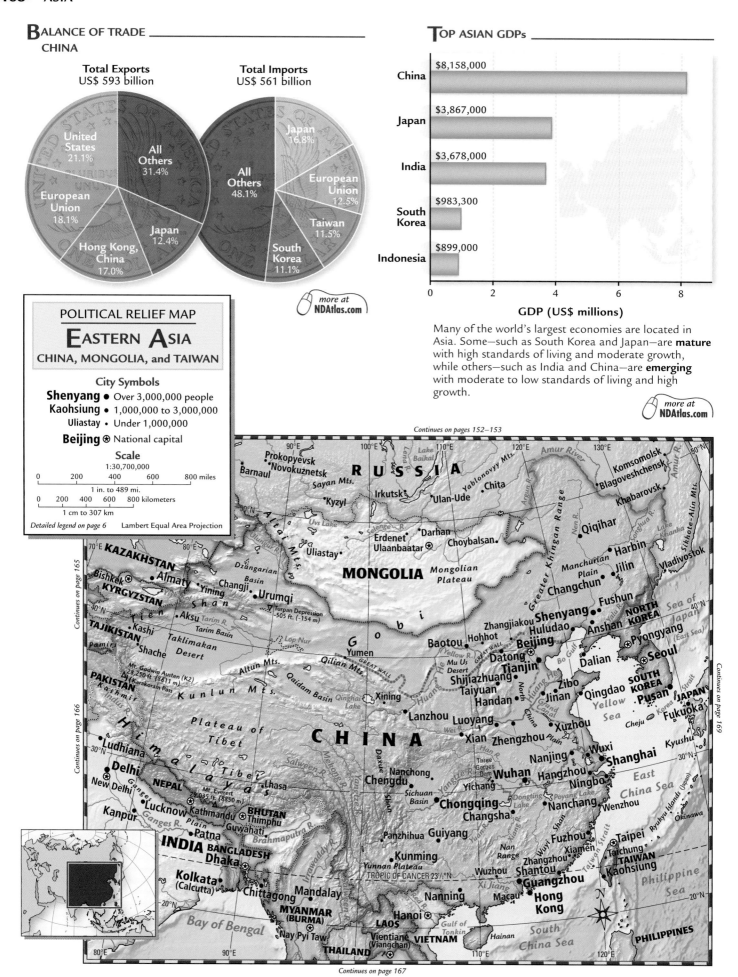

Continues on pages 152–153

Continues on page 165

Continues on page 166

Continues on page 169

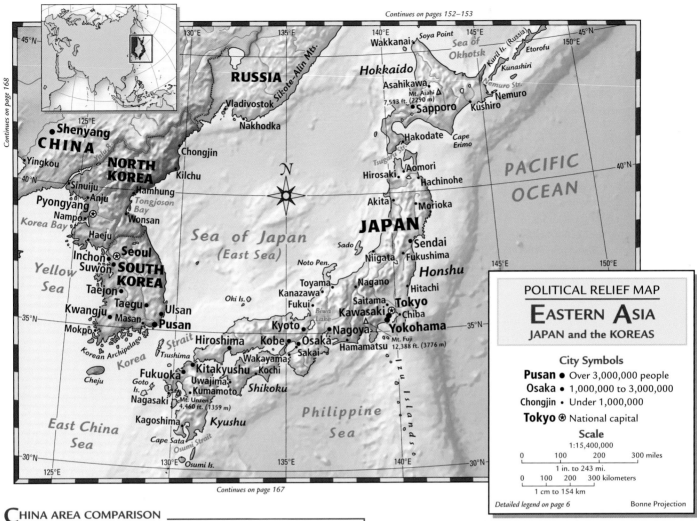

Continues on pages 152–153

RUSSIA
Sikote-Alin Mts.
Vladivostok
Nakhodka
Sea of Okhotsk
Soya Point
Wakkanai
Kuril Is. (Russia)
Etorofu
Nemuro Str.
Kunashiri
Hokkaido
Asahikawa
Mt. Asahi △
7,513 ft. (2290 m)
Sapporo
Kushiro
Nemuro

Shenyang
CHINA
Yingkou
Sinuiju
Anju
Pyongyang
Nampo
Korea Bay
Haeju
NORTH KOREA
Chongjin
Kilchu
Hamhung
Tongjoson Bay
Wonsan

Hakodate
Cape Erimo
Tsugaru Str.
Aomori
Hirosaki
Hachinohe
Akita
Morioka

JAPAN
Sendai
Fukushima
Niigata
Honshu
Hitachi

PACIFIC OCEAN

Sea of Japan (East Sea)
Sado
Noto Pen.
Toyama
Nagano
Kanazawa
Fukui
Saitama
Tokyo
Kawasaki
Chiba
Yokohama

Inchon
Seoul
Suwon
SOUTH KOREA
Taejon
Taegu
Kwangju
Masan
Ulsan
Pusan
Mokpo
Yellow Sea
Korean Archipelago
Cheju
Korea Strait
Tsushima
Fukuoka
Goto Is.
Uwajima
Kumamoto
Nagasaki
Mt. Unzen
4,460 ft. (1359 m)
Kagoshima
Cape Sata
Osumi Strait
Osumi Is.

Oki Is.
Biwa Lake
Kyoto
Nagoya
Kobe
Osaka
Sakai
Hamamatsu
Wakayama
Kochi
Kitakyushu
Hiroshima
Shikoku
Kyushu
Mt. Fuji 12,388 ft. (3776 m)
Izu Islands
Philippine Sea
East China Sea

Continues on page 168
Continues on page 167

POLITICAL RELIEF MAP
EASTERN ASIA
JAPAN and the KOREAS
City Symbols
Pusan ● Over 3,000,000 people
Osaka ● 1,000,000 to 3,000,000
Chongjin • Under 1,000,000
Tokyo ⊗ National capital
Scale
1:15,400,000
0 100 200 300 miles
1 in. to 243 mi.
0 100 200 300 kilometers
1 cm to 154 km
Detailed legend on page 6   Bonne Projection

CHINA AREA COMPARISON

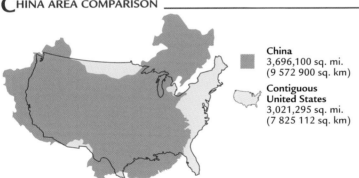

China 3,696,100 sq. mi. (9 572 900 sq. km)
Contiguous United States 3,021,295 sq. mi. (7 825 112 sq. km)

ETHNIC COMPOSITION
SOUTH KOREA

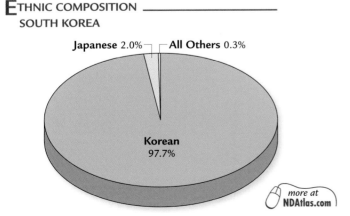

Japanese 2.0% — All Others 0.3%
Korean 97.7%

more at NDAtlas.com

The Japanese have one of the world's highest levels of personal income. These teenagers in Tokyo stop by a mall on the way home from school.

ISSUES ◄► TODAY

How can population growth be controlled?

Asia, the most populated continent on Earth, is home to more than half of the world's people. Its population is projected to reach 5.2 billion by 2050. Unfortunately, Asia's population places a major strain on economic development and the environment. High population density has resulted in a loss of cropland and an increase in waste and pollution. Overpopulation also has reduced access to such basics as food, water, and health care. Should Asian countries carry out policies to slow population growth? There are many perspectives on this issue. Here are two of them.

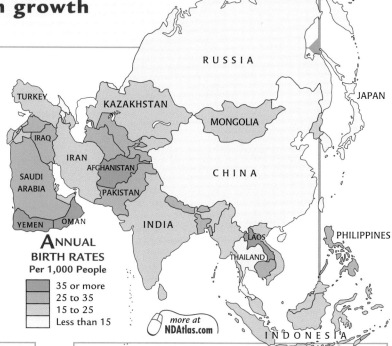

ANNUAL BIRTH RATES
Per 1,000 People

- 35 or more
- 25 to 35
- 15 to 25
- Less than 15

more at NDAtlas.com

Government policy can greatly reduce birth rates.

- In most developing countries, people are encouraged to have many children. Legal and political pressures are needed to counteract these long-standing customs.

- China's planned birth policy (known in the West as the "One-child" policy) uses political sanctions to curtail its rapidly increasing population. Since 1979 the policy has prevented about 300 million births.

- Today over 80 percent of all married women in China use contraception, compared to 33 percent in other developing countries.

- Since 1979 China has experienced a tenfold increase in GDP (Gross Domestic Product) and now has the second-largest economy in the world.

POPULATION PYRAMIDS

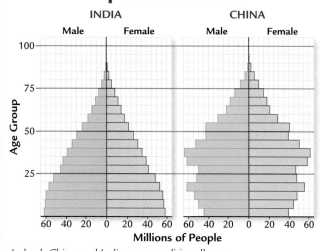

INDIA   CHINA

In both China and India, sons traditionally are valued more than daughters. Female infanticide and selective abortion are not uncommon.

more at NDAtlas.com

Education will control population growth.

- The ability to "found a family" is a basic human right, declared by the United Nations. Education respects that right by allowing people to make their own choices.

- Education helps people make informed choices about their own reproductive health and their children's health.

- High birth rates often compensate for high infant mortality. Reproductive education results in healthier women and healthier babies. With more survivors, parents do not feel the need to have more children.

- India was the first developing country to sponsor a family planning program. Since the 1960s, its annual birth rate has dropped from 40 births to 22 births per 1000.

As part of India's population policy, a doctor discusses family planning methods in a rural village, where two-thirds of the women use no contraception.

AUSTRALIA & OCEANIA

Australia and Oceania—the central and south Pacific—are famous for their thousands of beautiful tropical islands and for their diverse cultures and languages. Unique plants and animals can be found throughout the isolated islands of the region.

PHYSICAL FEATURES

Mountains
Highest peak: Jaya Peak 16,503 ft. (5 030 m)
Longest range: Great Dividing Range 2,300 mi. (3 700 km)

Largest Islands
New Guinea 342,000 sq. mi. (885 780 sq. km)
South Island (New Zealand) 58,385 sq. mi. (151 215 sq. km)

Major Archipelagos
Hawaiian Islands
Tuamotu Archipelago
New Hebrides

Largest Lake
Lake Eyre* 3,700 sq. mi. (9 583 sq. km)

Longest Rivers
Murray 1,200 mi (1 930 km)
Darling* 1,160 mi (1 879 km)

Other Key Physical Features
Great Artesian Basin
Nullarbor Plain
Western Plateau
Kimberly Plateau

CULTURAL FEATURES

Population 33,100,000

Largest Country
By area: Australia 2,969,978 sq. mi. (7 692 208 sq. km)★
By population: Australia 20,264,082

Population Density
Most densely populated: Nauru
1,620.4 people per sq. mi. (626.7 per sq. km)
Least densely populated: Australia
6.8 people per sq. mi. (2.6 per sq. km)

Largest Urban Areas
Sydney, Australia 4,331,000
Melbourne, Australia 3,626,000

★ Among the world's largest. See the inside front cover.

* Seasonal

more at
NDAtlas.com
For more maps, graphs, and photos of Australia and Oceania, go to NystromDeskAtlas.com.

AREA COMPARISON

■ Australia
2,969,978 sq. mi.
(7 692 208 sq. km)

Contiguous
United States
3,021,295 sq. mi.
(7 825 112 sq. km)

World Extreme The Great Barrier Reef is the largest coral reef system in the world. It consists of more than 2000 individual reefs and extends about 1240 miles (2000 kilometers) along the northeast coast of Australia.

REGIONAL MAPS OF AUSTRALIA AND OCEANIA

1 Australia • page 179   **2 New Zealand** • page 179

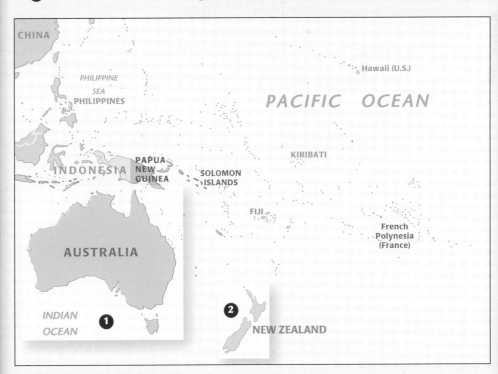

Chengdu · Nanjing · 120°E · JAPAN · 135°E · 150°E · 165°E

CHINA · Wuhan · Shanghai · PACIFIC OCEAN

Chongqing · Changsha · Nanchang · East China Sea

ASIA · Fuzhou · Okinawa · Bonin Islands (Japan)

Nanning · Guangzhou · Taipei · Ryukyu Islands (Japan) · Volcano Islands (Japan) · Iwo To (Iwo Jima) (Japan) · Minami Tori Shima (Japan)

Macau · Hong Kong · TAIWAN · Kaohsiung · TROPIC OF CANCER 23½°N

Hanoi · Luzon Strait · Babuyan Is. · Okino Tori Shima (Japan) · Wake (U.S.)

LAOS · Vientiane (Viangchan) · Hainan · Luzon · Farallon de Pajaros · Maug Is. · Asuncion I. · Northern Mariana Islands (U.S.) · MARSHALL ISLANDS

THAILAND · Da Nang · Baguio · Agrihan I. · Taongi Atoll · Bikini Atoll · Ratak Chain

VIETNAM · Quezon City · Pagan I. · Alamagan I. · Enewetak Atoll

15°N · Manila · PHILIPPINES · Guguan I. · Farallon de Medinilla · Ujelang Atoll · Kwajalein Atoll · Ralik Chain

CAMBODIA · Anatahan I. · Saipan I. · Tinian I. · Saipan · Majuro · Majuro Atoll

Phnom Penh · Ho Chi Minh City · Palawan · Cebu · Guam (U.S.) · Hagatna (Agana) · Jaluit Atoll

Mindanao · FEDERATED STATES OF MICRONESIA

Kota Kinabalu · Sandakan · Davao · Ulithi Atoll · Namonuito Atoll · Hall Islands · Oroluk Atoll · Pohnpei Islands

Bandar Seri Begawan · Yap Is. · Sorol Atoll · Ngulu Atoll · Palikir

Kuala Lumpur · BRUNEI · Babelthuap · Koror · Melekeok · Ifalik Atoll · Pulusuk Atoll · Chuuk (Truk) Islands · Mortlock Islands · Ngatik Atoll · Kosrae I.

MALAYSIA · Sibu · Celebes Sea · Sonsorol Is. · Caroline · PALAU · Islands · Kapingamarangi Atoll

SINGAPORE · EQUATOR · Manado · Halmahera

0° · Samarinda · Palu · Molucca Sea · Ninigo Group · St. Matthias Group · Lyra Reef · Yaren District (unofficial) · Gilbert

Sumatra · Pontianak · Borneo · Sulawesi (Celebes) · Sorong · Admiralty Is. · Manus I. · New Hanover · NAURU · Banaba I.

Bangka · Banjarmasin · Buru I. · Ambon · Jayapura · Wewak · Bismarck Archipelago · New Ireland

Palembang · Belitung · INDONESIA · Ceram · Ceram Sea · New Guinea · PAPUA NEW GUINEA · Madang · Bismarck Sea · Rabaul · Buka I. · Solomon · Ontong Java Atoll · SOLOMON ISLANDS

Jakarta · Java Sea · Semarang · Makassar · Banda Sea · Aru Is. · Lae · New Britain · Bougainville · Choiseul I. · Santa Isabel · Reef Islands · Duff Islands

Bandung · Surabaya · Flores Sea · Tanimbar Is. · Dolak I. · Port Moresby · Solomon Sea · Woodlark I. · New Georgia Group · Honiara · Santa Cruz Islands · Vanikolo Is.

Malang · Java · Bali · Sumbawa · Kupang · Dili · EAST TIMOR · Merauke · Gulf of Papua · Fergusson I. · Guadalcanal · Nendo I.

Christmas I. (Australia) · Lombok · Sumba · Timor · Arafura Sea · Torres Strait · Louisiade Archipelago · San Cristobal · Rennell I. · Indispensable Reefs

Timor Sea · Cape York · Coral Sea

INDIAN OCEAN · Darwin · Gulf of Carpentaria · Groote Eylandt · Great Barrier Reef · Torres Islands · Banks Islands · VANUATU

15°S · Kuri Bay · Katherine · Wellesley Is. · Mitchell R. · Cairns · Espiritu Santo · Maewo I. · Pentecost I. · Ambrym I.

Broome · Lake Argyle · Great Dividing Range · Chesterfield Isles · Malakula I. · Epi I. · Port-Vila · Efate I. · Erromango

Eighty Mile Beach · Fitzroy R. · Belep Is. · Tanna I. · Anatom

North West Cape · Port Hedland · Great Sandy Desert · Townsville · Mackay · Ouvea Atoll · New Caledonia · Noumea · Lifou I. · Loyalty Is. · Mare I.

TROPIC OF CAPRICORN 23½°S · Western · Macdonnell Ranges · New Caledonia (France) · Isle of Pines · Walpole I.

Gibson Desert · Alice Springs · Central · Rockhampton

AUSTRALIA · Plateau · Great Artesian Basin · Bundaberg · Norfolk I. (Australia)

Geraldton · Great Victoria Desert · AUSTRALIA · Toowoomba · Brisbane · Gold Coast

30°S · Lake Eyre -52 ft. (-16 m) · Lowlands · Darling R. · Coffs Harbor

Kalgoorlie · Woomera · Tamworth · Lord Howe I. (Australia)

Perth · Mandurah · Whyalla · Murray R. · Newcastle · Gosford · Sydney

Bunbury · Great Australian Bight · Spencer Gulf · Mildura · Albury · Canberra · Tasman Sea

Cape Leeuwin · Albany · Adelaide · Australian Alps · Gulf St. Vincent · Kangaroo I. · Ballarat · Geelong · Melbourne

Bass Strait · NEW ZEALAND

INDIAN OCEAN · Tasmania · Launceston · South Island

Hobart · Milford Sound · Southern Alps · Dunedin

45°S

105°E · 120°E · 135°E · 150°E · 165°E

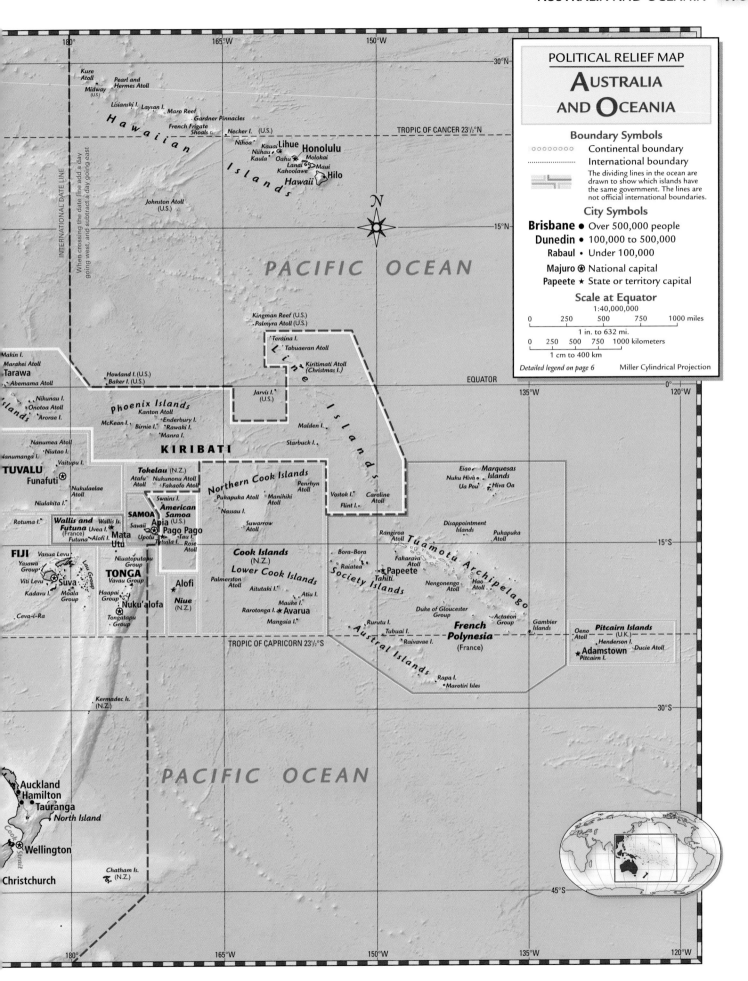

POLITICAL RELIEF MAP

AUSTRALIA AND OCEANIA

Boundary Symbols
○○○○○○○○ Continental boundary
·················· International boundary

The dividing lines in the ocean are drawn to show which islands have the same government. The lines are not official international boundaries.

City Symbols
Brisbane ● Over 500,000 people
Dunedin ● 100,000 to 500,000
Rabaul · Under 100,000

Majuro ⊗ National capital
Papeete ★ State or territory capital

Scale at Equator
1:40,000,000
0   250   500   750   1000 miles
1 in. to 632 mi.
0   250 500 750 1000 kilometers
1 cm to 400 km

Detailed legend on page 6   Miller Cylindrical Projection

180°   165°W   150°W   30°N

Kure Atoll
Midway (U.S.)
Pearl and Hermes Atoll
Lisianski I.   Laysan I.   Maro Reef
Gardner Pinnacles
French Frigate Shoals
Necker I. (U.S.)   TROPIC OF CANCER 23½°N
Nihoa I.
Kauai **Lihue**   **Honolulu**
Niihau   Oahu ★
Kaula   Molokai
Lanai   Maui
Kahoolawe   **Hilo**
Hawaii ●

Hawaiian Islands

INTERNATIONAL DATE LINE
When crossing the date line add a day going west, and subtract a day going east

Johnston Atoll (U.S.)

15°N

PACIFIC OCEAN

Kingman Reef (U.S.)
Palmyra Atoll (U.S.)

Teraina I.
Tabuaeran Atoll
Kiritimati Atoll (Christmas I.)

Line Islands

Makin I.
Marakei Atoll
Tarawa ⊗
Abemama Atoll

Howland I. (U.S.)
Baker I. (U.S.)

Jarvis I. (U.S.)

EQUATOR   135°W   120°W   0°

Nikunau I.
Onotoa Atoll
Arorae I.

Phoenix Islands
Kanton Atoll
McKean I.   Enderbury I.
Birnie I.   Rawaki I.
Manra I.

Malden I.

Starbuck I.

KIRIBATI

Nanumea Atoll
Nanumanga I.   Niutao I.
Vaitupu I.

Eiao   **Marquesas Islands**
Nuku Hiva
Ua Pou   Hiva Oa

TUVALU ⊗
Funafuti

Nukulaelae Atoll
Niulakita I.

Tokelau (N.Z.)
Atafu Atoll   Nukunonu Atoll
Fakaofo Atoll

Northern Cook Islands
Pukapuka Atoll   Manihiki Atoll
Penrhyn Atoll

Vostok I.
Caroline Atoll
Flint I.

Rotuma I.

Swains I.
American Samoa (U.S.)
SAMOA   Savaii ★
Apia ⊗
Upolu   **Pago Pago** ★
Tau I.
Rose Atoll

Nassau I.

Suwarrow Atoll

Rangiroa Atoll

Disappointment Islands

Pukapuka Atoll

Wallis and Futuna (France)
Uvea I. ★   Wallis Is.
Futuna   Alofi I.
Mata Utu

FIJI   Vanua Levu
Yasawa Group
Viti Levu ★
Suva
Kadavu I.   Moala Group
Ceva-i-Ra

Lau Group

Niuatoputapu Group

Cook Islands (N.Z.)
Lower Cook Islands
Palmerston Atoll

Bora-Bora
Raiatea   *Society Islands*
Tahiti ★ **Papeete**

Fakarava Atoll
Tuamotu Archipelago
Hao Atoll

15°S

TONGA
Vavau Group
Haapai Group
Niuatoputapu Group

Alofi ★

Niue (N.Z.)

Aitutaki I.
Mauke I.   Atiu I.
Rarotonga I. ★ **Avarua**
Mangaia I.

Nengonengo Atoll   Actaeon Group

Duke of Gloucester Group

Gambier Islands

Oeno Atoll   **Pitcairn Islands (U.K.)**
Henderson I.
★ **Adamstown**   Ducie Atoll
Pitcairn I.

Haapai Group
Nuku'alofa ⊗
Tongatapu Group

Rurutu I.
Tubuai I.   **French Polynesia (France)**
Raivavae I.

Austral Islands

TROPIC OF CAPRICORN 23½°S

Kermadec Is. (N.Z.)

Rapa I.
Marotiri Isles

30°S

PACIFIC OCEAN

Auckland ●
Hamilton ●
Tauranga ●
North Island

Cook Strait
⊗ **Wellington**

Chatham Is. (N.Z.)

Christchurch ●

45°S

180°   165°W   150°W   135°W   120°W

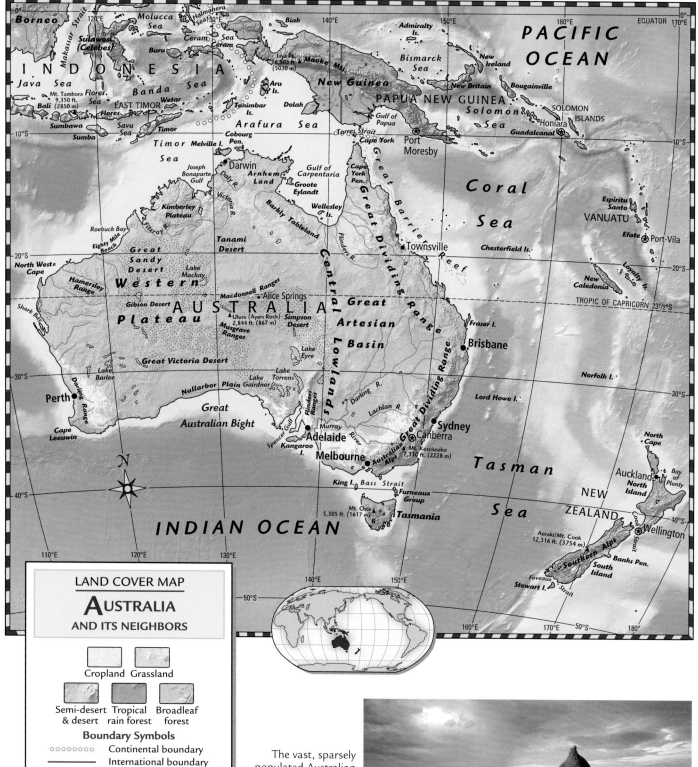

PACIFIC OCEAN

INDONESIA

Borneo

Makassar Strait

Molucca Sea

Halmahera Sea

Sulawesi (Celebes)

Buru

Ceram Sea

Ceram

Biak

Admiralty Is.

New Ireland

Bismarck Sea

New Britain

Bougainville

SOLOMON ISLANDS

Java Sea

Mt. Tambora 9,350 ft. (2850 m)

Bali

Flores Sea

EAST TIMOR

Wetar

Flores

Sumbawa

Savu Sea

Sumba

Timor

Melville I.

Cobourg Pen.

Timor Sea

Arafura Sea

Tanimbar Is.

Dolak

Aru Is.

Maoke Mts. Jaya Pk. 16,503 ft. (5030 m)

New Guinea

PAPUA NEW GUINEA

Gulf of Papua

Torres Strait

Cape York

Port Moresby

Solomon Sea

Guadalcanal

Honiara

Coral Sea

VANUATU

Espiritu Santo

Efate Port-Vila

Loyalty Is.

New Caledonia

Chesterfield Is.

Darwin

Joseph Bonaparte Gulf

Arnhem Land

Groote Eylandt

Daly R.

Victoria R.

Gulf of Carpentaria

Wellesley Is.

Cape York Pen.

Great Barrier Reef

Townsville

Kimberley Plateau

Roebuck Bay

Fitzroy R.

Eighty Mile Beach

Great Sandy Desert

Lake Mackay

Barkly Tableland

Flinders R.

Tanami Desert

Central Lowlands

Great Dividing Range

TROPIC OF CAPRICORN 23½°S

North West Cape

Hamersley Range

Shark Bay

Western Plateau

Gibson Desert

Macdonnell Ranges

Alice Springs

Uluru (Ayers Rock) 2,844 ft. (867 m)

Musgrave Ranges

Simpson Desert

AUSTRALIA

Great Artesian Basin

Fraser I.

Brisbane

Norfolk I.

Great Victoria Desert

Lake Eyre

Lake Torrens

Darling R.

Lachlan R.

Great Dividing Range

Lord Howe I.

Lake Barlee

Perth

Darling Range

Cape Leeuwin

Nullarbor Plain

Lake Gairdner

Flinders Ranges

Murray River

Sydney

Canberra

Great Australian Bight

Spencer Gulf

Kangaroo I.

Adelaide

Melbourne

Australian Alps

Mt. Kosciuszko 7,310 ft. (2228 m)

Tasman Sea

North Cape

Auckland

Bay of Plenty

NEW ZEALAND

North Island

INDIAN OCEAN

King I.

Bass Strait

Furneaux Group

Mt. Ossa 5,305 ft. (1617 m)

Tasmania

Aoraki/Mt. Cook 12,316 ft. (3754 m)

Southern Alps

South Island

Foveaux Strait

Stewart I.

Cook Strait

Wellington

Banks Pen.

EQUATOR

LAND COVER MAP

AUSTRALIA

AND ITS NEIGHBORS

Cropland   Grassland

Semi-desert & desert   Tropical rain forest   Broadleaf forest

Boundary Symbols

○○○○○○○○ Continental boundary

——————— International boundary

Scale

1:35,800,000

0   200   400   600   800 miles

1 in. to 565 mi.

0   200   400   600   800 kilometers

1 cm to 358 km

Detailed legend on page 6   Lambert Equal Area Projection

The vast, sparsely populated Australian **outback** covers about 80 percent of the continent. It consists mostly of large deserts and is known for its unusual wildlife. Here, an enormous termite mound in the Tanami Desert in north central Australia dominates the landscape.

ELEVATION MAP

AUSTRALIA
AND ITS NEIGHBORS

Meters Above Sea Level	Feet Above Sea Level
Over 3000	Over 10,000
1500 to 3000	5,000 to 10,000
600 to 1500	2,000 to 5,000
300 to 600	1,000 to 2,000
150 to 300	500 to 1,000
0 to 150	0 to 500
Below sea level	Below sea level

Scale
1:35,800,000

0   200   400   600   800 miles
1 in. to 565 mi.
0   200   400 600   800 kilometers
1 cm to 358 km

Detailed legend on page 6 Lambert Equal Area Projection

CROSS SECTION
Vertical exaggeration 78 to 1
Scale at 24°S: 1 in. to 470 mi., 1 cm to 298 km

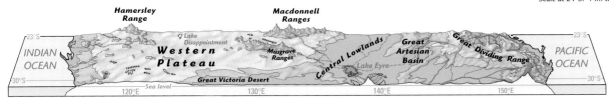

Drawing Lines

Alfred Russel Wallace, a British naturalist, discovered that animals in Indonesia are divided into two groups of species. He drew a line that runs through the Maskassar Strait and matches the geological history of the region. Species to the west of the **Wallace Line** are related to the animals of Asia, while those east of the line are relatives of Australian animals.

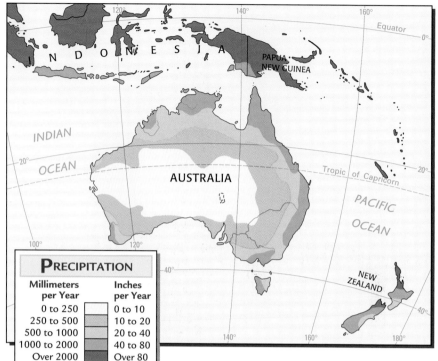

CLIMOGRAPHS

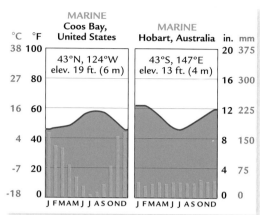

There is a six-month difference in seasons between Coos Bay and Hobart. This is because the Southern Hemisphere experiences winter when the Northern Hemisphere has summer. (For more information, see page 21.)

more at **NDAtlas.com**

PRECIPITATION

Millimeters per Year	Inches per Year
0 to 250	0 to 10
250 to 500	10 to 20
500 to 1000	20 to 40
1000 to 2000	40 to 80
Over 2000	Over 80

Tropical rain forests, such as this one in Papua New Guinea, exist only in regions that have high temperatures and high precipitation year-round. Tropical rain forests are the most biologically diverse ecosystems in the world. (For more information, see pages 30 and 120.)

Stations Down Under

In Australia and New Zealand, large cattle or sheep ranches are called **stations**. Cattle stations are usually much larger than sheep stations. Anna Creek in South Australia, Australia's largest cattle station, covers about 11,600 square miles (30 100 square kilometers) and is larger than the state of Maryland.

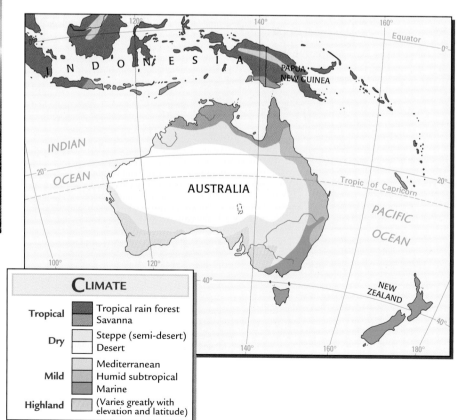

CLIMATE

Tropical		Tropical rain forest
		Savanna
Dry		Steppe (semi-desert)
		Desert
Mild		Mediterranean
		Humid subtropical
		Marine
Highland		(Varies greatly with elevation and latitude)

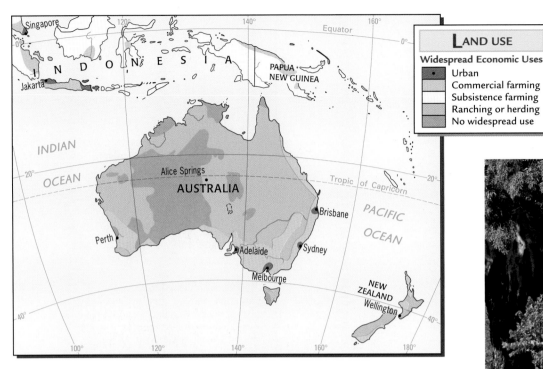

LAND USE

Widespread Economic Uses

- Urban
- Commercial farming
- Subsistence farming
- Ranching or herding
- No widespread use

Winemaking is a rapidly growing industry in Australia. The Barossa Valley, northeast of Adelaide in South Australia, produces more than 20 percent of the wine in the country.

BALANCE OF TRADE

AUSTRALIA

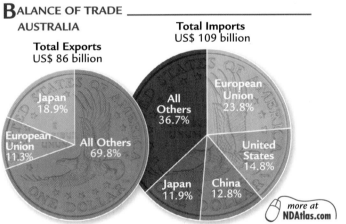

Total Exports
US$ 86 billion

- Japan 18.9%
- European Union 11.3%
- All Others 69.8%

Total Imports
US$ 109 billion

- All Others 36.7%
- European Union 23.8%
- United States 14.8%
- China 12.8%
- Japan 11.9%

more at NDAtlas.com

ENERGY RESOURCES AND METALS

- Coal
- Oil (petroleum)
- Natural gas
- Uranium
- Aluminum (bauxite)
- Copper
- Gold
- Iron
- Lead
- Manganese
- Nickel
- Silver
- Tin
- Zinc

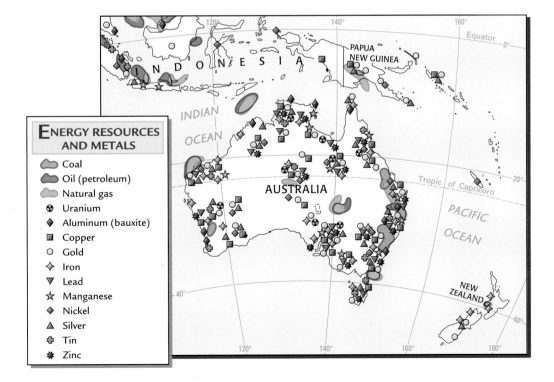

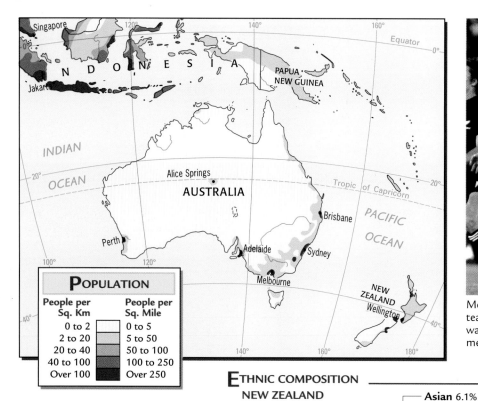

POPULATION

People per Sq. Km	People per Sq. Mile
0 to 2	0 to 5
2 to 20	5 to 50
20 to 40	50 to 100
40 to 100	100 to 250
Over 100	Over 250

Members of New Zealand's international rugby team, the All Blacks, perform a traditional Maori war chant at the start of each game. Several members of the team are Maori.

ETHNIC COMPOSITION
NEW ZEALAND

Asian 6.1%
All Others 0.6%
Other Polynesian 6.0%
Maori 13.5%
European 73.8%

more at NDAtlas.com

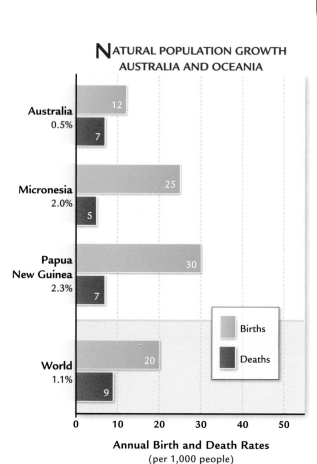

NATURAL POPULATION GROWTH
AUSTRALIA AND OCEANIA

Australia 0.5% — Births 12, Deaths 7

Micronesia 2.0% — Births 25, Deaths 5

Papua New Guinea 2.3% — Births 30, Deaths 7

World 1.1% — Births 20, Deaths 9

Births
Deaths

0   10   20   30   40   50

Annual Birth and Death Rates
(per 1,000 people)

INDIGENOUS PEOPLE
MICRONESIANS Major group
Hawaiians Smaller group

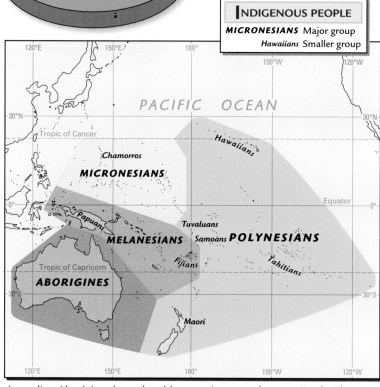

Australian Aborigines have the oldest continuous culture on Earth. They arrived in Australia at least 50,000 years ago. Papuans occupied New Guinea about 40,000 years ago. However, some distant islands in Oceania were occupied much later. For example, Hawaii was first settled 2000 years ago.

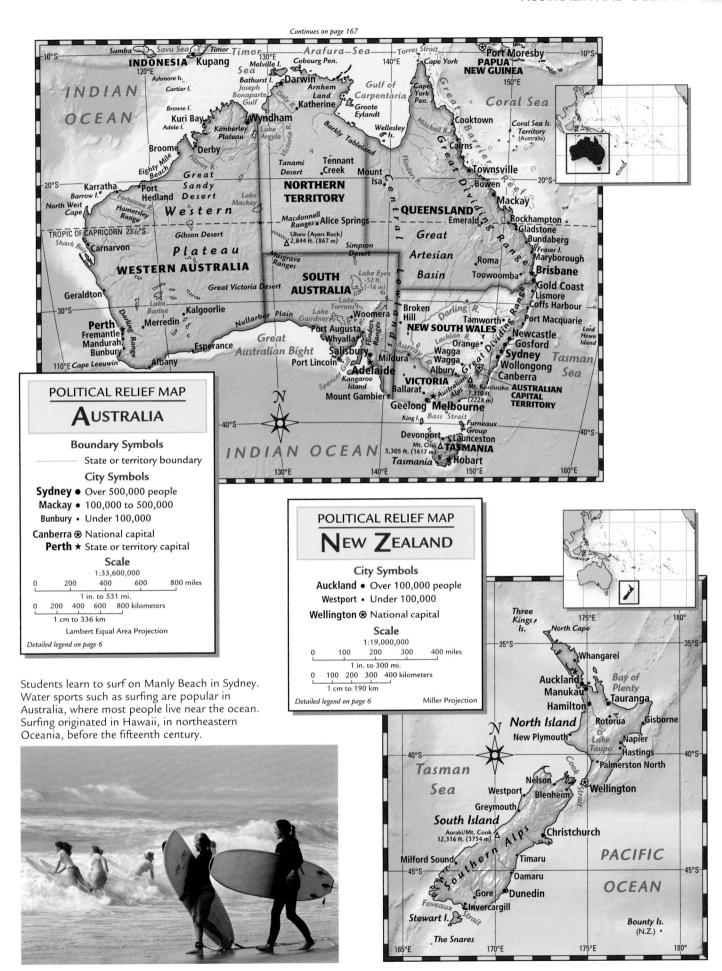

Continues on page 167

POLITICAL RELIEF MAP

AUSTRALIA

Boundary Symbols

················· State or territory boundary

City Symbols

Sydney ● Over 500,000 people

Mackay ● 100,000 to 500,000

Bunbury • Under 100,000

Canberra ⊗ National capital

Perth ★ State or territory capital

Scale
1:33,600,000

0   200   400   600   800 miles

1 in. to 531 mi.

0   200 400 600 800 kilometers

1 cm to 336 km

Lambert Equal Area Projection

Detailed legend on page 6

POLITICAL RELIEF MAP

NEW ZEALAND

City Symbols

Auckland ● Over 100,000 people

Westport • Under 100,000

Wellington ⊗ National capital

Scale
1:19,000,000

0   100   200   300   400 miles

1 in. to 300 mi.

0   100 200 300 400 kilometers

1 cm to 190 km

Detailed legend on page 6   Miller Projection

Students learn to surf on Manly Beach in Sydney. Water sports such as surfing are popular in Australia, where most people live near the ocean. Surfing originated in Hawaii, in northeastern Oceania, before the fifteenth century.

ISSUES ▸ TODAY

What should be done about introduced species?

Introduced species are living things brought to non-native environments. When these species breed quickly and have few or no natural enemies, they can become *invasive*. They compete with native species for food and other resources. Do introduced species damage native ecosystems, or are they important resources? There are many perspectives on this issue. Here are two of them.

RANGE OF INTRODUCED SPECIES

- European wild rabbit
- Sheep
- Feral pig

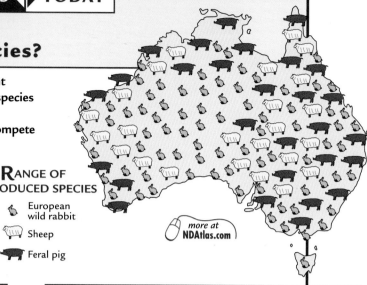

more at NDAtlas.com

All new species must be kept out.

- Because the continent of Australia shares no point of contact with any other land mass, native species have evolved over millions of years in isolation. Any introduction of new species has the potential to be catastrophically disruptive.

- It is nearly impossible to predict which introduced species will harm the environment. For example, the cane toad was introduced to Australia to control the cane beetle population. However, the cane toad population exploded, threatening many native species.

- Measures to control invasive species, such as chemicals and traps, often harm native species as well.

- Invasive species of plants cost Australia over US$3 billion annually in lost production and in control management. Invasive species of pest animals, such as wild rabbits and feral camels, cost Australia over US$550 million a year.

DAMAGE BY INVASIVE SPECIES

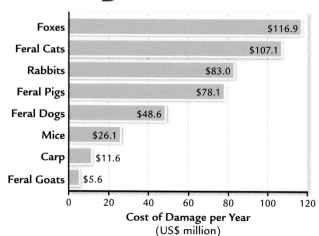

Species	Cost
Foxes	$116.9
Feral Cats	$107.1
Rabbits	$83.0
Feral Pigs	$78.1
Feral Dogs	$48.6
Mice	$26.1
Carp	$11.6
Feral Goats	$5.6

Cost of Damage per Year
(US$ million)

Invasive animals eat plants and other animals, dig tunnels, and foul water. Management strategies including trapping them, poisoning their food, and destroying their nests.

Not all introduced species are bad.

- Australia is one of the most biologically diverse places on Earth, but native species on the continent were never domesticated. As a result, all domesticated species currently found in Australia—including key crops, livestock, and pets—were introduced from abroad.

- European settlers introduced a host of economically important species to Australia, including wheat, sheep, cattle, and grapes.

- Today, agriculture is an important contributor to the Australian economy. The farming industry generates about US$30 billion each year and employs about 370,000 people.

- Introduced species can be used against each other to limit damage to the environment and to native species. Goats consume blackberries and other highly invasive weeds, cats and foxes help control the rabbit population, and cats eat pests such as mice and rats.

WOOL AND WHEAT EXPORTS

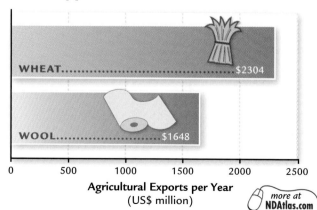

WHEAT..........$2304

WOOL..........$1648

Agricultural Exports per Year
(US$ million)

more at NDAtlas.com

Australia is the world's leading producer of wool. Sheep were first brought to the continent in 1788 by the British.

Antarctica

Antarctica is a single continent located almost entirely south of the Antarctic Circle. It is the world's coldest region.

Antarctica's Features

Mountains

Highest peak: Vinson Massif 16,864 ft. (5 140 m)

Longest range: Transantarctic Mountains 1,900 mi. (3 000 km)

Largest Ocean
Southern Ocean
7,848,000 sq. mi. (20 327 000 sq. km)

Other Key Physical Features
Bentley Subglacial Trench
8,383 ft. below sea level (2 555 m)

Polar Plateau

Antarctic Peninsula

Largest Country
There are no countries in Antarctica.

Largest Research Station
McMurdo (U.S.) temporary population:
250 people (winter), 1,000 people (summer)

AREA COMPARISON

■ **Antarctica**
5,400,000 sq. mi.
(14 000 000 sq. km)

**Contiguous
United States**
3,021,295 sq. mi.
(7 825 112 sq. km)

AFRICA

SOUTH AMERICA

ANTARCTIC CIRCLE

ANTARCTICA

AUSTRALIA

Antarctica • page 182

Antarctica is on land. Notice the exposed ground in the foreground. The ice and snow that cover 98 percent of Antarctica's land account for 70 percent of the world's fresh water.

. . . AND THE ARCTIC

The Arctic includes the islands, northern areas of three continents, and sea ice north of the Arctic Circle.

Arctic's Features

Land Area
Most of the area north of the Arctic Circle is water, not land.

Largest Island
Greenland
836,330 sq. mi. (2 166 066 sq. km)

Largest Ocean
Arctic Ocean
5,427,000 sq. mi. (14 056 000 sq. km)

Largest City
Murmansk, Russia
382,700 people

**more at
NDAtlas.com**
For more maps, graphs, and photos of Antarctica and the Arctic, go to NystromDeskAtlas.com.

ASIA

EUROPE

ARCTIC CIRCLE

Arctic •
page 183

NORTH AMERICA

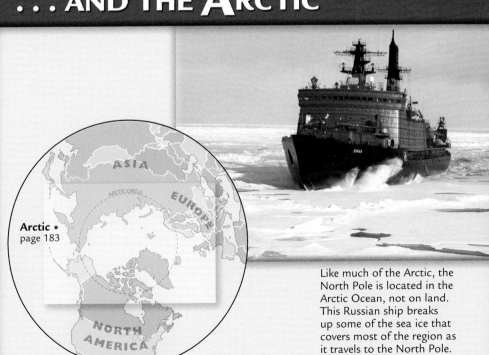

Like much of the Arctic, the North Pole is located in the Arctic Ocean, not on land. This Russian ship breaks up some of the sea ice that covers most of the region as it travels to the North Pole.

CLIMOGRAPHS

Antarctica's average elevation is 7500 feet (2300 meters), while most of the Arctic is at or near sea level. Antarctica is much colder due to its higher elevation. The world's coldest recorded temperature, -128.6°F (-89.2°C), was measured at Vostok.

more at NDAtlas.com

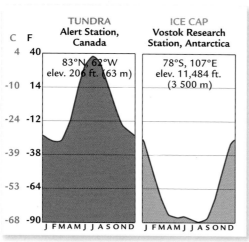

	TUNDRA Alert Station, Canada	ICE CAP Vostok Research Station, Antarctica

83°N, 62°W elev. 206 ft. (63 m)

78°S, 107°E elev. 11,484 ft. (3 500 m)

C	F
4	40
-10	14
-24	-12
-39	-38
-53	-64
-68	-90

J F M A M J J A S O N D   J F M A M J J A S O N D

Calving is the fracturing of large pieces of ice off the edge of a glacier as it reaches the sea. These chunks become icebergs. This Antarctic glacier is calving into Paradise Bay on the Antarctic Peninsula.

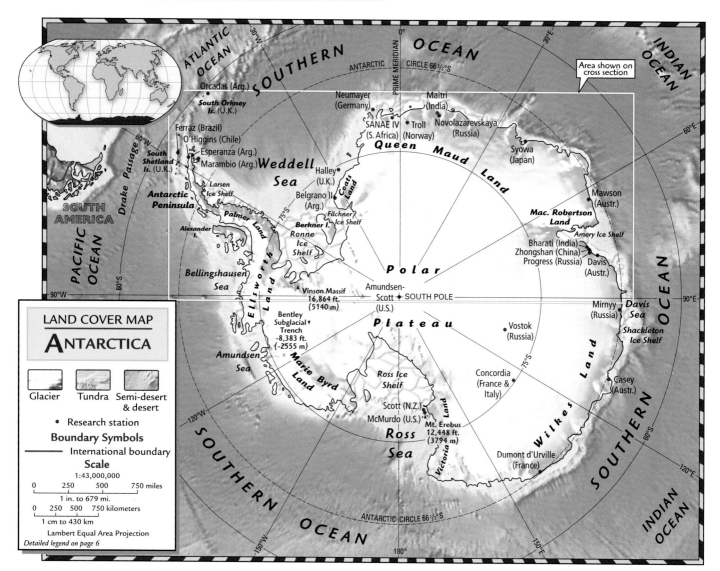

LAND COVER MAP
ANTARCTICA

Glacier   Tundra   Semi-desert & desert

• Research station

Boundary Symbols

International boundary

Scale

1:43,000,000

0   250   500   750 miles

1 in. to 679 mi.

0   250   500   750 kilometers

1 cm to 430 km

Lambert Equal Area Projection

Detailed legend on page 6

The ice cap on the Polar Plateau is up to 2½ miles (4 km) thick.

CROSS SECTION

Vertical exaggeration 37 to 1
Scale at 90°E/W: 1 in. to 690 mi., 1 cm to 437 km

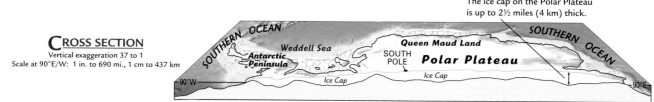

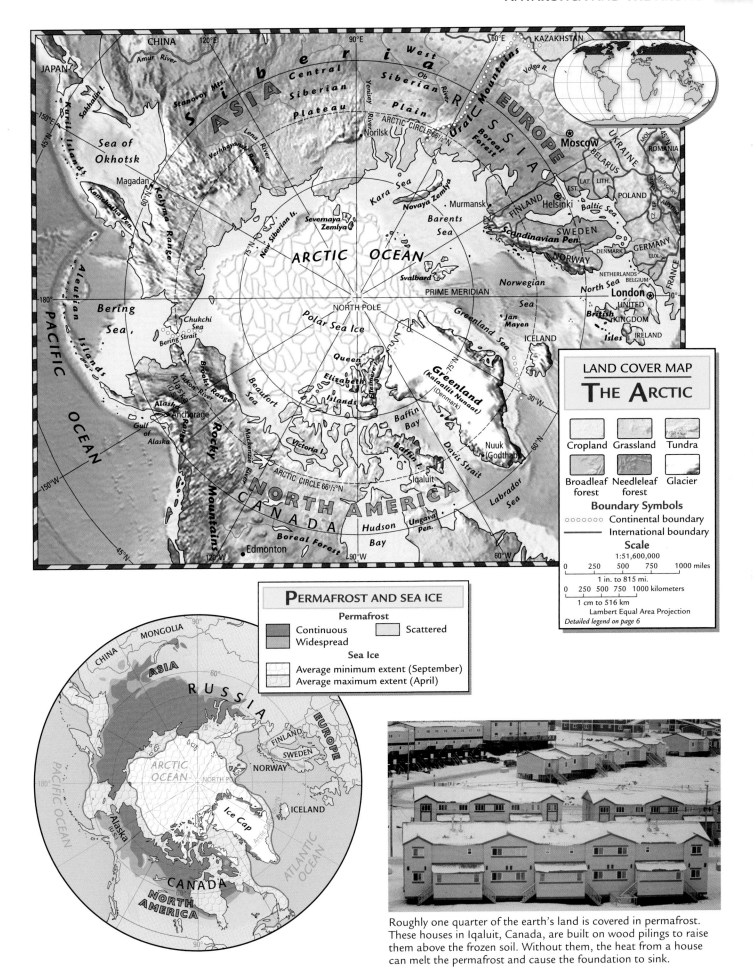

LAND COVER MAP
THE ARCTIC

Cropland   Grassland   Tundra

Broadleaf   Needleleaf   Glacier
forest   forest

Boundary Symbols
○○○○○○ Continental boundary
———— International boundary

Scale
1:51,600,000

0   250   500   750   1000 miles
1 in. to 815 mi.

0   250 500 750 1000 kilometers
1 cm to 516 km
Lambert Equal Area Projection
Detailed legend on page 6

PERMAFROST AND SEA ICE

Permafrost

Continuous   Scattered
Widespread

Sea Ice

Average minimum extent (September)
Average maximum extent (April)

Roughly one quarter of the earth's land is covered in permafrost. These houses in Iqaluit, Canada, are built on wood pilings to raise them above the frozen soil. Without them, the heat from a house can melt the permafrost and cause the foundation to sink.

UNDERSTANDING MAP PROJECTIONS

Because the earth is a nearly perfect sphere, a globe is its only true model. It accurately shows the earth's shape, size, and direction. No flat map can do the same.

▶ Map projections are the means by which the curved surface of a globe is transferred onto the flat surface of a map.

▶ There are hundreds of map projections. They are often classified by their properties.

▶ **Conformal** projections show true shapes, but distort sizes.

▶ **Equal-area** projections show all areas in their true relative sizes, but distort shapes.

▶ **Compromise** projections allow some size distortions in order to portray shapes more accurately.

▶ Map legends often identify the projection used for the map.

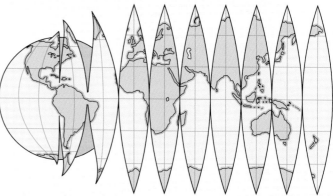

A map of a round object would be like a peeled and flattened orange peel if cartographers could not transform the information from the segments to make them fit together.

SHAPE AND SIZE

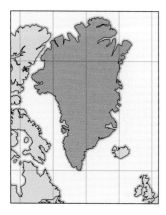

This **Mercator** view of Greenland shows its **shape** fairly accurately. Mercator is a conformal projection.

The **globe** view of Greenland accurately shows both size and shape. Compare it with the Mercator on the left and the Eckert IV on the right.

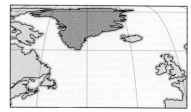

This **Eckert IV** view of Greenland accurately shows its **size**. Eckert IV is an equal-area projection.

DIRECTION

Follow the longitude grid lines (meridians) to find true north on a map.

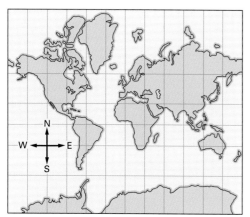

On **cylindrical** projections, such as the **Mercator**, both the parallels and meridians are straight lines. The North Pole is all along the top edge of the map.

On **pseudocylindrical** projections, such as the Robinson, the parallels are straight, but the meridians are curved. On world maps, the North Pole is along the top edge of the map.

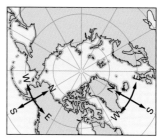

On **azimuthal** projections the parallels are circular lines and the meridians are straight. On this **orthographic** map, the North Pole is in the exact center of the map.

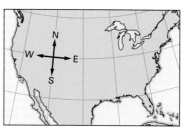

On **conic** projections, such as the **Albers Equal-Area**, parallels are curved, but the meridians are straight. The North Pole, if it appeared, would be in the top center of the map.

Some Map Projections Used in *The Nystrom Desk Atlas*

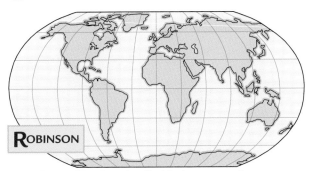

ROBINSON

Properties: Pseudocylindrical, compromise
Shape: Some shape distortion, especially near poles
Size: Minor area distortions
Direction: True along all parallels and Prime Meridian
Scale: Accurate at 38°N and 38°S
Examples: World Political Relief, Land Cover, and Elevation maps, pages 8–13

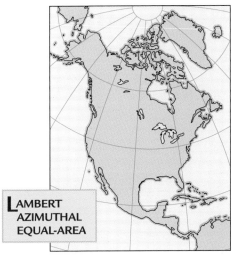

Properties: Azimuthal, equal-area
Shape: Relatively little distortion
Size: True relative size
Direction: True only for the center point
Scale: Accurate at center point
Examples: North America, South America, Africa, Asia maps, pages 46, 112, 122, 152–153

LAMBERT AZIMUTHAL EQUAL-AREA

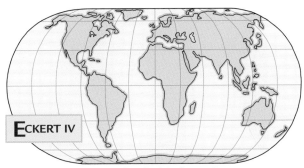

ECKERT IV

Properties: Pseudocylindrical, equal-area
Shape: Relatively minor distortions near Equator and poles
Size: True relative size
Direction: True along all parallels and Prime Meridian
Scale: Accurate at 40°N and 40°S
Examples: World thematic maps, pages 16–21, 24–44

BONNE

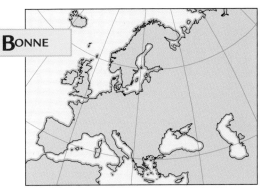

Properties: Pseudoconic, equal-area
Shape: Fairly accurate shapes at mid-latitudes
Size: True relative size
Direction: True at center meridian
Scale: Accurate along center meridian
Examples: Europe map, pages 134–135

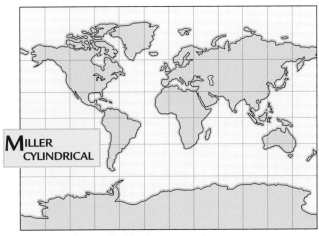

MILLER CYLINDRICAL

Properties: Cylindrical, compromise
Shape: Not as accurate Mercator
Size: Fairly accurate at mid-latitudes
Direction: Only true at the Equator
Scale: Accurate only at the Equator
Examples: Australia and Oceania, Time Zone maps, pages 172–173, 193

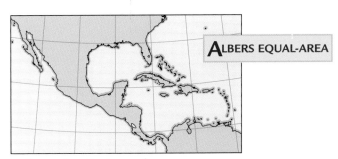

ALBERS EQUAL-AREA

Properties: Conic, equal-area
Shape: Good for regions that extend further east-west than north-south
Size: True relative size
Direction: True on both standard parallels
Scale: Accurate along the standard parallels
Examples: Middle America map, pages 100–101

COUNTRY TABLES

COUNTRY, Dependency *Official Name (if different)*	CAPITAL(S) (Island location)	PRINCIPAL LANGUAGES OFFICIAL and other languages	AREA mi²/km²	POPULATION	POPULATION DENSITY per mi²/km²	NATURAL POP. GROWTH % gain	LIFE EXPECTANCY Male Female	
AFRICA (For country locations, see page 122.)								
ALGERIA *People's Democratic* *Republic of Algeria*	Algiers	ARABIC, French, Berber	919,595 2 381 741	32,930,091	35.8 13.8	1.3	71.7	74.9
ANGOLA *Republic of Angola*	Luanda	PORTUGUESE, Ovimbundu (Umbundu), Mbundu, Kongo	481,354 1 246 700	12,127,071	25.2 9.7	2.1	37.5	39.8
BENIN *Republic of Benin*	Porto-Novo, Cotonou	FRENCH, Fon, Yoruba (Nago), Adja	43,483 112 622	7,862,944	180.8 69.8	2.7	51.9	54.2
BOTSWANA *Republic of Botswana*	Gaborone	ENGLISH, Tswana	224,848 582 356	1,639,833	7.3 2.8	-0.6	33.9	33.6
BURKINA FASO	Ouagadougou	FRENCH, Moore (Mossi), Fula (Fulani)	103,456 267 950	13,902,972	134.4 51.9	3.0	47.3	50.4
BURUNDI *Republic of Burundi*	Bujumbura	RUNDI, FRENCH, Hutu	10,740 27 816	8,090,068	753.3 290.8	2.9	50.1	51.6
CAMEROON *Republic of Cameroon*	Yaounde	ENGLISH, FRENCH, Fang, Bamileke, Duala, Fula (Fulani), Tikar	183,569 475 442	17,340,702	94.5 36.5	2.1	51.0	51.3
CAPE VERDE *Republic of Cape Verde*	Praia (on Santiago)	Portuguese, Crioulo (Portuguese Creole)	1,557 4 033	420,979	270.4 104.4	1.9	67.4	74.2
CENTRAL AFRICAN REPUBLIC	Bangui	SANGO, FRENCH, Gbaya (Baya), Banda	240,324 622 436	4,303,356	17.9 6.9	1.6	43.5	43.6
CHAD *Republic of Chad*	N'Djamena	FRENCH, ARABIC, Sara, Mayo-Kebbi	495,755 1 284 000	9,944,201	20.1 7.7	2.9	45.9	49.2
COMOROS *Union of the Comoros*	Moroni (on Grande Comore)	COMORIAN, FRENCH, ARABIC	719 1 862	690,948	961.0 371.1	2.9	60.0	64.7
CONGO REPUBLIC *Republic of Congo*	Brazzaville	FRENCH, Monokutuba, Lingala, Kongo	132,047 342 000	3,702,314	28.0 10.8	3.0	51.7	54.0
CÔTE D'IVOIRE (Ivory Coast) *Republic of Côte d'Ivoire*	Yamoussoukro, Abidjan	FRENCH, Akan, Gur, Malinke, Kru	123,863 320 803	17,654,843	142.5 55.0	2.1	46.2	51.5
DEMOCRATIC REPUBLIC OF THE CONGO	Kinshasa	FRENCH, ENGLISH, Lingala, Swahili, Kongo, Luba	905,354 2 344 858	62,660,551	69.2 26.7	3.1	50.0	52.9
DJIBOUTI *Republic of Djibouti*	Djibouti	FRENCH, ARABIC, Somali, Afar	8,950 23 200	486,530	54.4 21.0	2.1	41.9	44.5
EGYPT *Arab Republic of Egypt*	Cairo	ARABIC	385,229 997 739	78,887,007	204.8 79.1	1.8	68.8	73.9
EQUATORIAL GUINEA *Republic of Equatorial Guinea*	Malabo	SPANISH, FRENCH, Fang	10,831 28 051	540,109	49.9 19.3	2.1	48.0	51.1
ERITREA *State of Eritrea*	Asmara	Tigrinya, Tigre	46,760 121 100	4,786,994	102.4 39.5	2.5	57.4	60.7
ETHIOPIA *Federal Democratic* *Republic of Ethiopia*	Addis Ababa	Oromo (Oromifa), Amharic	435,186 1 127 127	74,777,981	171.8 66.3	2.4	47.9	50.2
GABON *Gabonese Republic*	Libreville	FRENCH, Fang	103,347 267 667	1,424,906	13.8 5.3	2.4	53.2	55.8
GAMBIA *Republic of The Gambia*	Banjul	ENGLISH, Malinke, Fula (Fulani), Wolof	4,127 10 689	1,641,564	397.8 153.6	2.7	52.3	56.0
GHANA *Republic of Ghana*	Accra	ENGLISH, Hausa, Akan	92,098 238 533	22,409,572	243.3 93.9	2.1	58.1	59.7
GUINEA *Republic of Guinea*	Conakry	FRENCH, Fula (Fulani), Malinke, Susu	94,919 245 836	9,690,222	102.1 39.4	2.6	48.3	50.7
GUINEA-BISSAU *Republic of Guinea-Bissau*	Bissau	PORTUGUESE, Crioulo (Portuguese Creole), Balante, Fula (Fulani)	13,948 36 125	1,442,029	103.4 39.9	2.1	45.1	48.8
KENYA · *Republic of Kenya*	Nairobi	SWAHILI, ENGLISH, Kikuyu, Luhya, Luo	224,961 582 646	34,707,817	154.3 59.6	2.5	49.8	48.1
LESOTHO *Kingdom of Lesotho*	Maseru	SOTHO, ENGLISH, Zulu	11,720 30 355	2,022,331	172.6 66.6	-0.4	35.6	33.2
LIBERIA *Republic of Liberia*	Monrovia	ENGLISH, Krio (English Creole), Kpelle, Bassa	38,250 99 067	3,042,004	79.5 30.7	2.2	38.0	41.4
LIBYA *Socialist People's Libyan* *Arab Jamahiriya*	Tripoli	ARABIC, Berber	679,362 1 759 540	5,900,754	8.7 3.4	2.3	74.5	79.0
MADAGASCAR *Republic of Madagascar*	Antananarivo	Malagasy, French	226,658 587 041	18,595,469	82.0 31.7	3.0	54.9	59.8

COUNTRY, Dependency: all independent countries, as well as selected dependencies; includes both conventional and official forms of country names. **CAPITALS:** all national capitals, with island location when applicable. **PRINCIPAL LANGUAGE(S):** all official languages, as well as primary languages spoken by a substantial proportion of the population. **POPULATION DENSITY:** computed as population divided by area; given per square mile and per square kilometer. **NATURAL POP. GROWTH:** annual population increase; does not include population change due to immigration or emigration. **LIFE EXPECTANCY:** average length of life in years at birth; given for males and females.

COUNTRY, Dependency Official Name (if different)	CAPITAL(S) (Island location)	PRINCIPAL LANGUAGES OFFICIAL and other languages	AREA mi²/km²	POPULATION	POPULATION DENSITY per mi²/km²	NATURAL POP. GROWTH % gain	LIFE EXPECTANCY Male	Female
MALAWI Republic of Malawi	Lilongwe	ENGLISH, Chewa, Lomwe, Yao	45,747 118 484	13,013,926	284.5 109.8	2.4	41.9	41.5
MALI Republic of Mali	Bamako	FRENCH, Bambara	482,077 1 248 574	11,716,829	24.3 9.4	3.3	47.1	51.0
MAURITANIA Islamic Republic of Mauritania	Nouakchott	ARABIC, Hassaniya Arabic	398,000 1 030 700	3,177,388	8.0 3.1	2.9	50.9	55.4
MAURITIUS Republic of Mauritius	Port Louis	ENGLISH, French, Creole, Bhojpuri	788 2 040	1,240,827	1,574.7 608.2	0.9	68.7	76.7
MOROCCO Kingdom of Morocco	Rabat	ARABIC, French, Berber	172,414 456 550	33,241,259	192.8 72.8	1.7	68.6	73.4
MOZAMBIQUE Republic of Mozambique	Maputo	PORTUGUESE, Makua	313,661 812 379	19,686,505	62.8 24.2	1.5	39.5	40.1
NAMIBIA Republic of Namibia	Windhoek	ENGLISH, Ovambo, Nama, Kavango, Afrikaans	318,580 825 118	2,044,147	35.8 6.4	0.7	44.5	42.3
NIGER Republic of Niger	Niamey	FRENCH, Hausa, Songhai, Zerma	459,286 1 189 546	12,525,094	27.3 10.5	3.0	43.8	43.7
NIGERIA Federal Republic of Nigeria	Abuja	ENGLISH, Hausa, Yoruba, Igbo (Ibo), Fula (Fulani)	356,669 923 768	131,859,731	369.7 142.7	2.3	46.5	47.7
RWANDA Republic of Rwanda	Kigali	RWANDA, FRENCH, ENGLISH	10,169 26 338	8,648,248	850.5 328.4	2.4	46.3	48.4
SAO TOME AND PRINCIPE Democratic Republic of Sao Tome and Principe	Sao Tome	PORTUGUESE, Crioulo (Portuguese Creole)	386 1 001	193,413	501.1 193.2	3.4	65.7	69.0
SENEGAL Republic of Senegal	Dakar	FRENCH, Wolof, Fula (Fulani)-Tukulor	75,955 196 722	11,987,121	157.8 60.9	2.4	57.7	60.9
SEYCHELLES Republic of Seychelles	Victoria (on Mahe)	French, English, Seselwa (French Creole)	176 455	81,541	463.3 179.2	1.0	66.7	77.6
SIERRA LEONE Republic of Sierra Leone	Freetown	ENGLISH, Krio (English Creole), Mende, Temne	27,699 71 740	6,005,250	216.8 83.7	2.3	38.1	42.5
SOMALIA	Mogadishu	SOMALI, ARABIC	246,000 637 000	8,863,338	36.0 13.9	2.9	46.7	50.3
SOUTH AFRICA Republic of South Africa	Pretoria (Tshawane), Cape Town, Bloemfontein	ZULU, XHOSA, AFRIKAANS, SOTHO, TSWANA, ENGLISH, TSONGA, VENDA, SWASI, NDEBELE	470,693 1 219 090	44,187,637	93.9 36.2	-0.3	43.3	42.2
SOUTH SUDAN Republic of South Sudan	Juba	ARABIC, ENGLISH, Juba Arabic, Dinka, Nver, Zande, Bari, Shiluk	248,777 644 329	8,260,490	33.2 12.8	no data	no data	no data
SUDAN Republic of the Sudan	Khartoum	ARABIC, Nubian languages, Beja	718,723 1 816 484	36,787,012	51.2 19.8	no data	no data	no data
SWAZILAND Kingdom of Swaziland	Mbabane, Lobamba	SWAZI, ENGLISH	6,704 17 364	1,136,334	169.5 65.4	-0.1	32.1	33.2
TANZANIA United Republic of Tanzania	Dar es Salaam, Dodoma	SWAHILI, ENGLISH, Nyamwesi (Sukuma)	364,017 942 799	37,445,392	102.9 39.7	2.1	44.9	46.4
TOGO Togolese Republic	Lome	FRENCH, Ewe, Kabre	21,925 56 785	5,548,702	253.1 97.7	2.7	55.4	59.5
TUNISIA Republic of Tunisia	Tunis	ARABIC, French	63,170 163 610	10,175,014	161.1 62.2	1.0	73.4	77.0
UGANDA Republic of Uganda	Kampala	ENGLISH, Swahili, Ganda (Luganda)	93,065 241 038	28,195,754	303.0 117.0	3.5	51.7	53.7
Western Sahara (adm. Morocco) Sahrawi Arab Democratic Republic	El Aauin (Laayoune)	Arabic	102,700 266 000	273,008	2.7 1.0	no data	no data	no data
ZAMBIA Republic of Zambia	Lusaka	ENGLISH, Bemba, Nyanja, Tonga	290,585 752 612	11,502,010	39.6 15.3	2.1	39.8	40.3
ZIMBABWE Republic of Zimbabwe	Harare	ENGLISH, Shona, Ndebele	150,872 390 757	12,236,805	81.1 31.3	0.6	40.4	38.2

ASIA (For country locations, see pages 152–153.)

COUNTRY, Dependency Official Name (if different)	CAPITAL(S) (Island location)	PRINCIPAL LANGUAGES OFFICIAL and other languages	AREA mi²/km²	POPULATION	POPULATION DENSITY per mi²/km²	NATURAL POP. GROWTH % gain	LIFE EXPECTANCY Male	Female
AFGHANISTAN Islamic Republic of Afghanistan	Kabul	PASHTO, DARI (Persian), Tajik, Hazara, Uzbek	249,347 645 807	31,056,997	124.6 48.1	2.6	43.2	43.5
ARMENIA Republic of Armenia	Yerevan	ARMENIAN	11,484 29 743	2,976,372	259.2 100.1	0.4	68.3	76.0
AZERBAIJAN Republic of Azerbaijan	Baku	AZERBAIJANI (Azeri)	33,400 86 600	7,961,619	238.4 91.9	1.1	59.8	68.1
BAHRAIN Kingdom of Bahrain	Manama	ARABIC	277 718	698,585	2,522.0 973.0	1.4	72.0	77.0
BANGLADESH People's Republic of Bangladesh	Dhaka	BANGLA (Bengali)	56,977 147 570	147,365,352	2,586.4 998.6	2.2	62.5	62.5
BHUTAN Kingdom of Bhutan	Thimphu	DZONGKHA, Nepali (Hindi)	14,824 38 394	2,279,723	153.8 59.4	2.1	55.0	54.5
BRUNEI State of Brunei, Abode of Peace	Bandar Seri Begawan	MALAY, English, Chinese	2,226 5 765	379,444	170.5 65.8	1.6	72.6	77.6
CAMBODIA Kingdom of Cambodia	Phnom Penh	KHMER	69,898 181 035	13,881,427	198.6 76.7	1.8	57.4	61.3

COUNTRY, Dependency *Official Name (if different)*	CAPITAL(S) (Island location)	PRINCIPAL LANGUAGES OFFICIAL and other languages	AREA mi²/km²	POPULATION	POPULATION DENSITY per mi²/km²	NATURAL POP. GROWTH % gain	LIFE EXPECTANCY Male Female	
CHINA *People's Republic of China*	Beijing	MANDARIN, Chinese (Han), Wu, Cantonese (Yue)	3,696,100 9 572 900	1,313,973,713	355.5 137.3	0.6	70.9	74.5
CYPRUS *Republic of Cyprus*	Nicosia	GREEK, TURKISH	2,276 5 896	784,301	344.6 133.0	0.5	75.4	80.3
EAST TIMOR *Democratic Republic of Timor-Leste*	Dili	Tetum (Tetun), Portuguese	5,639 14 604	1,062,777	188.5 72.8	2.1	64.0	68.7
GEORGIA	Tbilisi	GEORGIAN, Russian, Armenian	27,086 70 152	4,661,473	172.1 66.4	0.1	72.8	79.9
INDIA *Republic of India*	New Delhi	HINDI, ENGLISH, Bangla (Bengali), Telugu, Marathi, Tamil, Urdu, Gujarati	1,222,559 3 166 414	1,095,351,995	896.0 345.9	1.4	63.9	65.6
INDONESIA *Republic of Indonesia*	Jakarta (on Java)	INDONESIAN (Malay), Javanese, Sundanese	730,024 1 890 754	245,452,739	336.2 129.8	1.4	67.4	72.5
IRAN *Islamic Republic of Iran*	Tehran	FARSI (Persian), Azerbaijani (Azeri)	629,272 1 629 807	68,688,433	109.2 42.1	1.1	68.9	71.7
IRAQ *Republic of Iraq*	Baghdad	ARABIC, Kurdish	167,618 434 128	26,783,383	159.8 61.7	2.7	67.8	70.3
ISRAEL *State of Israel*	Jerusalem	HEBREW, ARABIC	8,367 21 671	6,352,117	759.2 293.1	1.2	77.3	81.7
JAPAN	Tokyo (on Honshu)	JAPANESE	145,898 377 873	127,463,611	873.6 337.3	0.1	78.0	84.7
JORDAN *Hashemite Kingdom of Jordan*	Amman	ARABIC	34,495 89 342	5,906,760	171.2 66.1	1.9	75.9	81.1
KAZAKHSTAN *Republic of Kazakhstan*	Astana	KAZAKH, Russian	1,052,100 2 724 900	15,233,244	14.5 5.6	0.6	61.6	72.5
KUWAIT *State of Kuwait*	Kuwait	ARABIC	6,880 17 818	2,418,393	351.5 135.7	1.9	76.1	78.3
KYRGYZSTAN *Kyrgyz Republic*	Bishkek	KYRGYZ, RUSSIAN, Uzbek	77,199 199 945	5,213,898	67.5 26.1	1.5	64.5	72.7
LAOS *Lao People's Democratic Republic*	Vientiane (Viangchan)	LAO-LUM (Lao), Lao-Theung	91,429 236 800	6,368,481	69.7 26.9	2.4	53.5	57.6
LEBANON *Lebanese Republic*	Beirut	ARABIC, French	4,016 10 400	3,874,050	964.7 372.5	1.3	70.4	75.5
MALAYSIA	Kuala Lumpur	MALAY, English	127,355 329 847	24,385,858	191.5 73.9	1.8	69.8	75.4
MALDIVES *Republic of Maldives*	Male (on Male)	DIVEHI (Maldivian)	115 298	359,008	3,121.8 1 204.7	2.8	63.1	65.8
MONGOLIA	Ulaanbaatar	KHALKHA (Mongolian)	603,930 1 564 160	2,832,224	4.7 1.8	1.4	62.6	67.3
MYANMAR (Burma) *Union of Myanmar*	Nay Pyi Taw, Yangon (Rangoon)	BURMESE	261,228 676 577	47,382,633	181.4 70.0	0.8	58.1	64.0
NEPAL *Federal Democratic Republic of Nepal*	Kathmandu	NEPALI, English	56,827 147 181	28,287,147	497.8 192.2	2.2	60.4	59.9
NORTH KOREA *Democratic People's Republic of Korea*	Pyongyang	KOREAN	47,399 122 762	23,113,019	487.6 188.3	0.9	68.9	74.5
OMAN *Sultanate of Oman*	Muscat	ARABIC	119,500 309 500	3,102,229	26.0 10.0	3.3	71.1	75.7
PAKISTAN *Islamic Republic of Pakistan*	Islamabad	URDU, Punjabi, Pashto, Sindhi, English, Saraiki	307,374 796 096	165,803,560	539.4 208.3	2.2	62.4	64.4
PHILIPPINES *Republic of the Philippines*	Manila (on Luzon)	PILIPINO, ENGLISH, Cebuano	122,121 316 294	89,468,677	732.6 282.9	2.0	67.3	73.2
QATAR *State of Qatar*	Doha	ARABIC	4,412 11 427	885,359	200.7 77.5	1.1	71.4	76.6
SAUDI ARABIA *Kingdom of Saudi Arabia*	Riyadh	ARABIC	830,000 2 149 690	27,019,731	32.6 12.6	2.7	73.7	77.8
SINGAPORE *Republic of Singapore*	Singapore	MANDARIN, ENGLISH, MALAY, TAMIL, Chinese	269 697	4,492,150	16,699.4 6 445.0	0.5	79.1	84.5
SOUTH KOREA *Republic of Korea*	Seoul	KOREAN	38,572 99 900	48,846,823	1,266.4 489.0	0.4	73.6	80.8
SRI LANKA *Democratic Socialist Republic of Sri Lanka*	Colombo, Sri Jayewardenepura Kotte	SINHALA, TAMIL	25,332 65 610	20,222,240	798.3 308.2	0.9	70.8	76.1
SYRIA *Syrian Arab Republic*	Damascus	ARABIC	71,498 185 180	18,881,361	264.1 102.0	2.3	69.0	71.7
TAIWAN *Republic of China on Taiwan*	Taipei	MANDARIN, Min, Hakka	13,969 36 179	23,036,087	1,649.1 636.7	0.6	74.7	80.5
TAJIKISTAN *Republic of Tajikistan*	Dushanbe	TAJIK, Uzbek	55,300 143 100	7,320,815	132.4 51.2	2.4	62.0	68.0
THAILAND *Kingdom of Thailand*	Bangkok	THAI (Siamese), Lao, Chinese	198,117 513 120	64,631,595	326.2 126.0	0.7	70.0	74.7
TURKEY *Republic of Turkey*	Ankara	TURKISH, Kurdish	299,158 774 815	70,413,958	235.4 90.9	1.1	70.2	75.2
TURKMENISTAN	Ashgabat	TURKMEN	188,500 488 100	5,042,920	26.8 10.3	1.9	58.4	65.4
UNITED ARAB EMIRATES	Abu Dhabi	ARABIC	32,280 83 600	2,602,713	80.6 31.1	1.5	72.9	78.1

COUNTRY, Dependency *Official Name (if different)*	CAPITAL(S) (Island location)	PRINCIPAL LANGUAGES OFFICIAL and other languages	AREA mi²/km²	POPULATION	POPULATION DENSITY per mi²/km²	NATURAL POP. GROWTH % gain	LIFE EXPECTANCY Male Female	
UZBEKISTAN *Republic of Uzbekistan*	Tashkent	UZBEK	172,700 447 400	27,307,134	158.1 61.0	1.8	61.2	68.1
VIETNAM *Socialist Republic of Vietnam*	Hanoi	VIETNAMESE	128,379 332 501	84,402,966	657.5 253.8	1.1	68.1	73.9
YEMEN *Republic of Yemen*	Sanaa	ARABIC	214,300 555 000	21,456,188	100.1 38.7	3.5	60.2	64.1

AUSTRALIA AND OCEANIA (For country locations, see pages 172–173.)

COUNTRY, Dependency *Official Name (if different)*	CAPITAL(S) (Island location)	PRINCIPAL LANGUAGES OFFICIAL and other languages	AREA mi²/km²	POPULATION	POPULATION DENSITY per mi²/km²	NATURAL POP. GROWTH % gain	LIFE EXPECTANCY Male Female	
AUSTRALIA *Commonwealth of Australia*	Canberra	ENGLISH	2,969,978 7 692 208	20,264,082	6.8 2.6	0.5	77.6	83.5
FIJI *Republic of the Fiji Islands*	Suva (on Viti Levu)	ENGLISH, Fijian, Hindi	7,055 18 272	905,949	128.4 49.6	1.7	67.3	72.5
French Polynesia (Fr.)	Papeete (on Tahiti)	FRENCH. TAHITIAN, Polynesian languages	1,544 4 000	274,578	177.8 68.6	1.2	73.7	78.6
KIRIBATI *Republic of Kiribati*	Tarawa (on Tarawa)	ENGLISH, Kiribati	313 811	105,432	336.8 130.0	2.2	59.1	65.2
MARSHALL ISLANDS *Republic of the Marshall Islands*	Majuro (on Majuro)	MARSHALLESE, ENGLISH	70 181	60,422	863.2 333.8	2.9	68.3	72.4
MICRONESIA *Federated States of Micronesia*	Palikir (on Pohnpei)	Chuukese/Mortlockese, Pohnpeian	271 701	108,004	398.5 154.1	2.0	68.2	72.0
NAURU *Republic of Nauru*	Yaren District (unofficial)	English, Nauruan	8 21	13,287	1,620.4 626.7	1.8	59.5	66.8
New Caledonia (Fr.)	Noumea	FRENCH, Melanesian and Polynesian languages	7,172 18 575	219,246	30.6 11.8	1.3	71.3	77.4
NEW ZEALAND	Wellington (on North Island)	ENGLISH, MAORI	104,454 270 534	4,076,140	39.0 15.1	0.6	75.8	81.9
PALAU *Republic of Palau*	Melekeok (on Babelthuap)	PALAUAN, ENGLISH	188 488	20,579	109.5 42.2	1.2	67.3	73.8
PAPUA NEW GUINEA *Independent State of Papua New Guinea*	Port Moresby (on New Guinea)	ENGLISH, Tok Pisin (English Creole), Papuan and Melanesian languages	178,704 462 840	5,670,544	31.7 12.3	2.3	63.1	67.6
SAMOA *Independent State of Samoa*	Apia (on Upolu)	SAMOAN, ENGLISH	1,093 2 831	176,908	161.9 62.5	0.9	68.2	73.9
SOLOMON ISLANDS	Honiara (on Guadacanal)	ENGLISH, Melanesian languages	10,954 28 370	552,438	50.4 19.5	2.7	70.4	75.6
TONGA *Kingdom of Tonga*	Nuku'alofa (on Tongatapu)	TONGAN, ENGLISH	290 750	114,689	395.5 152.9	2.0	67.3	72.5
TUVALU	Funafuti (on Funafuti)	Tuvaluan	10 26	11,810	1,192.9 461.3	1.5	66.1	70.7
VANUATU *Republic of Vanuatu*	Port-Vila (on Efate)	BISLAMA (English Creole), ENGLISH, FRENCH	4,707 12 190	208,869	44.4 17.1	1.5	61.3	64.4

EUROPE (For country locations, see pages 134–135.)

COUNTRY, Dependency *Official Name (if different)*	CAPITAL(S) (Island location)	PRINCIPAL LANGUAGES OFFICIAL and other languages	AREA mi²/km²	POPULATION	POPULATION DENSITY per mi²/km²	NATURAL POP. GROWTH % gain	LIFE EXPECTANCY Male Female	
ALBANIA *Republic of Albania*	Tirana	ALBANIAN	11,082 28 703	3,581,655	323.2 124.8	1.0	74.8	80.3
ANDORRA *Principality of Andorra*	Andorra la Vella	CATALAN, Spanish	179 464	71,201	397.8 153.5	0.3	80.6	86.6
AUSTRIA *Republic of Austria*	Vienna	GERMAN	32,383 83 871	8,192,880	253.0 97.7	-0.1	76.2	82.1
BELARUS *Republic of Belarus*	Minsk	BELARUSIAN, RUSSIAN	80,200 207 600	10,293,011	128.3 49.6	-0.3	63.5	75.0
BELGIUM *Kingdom of Belgium*	Brussels	DUTCH, FRENCH, GERMAN	11,787 30 528	10,379,067	880.6 340.0	0.0	75.6	82.1
BOSNIA AND HERZEGOVINA	Sarajevo	BOSNIAN, SERBIAN, CROATIAN	19,772 51 209	4,498,976	227.5 87.9	0.1	74.4	81.9
BULGARIA *Republic of Bulgaria*	Sofia	BULGARIAN	42,858 111 002	7,385,367	172.3 66.5	-0.5	68.7	76.1
CROATIA *Republic of Croatia*	Zagreb	SERBO-CROATIAN (Croatian)	21,851 56 594	4,494,749	205.7 79.4	-0.2	71.0	78.5
CZECH REPUBLIC	Prague	CZECH, Moravian	30,450 78 866	10,235,455	336.1 129.8	-0.1	72.9	79.7
DENMARK *Kingdom of Denmark*	Copenhagen	DANISH	16,640 43 098	5,450,661	327.6 126.5	0.1	75.5	80.2
ESTONIA *Republic of Estonia*	Tallinn	ESTONIAN, Russian	16,769 43 431	1,324,333	79.0 30.5	-0.3	66.6	77.8
FINLAND *Republic of Finland*	Helsinki	Finnish, Swedish	130,559 338 145	5,231,372	40.1 15.5	0.1	75.0	82.2
FRANCE *French Republic*	Paris	FRENCH	210,026 543 965	60,876,136	289.9 111.9	0.3	76.1	83.5
GERMANY *Federal Republic of Germany*	Berlin	GERMAN	137,847 357 023	82,422,299	597.9 230.9	-0.2	75.8	82.0
GREECE *Hellenic Republic*	Athens	GREEK	50,949 131 957	10,688,058	209.8 81.0	0.0	76.7	81.9

COUNTRY, Dependency *Official Name (if different)*	CAPITAL(S) (Island location)	PRINCIPAL LANGUAGES OFFICIAL and other languages	AREA mi²/km²	POPULATION	POPULATION DENSITY per mi²/km²	NATURAL POP. GROWTH % gain	LIFE EXPECTANCY Male	Female
HUNGARY	Budapest	HUNGARIAN	35,919 93 030	9,981,334	277.9 107.3	-0.3	68.5	77.1
ICELAND *Republic of Iceland*	Reykjavik	ICELANDIC	39,741 102 928	299,388	7.5 2.9	0.7	78.2	82.5
IRELAND	Dublin	ENGLISH, IRISH	27,133 70 273	4,062,235	149.7 57.8	0.7	75.1	80.5
ITALY *Italian Republic*	Rome	ITALIAN	116,324 301 277	58,133,509	499.8 193.0	-0.1	76.9	82.9
KOSOVO *Republic of Kosovo*	Pristina	ALBANIAN, SERBIAN Bosnian, Turkish	4,203 10,887	2,126,708	506.0 195.3	no data	no data	no data
LATVIA *Republic of Latvia*	Riga	LATVIAN, Russian	24,938 64 589	2,274,735	91.2 35.2	-0.5	66.1	76.9
LIECHTENSTEIN *Principality of Liechtenstein*	Vaduz	GERMAN	62 160	33,987	548.2 212.4	0.3	76.1	83.3
LITHUANIA *Republic of Lithuania*	Vilnius	LITHUANIAN	25,212 65 300	3,585,906	142.2 54.9	-0.2	69.2	79.5
LUXEMBOURG *Grand Duchy of Luxembourg*	Luxembourg	Luxemburgian, Portuguese	999 2 586	474,413	474.9 183.5	0.4	75.6	82.4
MACEDONIA *Republic of Macedonia*	Skopje	MACEDONIAN, Albanian	9,928 25 713	2,050,554	206.5 79.7	0.3	71.5	76.6
MALTA *Republic of Malta*	Valletta	MALTESE, ENGLISH	122 315	400,214	3,280.4 1 270.5	0.2	76.8	81.3
MOLDOVA *Republic of Moldova*	Chisinau	ROMANIAN (Moldovan), Russian	13,068 33 845	4,466,706	341.8 132.0	0.2	61.6	69.9
MONACO *Principality of Monaco*	Monaco	FRENCH, Italian, Monegasque	0.75 1.95	32,543	43,390.7 16 688.7	-0.3	75.9	83.7
MONTENEGRO *Republic of Montenegro*	Podgorica	SERBIAN	5,333 13 812	630,548	118.2 45.7	0.3	no data	no data
NETHERLANDS *Kingdom of The Netherlands*	Amsterdam, The Hague	DUTCH	16,034 41 528	16,491,461	1,028.5 397.1	0.2	76.4	81.7
NORWAY *Kingdom of Norway*	Oslo	NORWEGIAN	125,004 323 758	4,610,820	36.9 14.2	0.2	76.9	82.3
POLAND *Republic of Poland*	Warsaw	POLISH	120,728 312 685	38,536,869	319.2 123.2	0.0	71.0	79.2
PORTUGAL *Portuguese Republic*	Lisbon	PORTUGUESE	35,580 92 152	10,605,870	298.1 115.1	0.0	74.4	81.2
ROMANIA	Bucharest	ROMANIAN	92,043 238 391	22,303,552	242.3 93.6	-0.1	68.1	75.3
RUSSIA *Russian Federation*	Moscow	RUSSIAN	6,592,800 17 075 400	142,893,540	21.7 8.4	-0.5	60.5	74.1
SAN MARINO *Most Serene Republic* *of San Marino*	San Marino	ITALIAN (Romagnolo)	24 61	29,251	1,218.8 479.5	0.2	78.2	85.5
SERBIA *Republic of Serbia*	Belgrade	SERBO-CROATIAN (Serbian)	29,913 77 474	8,023,557	268.2 103.6	-0.5	71.0	76.0
SLOVAKIA *Slovak Republic*	Bratislava	SLOVAK	18,933 49 035	5,439,448	287.3 110.9	0.1	70.8	78.9
SLOVENIA *Republic of Slovenia*	Ljubljana	SLOVENE	7,827 20 273	2,010,347	256.8 99.2	-0.1	72.6	80.3
SPAIN *Kingdom of Spain*	Madrid	CASTILIAN SPANISH, Catalan, Galician	195,363 505 988	40,397,842	206.8 79.8	0.0	76.3	83.2
SWEDEN *Kingdom of Sweden*	Stockholm	SWEDISH	173,860 450 295	9,016,596	51.9 20.0	0.0	78.3	82.9
SWITZERLAND *Swiss Confederation*	Bern, Lausanne	GERMAN, FRENCH, ITALIAN	15,940 41 284	7,523,934	472.0 182.2	0.1	77.7	83.5
UKRAINE	Kiev	UKRAINIAN, Russian	233,062 603 628	46,710,816	200.4 77.4	-0.6	64.7	75.6
UNITED KINGDOM *United Kingdom of Great* *Britain and Northern Ireland*	London (on Great Britain)	ENGLISH	93,788 242 910	60,609,153	646.2 249.5	0.1	76.1	81.1
VATICAN CITY *The Holy See (State* *of the Vatican City)*	Vatican City	Italian, Latin, French	0.17 0.44	932	5,482.4 2 118.2	0.0	no data	no data

NORTH AMERICA   (For country locations, see page 46.)

COUNTRY, Dependency *Official Name (if different)*	CAPITAL(S) (Island location)	PRINCIPAL LANGUAGES OFFICIAL and other languages	AREA mi²/km²	POPULATION	POPULATION DENSITY per mi²/km²	NATURAL POP. GROWTH % gain	LIFE EXPECTANCY Male	Female
ANTIGUA AND BARBUDA	Saint John's (on Antigua)	ENGLISH, English Creole	171 442	69,108	404.1 156.4	1.2	69.8	74.7
Aruba (Neth.)	Oranjestad	DUTCH, Papiamento	75 193	71,891	958.5 372.5	0.5	76.0	82.8
BAHAMAS *Commonwealth of the Bahamas*	Nassau (on New Providence)	ENGLISH, English Creole	5,382 13 939	303,770	56.4 21.8	0.9	62.2	69.0
BARBADOS	Bridgetown	ENGLISH, Bajan (English Creole)	166 430	279,912	1,686.2 651.0	0.4	70.8	74.8
BELIZE	Belmopan	ENGLISH, English Creole, Spanish	8,867 22 965	287,730	32.4 12.5	2.4	66.4	70.3
CANADA	Ottawa	ENGLISH, FRENCH	3,855,103 9 984 670	33,098,932	8.6 3.3	0.3	76.9	83.7
COSTA RICA *Republic of Costa Rica*	San Jose	SPANISH	19,730 51 100	4,075,261	206.6 79.8	1.4	74.4	79.7

COUNTRY, Dependency Official Name (if different)	CAPITAL(S) (Island location)	PRINCIPAL LANGUAGES OFFICIAL and other languages	AREA mi²/km²	POPULATION	POPULATION DENSITY per mi²/km²	NATURAL POP. GROWTH % gain	LIFE EXPECTANCY Male	Female
CUBA *Republic of Cuba*	Havana	SPANISH	42,804 110 861	11,382,820	265.9 102.7	0.5	75.1	79.9
Curacao (Neth.)	Willemstad	DUTCH, Papiamento	171 444	142,180	831.5 319.0	0.5	72.4	80.1
DOMINICA *Commonwealth of Dominica*	Roseau	ENGLISH, English Creole, French Creole	285 739	68,910	241.8 93.2	0.9	72.0	77.9
DOMINICAN REPUBLIC	Santo Domingo	SPANISH	18,792 48 671	9,183,984	488.7 188.7	1.8	70.2	73.3
EL SALVADOR *Republic of El Salvador*	San Salvador	SPANISH	8,124 21 042	6,822,378	839.8 324.2	2.1	67.9	75.3
Greenland (Kalaallit Nunaat) (Den.)	Nuuk (Godthab)	GREENLANDIC, Danish	836,330 2 166 086	56,361	0.1 0.0	0.8	66.4	73.6
GRENADA	Saint George's	ENGLISH, English Creole	133 344	89,703	674.5 260.8	1.5	63.1	66.7
Guadeloupe (Fr.) *Department of Guadeloupe*	Basse-Terre	FRENCH, French Creole	658 1 705	452,776	688.1 265.6	0.9	74.9	81.4
GUATEMALA *Republic of Guatemala*	Guatemala City	SPANISH, Quiche, Cakchiquel, Kekchi, Mam	42,130 109 117	12,293,545	291.8 112.7	2.5	67.7	71.2
HAITI *Republic of Haiti*	Port-au-Prince	HAITIAN (French Creole), FRENCH	10,695 27 700	8,308,504	776.9 299.9	2.4	51.9	54.6
HONDURAS *Republic of Honduras*	Tegucigalpa	SPANISH	43,433 112 492	7,326,496	168.7 65.1	2.4	67.8	71.0
JAMAICA	Kingston	ENGLISH, English Creole	4,244 10 991	2,758,124	649.9 250.9	1.5	71.5	75.0
Martinique (Fr.) *Department of Martinique*	Fort-de-France	FRENCH, French Creole	436 1 128	436,131	1,000.3 386.6	0.8	79.5	78.9
MEXICO *United Mexican States*	Mexico City	SPANISH, Aztec (Nahuatl), Yucatec (Mayan)	758,449 1 964 375	107,449,525	141.7 54.7	1.6	72.6	78.3
NICARAGUA *Republic of Nicaragua*	Managua	SPANISH	50,337 130 373	5,570,129	110.7 42.7	2.0	68.6	72.8
PANAMA *Republic of Panama*	Panama City	SPANISH, English Creole	28,973 75 040	3,191,319	110.1 42.5	1.7	72.7	77.9
Puerto Rico (U.S.) *Commonwealth of Puerto Rico*	San Juan	SPANISH, ENGLISH	3,515 9 104	3,927,188	1,117.3 431.4	0.5	74.5	82.5
SAINT KITTS AND NEVIS *Federation of St. Kitts (Christopher) and Nevis*	Basseterre (on St. Kitts)	ENGLISH, English Creole	104 269	39,129	376.2 145.5	1.0	69.6	75.4
SAINT LUCIA	Castries	ENGLISH, English-French Creole	238 617	168,458	707.8 273.0	1.5	70.3	77.7
SAINT VINCENT AND THE GRENADINES	Kingstown (on St. Vincent)	ENGLISH, English Creole	150 389	117,848	785.7 303.0	1.0	72.0	75.8
Sint Maarten (Neth.)	Philipsburg	DUTCH, ENGLISH, Papiamento	13.1 34	37,429	2,857.1 1,100.9	1.0	73.1	78.2
TRINIDAD AND TOBAGO *Republic of Trinidad and Tobago*	Port-of-Spain (on Trinidad)	ENGLISH, Trinidad English	1,980 5 127	1,065,842	538.3 207.9	0.2	65.7	67.9
UNITED STATES *United States of America*	Washington, D.C.	English, Spanish	3,676,487 9 522 058	304,059,728	81.2 31.3	0.6	75.0	80.8

SOUTH AMERICA (For country locations, see page 112.)

COUNTRY, Dependency Official Name (if different)	CAPITAL(S) (Island location)	PRINCIPAL LANGUAGES OFFICIAL and other languages	AREA mi²/km²	POPULATION	POPULATION DENSITY per mi²/km²	NATURAL POP. GROWTH % gain	LIFE EXPECTANCY Male	Female
ARGENTINA *Argentine Republic*	Buenos Aires	SPANISH	1,073,400 2 780 092	39,921,833	37.2 14.4	0.9	72.4	80.1
BOLIVIA *Republic of Bolivia*	La Paz, Sucre	SPANISH, QUECHUA, AYMARA	424,164 1 098 581	8,989,046	21.2 8.2	1.6	63.2	68.6
BRAZIL *Federative Republic of Brazil*	Brasilia	PORTUGUESE	3,287,612 8 514 877	188,078,227	57.2 22.1	1.1	68.0	76.1
CHILE *Republic of Chile*	Santiago	SPANISH, Araucanian (Mapuche)	291,930 756 096	16,134,219	55.3 21.3	1.0	73.5	80.2
COLOMBIA *Republic of Colombia*	Bogota	SPANISH	440,762 1 141 568	43,593,035	98.9 38.2	1.5	68.2	76.0
ECUADOR *Republic of Ecuador*	Quito	SPANISH, Quechuan	105,037 272 045	13,547,510	129.0 49.8	1.8	73.6	79.4
French Guiana (Fr.) *Department of French Guiana*	Cayenne	FRENCH, French Creole	32,253 83 534	199,509	6.2 2.4	1.6	74.0	80.8
GUYANA *Co-operative Republic of Guyana*	Georgetown	ENGLISH, English Creole	83,044 215 083	767,245	9.2 3.6	1.0	63.2	68.7
PARAGUAY *Republic of Paraguay*	Asuncion	GUARANI, SPANISH	157,048 406 752	6,506,464	41.4 16.0	2.5	72.6	77.8
PERU *Republic of Peru*	Lima	SPANISH, QUECHUA, AYMARA	496,225 1 285 216	28,302,603	57.0 22.0	1.5	68.1	71.7
SURINAME *Republic of Suriname*	Paramaribo	DUTCH, English Creole	63,251 163 820	439,117	6.9 2.7	1.1	66.7	71.5
URUGUAY *Oriental Republic of Uruguay*	Montevideo	SPANISH	68,037 176 215	3,431,932	50.4 19.5	0.5	73.1	79.7
VENEZUELA *Bolivarian Republic of Venezuela*	Caracas	SPANISH	353,841 916 445	25,730,435	72.7 28.1	1.4	71.5	77.8

Glossary

acid rain Rain or snow that carries acids formed from chemical pollutants in the atmosphere.

Antarctic Circle Imaginary line of latitude located at 66½°S, approximately 1,630 miles (2620 kilometers) from the South Pole.

Arctic Circle Imaginary line of latitude located at 66½°N, approximately 1,630 miles (2620 kilometers) from the North Pole.

ANTARCTIC CIRCLE (66 ½°S)   ARCTIC CIRCLE (66½°N)

atoll Low, ring-shaped island formed by coral reefs.

balance of trade Difference between the value of a country's exports and the value of its imports, commonly measured in U.S. dollars. A country that exports more than it imports has a positive balance of trade, or *trade surplus*. A country that imports more than it exports has a negative balance of trade, or *trade deficit*.

basin 1. Area drained by a river and its branches. 2. Area surrounded by higher land.

biofuel Renewable alternative fuel that is made from recently living plant or animal material.

broadleaf forest Forest whose trees have broad leaves. In places with cold winters, broad leaves change color and fall off each autumn.

cartogram Special map that shows countries at equal scale—not by area but by another attribute, such as population.

climate Pattern of weather conditions for a place or region in a typical year. Climate is affected by latitude, elevation, topography, ocean currents, and wind.

climograph Graph showing annual patterns of temperature and precipitation for a specified place.

combustion Burning or other process that produces heat and light.

commercial farming Growing crops or raising livestock, largely for sale to others.

cropland Region used mainly to grow crops.

culture Beliefs, practices, and customs of a group of people.

deforestation Removal of all trees from a vast area of forest.

desert Dry region receiving little or no precipitation and with little or no vegetation.

dispossession Seizure of land from a person or group.

elevation Height above sea level.

emigration Movement of people away from their native country or region to a new home elsewhere. The people moving away are called *emigrants*.

Equator Imaginary line that divides the earth into the Northern and Southern Hemispheres. All points along the Equator have a latitude of 0°.

ethanol Alternative energy source made from plants, often corn or sugar cane.

ethnicity Group identity based on ancestral homeland, language, religion, and/or race.

European Union (EU) Group of European countries whose main goal is to establish themselves, for trading purposes, as a single market. (See map on page 141.)

export Sale of goods to a foreign country.

fault Boundary between plates of the earth's crust. An area where this boundary is indistinct is a *fault zone*.

feral Regarding a domesticated animal that has returned to the wild or one of its descendants.

forestry Use of forests for lumber, paper, and other products.

fossil fuels Natural fuels that were formed from the remains of plants and animals over millions of years. Principal fossil fuels are petroleum, natural gas, and coal.

free trade System of buying and selling of goods across international borders without restrictions.

glacier Large body of ice formed from a long-lasting accumulation of snow on mountains and in polar regions.

global warming Increase in worldwide air temperature, thought to be caused by pollution and the greenhouse effect.

grassland Region where grass grows, sometimes mixed with scattered trees and shrubs. Grasslands are often used for grazing.

greenhouse effect Trapping of solar radiation in the atmosphere due to high concentrations of gases that absorb heat, such as carbon dioxide, methane, and water vapor.

Greenwich Mean Time (GMT) Time of day along the Prime Meridian, also called Universal Time or Zulu Time. All other time zones are identified in hours before or after GMT.

gross domestic product (GDP) Annual value of all goods and services produced within a country's borders. GDP includes production by foreign-owned facilities.

immigration Movement of people into a new country of residence. The people moving in are called *immigrants*.

import Purchase of goods produced in a foreign country.

indigenous Native to a particular region. Indigenous peoples are related to the earliest known inhabitants of a region.

International Date Line Imaginary line located along and near 180° longitude that divides calendar days. Places west of the line are 24 hours ahead of places east of the line.

land cover Vegetation, deserts, and glaciers covering the earth's surface.

land use Principal economic activity in an area. It is not the only activity, but it is the most significant or widespread.

landform Natural feature of the landscape, such as a mountain, plain, or island.

latitude Distance from the Equator measured in degrees. Lines of latitude, or *parallels*, are numbered north and south from the Equator and appear on maps as east-west lines.

life expectancy Average number of years that people born today may expect to live based on the prevailing death rates for that population. Life expectancy reflects the group's general health and welfare.

literacy Ability to both read and write. The percentage of literate people is a good indicator of a country's educational level; literacy standards vary by country.

longitude Distance from the Prime Meridian measured in degrees. Lines of longitude, or *meridians*, are numbered east and west from the Prime Meridian and appear on maps as north-south lines.

map projection Any system for drawing lines of latitude, lines of longitude, and earth features on a map. Projections are never completely accurate, distorting either sizes or shapes of the earth's land and water features.

metal Element that reflects light, conducts electricity and heat, and can be manipulated into new shapes. Metal and metal-bearing ores are mined at and below the earth's surface.

migration Mass movement from one region or country to another.

national poverty line Poverty as defined by a government for an entire country. National poverty lines are a measure of *relative poverty*.

natural population growth (NPG) Annual difference between the number of births and the number of deaths in a country or region; does not include change due to population movement.

needleleaf forest Forest of needleleaf trees, such as pines and other evergreens.

nomadic herding Raising herds of animals, moving them in a yearly cycle from one seasonal source of food and water to the next.

Oceania Collective name for islands of the central and southern Pacific Ocean, usually including New Zealand and sometimes also including Australia.

Organization of Petroleum Exporting Countries (OPEC) Association of countries that control most of the world's known oil reserves. (See maps on page 160.)

pandemic Disease spread over a wide geographic area.

permafrost Ground that is frozen most or all of the year.

plain Broad area of land that is gently rolling or almost flat.

plate Any of the sections of the earth's crust that float above the molten interior of the planet. Lighter and thicker areas of the plates form the continents, while denser and thinner areas form ocean floors.

plateau Elevated plain, usually with at least one steeply dropping or rising side; tableland.

population density The number of people living in a given area such as a square mile or square kilometer.

poverty Inability to acquire basic human needs, such as food and housing. In global terms, poverty is defined as living on the equivalent of less than US$1 a day.

precipitation Water from the atmosphere that accumulates on the earth's surface as rain, snow, hail, sleet, or dew.

Prime Meridian Imaginary line of longitude, the 0° meridian, which passes through Greenwich, United Kingdom.

rain forest Dense forest that receives great amounts of rain and stays green throughout the year, can be tropical or temperate.

ranching and herding Raising herds of livestock on large, open ranches. The livestock graze or feed on the natural grasses growing there.

region Large area that is different from the areas around it. A region can be defined by a single feature or by several features, either physical or cultural.

renewable energy resource Power source that can be grown, such as firewood, or that cannot by used up, such as wind.

rural Relating to the countryside, as opposed to cities.

Sahel Narrow, semi-arid region south of Africa's Sahara that extends east-west between Somalia and Senegal.

scale Relationship between an actual distance on the earth and the same distance as shown on a map.

semi-desert Region covered by scattered vegetation but too dry for crops without irrigation. Also called *semi-arid*.

staple food Foodstuff that constitutes a major part of the diet for a region's population.

subsistence farming Agriculture that produces only enough for the needs of a farmer and his or her family, with little or nothing left to sell.

surface current Continuous flow of water at or near the surface of an ocean.

territory **1.** Part of a country that does not have the rights of a state or province. **2.** Any large region, often with poorly defined boundaries.

thermal energy Energy derived from a heat source, usually natural, to create electricity.

time zone Region that shares the same time of day, usually one hour earlier than the zone to the west. Time zones are roughly centered on lines of longitude 15° apart.

trade organization Group established by an agreement between governments to promote trade. Examples include EU and OPEC.

Tropic of Cancer Imaginary line of latitude located at 23½°N. It marks the northern boundary of the tropics.

Tropic of Capricorn Imaginary line of latitude located at 23½°S. It marks the southern boundary of the tropics.

tropical rain forest Dense forest in or near the tropics that receives great amounts of rain and stays green year round.

tundra **1.** Polar or mountainous area with no glaciers but too cold for trees to grow. **2.** Small plants that grow close to the ground in places that are cool or cold most of the year.

urban Relating to cities and their surrounding suburbs, the opposite of rural.

urbanization Change at a place as it grows into a city or is absorbed by an expanding city nearby.

vertical exaggeration **1.** Increase in the height of a cross section or other diagram on order to show landforms more clearly. **2.** Ratio of vertical scale to horizontal scale. If vertical exaggeration is 32:1, one vertical mile appears 32 times larger than one horizontal mile.

weather Temperature, rainfall, and other conditions of the atmosphere over a short time in one place.

wetland Transition zone between land and water where the water level remains near or above the ground's surface for most of the year. Wetlands include swamps, marshes, and bogs.

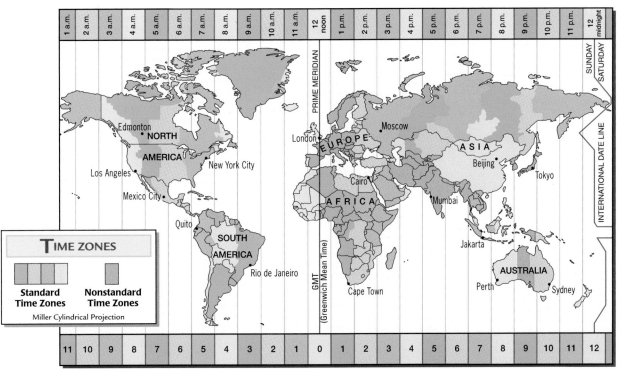

Subtract time zone number from GMT to obtain local time.   Add time zone number to GMT to obtain local time.

INDEX

The index lists all the place names that appear in the atlas. Entries for physical features are alphabetized by the proper part of their names, not by the descriptive part. For example, Lake Superior is listed as **Superior, L.** Entries for cities, however, are alphabetized by the first word in their names. So the city of Lake Charles is listed as **Lake Charles**. Similarly, foreign names, such as Rio Grande, are alphabetized by the first word in the name. Names beginning with St. are spelled **Saint** in the index. Abbreviations used in the index and in other parts of the atlas are listed on page 224.

Name (Pronunciation), Description (Lat., Long.)   Page

ABBREVIATIONS

&	and
AB	Alberta
A.D.	Anno Domini (year of the Lord)
adm.	administered by
AIDS	Acquired Immunodeficiency Syndrome
AK	Alaska
AL	Alabama
Alb.	Albania
a.m.	ante meridiem (before noon)
Am. Samoa	American Samoa
Ang.	Angola
AR	Arkansas
Arch.	archipelago
Arg.	Argentina
Arm.	Armenia
Aus.	Austria
Austr.	Australia
AZ	Arizona
Azer.	Azerbaijan
B.C.	Before Christ
BC	British Columbia
Bos., Bosnia	Bosnia-Herzegovina
Bulg.	Bulgaria
C	Celsius
C. Afr. Rep.	Central African Republic
CA	California
cm	centimeter
CO	Colorado
Congo Rep.	Congo Republic
Cro.	Croatia
CT	Connecticut
Cz., Cz. Rep.	Czech Republic
D.C.	District of Columbia
DE	Delaware
Dem. Rep. Congo	Democratic Republic of the Congo
Den.	Denmark
Dom. Rep.	Dominican Republic
E	East
elev.	elevation
Eq. Guinea	Equatorial Guinea
Est.	Estonia

F	Fahrenheit
Fk.	Fork
FL	Florida
Fr.	France or French
ft.	foot or feet
GA	Georgia (U.S. state)
GDP	Gross Domestic Product
GMT	Greenwich Mean Time
HI	Hawaii
HIV	Human immunodeficiency virus
I., Is.	island, islands
IA	Iowa
ID	Idaho
IL	Illinois
IN	Indiana
in.	inch or inches
Intl.	International
km	kilometer or kilometers
KS	Kansas
Kos.	Kosovo
KY	Kentucky
L.	lake
LA	Louisiana
Lat.	Latvia
Liech.	Liechtenstein
Lith.	Lithuania
Lux.	Luxembourg
m	meter or meters
MA	Massachusetts
Mac.	Macedonia
MB	Manitoba
MD	Maryland
ME	Maine
Mex.	Mexico
MI	Michigan
mi.	mile or miles
mm	millimeter or millimeters
MN	Minnesota
MO	Missouri
Mol.	Moldova

Mon.	Montenegro
MS	Mississippi
MT	Montana
Mt., Mts.	mount, mont, mountain, or mountains
N	North
Nat.	National
NB	New Brunswick
NC	North Carolina
ND	North Dakota
NE	Nebraska
Neth.	Netherlands
NH	New Hampshire
NJ	New Jersey
NL	Newfoundland and Labrador
NM	New Mexico
Nor.	Norway
N.P.	National Park
NS	Nova Scotia
NT	Northwest Territories
NU	Nunavut
NV	Nevada
NY	New York
N.Z.	New Zealand
O.	ocean
OH	Ohio
OK	Oklahoma
ON	Ontario
OR	Oregon
PA	Pennsylvania
Pak.	Pakistan
PE	Prince Edward Island
Pen.	peninsula
Pk.	peak
p.m.	post meridiem (after noon)
Pop.	Population
Port.	Portugal
poss.	possession
P.P.	Provincial Park
Prov.	Province, Provincial
Pt.	point
P.W.P.	Provincal Wilderness Park

QC	Québec
R.	river
Ra.	range
Rep.	republic
Res.	reservoir
RI	Rhode Island
S	South
S. Afr.	South Africa
SC	South Carolina
SD	South Dakota
Sd.	sound
Serb.	Serbia
SK	Saskatchewan
Sl., Slovak.	Slovakia
Slov.	Slovenia
Sp.	Spain
sq.	square
St., Ste.	Saint, Sainte
Str.	strait
Switz.	Switzerland
Terr.	territory
TN	Tennessee
TX	Texas
U.A.E.	United Arab Emirates
U.K.	United Kingdom
U.S.	United States
US$	United States dollars
UT	Utah
VA	Virginia
Ven.	Venezuela
VT	Vermont
W	West
WA	Washington
WI	Wisconsin
W.P.P.	Wilderness Provincial Park
WV	West Virginia
WY	Wyoming
YT	Yukon